Accounting, Innovation and Inter-Organisational Relationships

Successful innovation is a true challenge and especially when today's companies are intertwined in close inter-organisational relationships and networks with e.g. customers and suppliers. Research has indicated that accounting can play important roles in such innovation processes, but there is little in-depth systematic knowledge about this issue.

Accounting, Innovation and Inter-Organisational Relationships gathers leading researchers from all around the world to, based on in-depth field work, explore the interconnections between accounting, innovation and inter-organisational relationships.

Accounting, Innovation and Inter-Organisational Relationships thus becomes an important source for researchers and practitioners interested in accounting and inter-organisational relationships as well as the related disciplines of management, marketing, innovation and strategy.

Martin Carlsson-Wall is an Associate Professor in the Department of Accounting at the Stockholm School of Economics, Sweden.

Håkan Håkansson is a Professor of International Management at the BI Norwegian Business School, Norway.

Kalle Kraus is a Professor in the Department of Accounting at the Stockholm School of Economics, Sweden, and in the Department of Accounting at Monash University, Monash Business School, Australia.

Johnny Lind is a Professor in the Department of Accounting at the Stockholm School of Economics, Sweden.

Torkel Strömsten is an Associate Professor in the Department of Accounting at the Stockholm School of Economics, Sweden.

Routledge Studies in Accounting

A Philosophy of Management Accounting
A Pragmatic Constructivist Approach
Edited by Hanne Nørreklit

Cost Accounting in Government
Theory and Applications
Edited by Zachary Mohr

Auditing Teams
Dynamics and Efficiency
Mara Cameran, Angela Kate Pettinicchio and Angelo Detillo

The History and Tradition of Accounting in Italy
Edited by David Alexander, Roberto Di Pietra, Stefano Adamo and Roberta Fasiello

The Social Function of Accounts
Reforming Accountancy to Serve Mankind
John Flower

The Role of the Management Accountant
Local Variations and Global Influences
Lukas Goretzki and Erik Strauss

Interventionist Management Accounting Research
Theory Contributions with Societal Impact
Jouni Lyly-Yrjänäinen, Petri Suomala, Teemu Laine and Falconer Mitchell

Accounting, Innovation and Inter-Organisational Relationships
Edited by Martin Carlsson-Wall, Håkan Håkansson, Kalle Kraus, Johnny Lind and Torkel Strömsten

For more information about this series, please visit: www.routledge.com/Routledge-Studies-in-Accounting/book-series/SE0715

Accounting, Innovation and Inter-Organisational Relationships

Edited by Martin Carlsson-Wall, Håkan Håkansson, Kalle Kraus, Johnny Lind and Torkel Strömsten

Routledge
Taylor & Francis Group
NEW YORK AND LONDON

First published 2018
by Routledge
605 Third Avenue, New York, NY 10017

and by Routledge
2 Park Square, Milton Park, Abingdon, Oxon, OX14 4RN

First issued in paperback 2020

Routledge is an imprint of the Taylor & Francis Group, an informa business

Library of Congress Cataloging-in-Publication Data
A catalog record for this book has been requested

ISBN 13: 978-0-367-73469-5 (pbk)
ISBN 13: 978-1-138-08261-8 (hbk)

Typeset in Sabon
by Apex CoVantage, LLC

Contents

1 Introduction

Accounting, Innovation and Inter-Organisational Relationships

Martin Carlsson-Wall, Håkan Håkansson, Kalle Kraus, Johnny Lind and Torkel Strömsten

Dreams of glory, yes, but innovation projects are often characterised by problems and frustration. Companies often underestimate the complexity and end up in situations with no obvious way out. From a financial perspective, innovation projects are therefore high-risk endeavors as they require a hefty development budget at the same time as they strongly affect future revenues and costs (Davila, 2000, 2005); innovation projects separate winners from losers (Davila et al., 2009b; Chenhall and Moers, 2015). The Finnish company Nokia is a case in point. In 2007, Nokia had a global market share of 50% and had become a leading "best practice company" (www.statista.com; Vuori and Huy, 2016). However, Nokia faced its own innovation failures at the same time as Apple and Samsung introduced new, exciting products, and Nokia quickly lost market share. In 2013, Nokia's market share fell below three percent, and the company was sold to Microsoft. A winner had suddenly become a loser.

Boeing is another company that has experienced the glory as well as the problems and frustration of innovation. When the 787 Dreamliner project started in April 2004, it was one of Boeing's largest innovation projects ever. The development budget was nearly 20 billion dollars, and with its radical lightweight design, Boeing promised to reduce airplane fuel consumption and operating costs (Shenhar et al., 2016). In 2007, three years after the project was launched, Boeing had sold more than 500 airplanes, and it looked like a smashing success (Elahi et al., 2014). However, the Dreamliner project turned into a nightmare with technical problems and constant delays (Harrigan, 2014). When the airplane was finally ready to fly in 2011, the development costs had doubled to nearly 40 billion dollars (Shenhar et al., 2016).

Importantly, the Dreamliner project is not a story about innovation in relation to one company; rather, *it is a story about accounting, innovation and inter-organisational relationships*. Consider All Nippon Airways (ANA): This Japanese airline wanted to be the first customer for the 787 Dreamliner and therefore placed a large order to make the maiden journey before the Beijing Olympics in 2008. In addition to an expectation of public relations benefits, ANA made a bet that the lower operating costs would help it expand its business to new destinations without sacrificing profits.

When Boeing had to postpone the deliveries, this highly affected the financial performance of ANA. Interestingly, suppliers two or three tiers down the supply chain were also affected. For many of these small component suppliers, a three-year delay almost meant they went bankrupt because Boeing did not pay any suppliers before customers such as ANA could pay them. So, not only gave accounting measures such as revenue growth and operating costs impulses and justification for Boeing to start the Dreamliner project, but the delays also almost turned an entire airplane ecosystem from financial winners to financial losers. With such practical relevance and with great potential to make theoretical contributions (c.f., Chenhall and Moers, 2015; Moll, 2015), the focus of this book is therefore to explore the interconnections between accounting, innovation and inter-organisational relationships.

We take a broad perspective on accounting, including archetypes, control systems and specific techniques (c.f., Caglio and Ditillo, 2008). This broad and more holistic view is suitable when a research conversation is in a nascent stage (Edmondson and McManus, 2007), but it also follows how accounting is conceptualised in related research domains such as "accounting and inter-organisational relationships" (Caglio and Ditillo, 2008; Håkansson et al., 2010a) and "accounting and innovation" (Davila et al., 2009a; Chenhall and Moers, 2015; Moll, 2015).

When it comes to our perspective on innovation, an obvious starting point is the unit of analysis in that our focus is on innovation that occurs *between* organisations (Håkansson and Waluszewski, 2002; Hoholm and Araujo, 2011). Such inter-organisational innovation includes innovation in dyads, such as the collaboration between Boeing and ANA, as well as innovation in networks in which a number of companies are connected to each other directly and indirectly. Another aspect when it comes to our perspective on innovation is whether to focus primarily on the outcome or the process of inter-organisational innovation. For example, an important outcome of inter-organisational innovation is the various forms of interdependencies that are created. Sometimes these interdependencies are strong, creating problems of overembeddedness (Uzzi, 1997), but there are also situations when the lack of mutual adaptations results in poor quality or increased costs (Tomkins, 2001). Having a process focus, on the other hand, is about studying how organisations are coping and trying to navigate in this complex web of interdependencies. Often, due to incomplete knowledge about outcomes, such a process perspective can be expected to highlight the need for pragmatic compromises. It is not possible to have clear winners and losers because inter-organisational innovation is about interactively finding compromises, i.e., temporary solutions, that two or more parties can 'live with'. In this book, we focus on such a process perspective, highlighting that that inter-organisational innovation can be characterised as a messy and unpredictable process that is guided by pragmatic compromises concerning which interdependencies that should be increased or reduced when resources are combined across organisational boundaries.

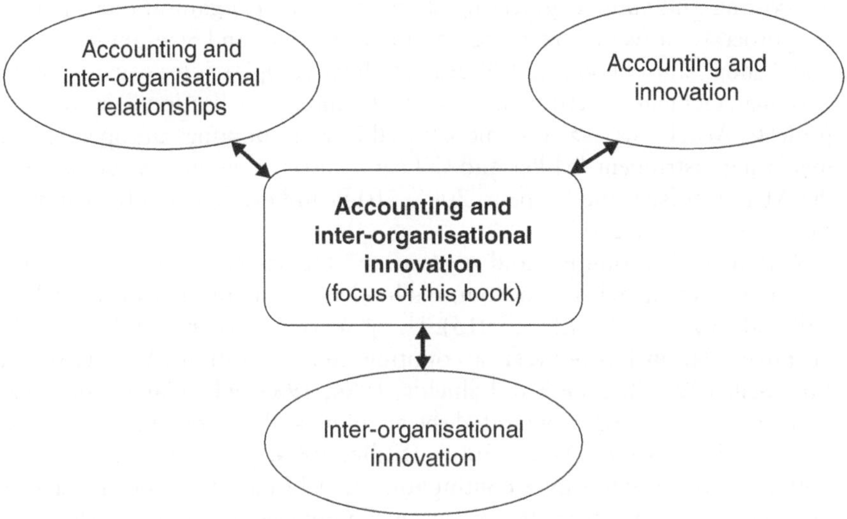

Figure 1.1 Focus of this book and related research domains.

Figure 1.1 illustrates how accounting and inter-organisational innovation relates to other research conversations. To start with, in the upper left corner, we have the "accounting and inter-organisational relationships" literature (Caglio and Ditillo, 2008; Håkansson et al., 2010a). This literature emerged in the mid-1990s when accounting scholars began to pay more attention to various forms of inter-organisational arrangements such as strategic partnerships, alliances, outsourcing relationships and joint ventures. An early milestone was a special issue in *Accounting, Organizations and Society* in 1996 edited by Anthony Hopwood, and since then a research conversation has evolved covering different theoretical perspectives, empirical settings and research methodologies. As a way to summarise this type of research, we published the book *Accounting in Networks* in 2010. A central part of that book was different theoretical perspectives with chapters covering Transaction Cost Economics (Anderson and Dekker, 2010), The Industrial Network Approach (Håkansson et al., 2010b), Actor Network Theory (Mouritsen et al., 2010) and Institutional Theory (Scapens and Varoutsa, 2010). When reading our 2010 book as well as the published journal articles in this domain, it was evident that many of the chapters and articles, explicitly or implicitly, described inter-organisational innovation. In the 2010 book, for example, Van der Meer-Kooistra and Kamminga (2010) discussed innovation in joint ventures, Mouritsen et al. (2010) used innovation examples from LeanTech and Intel and Carlsson-Wall and Kraus (2010) showed how underlying assumptions about the product development process could help to theorise guiding and synchronising roles of inter-organisational target costing. When it comes to the journal articles, Mouritsen et al.'s (2001) article about target costing and value engineering shows how inter-organisational innovation processes affect firm strategy, and both Cooper and Slagmulder (2004) and Agndal and Nilsson (2009) describe how complex inter-organisational cost management practices are related to inter-organisational innovation projects. Articles have also demonstrated how accounting can operate as a mediating instrument (Miller and O'Leary, 2007), a minimal structure (van der Meer-Kooistra and Scapens, 2008, 2015) and evaluative infrastructures (Kornberger et al., 2017).

Within the "accounting and innovation" literature, a central theme has been to investigate whether accounting hinders or support innovation (Chenhall and Moers, 2015; Moll, 2015). Using surveys, early research showed a negative relationship between accounting and innovation (Abernethy and Brownell, 1997; Rockness and Shields, 1984, 1988) while later more case-based research have demonstrated the enabling and supporting role of innovation (Nixon, 1998; Davila, 2000; Ditillo, 2004; Jörgensen and Messner, 2009, 2010). An interesting continuation that bridges these perspectives is an emerging stream that shows that accounting does indeed interfere and shape innovation processes (Mouritsen et al., 2009, Christner and Strömsten, 2015; Revellino and Mouritsen, 2015) regardless of whether accounting is 'hindering' or 'enabling'. Accounting is *there*, and it will influence decision-making regarding *what* innovation projects that will be undertaken and *how* these processes will be organised over time. Even though the majority of studies within this domain have focused on intra-organisational innovation, a few studies go beyond firm boundaries. For example, Mouritsen et al. (2009) describe how accounting calculations impact both intra- and inter-organisational innovation processes, and Revellino and Mouritsen (2009) demonstrate how different forms of accounting were part of coordinating the inter-organisational innovation process in the development of the Italian Autostrade's Telepass system.

Finally, with regards to the "inter-organisational innovation" literature, industrial marketing and purchasing researchers have studied such innovation for a long time (Håkansson and Snehota, 1995; Håkansson and Waluszewski, 2002, 2007; Laage-Hellman 1989; Öberg, 2013). An important contribution within this literature has been to highlight the unpredictable and interactive nature of the innovation process (Dubois and Araujo, 2006; Hoholm and Araujo, 2011; Hoholm and Olsen, 2012; La Rocca and Snehota, 2014). For example, studying the development of green paper technology, Håkansson and Waluszewski (2002) show how the innovation process requires coordination on multiple levels. Because of the inherent uncertainty, many different innovation paths are possible, and therefore the innovation process is characterised by an uneven development rhythm in which some companies experience high degrees of time pressure while others are frustrated by delays. However, even though accounting has generally not been the focus in this literature, there are some exceptions (Baraldi and

Strömsten, 2009; Baraldi et al., 2014; Perna et al., 2015; Strömsten and Waluszewski, 2012). For example, Baraldi and Strömsten (2009) explored how resources were controlled and combined in a biotech network spanning from Uppsala in Sweden to Palo Alto in the US. Analysing result, action and personnel controls, the authors describe the complexities of controlling a network of companies with traditional cybernetic forms of control. Focusing on target costing in distributed product development, Carlsson-Wall et al. (2009) came to a similar conclusion. Studying the development of industrial robots, they distinguished between the traditional and hierarchical model of target costing and an interactive model in which more focus is on improvisation and temporary compromises. Recent work has further extended this line of thinking and problematised the role of accounting in the fuzzy front end of innovation (Carlsson-Wall and Kraus, 2015); network dynamics (Lind, 2017); and how innovation relates to money (Perna et al., 2015), business deals (Håkansson and Olsen, 2015) and ownership (Strömsten and Waluszewski, 2012).

Focus of This Book

As mentioned earlier, our previous book *Accounting in Networks* (Håkansson et al., 2010a) was about accounting and inter-organisational relationships. At that time there was already a large body of work published on this topic; hence, there was a need for synthesising this prior literature. This time it is different. Because the interconnections between accounting and inter-organisational innovation are relatively neglected in prior research, we decided that our book should take its point of departure in interesting empirical cases. That is, instead of traditional reviews of theoretical perspectives and empirical contexts, we have this time asked authors (many of them contributors in the previous book) to focus on rich empirical descriptions. We believe this is appropriate because in an emergent field the central focus is on exploration (Edmondson and McManus, 2007; Power, 2015). Each of the 13 chapters therefore contains a detailed case, and reflections are made based on each case.

Across the chapters, the following broad themes are explored: Taking its starting point in inter-organisational innovation being a 'novel' context, what are the consequences for the design and use of accounting? More specifically, as inter-organisational innovation is characterised by uncertainty, messiness, interaction and different development rhythms, how does this affect accounting? What do actors account for? When do they see a need for 'accounts'? In 1998, Peter Miller (1998, p. 605) wrote: "Accounting is most interesting at its margins. For it is at the margins that we see new calculative practices added to the repertoire of accounting." This book focuses on inter-organisational innovation, which up until now has been 'at the margins' of accounting scholarship. In recent reviews, Chenhall and Moers (2015) call for more research on accounting in open innovation and Moll (2015) argue that future research should focus on accounting in collaborative research and development (R&D) projects. Another interesting theme is how accounting affects inter-organisational innovation. For example, even though inter-organisational innovation can be difficult to capture in valuation models, we still see how both entrepreneurs and venture capitalists need a language to discuss how much a company is worth at a specific point of time. The constant dynamics in a business network needs to be accounted for in one way or another. How is this done? Who are involved, and when is accounting important?

There are 13 empirical chapters in the book from a variety of contexts. Chapters 2–5 detail a start-up context. In Chapter 2, Andrea Perna and Alexandra Waluszewski analyse the Q-Linea project, an innovation for a new type of diagnostic technology for rapid characterisation of bloodstream infections. The authors found that the challenges involved in accounting for a potentially successful innovation were tackled through what they call 'accounting based on limitations'. Two separate accounting systems were established, and non-financial measures, such as number of publications and patents, were mobilised to find support for the innovation despite constant 'red numbers'. In Chapter 3, Carl Henning Christner, Johnny Lind and Torkel Strömsten detail Pyrosequencing's development of a new and innovative way to sequence and analyse DNA. They find that calculations, deals and inter-organisational innovation processes influence each other in the formation of temporary solutions. Calculations can both hinder and facilitate the innovation process, it depends on the time horizon of the judgement. In Chapter 4, Per Ingvar Olsen analyses the scaling of innovative technology start-ups to global business activities through rapidly accelerated innovation processes. The author details the importance of various accounting techniques at work in the industry, such as portfolio management systems and syndicated investment systems, to discipline the actors and thereby speed up the innovation and scaling processes. In Chapter 5, Marc Wouters and Michael Pelz examine the Bosch startup platform, a corporate program that lets employees start new businesses as if they are independent startups. The platform did not have to produce detailed monthly reports for Bosch headquarters; it could focus on cash-flow based metrics and could implement specific non-financial metrics which were not used elsewhere within Bosch. There was a delicate balance between stimulating experimentation on the one hand and creating market pressures and stop startup investments if needed on the other hand. Accounting helped achieve what the authors call 'balanced experimentation'.

Chapters 6–8 detail a more traditional production context. In Chapter 6, Jodie Moll and Fiona Harrigan examine the development of the Boeing Dreamliner. They found that Boeing and its collaborating partners had grossly overestimated the power of accounting systems to facilitate the coordination of R&D and the manufacture of integrated components by a global supply chain. In Chapter 7, Martin Carlsson-Wall and Kalle Kraus analyse how accounting is involved in innovation conducted between ABB Robotics, a producer of industrial robots, and its close customers and suppliers. They found the importance of time in inter-organisational innovation and that accounting helped establish time-based compromises by relating estimated revenues of customer contracts to what were perceived to be 'reasonable costs'. In Chapter 8, Jan Mouritsen and Kim S. Hald study inter-organisational innovation based on the interaction between a manufacturer of advanced hearing aids and its suppliers. They detail how accounting was an 'engine' for the development of innovative capabilities in inter-organisational relationships. Innovation is therefore argued to be an effect of how accounting mediates relations between a focal firm and its suppliers.

In Chapters 9–11, a services context is examined. In Chapter 9, Angelo Ditillo and Ariela Caglio analyse an innovation project about the customisation of existing software for the billing and customer care activities of a mobile operator's telecommunication division. They found that traditional variables (i.e., asset specificity, interdependence) used to explain the adoption of inter-organisational accounting need to be complemented by another key variable: the characteristics of the knowledge provided by the parties involved in innovation. In Chapter 10, Sander van Triest and Jacco Blom examine how accounting was used in innovation related to logistics services. More specifically, a supplier used open book accounting to convince the buyer to adjust its operations and thereby created the starting point for innovating in the supply chain. In Chapter 11, Anna Dubois and Lars-Erik Gadde study a local service unit of a large multinational company and a number of individual suppliers of the company. They found that accounting played a significant role in inter-organisational innovation, more specifically detailing accounting for indirect effects, accounting for prioritisation and accounting for the networking activities of firms.

Chapters 12–14 include a discussion of governmental agencies when analysing accounting and inter-organisational innovation. In Chapter 12, Jens Eklinder-Frick and Alexandra Waluszewski analyse a governmental agency's accounting for the outcome of innovation policy support. The found that the agency's accounting for innovation success was focused on early phase projects, while the most important interfaces for the survival and benefits of the innovation—the producer–user interfaces—were left out of the analysis. In Chapter 13, Jeltje van der Meer-Kooistra and Robert W. Scapens examine the development of a desktop electron microscope and new applications for inkjet technology. Both projects involved the local development agency. They found that accounting functioned as a 'minimal structure' providing flexibility as well as structure for inter-organisational innovation and the importance of good working relationships among the participating parties at three levels: senior management, participants cooperating on a day-to-day basis and individuals working in the project and colleagues working on other projects. In Chapter 14, Paul Andon, Jane Baxter and Wai Fong Chua analyse an inter-organisational network designed to address a government's social housing needs in an innovative but economically defensible way. They find that accounting and affect were intertwined in inter-organisational networks concerned with innovation. The adoption of a public private partnership stemmed from the hope in the potential of inter-organisational networks to deliver innovation, that is, affective ties between members of governmental departments and other organisations significantly influenced the role accounting played in innovation processes.

In Chapter 15, we compare and contrast the findings from the empirical chapters. What patterns, if any, can be seen? Chapter 16 then returns to Figure 1.1 (with the three research domains) and reflects on how the findings from the empirical chapters can fruitfully open up new research avenues in the three domains: "accounting and inter-organisational relationships," "accounting and innovation" and "inter-organisational innovation." We hope that this book will inspire and initiate a large body of scholarly work on accounting, innovation and inter-organisational relationships.

References

Abernethy, M., and Brownell, P. (1997). Management control systems in research and development organizations: The role of accounting, behavioural and personnel controls. *Accounting, Organizations and Society*, Vol. 22, Issue 3–4, pp. 233–248.

Agndal, H., and Nilsson, U. (2009). Interorganizational cost management in the exchange process. *Management Accounting Research*, Vol. 20, Issue 1, pp. 85–101.

Anderson, S., and Dekker, H. (2010). Accounting in networks—The transaction cost perspective. *Accounting in Networks*, Eds. Håkansson, H., Kraus, K., and Lind, J., pp. 235–268. New York: Routledge.

Baraldi, E., Ingemansson, M., and Launberg, A. (2014). Controlling the commercialisation of science across inter-organisational borders: Four cases from two major Swedish universities. *Industrial Marketing Management*, Vol. 43, pp. 382–391.

Baraldi, E., and Strömsten, T. (2009). Controlling and combining resources in networks. From Uppsala to Stanford, and back again: The case of a biotech innovation. *Industrial Marketing Management*, Vol. 38, Issue 5, pp. 541–552.

Caglio, A., and Ditillo, A. (2008). A review and discussion of management control in inter-firm relationships: Achievements and future directions. *Accounting, Organization and Society*, Vol. 33, Issue 7–8, pp. 868–898.

Carlsson-Wall, M., and Kraus, K. (2010). Target costing in inter-organizational relationships and networks. *Accounting in Networks*, Eds. Håkansson, H., Kraus, K., and Lind, J., pp. 184–210. New York: Routledge.

Carlsson-Wall, M., and Kraus, K. (2015). Opening the black box of the role of accounting practices in the fuzzy front-end of product innovation. *Industrial Marketing Management*, Vol. 45, pp. 184–194.

Carlsson-Wall, M., Kraus, K., and Lind, J. (2009). Accounting and distributed product development. *The IMP Journal*, Vol. 3, Issue 1, pp. 2–27.

Chenhall, R., and Moers, F. (2015). The role of innovation in the evolution of management accounting and its integration into management control. *Accounting, Organizations and Society*, Vol. 47, pp. 1–15.

Christner, H., and Strömsten, T. (2015). Scientists, venture capitalists and the stock exchange: The mediating role of accounting in product development. *Management Accounting Research*, Vol. 28, pp. 50–67.

Cooper, R., and Slagmulder, R. (2004). Interorganizational cost management and relational context. *Accounting, Organization and Society*, Vol. 29, Issue 1, pp. 1–26.

Davila, A. (2000). An empirical study on the drivers of management control systems' design in new product development. *Accounting, Organizations and Society*, Vol. 25, Issue 4–5, pp. 383–409.

Davila, A. (2005). The promise of management control systems for innovation and strategic change. *Controlling Strategy—Management Accounting, and Performance Measurement*, Ed. Chapman, C., pp. 37–61. Oxford: Oxford Press.

Davila, A., Foster, G., and Li, M. (2009b). Reasons for management control system adoption: Insights from product development systems choice by early-stage entrepreneurial companies. *Accounting, Organizations and Society*, Vol. 34, pp. 322–347.

Davila, A., Foster, G., and Oyon, D. (2009a). Accounting and control, entrepreneurship and innovation: Venturing into new research opportunities. *European Accounting Review*, Vol. 18, Issue 2, pp. 281–311.

Ditillo, A. (2004). Dealing with uncertainty in knowledge-intensive firms: The role of management control systems as knowledge integration mechanisms. *Accounting, Organizations and Society*, Vol. 29, Issue 3–4, pp. 401–422.

Dubois, A., and Araujo, L. (2006). The relationship between technical and organisational interfaces in product development. *The IMP Journal*, Vol. 1, Issue 1, pp. 28–51.

Edmondson, A., and McManus, S. (2007). Methodological fit in management field research. *Academy of Management Review*, Vol. 32, Issue 4, pp. 1155–1179.

Elahi, E., Sheikhzadeh, M., and Lamba, N. (2014). An integrated outsourcing framework: Analyzing Boeing's outsourcing program for Dreamliner (B787). *Knowledge and Process Management*, Vol. 21, Issue 1, pp. 13–28.

Håkansson, H., Kraus, K., and Lind, J. (2010a). *Accounting in Networks*. New York: Routledge.

Håkansson, H., Kraus, K., Lind, J., and Strömsten, T. (2010b). Accounting in networks—The industrial network approach, *Accounting in Networks*, Eds. Håkansson, H., Kraus, K., and Lind, J., pp. 269–291. New York: Routledge.

Håkansson, H., and Olsen, P. (2015). The roles of money and business deals in network structures. *Industrial Marketing Management*, Vol. 45, pp. 207–217.

Håkansson, H., and Snehota, I. (1995). *Developing Relationships in Business Networks*. London: Routledge.

Håkansson, H., and Waluszewski, A. (2002). *Managing Technological Development: IKEA, the Environment and Technology*. London: Routledge.

Håkansson, H., and Waluszewski, A. (2007). *Knowledge and Innovation in Business and Industry: The Importance of Using Others*. London, New York: Routledge.

Harrigan, F. (2014). Evolution of accounting controls in a de-integrated project structure: A case of hybridization. *Journal of Information Systems*, Vol. 28, Issue 2, pp. 329–355.

Hoholm, T., and Araujo, L. (2011). Studying innovation processes in real-time: The promises and challenges of ethnography. *Industrial Marketing Management*, Vol. 40, pp. 933–939.

Hoholm, T., and Olsen, P. (2012). The contrary forces of innovation: A conceptual model for studying networked innovation processes. *Industrial Marketing Management*, Vol. 41, pp. 344–356.

Hopwood, A. (1996). Looking across rather than up and down: On the need to explore the lateral processing of information. *Accounting, Organizations and Society*, Vol. 21, Issue 6, pp. 589–590.

Jörgensen, B., and Messner, M. (2009). Management control in new product development: The dynamics of managing flexibility and efficiency. *Journal of Management Accounting Research*, Vol. 22, Issue 1, pp. 99–124.

Jörgensen, B., and Messner, M. (2010). Accounting and strategising: A case study from new product development. *Accounting Organizations and Society*, Vol. 35, Issue 2, pp. 184–204.

Kornberger, M., Pfluger, D., and Mouritsen, J. (2017). Evaluative infrastructures: Accounting for platform organization. *Accounting, Organizations and Society*, Vol. 60, pp. 79–95.

La Rocca, A., and Snehota, I. (2014). Relating in business networks: Innovation in practice. *Industrial Marketing Management*, Vol. 43, pp. 441–447.

Laage-Hellman, J. (1989). *Technological Development in Industrial Networks*. Doctoral Thesis, Uppsala, Sweden.

Lind, J. (2017). The role of accounting for managing innovation processes when relationships matter. *The IMP Journal*, Vol. 11, pp. 7–24.

Miller, P. (1998). The margins of accounting. *The Sociological Review*, pp. 174–193.

Miller, P., and O'Leary, T. (2007). Mediating instruments and making markets: Capital budgeting, science and the economy. *Accounting, Organizations and Society*, Vol. 32, Issues 7–8, pp. 701–734.

Moll, J. (2015). Editorial: Special issue on innovation and product development. *Management Accounting Research*, Vol. 28, pp. 2–11.

Mouritsen, J., Chua, W., and Habib, M. (2010). Actor-network theory and the study of inter-organisational network-relations, *Accounting in Networks*, Eds. Håkansson, H., Kraus, K., and Lind, J., pp. 292–313. New York: Routledge.

Mouritsen, J., Hansen, A., and Hansen, C.Ø. (2001). Interorganizational controls and organizational competencies: Episodes around target cost management/functional analysis and open book accounting. *Management Accounting Research*, Vol. 12, Issue 2, pp. 221–244.

Mouritsen, J., Hansen, A., and Hansen, C.Ø. (2009). Short and long translations: Management accounting calculations and innovation management. *Accounting, Organization and Society*, Vol. 34, Issues 6–7, pp. 738–754.

Nixon, B. (1998). Research and development performance measurement: A case study. *Management Accounting Research*, Vol. 3, Issue 3, pp. 329–355.

Öberg, C. (2013). Competence integration in creative processes. *Industrial Marketing Management*, Vol. 42, pp. 113–124.

Perna, A., Baraldi, A., and Waluszewski, A. (2015). Is the value created necessarily associated with money? On the connections between an innovation process and its monetary dimension: The case of Solibro's thin-film solar cells. *Industrial Marketing Management*, Vol. 46, pp. 108–121.

Power, M. (2015). How accounting begins: Object formation and the accretion of infrastructure. *Accounting, Organizations and Society*, Vol. 47, pp. 43–55.

Revellino, S., and Mouritsen, J. (2009). The multiplicity of controls and the making of innovation. *European Accounting Review*, Vol. 18, Issue 2, pp. 341–369.

Revellino, S., and Mouritsen, J. (2015). Accounting as an engine. The performativity of calculative action and the dynamics of innovation. *Management Accounting Research*, Vol. 28, pp. 31–49.

Rockness, H.O., and Shields, M. (1984). Organizational control systems in research and development. *Accounting, Organizations and Society*, Vol. 9, Issue 2, pp. 165–177.

Rockness, H.O., and Shields, M. (1988). An empirical analysis of the expenditure budget in research and development. *Contemporary Accounting Research*, Vol. 4, Issue 2, pp. 568–581.

Scapens, R., and Varoutsa, E. (2010). Accounting in inter-organisational relationships—The institutional theory perspective, *Accounting in Networks*, Eds. Håkansson, H., Kraus, K., and Lind, J., pp. 314–341. New York: Routledge.

Shenhar, A., Holzmann, V., Melamed, B., and Zhao, Y. (2016). The challenge of innovation in highly complex projects: What can we learn from Boeing's Dreamliner experience? *Project Management Journal*, Vol. 47, Issue 2, pp. 62–78.

Strömsten, T., and Waluszewski, A. (2012). Governance and resource interaction in networks. The role of venture capital in a biotech start-up. *Journal of Business Research*, Vol. 65, pp. 232–244.

Tomkins, C. (2001). Interdependencies, trust and information in relationships, alliances and networks. *Accounting, Organizations and Society*, Vol. 26, Issue 2, pp. 161–191.

Uzzi, B. (1997). Social structure and competition in interfirm networks: The paradox of embeddedness. *Administrative Science Quarterly*, Vol. 42, pp. 35–67.

Van der Meer-Kooistra, J., and Kamminga, P. (2010). The role of management accounting in joint venture relationships: A dynamic perspective, *Accounting in Networks*, Eds. Håkansson, H., Kraus, K., and Lind, J., pp. 184–210. New York: Routledge.

Van der Meer-Kooistra, J., and Scapens, R. (2008). The governance of lateral relationships between and within organizations. *Management Accounting Research*, Vol. 19, Issue 4, pp. 365–384.

Van der Meer-Kooistra, J., and Scapens, R. (2015). Governing product co-development projects: The role of minimal structures. *Management Accounting Research*, Vol. 28, pp. 68–91.

Vuori, T., and Huy, Q. (2016). Distributed attention and shared emotions in the process: How Nokia lost the smart phone battle. *Administrative Science Quarterly*, Vol. 61, Issue 1, pp. 9–51.

2 The Interplay Between Innovation and Accounting

The Border-Crossing Q-Linea Project and Its Within-Border Accounting

Andrea Perna and Alexandra Waluszewski

Introduction

"Do you need antibiotics, and if so, what kind? Q-Linea develops a system that can give the answer within a few hours. Moreover, it calculates the right dose" (Ny Teknik, April 13, 2013[1]). The quotation above was published in Sweden's largest new-technology-focused newspaper and is just one in a list of positive statements made about Q-Linea and the diagnostic product system it developed for use in the health care and military sectors. In 2016, for the third year in a row, the company was placed on the so-called "33-list' of the most promising young innovation companies by two of Sweden's largest business and technology magazines.[1]

Q-Linea's main engagement is the development of a new type of diagnostic technology for rapid characterisation of bloodstream infections (e.g., sepsis), based on DNA and protein detection. An important aim of this innovation effort is to contribute to combating antibiotic resistance. The goal is to deliver a diagnostic system that rapidly identifies exactly what pathogen a patient is infected with and then identify exactly what antibiotic should be used to combat it. Along with its engagement in this so-called 'Astrid' blood infection diagnostic system, Q-Linea is still engaged in its first innovation application, development of a system to identify bio-warfare agents, based on a related technology.

Early in its innovation engagement Q-Linea, which still has not launched any finalised product system, became surrounded by positive external estimations of its ability to be successful. However, a somewhat different evaluation was made by the company that initially hosted the innovation attempt: *Olink Bioscience AB* (Olink). The latter company's interpretation was the project, at that time directed to the military application, that rested on a rather shaky economic ground. To protect Olink's economy, the idea emerged to create a separate economy and accounting system for Q-Linea's innovation activities. In 2008, the company Q-Linea was established, and its economy and accounting system was isolated from Olink (despite the owner involvement).

The different accounting systems and ownership structure were initially the only main differences between the two companies. The main technological and organisational activities of Olink and Q-Linea were still located in the same place, Olink's facilities in Uppsala Science Park. The technological roots of the innovation engagements of Olink and Q-Linea were also the same—research advancements made by a research group at Uppsala University's Rudbeck Laboratory. Hence, both companies' innovation journeys took off in an interdisciplinary, publicly financed research environment. Professor Ulf Landgren, one of the research leaders at the Rudbeck Laboratory, was involved in developing new and improved methods for molecular diagnostics and new therapies in the area of DNA and protein analysis and was also dedicated to spreading their use through commercialisation and transformation into automatised product systems. As we will see later, there were also owner relationships between professor Landegren and the two firms. Both companies' innovation efforts also received financial and organisational support from Uppsala University's holding company, Uppsala *University Holding AB* (UUAB), which was owned by the state but controlled by the university.

Hence, the Q-Linea innovation journey goes hand in hand with mobilising the social, material and financial resources necessary to carry out the system development and to cover costs that appear long before any finalised product is ready for sales and billing customers—a process that is closely related to how the pros and cons are accounted for by related actors. The aim of this chapter is to highlight the interplay between the Q-Linea innovation journey and how it is accounted for by related involved actors, including how this interplay affects its direction and content and the establishment of deals. The overall research question is: *How is the direction and content of the Q-Linea innovation journey influenced by—and influencing—how it is accounted for by related actors? What types of deals does this accounting give rise to?*

Theoretical Points of Departure

The theoretical points of departure of this project are the IMP approach and the key assumptions of resource heterogeneity and an interactive business landscape (Håkansson et al., 2009). In this perspective, innovation is approached as an embedding process in which a) establishment of related interfaces among a potential innovation in a using *setting*, a producing *setting* and a *developing setting* is critical (Håkansson and Waluszewski, 2002; 2007), something that in turn underlines the importance of b) establishment of deals giving rise to a monetary dimension (Håkansson and Olsen, 2015; Perna et al., 2015).

These empirical settings are characterised by different but related social and material investments in place in each setting, transcending company and organisational borders (Håkansson and Waluszewski, 2002; Håkansson et al., 2009; Baraldi et al., 2011). Therefore, embedding a potential innovation into a large-scale producing and using setting requires connections with both a social-material structure and a monetary deal structure, the latter being needed even before social-material interfaces in a producing and a using setting were established.

While the connection between the value that an innovation creates in a social-material structure and its monetary dimensions is seen as rather straightforward in approaches close to mainstream economic thinking, the research carried out in the IMP setting suggests that this relationship is much more complicated. The value of an innovation is created in interaction, heavily influenced by what the new can add to investments in place (Håkansson et al., 2009), and the economic deals are negotiated based on propositions of what the innovation will contribute in a social-material structure (Håkansson and Olsen, 2015; Perna et al., 2015; Lind, 2017).

This implies that the accounting for economic *pros and cons* of an emerging innovation is one of the most important questions for its stakeholders in a using, a producing and a developing setting (Håkansson and Waluszewski, 2007). In all these settings, accounting has an important impact on the ability to mobilise social, material and financial resources for the innovation attempt.

But how can necessary underlying accounting information be achieved and dealt with when the costs and benefits in a large-scale producing and using setting are difficult to estimate and the costs for testing at least a prototype in these settings appear long before any gains are realised? Although this question might appear tricky, each stakeholder of a particular innovation process must consider them, including in what interest and from what perspective a certain account was created.

Cross-Boundary Innovation and Within-Boundary Accounting

An interesting challenge that we already touched upon in the introduction is that, per definition, the innovation process is border crossing, while accounting is made within organisational borders. Furthermore, the pros and cons accounted for radical differences among the using, producing and developing settings of an innovation. In the *developing setting*, the benefits accounted for are related to the ability to contribute to knowledge advances. If the development takes place in an academic research unit, the benefits are accounted for in terms of the number of publications, numbers of citations, attraction of external research funding and attraction of skilled researchers. For those engaged in the *commercialisation of knowledge advancements*, the benefits of the same innovation are based on the ability to create a positive exit, for example, accounted for in terms of estimation of future market share and price in relation to development cost.

In the *producing setting*, the benefits of the innovation are related to its ability to contribute to supplying and producing investments in place. In each firm engaged as an end-producer (as supplier and sub-supplier), the adapting and delivering solutions of the end-product must cover the costs, accounted for in terms of estimations of current production volume, cost of adaptations and production costs.

In the *using setting*, the benefits of the same innovation are related to the impact on existing user systems if it increases the value of the established user system or if it challenges its value. If the using setting is public hospital clinics, as in this chapter, before a purchase actually is done, it has to pass a number of accounting systems as well as several types of medical regulations; it will be exposed to a public procurement procedure, in which its benefits are accounted for in terms of price and function in relation to established technologies.

Hence, an emerging innovation can have accountable benefits in a developing setting and in a venture capital financed start-up setting, long before its pros and cons as an established product or service embedded into a large-scale producing and using setting are proven. In all of these settings, the related accounting systems will have an impact on the content and direction of the innovation efforts (Lind, 2017). The interplay between the accounting systems of the involved actors and the cross-boundary innovation journey can lead both to a stabilising and destabilising of the latter, depending on what financial and nonfinancial accounting estimations are made.

As already indicated, a challenging issue is that the pros and cons of an innovation process present differently over time and space and are accounted for differently in user, producer and developing settings. Hence, the full range of consequences of engaging in and accounting for an innovation project cannot be outlined until the innovation is embedded in a large-scale producing and a using setting.

Thus, an important question for the emergence and direction of an innovation is which costs and which gains are accounted for at what time, within what settings and within what organisational borders. A related question regards the establishment of deals, that is, the translation of estimated social-material values into a monetary dimension (Håkansson and Olsen, 2015; Perna et al., 2015). The creation of deals that are the result of a translating and negotiating process giving rise to a monetary flow, as underlined earlier, is necessary for innovation attempts to occur within a developing setting and for an innovation to become finalised and embedded into a producing and using settings. In this translation, financial and nonfinancial accounting, as Lind (2017) shows, plays a key role.

Research Design

The research design of this investigation follows what is expressed in the first IMP project: that the methodology is a consequence of the overall research question and how it is approached theoretically (Håkansson, 1982, pp. 28–53). To capture the interactive aspects of an innovation journey and, more precisely, the interplay between attempts to develop and embed something new in a producing and using setting and related accounting system, we used the Activity, Resource and Actor (ARA) model (Håkansson and Johanson, 1992; Håkansson and Snehota, 1995) and the distinction of the different economic logics of a developing, producing and using setting (Håkansson and Waluszewski, 2007) as a conceptual *and* methodological foundation.

We used the ARA model in the identification of the interactive aspects of the innovation process focusing on attempts to transform a scientific advancement, considered as successful, in an academic developing setting to a commercial producing and using setting and how it is related to financial and nonfinancial accounting and the establishment of deals. To catch the interplay between the innovation journey and the related accounting system, we used some IMP studies that directly or indirectly touch on how it is related to different types of financial and nonfinancial control systems (Lind, 2017; Strömsten and Waluszewski, 2012; Baraldi and Strömsten, 2009; Ingemansson and Waluszewski, 2009). To highlight what types of deals this accounting gives rise to, we used some recent studies (Håkansson and Olsen, 2015; Perna et al., 2015) capturing deals as an entity representing the "result of an interactive business relationship where the basic problem is the difficulty of relating the heterogeneous social—material interactions to the homogeneous monetary sub-processes" (Håkansson and Olsen, 2015, p. 215).

The Q-Linea innovation journey stretches across an academic development setting and an emerging commercial producing and using setting and the interplay with a related accounting system. Although we named it the 'Q-Linea innovation journey,' we also investigate how this unfolds outside the focal company's borders. As previously mentioned, the aim of the empirical study is not to evaluate the success or failure of an innovation journey; rather, we are interested in elaborating on the multiple roles played by accounting in this process.

The data collection carried out in the developing, producing and using setting focused on a) identifying emerging resource ties, activity links and actors' bonds here and b) what financial and nonfinancial accounting they were related to and c) what types of deals were established. The main source of data was in-depth interviews with focal representatives in the three empirical settings. This data were complemented by internal documents, the company's website and public reports from Swedish authorities. We also relied on several email exchanges with one of the Q-Linea stakeholders, posing some initial questions focused on investigating the major motivations that led the investor to engage with the new venture. The data collection was carried out from November 2015 to July 2016.

We conducted 18 face-to-face interviews of between 30 and 60 minutes each, seven of which were conducted at Q-Linea, that is, in the emerging producing setting. Informants at Q-Linea were the company's CEO, the marketing manager, the head of finance, the production manager and two representatives of the company's board. In the developing setting, we interviewed the scientist Ulf Landgren at Uppsala University's Rudbeck Laboratory, who held most of the technologies behind Olink and Q-Linea and representatives of Uppsala University's innovation support unit UUAB. We also interviewed a potential user of the technology at Uppsala Academic Hospital.

Interview guides were prepared before each interview and adjusted according to the outcomes we received. For instance, in the late stage of our research, we explicitly focused on accounting and the innovation journey. All 18 interviews were recorded and transcribed for the analysis. We also followed up on our interviews by exchanging several emails with our informants. On some occasions, we collected confidential material that contributed more precise information, especially regarding the financial and nonfinancial features. As for the secondary data sources, we employed data from company and official university documents and websites, from which we collected important information regarding the connections among UU AB, Olink and Q-Linea.

Innovation, Accounting and Deals—The Q-Linea Case

The Q-Linea innovation journey began with research carried out at the university's Rudbeck Laboratory, led by Professor Ulf Landegren. The Rudbeck Laboratory is an interdisciplinary research environment related to the medical faculty, with the overall goal of developing new and improved methods for molecular diagnostics and therapies. Or as Ulf Landegren presents the group and its research:

> Molecular tools for molecular medicine are in rapid development. Radically improved methods can offer entirely new biological insights, reveal disease processes at potentially curable stages, and serve to evaluate new drugs and monitor responses to therapy.[2]

Ulf Landegren and his research group are recognised in the international scientific community, and for their strong engagement in making the techniques available for users in the academic, business and health care setting:

> Our lab also very actively disseminates the techniques we develop; for example by making them available nationwide as services via the Science for Life Laboratory organisation, or through licensing leading international biotech and diagnostic companies, or via the seven companies we have so far spun out.[3]

One of the seven spin-out companies was Olink AB, which became the first business unit within which the commercialisation of the Q-Linea project took off. Olink was established to transform the technologies developed at Rudbeck Laboratory, depicted in a family of about 20 patents, to commercially available molecular tools. The Q-Linea project was based on an adaptation of this technology base to a product system for detection of agents such as bacteria, spores, viruses and toxins, later spun off to Q-Linea. As we will see, from the perspective of Rudbeck Laboratory, Uppsala University and its innovation agency UUAB, the commercialisation of these 20 patents was accounted for as the result of a successful innovation.

Research Advance Accounted for as Innovation

Based on the desire to transform research advances made in the area of so-called biomarkers to analytical techniques available for users engaged in DNA and protein detection in research laboratories in the academic as well as business settings, Ulf Landegren and four research colleagues at Rudbeck Laboratory (Simon Fredriksson, Mats Gulberg, Jonas Jarvius and Mats Nilsson) engaged in the establishment of Olink in 2004. With two people with a background in Uppsala's biotech industry, Mårten Winge and Björn Ekström, the company *Olink* was established in 2004. With experience from spinning off the analytical instrument company Pyrosequencing from Pharmacia Biotech (today GE Healthcare) among others, Björn Ekström was appointed CEO.

The basic account for the possibilities of using biomarkers in panels for automated identification of protein signatures was the family of 20 patents that Professor Landegren and his colleagues transferred to Olink. Between 2004 and 2005, the estimated value of the patents transferred to Olink was approximately EUR 54,000 with the great expectation that potential incomes would be derived from the commercialisation of these technologies.

These accountings, along with the track record and judgements made by the researchers and business people involved in the project, made it possible to mobilise the first financiers, enabling the establishment of Olink. The financiers were Uppsala University's holding company UUAB, which contributed with a minor investment of EUR 100,000, along with two financing organisations controlled by the same family, the Anders Wall's Foundation and BeijerInvest. The primary market segments they identified were the academic research, the pharmaceutical and the diagnostic industries. The estimation made in 2004 referred to a worldwide market potential of roughly EUR 30b with an installation base of approximately 30,000 units.

The first year of operation mainly concerned how to transform the technological solutions described in the patents into an automated instrument, a work process that was estimated to require roughly EUR 72m. Hence, hand in hand with the technological challenges was the question of how to raise financial resources. Long before any prototype and any user applications existed, Olink had to present an accounting of the advantages of its emerging technological solution strong enough to attract a monetary flow to the company.

Based on past experiences with the vulnerability that follows being totally dependent on venture capital, the owners implemented another strategy.[4] The most promising technologies were developed in house, while others that did not seem to be critical for the instrument development were licensed out to gain capital to gain investment capital for the company.

The year after its establishment, in 2005, Olink signed an agreement with the California-based microarray technology company Affymetrix (formerly Rudbeck Laboratory related ParAllele[5] and part of Thermo Fisher Scientific, one of the world's largest suppliers of laboratory equipment). The licensing concerned the right to adopt a so-called 'Padlock Probe Technology', a method for capturing small segments of DNA, and along with being patented, it was presented by researchers at Rudbeck Laboratory in the publication *Science* 1994.[6] In October 2007, Olink announced that Applied Biosystems, another California-based company owned by Thermo Fisher Scientific, had licensed the so-called Proximity Ligation technology, which was developed for direct detection of proteins and presented in a publication by researchers at Rudbeck Laboratory in 2002.[7] The licensing deals made with Affymetrix and Applied Biosystems turned out to be very fruitful for Olink; it could avoid venture capital and still finance its own engagement in the development of a product system for biomarker discovery.

In late 2007, Olink launched its first very own product system, Duolink, a new method for detection of specific proteins, their interactions and modifications, with cancer research as its first targeted application area. The Duolink system, which implied an investment of between EUR 1,000 and 1,500 for the users (price range related to the selected primary antibody species and desired detection colour), immediately attracted attention in the user setting, and after the first year of commercialisation, it already counted thousands of customers all over the world. In 2015, when Duolink was sold to the American instrument company Sigma-Aldrich, about 1,000 research articles based on the instrument had been published. Like the licensing deals, the sell-out was made to facilitate the concentration on its new product systems, the so-called Proseek® Multiplex technology, for analysis of protein markers in several human diseases.

An Emerging Application Area and a Spin-Off: Detection for Military Purpose

One of the identified applications of the technologies developed at Rudbeck Laboratory, and further developed within Olink, was what we label the 'Q-Linea innovation path': the research and innovation field of military detection related to the so-called 'biological war defence' for the identification of agents such as bacteria, spores, viruses and toxins.

In 2007, one of the researchers behind the establishment of Olink, Jonas Jarvius, who also left the academic setting to work within this company, applied for research funding at the national military French authority—it was roughly less than EUR 1m—to get a research contract for developing a new generation of detecting systems.

The application was accepted, and Olink was connected with the French company Thales, one of the leading worldwide companies supplying special systems and solutions for the defence industry. In 2008, the French government gave Thales the task of organising a sub-suppliers network to fulfil an order, and Olink became involved as one of Thales' first-tier suppliers. However, what initially appeared as a promising opportunity soon turned out to be a tough economic requirement for the small start-up company to fulfil. Thales was required to unilaterally set all the terms concerning price, production and deliveries as well as penalties for missing milestones.

To protect Olink from possible liabilities, the idea emerged to create a separate economy and accounting system for the Q-Linea project through a spin-off for the detection engagement to a separate firm. In addition, both Jonas Jarvius and another of his former research colleagues, Magnus Nilsson, engaged in the establishment of Olink were attracted by the idea of engaging in application areas beyond the Olink business structure and saw the spin-off as an opportunity to develop their ideas. They also gained approval from Professor Landgren Rudbeck Laboratory who, together with the other co-founders, kept the ownership of Olink at 75% and a member of the Olink board, together with the rest of the Olink board to setup the new business. Hence, in 2008 the innovation journey that started within the organisational borders of Rudbeck Laboratory and then moved over to Olink took a next step over to Q-Linea AB.

The Olink board thought there were other reasons to create a separate financial system for the Q-Linea project rather than risking liabilities. The financial inability to support the required investments in the instrument development for the detection application amounted to about EUR 10m. Still, this was considered a business opportunity that should not be missed but preferably should be taken outside Olink's economy and accounting. So Olink's board decided to keep the focus on its core business of molecular tools for research on human diseases and leave the military detection technology application to continue at the spin-off named Q-Linea. Hence, by separating the accounting systems of Olink and the Q-Linea project, the latter was allowed to expand the application area of the Olink technologies in the military direction.

(The same year, another company based on the same technological roots was also spun off. This company was Halo Genomics, which was engaged in technology for preparation of DNA analysis; an area within which Olink had no desire to expand.)

A Project Becomes a Company

When the Q-Linea company was established in 2008, the initial business idea was to use the scientific advancements made at Rudbeck Laboratory as the base of Olink IP's along with the patents to develop and produce detection systems for the military industry. More specifically, Q-Linea's detection technique was based on two of Olink's 'proprietary amplification' technologies. The company Q-Linea was established in 2008 with Olink as a major owner of 38% of the shares. The remainder was divided among Professor Mats

Nilsson, Rudbeck Laboratory (22.2%) and PhD Jonas Jarvius (22.2%), who also became the CEO of the company. Then there were three minor shares: Uppsala University's holding company UUAB (3% of the shares for a total investment of EUR 26,000) and two PhD students who received about 7% of the ownership. According to one of the UUAB's managers, Q-Linea was spun out from a highly respected company that also had a very 'high' reputation on the academic level (world-leading research in their field) combined with an unusual commercial experience. Moreover, the business idea around Q-Linea seemed to be in an important field for society with a good business potential and was aligned with the core profile of Rudbeck Laboratory. This, together with the fact that the CEO Jonas Jarvius was considered to be a good leader with business-driving forces and good skills in the area of business, pushed UUAB to invest in Q-Linea. Dr. Jarvius was also recommended by the more experienced people in the 'mother company,' Olink.

Along with the commission to Thales, to which Q-Linea delivered components and technologies for detection of pathogens designed and assembled in house that turned out to provide some revenue, another military organisation showed interest in Q-Linea's technological solution. In 2008, Q-Linea got a request from the Swedish Defence Research Agency (FOI) related to one of its specific research programmes. In this programme, FOI's main task was to provide the Swedish Defence Materiel Administration (FMW), a civil authority that delivers instruments and tools to the Swedish army, with devices for detecting pathogens potentially used in biological weapons.

Q-Linea engaged in the project and in cooperation with FOI, Olink and researchers at Rudbeck Laboratory at Uppsala University, developed an instrument for the identification of a number of pathogens and designed and assembled the prototype in house. It was successfully presented in 2010. The project with the FOI provided about EUR 2m that was necessary for Q-Linea to continue its research and development (R&D).

The development of detection technologies delivered to FOI and Thales/the French military was essentially R&D funding and supported Q-Linea with financing during its first years. Q-Linea simply did not manage to attract any other investors. Hence, the main task of Q-Linea became to continue to engage in R&D to develop suggestions for detection instruments and to finalise some prototypes in cooperation with Olink.

In October 2013, after five years in business, Q-Linea managed to present a device developed for detecting pathogens in the air. The instrument, among others, was tested in a real site at the Prague subway where a simulated biological threat agent was aerosolised; the device successfully passed all the tests and was considered to be reliable and robust. However, after the two first years of working in relation to the military industry, Q-Linea's management realised how demanding it was for a small company with restricted resources, not least financial, to 'survive' as a developing partner and supplier in a context dominated by large and complex public and private organisations. From the research-based Q-Linea's point of view, the military sector, both the public and private sides, was considered slow in adopting new technological solutions and had very long purchasing cycles. Both the CEO and the board of Q-Linea considered these challenges too tough to cope with for a small company engaged in rapidly improving detection technologies. The solution became to search for other potential market applications.

Changing Innovation Direction: From Military to Medical Applications

The big question for Q-Linea was how to find an application area populated with a larger number and variety of paying customers. On one hand, the experience of developing and delivering solutions to the military industry was positive in terms of the ability to use the Rudbeck Laboratory and Olink technological base to develop applications and to raise R&D funding. On the other hand, the counterparts' long-term purchasing process and development demands putting significant demands on Q-Linea's economic endurance more or less forced the Q-Linea management to change innovation direction.

After two years of developing the technology within the frame of the Q-Linea company, with the main ambition to make the analytical items more stable and mature, in 2010, the management actively started to search for another application area. The intention was to make Q-Linea into a supplier of system solutions in the detection area, but a market analysis carried out by people from the marketing department saw that the company was still in its infancy of understanding what the technology could contribute to different using settings.

However, the expectations on potential user applications increased when the market study identified at least three possible areas within the life science setting. First, a potential was identified in the plant pathogens area, and the company soon applied for research money in that field at the European level. Second, there was an opportunity to engage in the antibiotic and antibiotic-resistance research area, in which Q-Linea's technology might contribute in terms of giving rapid answers regarding bacteria development. A third option was to use Q-Linea's technology to develop instruments for infectious disease diagnostics.

As for the antibiotic-resistant applications, in 2011, Q-Linea took part in a big international research project called RAPP-ID, initiated by the prestigious IMI[8] (Innovative Medicine Initiative). IMI represents a big public–private European platform focused on developing new drugs for patients, and RAPP-ID represented a specific attempt to develop tests for the detection of bacteria, viruses and fungi. Being efficient in developing cutting-edge and fast testing in that area would help to administer the correct antibiotic to patients and avoid developing antibiotic resistance. Q-Linea managed to acquire European funds of approximately EUR 430,000, with the goal of continuing to develop its single blood-molecule detection technology. Along with the IMI funding, smaller funding came from the Swedish Innovation agency (VINNOVA) that provided about EUR 260,000 in research grants.

Q-Linea Focuses on Diagnostic Applications: The Astrid Tool for Detecting Sepsis

The blood molecule detection area appeared as an interesting opportunity for Q-Linea. Before the engagement in the IMI project, the company had already received requests concerning the ability to use its technology as a diagnostic tool to rapidly identify which pathogen to treat with what kind of antibiotics from among colleagues at the Department of Microbiology at Uppsala University among others. Q-Linea determined that its technological base would be suitable for this application area, but it needed to be further developed in order to be embedded into an automated product system.

There were also positive indications concerning the economic aspect of engaging in this area. A market study carried out by Q-Linea revealed that the market size for such an application was about EUR 2b in the US and Europe, respectively. Hence, the Q-Linea management accounted for a successful commercialisation of its technology in infectious disease diagnostics, particularly in blood molecule analysis.

The most important characteristic of the diagnostic tool that Q-Linea had in the pipeline concerned the speed of the response provided in diagnosing certain specific bacteria. Through its involvement in the development of military detection applications Q-Linea gained experience in how to make rapid diagnostic tools for analysis of pathogens in the air, but it had less experience analysing pathogens in liquids.

The major issue was to sort out what specific diagnostic applications could fit Q-Linea's technology and which ones could also be the basis for creating a sustainable economy for the company. Many sources contributed to their judgement: years of research conducted at Rudbeck Laboratory in interaction with colleagues in the international research community, R&D within Olink in interaction with customers in academia and business, opinions from relevant stakeholders and suggestions from potential users and antibiotic resistance experts such as ReAct.[9] The experts at ReAct's headquarters in Uppsala contributed suggestions on how to set boundaries for the technological applications, for example, concerning which pathogens to include in the investigation panel and the typology of antibiotics.

All of these accounts were behind Q-Linea's interpretation that the technology had good opportunities for being used in the analysis of bloodstream infections or *sepsis*, a field strongly related to the question of how to tackle antibiotic resistance. The ambition was to develop a diagnostic product system that could rapidly identify the relevant pathogen and the corresponding antibiotic—something that would narrow down the antibiotic therapy and decrease the risk for resistance development. Beginning in 2012, Q-Linea became totally focused on developing a diagnostic instrument and applications for analysis of sepsis. Q-Linea's management estimated that the process from development to launch would require an investment of about EUR 21m.

A New Financial Actor Comes Into the Picture: The Venture Capitalist Next2B

Up to 2012 Q-Linea did not manage to attract any new investors, but a new share issue for about EUR 1.7m was made in mid-2012.

The Swedish private venture capital firm Next2 showed interest in taking over Q-Linea. This interest showed up when Q-Linea shifted its attention from the military industry to the Life Science business. Next2b was established by Mr. Bengt Ågerup in 2011, when he sold the medical technology company he had established in 1987, Q-med, to Galderma Nordic AB. The deal with Galderma provided enough financial resources to build up Next2b.

One of Next2b's first interests was Olink, and after intense negotiations with the main owner, Professor Ulf Landegren, who was keen on keeping the company in Sweden, Next2b acquired 49% of the shares. Among these were the shares owned by Uppsala University's holding company UUAB holding, which, through this affair, made a very good exit from the Olink investment. Afterwards, Next2B showed interest in an acquisition of Q-Linea, and it became the major owner with 68% of the shares. Between 2012 and 2015, Next2B invested roughly EUR 16m in Q-Linea.

Before the investment was made, Next2B wanted to develop a new business plan together with Q-Linea management and after the affair was settled, the new owner initiated several changes. For instance, managers from Next2B took major responsibility for driving the Q-Linea project forward in terms of arranging meetings with potential users and buyers to constantly amend the project plan according to identified user needs. Somehow, the Q-Linea focus on developing Astrid for the sepsis market was pushed ahead harder by Next2B.

The Astrid Technology and the Potential Users: An Intriguing and Complex Relationship

Within Q-Linea, the confidence in its technology and the ability to develop an application for analysis of sepsis was high, and so were the expectations from actors engaged in the antibiotic resistance issue, with ReAct in the forefront.

Sepsis is identified as a 'poisoned condition' resulting from the presence of pathogens—usually bacteria—in the human body. It is caused by the body's reaction to an infection, for example, in the lungs, kidneys or urinary tract, and can provoke tissue damage. The mortality rate for sepsis, which actually has been increasing in recent years, is estimated at 30% and to 80% for septic shock. Sepsis is treated with antibiotics, often in intensive care.

Early recognition and timely treatment of bloodstream pathogens are necessary for patient care. The sooner the antibiotics are prescribed, the lower the mortality rate of patients. Therefore, a central and key point is to identify and diagnose bacteria as fast as possible. The best state of the art, achieved in hospitals, is between 36 and 48 hours to diagnose the type of infection and related bacteria. Traditional and well-known techniques are called antimicrobial susceptibility tests, and they could even take more than 48 hours to provide results, but some years ago, new techniques were developed under the name of 'rapid' methods that should produce results in less than 8 hours.

With the Astrid technology, identifying the pathogen was possible within six to eight hours from blood sampling with a fully automatic workflow. It could even possibly decrease the timeframe up to four hours, but so far, the technology requires other improvements to get to that level. The complete prototype is not built yet, but according to the company, it will be ready by 2018.

Looking at the current situation, Q-Linea was fully involved in the R&D stage in terms of experiments, building instruments and finalising protocols. In 2017, Q-Linea will step into the next phase, which is to introduce a prototype and applications of the Astrid technology. So far, Q-Linea can basically show performance data of the technology, something that is useful for getting research funds and for attracting other investors. But according to the Q-Linea Diagnostic Project Manager, the big issue is reaching control over the production process—of the instrument, software and related consumables. After the prototype is finalised and is clinically validated in the hospital laboratory setting, the scaling up and production are assumed to be led by some of the established manufacturers in the diagnostic field. Some contacts have already been made between Q-Linea and an Australian partner that advises on risk management, risk validation and definition of the production process. The two companies have only set up agreements that are periodically re-negotiated, so it's not a long-term collaboration.

Some users have also been involved in analysing preliminary data and, according to the vice president, Mats Gullberg, Q-Linea has received some promising user feedback. Of course, company management is well aware that the process of getting the hospitals, laboratories and physicians to adopt the Astrid diagnostic system will be a long and rather costly process. Since 2012, Q-Linea has been exchanging experiences with four hospitals (three in Sweden and one in Denmark) and more specifically with its centralised microbiology labs. The operators of these labs are the practical users, the ones who interpret the results to the physicians, but the purchasing process of products, machines and new technologies usually involves the head of the microbiology lab. The heads of such units, together with the heads of the departments, usually make decisions as to whether or not to buy the machines. From the supplier side, it is rather difficult to influence the whole process because the head of the department only gets involved later in the final stage and usually doesn't talk with the supplier.

According to Q-Linea's CEO, beyond the complexity of the purchasing processes in the health care setting, another issue is quickly finding some basic applications: there might be different requests on the pathogen detection from users in different nations and regions. All in all, the Q-Linea management assumes that the estimated price for the Astrid product system—EUR 70,000—would be fair for hospitals, and from the perspective of the economic and social burdens of sepsis, the need to reduce antibiotic resistance included, the business opportunities for Q-Linea are considered as very promising.

Concluding Discussion

The investigation of the Q-Linea innovation journey revealed that the challenge of accounting for a potential innovation, that is for the cost and benefits of something new in a developing, producing and using setting *before* launch, has been solved by what can be labelled as 'accounting based on limitations'.

First the creation of a new organisational border between Olink and the Q-Linea innovation project, and consequently the establishment of two separated accounting systems, was made to save Olink from the losses of the Q-Linea innovation project. Despite the buzz created around Q-Linea and its promising innovation, hitherto the company, with its 40 employees, has only posted red figures; the total loss between 2008 and 2015 is EUR 10m.

Second, the accounts concerning Q-Linea's ability to cover its costs and deliver gains was based on its technology's contributions in a developing setting, that is, in public and private R&D. Publications and patents were used as proof of the significance of the new technology and in the mobilisation of social, material and financial resources, such as in terms of a number of successful research applications. Furthermore, patents were used in licensing of technological areas that Q-Linea were not aiming to develop further, giving rise to financial resources that allowed a further development of the Astrid technology. Hence, the type of deals that Q-Linea was able to establish based on this accounting were licensing agreements and R&D funding from the EU and national policy organisations.

However, the accounting for what the Astrid technology can contribute, if and when embedded into commercial producer–user interfaces, is still based on expectations. In contrast to the accounting of future benefits of potential innovations developed in the closely related Rudbeck lab and Olink environment, Q-Linea's accounting for future benefits in a producer–user setting had to be made with almost no experience in the focal application area.

This, in contrast to Rudbeck lab and Olink, which had a long history of heavy relationships with leading actors in their common focal application area, that is, with acknowledged users of molecular tools for research in public and private environments, as well as with some of the most acknowledged equipment suppliers. Hence, Rudbeck Laboratory and Olink accounting for novel product systems aimed to be embedded into molecular tools' producer–user interfaces could be made based on significant experiences of the economic logic of these settings.

However, Q-Linea lacked earlier experiences with supply and use of molecular tools for blood infection analysis, and neither within Q-Linea nor within Rudbeck Laboratory and Olink were there any main experiences of embedding novel products within this setting to rely on. The future benefits of Q-Linea's innovation were instead accounted for on estimations made in the developing setting—and on a beforehand-assumed market share of a user setting. However, in terms of mobilising social material and financial resources, this accounting turned out to be extremely successful for Q-Linea's founders; it resulted in the deal with a new owner, the venture capitalist Next2b.

If the future production of accounts concerning the benefits of Q-Linea's innovative product system, Astrid, will be based on trials to embed it into producer–user interfaces related to analysis of bloodstream infections in a hospital setting, or if, to create a successful sell-out for the new owners, Next2b, it will be based on accounts concerning its positive contributions in a developing setting combined with abstract estimations of a future market share, is still an open question. In the eyes of those responsible for Q-Linea's establishment of producer–user interfaces, the realisation of producer–user interfaces is still considered to be years ahead. Hence, for the moment, Q-Linea's potential innovation is surrounded by a positive buzz and red figures.

Notes

1. Stina Thor, OssDsign och Q-linea bland Sveriges 33 hetaste teknikbolag www.mynewsdesk.com/se/uppsala_innovation_centre_ab/pressreleases/ossdsign-och-Q-Linea-bland-sveriges-33-hetaste-teknikbolag-979774
2. www.igp.uu.se/research/molecular_tools/ulf_landegren/2016-11-10
3. www.igp.uu.se/research/molecular_tools/ulf_landegren/2016-11-10
4. The CEO, Björn Ekström, was one of the entrepreneurs behind the Pharmacia spin-off Pyrosequencing, which was totally financed by a venture capital company that also merged it with another of its investments, something that basically became the end of Pyrosequencing's innovation journey (the Pyrosequencing innovation journey is described in Ingemansson and Waluszewski, 2009, and the role of the venture capital investor in Strömsten and Waluszewski, 2012).
5. ParAllele Biosciences was established in 2001 in cooperation between Ulf Landegren and Mats Nilsson at Rudbeck Laboratory in Uppsala and five researchers led by Prof. Ronaghi at the Stanford Genome Technology Center (SGTC) of Stanford University to develop instruments for discovery and analysis of variations in the human genome
6. Nilsson, M., Malmgren, H., Samiotaki, M., Kwiatkowski, M., Chowdhary, B. P., and Landegren, U., 1994. Padlock probes: circularizing oligonucleotides for localized DNA detection. *Science*, Vol. 265, Issue 5181, pp. 2085–2088.
7. Fredriksson, S., Gullberg, M., Jarvius, J., Olsson, C., Pietras, K., Gústafsdóttir, S. M., Ostman, A., and Landegren, U., 2002 May. Protein detection using proximity-dependent DNA ligation assays. *Nature Biotechnology*, Vol. 20, Issue 5, pp. 473–477.

8. The IMI is Europe's largest public–private initiative aiming to speed up the development of better and safer medicines for patients, undertaken by the European Union and the pharmaceutical industry association EFPIA (www.imi.europa.eu).
9. ReAct is a global network of antibiotic resistance experts with nodes in five continents and headquarter in Uppsala (www.reactgroup.org/about-us).

References

Baraldi, E., Gregori, G. L., and Perna, A., 2011. 'Network evolution and the embedding of complex technical solutions: The case of the Leaf House network'. *Industrial Marketing Management*, Vol. 40, Issue 6, pp. 838–852.

Baraldi, E. and Strömsten, T. 2009. 'Controlling and combining resources in networks – from Uppsala to Stanford and back again: The case of a biotech innovation'. *Industrial Marketing Management*, Vol. 38, Issue 5, pp. 541–552.

Håkansson, H. (ed.), 1982. *International Marketing and Purchasing of Industrial Goods: An Interaction Approach*. New York: Wiley.

Håkansson, H., Ford, D., Gadde, L.-E., Snehota, I., and Waluszewski, A., 2009. *Business in Networks*. Chichester: Wiley & Sons.

Håkansson, H. and Johanson, J., 1992. 'A model of industrial networks'. In B. Axelsson and G. Easton (eds.), *Industrial Networks: A New View of Reality*. London: Routledge, 28–34.

Håkansson, H. and Olsen, O., 2015. 'The roles of money and business deals in network structures'. *Industrial Marketing Management*, Vol. 48, pp. 207–217.

Håkansson, H. and Snehota, I. (eds.), 1995. *Developing Relationships in Business Networks*. London: International Thomson.

Håkansson, H. and Waluszewski, A., 2002. *Managing Technological Development: IKEA, the Environment and Technology*. London: Routledge.

Håkansson, H. and Waluszewski, A., 2007. 'Interaction: The only means to create use'. In H. Håkansson and A. Waluszewski (eds.), *Knowledge and Innovation in Business and Industry: The Importance of Using Others*. London: Routledge, 147–167.

Horngren, T., Datar, S. M., Foster, G., Rajan, M., and Ittner, C., 2009. *Cost Accounting: A Managerial Emphasis*, 13th ed. Upper Saddle River, NJ: Pearson Prentice Hall.

Ingemansson, M., and Waluszewski, A. 2009. 'Success in science and burden in business. On the difficult relationship between science as a developing setting and business as a producer-user setting'. *IMP Journal*, Vol. 3, Issue 2, pp. 20–56.

Lind, J., 2017. 'The role of accounting for managing innovation processes when relationships matter'. *IMP Journal*, Vol. 11, Issue 1, pp. 7–24.

Perna, A., Baraldi, E., and Waluszewski, A., 2015. 'Is the value created necessarily associated with money? On the connections between an innovation process and its monetary dimension: The case of Solibro's thin-film solar cells'. *Industrial Marketing Management*, Vol. 46, pp. 108–121.

Strömsten, T., and Waluszewski, A. 2012. 'Resource interaction and innovation in networks: The role of venture capital governance in a biotech start-up'. *Journal of Business Research*, Vol. 65, Issue 2, pp. 232–244.

3 The Role of Deals and Economic Calculations for Temporary Solutions in Innovation Processes

Carl Henning Christner, Johnny Lind and Torkel Strömsten

Introduction

Researchers in management and marketing have long studied the importance of inter-organisational relationships for innovation processes (Rogers 1962, 2003; Håkansson 1989; von Hippel 1986). This research has shown how innovations are often developed and spread through the re-combination of resources in and among different organisations (Håkansson and Waluszewski 2002; Wedin 2001). Innovation is seen as a complex process that depends on the interaction between organisations and the adaptation of resources. Tension can arise because different actors have diverging interests and interpretations of the potential of an innovation. The actors involved need to find a mutual acceptable solution concerning the innovation that reconciles their different interests, relationships and resource dependencies, such that the development process can continue. Thus, inter-organisational innovation processes are often characterised by temporary solutions (Dubois and Araujo 2006; Hoholm and Olsen 2012). Studies have shown how inter-organisational relationships and resource interdependencies can lead to specific temporary solutions concerning product design and production, which in turn can push the development process in a certain direction (Håkansson and Waluszwski 2002).

However, while this line of research has demonstrated the importance of inter-organisational relationships in innovation processes, less attention has been devoted to accounting and the role of economic calculations (Baraldi and Strömsten 2009; Alenius et al. 2015). Financial matters have recently received renewed attention in marketing research with the concept of *business deals* (Håkansson and Olsen 2015; Perna et al. 2015; Olsen and Håkansson 2017). The concept of business deals highlights the importance of the contractual agreements that regulates the monetary flows associated with an innovation process, such as patenting, licensing and grants. A business deal is a negotiated agreement "regarding what the parties shall contribute and what they will receive in return from activities addressed by it" (Håkansson and Olsen 2015, p. 212). An organization may negotiate business deals with different counterparties during an innovation process. The ownership deal (Håkansson and Olsen 2015, p. 213) is important but not the only type of deal influencing inter-organisational innovation processes. The advantage of a business deal is that it could reduce the uncertainty and increase the predictability for the involved companies. However, business deals can also introduce rigidity, which could hinder the development process.

Financial calculations such as accounting have been considered to play a significant role in the monitoring and control of the business deals. These calculations are primarily seen here as a tool for measuring the monetary flows and the transactions of value among the different counterparties agreed upon in such deals (see Baraldi and Lind 2017), which Tomkins (2001) referred to as "the mastery of events." However, recent research in the accounting literature has suggested that accounting calculations may not only play a role as a measure of monetary value in business deals, but such calculations may also influence the innovation process by providing different representations of the innovation's commercial and economic potential (see Christner and Strömsten 2015; Miller and O'Leary 2007; Moll 2015; Mouritsen et al. 2009; Revellino and Mouritsen 2009. Calculations of an innovation's economic potential are important in the innovation process. Innovations are not only technical, but also economic, endeavours (see Hughes 1983). Different development trajectories are often motivated and justified in economic terms based on different calculations of the innovation's value. However, rather than only describing the innovation, these calculations also help to change it by envisioning certain possible futures. As Revellino and Mouritsen (2009, p. 31) note, financial calculations are "involved in luring actors into doing new things by their ability to inspire them to ask new questions and to see new opportunities." This is because different calculations embody certain economic ideas about when and how innovation should be conducted in time and space (see Miller and O'Leary 2007). For example, different calculations might embody assumption about the time value of money, making the near time more valuable than the long term. Furthermore, they may embody different assumptions about the value of the market and the customers, making certain design features desirable.

Taken together, these studies suggest that economic calculations might influence innovation processes. However, little is known about the interplay between business deals and economic calculations. Research on the importance of business deals in inter-organisational innovation processes suggest that the relation between value creation and the monetary flows decided by the deals is highly complex; the monetary gains distributed to a company is not so well correlated with the resources a company invests in the innovation process (Håkansson and Olsen 2015; Perna et al. 2015; Olsen and Håkansson 2017). However, the picture becomes even more complex if we also consider the different calculations which represent the commercial and economic potential of an innovation. Each of these calculations might suggest different potential directions for the development process, making different deals, relationships and design choices possible and desirable.

Based on a longitudinal in-depth case study of a potentially ground-breaking innovation in the biotech industry, we will examine how these different representations of the innovations economic value—in the form of deals and calculations—were implicated in the innovation process. We argue that these different forms of economic representations should not be understood as "an expression of deeper consistency" (Law and Akrich 1994). They were different deals and different calculations throughout the innovation processes. However, our study suggests that deals and economic calculations were not necessarily a coherent 'package', but there were intersections and tensions between them which pushed and pulled the development process in different directions. Certain economic calculations could motivate and inspire certain deals, which in turn could give arise to different economic calculations. We find that these interactions between deals and calculations had considerable influence on the development process, shaping different temporary solutions and eventually leading to the development of a particular type of innovation.

Hence, our main claim is that economic calculations are central in inter-organisational innovation processes. In addition, we demonstrate the need to be careful "not to treat 'the economic' in an undifferentiated manner" (Mennicken et al. 2008) because different economic calculations can have different consequences. Based on these observations, our study also contributes to the longstanding discussion in the accounting literature about whether financial calculations hinder or facilitate innovation. Early studies leaned more towards the conclusion that formal financial calculations were an obstacle to innovation (see Rockness and Shields 1984; Abernethy and Brownell 1997), since the emphasis on financial control was in contrast with the uncertain nature of innovation processes, which often deviated from preset plans (see Carlsson et al 2009; Carlsson-Wall and Kraus 2015; Ford et al. 1998; Hoholm and Olsen 2012). Later studies have shown that financial calculations can also play an enabling role in development processes by structuring the dialogue between different participants (see Davila, 2000, 2005; Ditillo 2004; Nixon 1998). However, it is only recently that there has been a growing recognition that accounting calculations can be both hindering and enabling at the same time or enabling at some point in time and hindering later on in the same innovation process (see Christner and Strömsten 2015; Mouritsen et al. 2009; Revellino and Mouritsen 2015). We extend this line of research by further exploring how deals and calculations not only shaped temporary solutions but also how these solutions created path dependencies for the actors involved in the innovation process. The temporary solutions opened up some paths but also closed some critical ones.

The remainder of the chapter is organised in the following way: In the next section, the case of Pyrosequencing will be presented. The case focuses on the innovation and development of a new and innovative technology for sequencing and analysing DNA, intended for scientific and commercial use. We follow the development process in four phases: The first phase begins in

1986 when one of the founders, Pål Nyrén, at the time a young researcher, came up with a new idea for sequencing human DNA. This phase ends with the formation of a commercial company built around this innovation, called Pyrosequencing AB, aiming to get as large market share as possible of the sequencing market. The second phase recounts how a venture capital firm, called HealthCap, became a main owner of Pyrosequencing AB. This phase describes how the internal rate of return (IRR) calculation linked the product development process to a new set of economic ideas and the interests of dispersed actors such as the venture capital firm and its investors. The third phase recounts how Pyrosequencing became a listed company on the stock exchange; it follows the manner in which the valuations performed on the stock market mediated decisions about product development activities in the company. In the final phase, the company's profit and loss statement is in focus as well as the company's cash reserve that in end led to a revered initial public offering (IPO). Thereafter follows a discussion, which draws together the main observations concerning deals, calculations and innovation from the four empirical phases. The chapter ends with some concluding remarks.

Pyrosequencing: The Role of Deals and Calculations in the Development of a New DNA Sequencing Method

This case is about an innovation going through several types of ownerships and how the innovation in different ways was influenced by the deals made, how the calculation used by these owners to motivate current and/or future deals and how the solutions, the outcomes from the deals and calculations, also affected the development path of the innovation in different ways. The case starts in the middle of the 1980s and continued to the middle of the 2000s. The study is mainly based on 35 interviews that were conducted in beginning of the 2000s. The interviewees held various positions within the studied company such as scientific founders, chief executive officer (CEO), chief financial officer (CFO), chief technological officer (CTO) and several project managers. Interviewees were also held with individuals from other actors related to the company such as investors, financial analysts, customers and suppliers. For a more detailed account of the research methods, see Christner and Strömsten (2015) and Strömsten and Waluszewski (2012).

Phase 1: Scientists and the Need for Funding

The case starts in 1986 when Pål Nyrén, a young post-doctoral student from Sweden, found himself working with analysing the bovine mitochondrial phosphate-carrier protein at the Laboratory for Molecular Biology in Cambridge. To his help he had a specific method, named after the Nobel prize winner in chemistry, Fredrick Sanger. The Sanger method was, and still is, widely used in laboratory work all over the world to analyse DNA sequences. While working in the laboratory, Nyrén found himself putting together tests, making manual work that took a lot of time. He was simply bored with the work that he thought could be made much more effective. While standing in the laboratory, he could not help himself starting to think about alternative ways of doing this activity to analyse DNA sequences.

Nyrén had previously studied biology and therefore came up with the idea of approaching the problem in a somewhat unorthodox way, by using an enzyme called pyrophosphate. This enzyme could identify if a base pair of nucleotides was merged in a DNA sequence (see Nyrén 2007).[1] This method had some benefits, or at least Nyrén thought so at the time. The idea would make the process simpler and faster than the traditional way of analysing DNA. Furthermore, Nyrén's idea also offered an instant analysis that was seen as somewhat revolutionary in this field. He kept the idea close to himself. If the idea had been revealed, it had belonged to the University of Cambridge. The Swedish system is different, since all ideas and innovations belong to the individual researcher.

Back in Sweden, Nyrén began searching and applying for research grants so that he could develop the method further. He searched for funding from different research foundations; the intention was to create "deals" with the research foundations, and his currency that he wanted to trade was his research ideas. Nyrén's aim was to create top-class research, and the foundations part was to fund his work. However, the research foundations had other ideas or were bound to procedures that did not fit Nyrén's research. The research foundation's aim was to fund "basic research," and this was not in line with what Nyrén was doing. "It was impossible to get funding," Nyrén recalled, ". . . I was focused on the technology, to develop a method for DNA sequencing, and it seemed, generally, to be harder to get money for that [kind of project]." Instead, Nyrén had to use money that he had received for a previous research project to fund the new one. He worked on his spare time to develop the method.

Since creating deals with the research foundations was hard. Development of the technology did not happen in an easy way. When Nyrén accepted a position at the Royal Institute of Technology in 1990, the development of the new technology took off. At this institution, he started to collaborate with Mattias Uhlén, a well-known scientist on the rise. Uhlén, was well funded and conducted research in a related area. Uhlén was also working with many PhD students in different projects and was able to allocate resources to Nyrén's idea about a new DNA sequencing method. They formed a research group and got going in materializing the idea of using pyrophosphate in DNA sequencing and analysis.

The initial intention was to create a better method than the one Nyrén had experienced as a postdoctoral fellow in Cambridge. A novel method that they believed would render high quality research and publications in the best journals. However, soon the two researchers realised that the method could have commercial value as well. Then they started to think about a market and potential buyers. Nyrén and Uhlén discussed what market they should aim for. Nyrén's idea was to go for a very general technology that could find different types of applications within the field of DNA sequencing and analysis. "I thought it would be the same as with computers," Nyrén explained, "in that, when people eventually would have access to this technology, they would figure out how they can use it."

Soon, however, they started to think more actively and in more concrete terms about a future market. They started to do simple calculations that showed that the technology had the potential to be successful also in financial terms. Nyrén and Uhlén imagined the market to be laboratories around the world that in different phases of the research needed quick and reliable analysis of DNA strands. There was a large number of such laboratories. The market share that they calculated was rather large, and the market was also projected to grow in the future. Hence, the simple calculations indicated that the technology had the potential to create an impressive profitability. The researchers had potential deals in mind when starting to design the product at this stage. It was at this stage a rather "clean" deal; even if it was only a potential, future deal, it was composed of two parties only, the researchers and their company and the laboratory buying the product.

Nyrén and Uhlén increased the detail in the calculations of the potential profitability of the technology through a comparison of its innovation with another technology, the PCR method.[2] The PCR method is a vital part of analysing DNA. PCR is used to increase or amplify the DNA sample to many (thousands) copies that can be analysed. Often the method used to analyse these was and still is based on the Sanger method. All laboratories that are conducting DNA analysis use a PCR equipment. By looking at the number of laboratories in the world that used PCR machines, Nyrén and Uhlén could calculate the potential market for their innovation and where future deals could be found:

> We looked at the PCR method that can be found in every lab [doing DNA analyses] all over the world. Our scenario was that researchers first needed a PCR machine in order to prepare the DNA, then they must have a Pyrosequencing machine that can perform the DNA sequencing. Our goal was that there should be a Pyrosequencing machine in every lab where there was a PCR machine—that's how we got a clear number [of the size of the potential market].
>
> (Pål Nyrén)

Based on this thinking, they remade their calculations and realised that even a smaller market share would lead to a financially viable company. A market share of 10 percent would be more than enough to generate a lot of sales. The calculation was based on a particular view of potential future deals and market share. The calculation suggested that Nyrén and Uhlén and their research would develop a certain type of their method. The method should be "general" and be able to address many different users. For example, the read length of DNA strands was one dimension that was incorporated in this calculation; the potential customers wanted a method that could analyse both short and long strands of DNA.

At the same time, the HUGO project (Human Genome Project), a world-wide research project with the ambition to map the human genome, was being finalised. The HUGO project had shown that genetic variation could be understood by studying so-called single nucleotide polymorphisms (SNPs). At this time, there were no market for SNPs, but the HUGO project pointed clearly in the direction of an increased need for better understanding of how genome variation could be understood. The role of SNPs in developing new drugs was considered to be of outmost importance.[3]

At this point in time, the research group had just made a breakthrough in the development process: they had discovered that a specific enzyme, apyrase, could be used to wash away unnecessary nucleotides with the result that four enzymes remained that created a light signal that detected DNA sequences. The research group now had a reliable form of method. This result was later published in the prestigious academic journal *Science* (Ronaghi et al. 1998), making it an academic success.

Now the researchers with Nyrén and Uhlén in the leading positions had to decide whether their technology would be geared towards SNPs (that represented short DNA sequences) or long strands of DNA sequences (that in turn could be more complicated to develop). Their initial ambition with the method was to develop a technology that could rival the Sanger method, would this have to be postponed while the technology was optimised to read short DNA sequences. However, the research group decided to maintain the focus on the whole-genome sequencing market. The target was still to increase the read length to 200 to 300 base pairs, which would appeal to a broader range of customers and make the technology more competitive on the general DNA sequencing market. The first prototype was constructed with such technical content and target market.

Phase 2: Forming a Company, Getting Money From Venture Capital, Paying Suppliers and Developing the Product for Future Deals

With the prototype ready to be tested, the researchers at the Royal Institute of Technology could see the potential in its innovation. However, they also realised also that there was a need for capital to make the innovation real and to commercialise the idea of DNA sequencing. Nyrén, Uhlén, some of their PhD students (Mostafa Ronaghi and Bertil Pettersson) and another person, who would function as the one who developed the method into a workable product, formed a company and called it Pyrosequencing, namned after the method that they had developed. Uhlén had just before been appointed a member of a newly founded venture capital company, HealthCap, as a scientific advisory board member and an industry expert. As soon as the new company Pyrosequencing AB was founded, he pitched the Pyrosequencing business case to HealthCap's management.[4]

With HealthCap as an owner, the development process took a somewhat new direction. For HealthCap, it was important to develop the new firm into a real firm that could be sold to another company or to make an IPO. Hence, the development process came to focus much on time. This corresponds to the way HealthCap and other venture capital firms calculate their investments. The most important measure that they focus on is the IRR. This is also the measure that investors follow and act upon. A venture capital fund with a higher IRR is considered better than one with a lower IRR. In the IRR calculation, time is built in, and this implies that the shorter time under management, the higher the IRR (everything else equal).

The board of Pyrosequencing AB was then filled with prominent people from the Swedish business sector and top-class researchers, among them a Noble Prize winner and a former CEO of one of Sweden's largest companies, who became the chairman. HealthCap was represented by two board members. Furthermore, HealthCap also recruited a CEO for the company that could in a short time create the administrative routines around a company. The chief technology officer was one of the founders, a person who previously had reviewed the technology for a potential acquisition by Pharmacia Biotech. The board and the management set a number of milestones that the company was to achieve within a certain time frame. The milestones were mainly related to product development, such as creating prototypes and beta versions within a certain time.

Time became a critical performance indicator overall. The interviewees related this to the involvement of a venture capital company with a clear focus on the exit.[5] An early exit would also improve the IRR measure, which was important when HealthCap was evaluated by its investors. This interest of keeping time down was translated into decisions and priorities when it came to product development, what to develop and how it was to be organised.

The strong emphasis on IRR and development time changed the direction of the innovation process. The focus shifted from the original vision of long or even whole-genome sequencing towards developing short DNA strands. This was from the founders' perspective a major strategic shift that created tensions between them and the management team. Despite this, Pyrosequencing and its management decided to focus on short SNPs, that is, shorter strands of DNA. The reason behind this strategic shift was that this application was easier to develop, and it was within reach timewise to meet in relation to the milestones that had been formulated. Basically, the focus on SNP was a more exploitative (March 1991) decision, while the choice to go for the longer read length involved much more exploration. The shorter development time for the innovation and the more focused customer offer reduced the perceived uncertainty of the calculation. The market for SNPs was considered to be booming commercially. Hence, the management was able to support this decision with positive financial numbers and a solid business case. The SNP was expected to be worth 750 million USD in 2004. Looking into the future in 1997, it was certainly bright for Pyrosequencing and its investors.

How Pyrosequencing was to reap a decent market share was not clear, however. In the end, the management and board decided to go for a so-called razor blade model, in which the inspiration could be found in other companies located in Uppsala (but also in the razor blade producer Gillette). In the end, the company board and management went for a physical product, a reagent kit consisting of the enzymes that were critical when doing the sequencing and a software program that would facilitate the actual analysis. The idea was to sell the physical product, a machine, relatively cheaply and then make most of the money on the reagent kits (the enzymes). This decision was discussed by one of the managers within Pyrosequencing:

> If you are bringing in venture capital, there must be something like this [a razor-blade business model]. Otherwise you run the risk of selling the whole idea away. The instrument must be easy for the customer to use, but then there should also be specific chemicals tied to the instrument that could be protected intellectually with patents.
>
> (Manager, Pyrosequencing)

As time became of outmost importance, it also influenced how product development was organised. It was decided that most of the development activities would be conducted by suppliers and partners that could be found in the close network of companies in the Uppsala region, where the company had been located. Contracts with the suppliers were signed; often these were well known and composed of small companies (one or two people) geographically close to Pyrosequencing. The reagent kits and the enzymes were considered so important from an intellectual property perspective that this development activity would be kept in house. One of the managers recalled:

> There was never a question of building up our own product development organisation. Instead, we used our network in the Uppsala region to get things done faster. Both the equipment and the software were developed by other firms, although I was overseeing it.

In addition, after having decided to focus on SNPs, the product package was discussed among top management. It was also possible to evaluate which steps of the DNA analysis that the product should involve. The basic question was if the product should incorporate all steps from design and preparation to coding and analysis of the whole cycle or focus on some of the steps. A product that incorporated design and preparation in the equipment would make customers buy a more integrated solution instead of being forced to handle separated steps in the process and would be a product that would simplify the process of DNA analysis for the potential customers. However, in the end, it was decided to go only for the coding and analysis step. These were the core steps in the whole cycle of activities and were the steps when Pyrosequencing could differentiate itself in relation to other alternatives. The main reason behind the decision to leave out design and preparation of tests was to the time saved in the development work; it was complex to integrate all the different activities in one machine. A shorter development time was viewed as the most important aspect in the IRR calculation, and a focus on the coding and analysis step reduced the perceived uncertainty in the IRR calculation.

Initially, the cost to develop an equipment and a reagent kit and a software was estimated to 7.5 million USD. In the end, development costs were closer to 25 million USD. HealthCap was a lead investor in three rounds. However, the increased cost was not a problem as long as the milestones for the product development time were kept. The financial numbers in the IRR calculation still indicated that the Pyrosequencing project was a profitable one for HealthCap. The development was finalised in the PSQ96 system that was bought by AstraZeneca as the first customer.

Phase 3: Pyrosequencing Moving Towards the Stock Exchange, the Use of Discounted Cash Flows and Aiming for a Mass Market

With well-known paying customers such as AstraZeneca, the board decided that Pyrosequencing was ready to go public through an IPO. The development process had so far been unexpectedly smooth; even if the initial budget for the project was heavily overrun, this was not considered a major drawback. Instead, the most important milestones were met, and the board started to plan for an IPO during 1999. Since Pyrosequencing even had buying customers, the company included more than just a high-class academic research. The company had proved that it could turn scientific research into a commercial product. Hence, deals with customers worked as a signal to the financial market to prove that Pyrosequencing was a good investment. It showed that the company was able to generate future cash flows. The deals with customers reduced the perceived uncertainty for the potential investors when they calculated the value of Pyrosequencing. The IPO of Pyrosequencing resulted in high returns for HealthCap and its investors. The share price more than doubled within the first six month after the IPO. The successful IPO of Pyrosequencing made it easier for HealthCap to raise new money from potential investors when it wanted to embark on a new fund.

The IPO was also further pressured the management to speed up product development. This was partly decided earlier, but in this process, further features were taken away from the equipment. One of the involved managers at Pyrosequencing commented:

> The product development was very effective and went very quickly. The price we paid for accelerating the product development was the lack of flexibility and lack of possibilities to adapt to alternative solutions . . . All these things require testing—and testing takes time.

When Pyrosequencing was listed on the stock exchange in June 2000, it was considered a big success by all involved parties, the media and other stakeholders. The IPO came close in time to the finalising of the HUGO project, and the media attention that was given to the HUGO project also spilled over to Pyrosequencing and its IPO. Pyrosequencing was simply everybody's darling at the time. It was given credit and attention in all different sorts of business press. One of the most prominent accolades came when Forbes listed Pyrosequencing as one of the world's "300 best small companies." The company took great pride in this and even sent out a press release about it.

However, even if success was sweet, being a listed company became also somewhat of a shock for top management and most specifically for the CEO and CFO. The CEO recalled how much time he spent on meetings with journalists and financial analysts.

> We are exposed to a 'world' with quarterly reporting, meetings with analysts, conferences, you name it. I spend 25 percent of my time on investor relations. It is a considerable amount of time.
>
> (CEO, Pyrosequencing)

Being listed on the stock exchange, the share price became of great importance for the company management. The successful IPO had resulted in a high market value, and the capital market expected Pyrosequencing to grow by 40 percent annually. This situation created stress among the management team. Discussions took place about how to defend the high valuation and how to find the growth that the financial market expected from the firm. If no growth was to be found, the share price would go down; this was clear for the management team. As a consequence of the pressure from the capital market, the top priority for the management was to increase sales. The management focused the company resources primarily on marketing and sales. The razor blade business model emphasises that in this phase of the business cycle the main task was to sell instruments, which later would generate sales of reagent kits. A key accounting metric in Pyrosequencing was the number of sold instruments to customers. Some interviewees even stated that it was more important to sell instruments than to educate the customers in how to use the instruments. The pressure from the capital market also influenced the company's communication to the financial market. "Good" news, such as big orders, was communicated, and this seemed to be especially important when a quarter was about to end and information to the market was expected, as explained by the first CFO of the company.

Even if the product was very well received by customers and users, they soon started to indicate that the features that had been developed and supplied were not enough. As most customers that Pyrosequencing was addressing were larger academic institutions and companies involved in drug discovery, it was important to handle large volumes of tests. Since the decision to only focus on the analysis and coding step had been taken, the activities that were needed to get there (design and test preparation) had been downplayed in the development work. Now customers asked for these features to be able to scale up their "production" of research. The product itself and the activities it performed were apparent, but the scale of its operations was not enough, forcing customers into a very labour-intensive processes. Furthermore, the customers also started to question the cost of the reagent kits that one had to buy from Pyrosequencing. Since variable cost per test was the focus for the customers, it was easy to compare the solution Pyrosequencing provided with alternatives, and here Pyrosequencing did not come out well.

From an initial good sales development, sales declined and did not live up to expectations. The idea was to sell the equipment for a low price and then make the money from the IP-protected reagent kits. However, even if the company sold more equipment, the sales of reagent kits did not take off. It was clear that something had to be done. Since the high-volume customers wanted more automatisation, the path for new products and solutions seemed to be in this segment. For these reasons, the company management started to work on developing the second generation of equipment that would address the issues identified and discussed above (integrate the whole customer process and the need to automated test preparation). This product would make it possible to run 384 tests at the same time compared with 96 in the original version. The process would further be automated and integrate all the steps asked for by customers.

Phase 4: Stopping the Bleeding and Selling the Company

The efforts to develop the new version of the equipment required large financial resources. The development and testing of the equipment took place both in Sweden and in US at Stanford University, where one of the founders now worked. The development seemed to work well, but the project was much more complex than the original one. The number of physical interfaces that had to work smoothly together had increased exponentially, and more work now had moved inside the company. Still many of the critical components and systems were managed and developed by outside suppliers. One of these systems, the automated of liquids from tests, created problems. The supplier responsible for this had been involved in the first version of the technology and had done a very good job. However, making the liquids automated did not go as well as the company management had hoped for. Several other issues came up along the way when developing the equipment. At the same time, the company now faced pressure from the financial market to increase sales, and when this growth never materialised, the stock price started to go down rapidly. Because the development work did not succeed, the stress increased inside the company. The development project was heavily delayed, and many technical issues were still unresolved.

Sales went down, and the customers waited for the new version (and updated version of the old system that also was delayed). Furthermore, the SNP market that Pyrosequencing had been targeting was not developing according to the pervious high expectations. Pyrosequencing's market share was lower than had been expected, only 5 to 10 percent of the market. The share price continued in accordance also to go down, and around 2002 the market valuation of Pyrosequencing was lower than the cash reserve in the company.

Something had to be done and the board decided to shift the direction of the company. Now cost cutting was the priority, and the company aimed for "near term profitability." A profit and loss calculation guided the management when it started to execute activities aimed at making Pyrosequencing a smaller but profitable company. The company started to cutting staff to reduce costs and increased short-term revenues. The ambition to increase short-term revenues had important strategic consequences because the decision was to license the right to conduct whole-genome sequencing based on the Pyrosequencing technology. The founders have since the start of Pyrosequencing argued that the company should allocate resources and develop such a product. The company management and the board had instead prioritised the SNP market and in the end licenced out the whole-genome sequencing. However, at this point, it was clear that the short-term profit and loss statement was emphasised by the management.

At the same time, HealthCap worked to find an exit for one of its other portfolio companies, Personal Chemistry. This company developed equipment and solutions for speeding up chemical reactions that could be used in drug discovery and in drug production. The idea came up to merge the two companies, Pyrosequencing and Personal Chemistry. It was clear that the idea behind the merger was not based on an industrial logic. The technologies that the two companies had developed had very little to do with each other, and commercially, the companies, addressed different customer groups and needs. There was further no technological platform that was common that could be exploited further. Instead, the main resource that HealthCap saw was the cash reserve that Pyrosequencing controlled in combination with its place on the stock exchange. Through this merger, Personal Chemistry would both get a place on the stock exchange and get control over the cash for future expansion.

The merger, that in technical terms was an acquisition of Personal Chemistry by Pyrosequencing, meant the end for Pyrosequencing as an independent company. From then on Pyrosequencing was a division within the newly formed company, which soon also acquired an American biotech tool manufacturer and then changed its name to Biotage.

The Pyrosequencing division changed direction again and now focused on the diagnostic market, in which different features of the technology were important and the small-scale samples were a viable way forward and were appreciated by customers. Even if the new technology now was working (with small samples sizes), the division sales after the strategic change were a fraction of the expectations a few years earlier. In 2008, the Pyrosequencing division was sold to the German biotech tool supply company Qiagen. Interestingly, the license to sequence the whole genome was now exploited by the company 454 Life Sciences. The vision to sequence long DNA strands was hence realised by another actor.

Discussion

The case study illustrates how the innovation processes consist of temporary solutions in the different phases. We further illustrate how calculations create deals and shape the innovation processes in certain directions. Our case illustrates how accounting and the calculations in the form of market shares, IRR, discounted cash flow valuation model and profit and loss statements and number of delivered instruments were critical for the scope and direction of the innovation process. Initially, the founders used a simple market share calculation to understand the commercial potential of the innovation. The venture capital firm then brought in the IRR to the company, which influenced the technology in different ways. On the stock exchange, Pyrosequencing was evaluated by DCF calculations, which influenced the company to prioritise growth in the forms of selling instruments, instead of developing features on the technology. And in the last phase, the owners made a more traditional profit and loss analysis to first stop the bleeding of the company and create near-term profitability and then an analysis that consisted of not only Pyrosequencing but also another portfolio company in its fund in combination. All these types of calculations shaped particular deals, which were related to the innovation efforts and temporary solutions.

The first phase showed how the prototype and the market share calculation formed the deal with the KTH team. However, the deals from research foundations that Nyrén searched for never materialised. The research foundations were not interested in the development of a tool for DNA sequencing. Instead, Nyrén mobilised a group of researchers at another university that had resources in terms of money but also infrastructure (laboratory facilities) and human resources. In the beginning, the deals that supported the innovation forced the researchers to focus on high-quality academic output. It meant that the new technology needed to be better than the existing Sanger method. Soon the idea Nyrén presented to the research group somewhat changed, when the researchers started to make simple calculations that showed the ideas' commercial potential. The calculations and possible future deals helped Nyrén and Uhlén to enrol both senior researchers as well as PhD students and the surrounding resources, including the money that

Uhlén had been very successful in securing through his research projects. After a while, new, more detailed calculations were developed that indicate that the idea had potential to create a viable company even with a smaller market share. The new calculation defined potential customers and specified the content of the technology. Possible customers were identified as all laboratories that have a PCR machine. The content of the technology was so general that it was able to addresses many different needs. In particular, the technology was able to analyse both short and long strands of DNA. This temporal solution made the founders start thinking about the application of the technology more seriously.

In the second phase, the deal with the venture capital firm HealthCap was imperative in founding the company, but the deal with HealthCap also created a new temporary solution in which the calculation, the RR, played an important role. The new technical design was related to the choice of a particular application area for the technology, which in turn was a consequence of how the company and the technology was represented in the calculation used by HealthCap. This calculation, the IRR, made it imperative to steer away from the temporal solution that was formulated in the first phase. The IRR calculation rendered the SNP solution more valuable. A focus on the SNP solution would reduce the development time. Hence, the deal with HealthCap, and the importance of the IRR calculation, made the product development process take a new route. Furthermore, the temporal solution created in this phase also facilitated the organisation of the new product development activities because it was easier to identify clear-cut physical interfaces between the different components of the product. The product was even narrowed down further when the development was focused on only the coding and analysis step of the usual DNA analysis.

In the third phase, the deal of going to the stock exchange, and the accounting calculations, most noteworthy the IRR calculation, that were related to this deal, formed a new temporal solution, which in end did not play out so well for Pyrosequencing as a company. The IPO deal was a success for HealthCap, and it resulted in a high market value for Pyrosequencing. The market share calculation and the IRR calculation used by the venture capital firm was in this phase combined with a cousin to the IRR calculation, the DCF. Both these techniques are based on the idea that there is time value of money and that cash flows are discounted back to a certain time. The DCF models are used for company valuations and to understand value drivers, often future-oriented value drives of the firm. Since the growth rate (everything the same) of a company is critical to understand the valuation of a company, the Pyrosequencing management wanted to please the capital market actors with a high future growth. This had to be translated into sales, and in particular the short-term sales of instruments. The management of Pyrosequencing used delivered instruments to customers as a key performance measure. The relationships with the customers were based on the temporary solution formed in the previous phase. It was an instrument, software and reagent kit for SNP solution, and it was focused on the coding and analysis step of the usual DNA analysis. However, soon it becomes clear that customers were not totally happy with this temporary solution. It had served its purposes in the previous phase, but now customer value was basically too low, and the customers, after they have bought an instrument and some reagent kits, don't buy repeatedly. The structure of the business deal with its razor blade model made it necessary to increase the sales of reagent kits or to change the business model. Pyrosequencing needed to change its customer offer and identified a new segment of companies going for high-throughput sequencing.

The last phase ends with the merger between Pyrosequencing and Personal Chemistry. The merger, which also is the major deal in this phase, was first based on a profit and loss calculation to save the company and then a calculation in which the cash reserve could be transferred from Pyrosequencing to a healthier company, Personal Chemistry. This analysis was made primarily from the perspectives of the venture capital company, HealthCap, and the other major owners. The alternative for the owners would have been to sell Pyrosequencing but then only to a very low price, which would create losses. By merging the two companies, this was avoided and the cash reserve could be used by Personal Chemistry in its expansion plans. The same cash reserve was now more valuable than before. The merger—the deal—had very little to do with industrial synergies. Instead, the merger was fully driven by a financial logic stemming from the venture capital owner, HealthCap. Hence, the cash reserves were critical to this deal. But another resource was also critical: the space that Pyrosequencing "owned" on the stock exchange. This was valuable for HealthCap and for its portfolio company, Personal Chemistry.

In the end, deals with other actors in the network around Pyrosequencing were critical. The deal with 454 Life Science meant that the whole-genome sequencing was sold, and Pyrosequencing had to focus on finding an application with SNPs. The temporary solution that was forced on Pyrosequencing was thus equipment with small sample size for a totally different market, namely for diagnostics.This market did not have the potential that once made Pyrosequencing famous and named as one of the world's most promising companies.

The various economic calculations used in the different phases, the different designs of the product, and the different deals that were made with various actors show how innovation can be seen as a temporary solution made up made these three components. A temporary solution is hence composed of both technical and social resources. The interfaces to other technical artefacts as well as social relationships are embedded in the technical solutions. The temporary solutions presented in this chapter are things that the actors at the specific time can live with and accept. What has not been investigated before, however, is how multiple temporary solutions relate to each other over both a product's and a company's life cycle. We have seen here how a series of temporary solutions gradually formed path-dependencies; certain possibilities that were open at certain stages were closed then because of decisions made earlier in the process. We have seen how the different calculations and deals set things in motion and took the innovation in certain directions. In the end, the calculations together with the deals created a certain momentum that took the innovation towards its destiny.

Concluding Remarks

From our case, we can conclude that innovations are temporary, but their temporality is built up by both social and technical dimensions. The product design changes over time, it economic value is assessed in different ways using different calculations, and it is embedded in different deals and relationships. We can also say something about how these building blocks interplay with each other.

First, we can conclude that a certain type of calculations shape and create a certain type of deals. The market share calculation, for instance, allowed for a broad and inclusive technical prototype. The founders' use of a market share calculation enabled the development of the first product, PSQ96. The IRR calculation then increased the need for speed in the development process, resulting in a successful IPO deal for the owners of Pyrosequencing. These deals opened some doors, but also closed some other future potential development paths. Second, deals shape and create a certain type of product design, which in turn will be the starting point for the next calculation. We can see patterns of loops between the building blocks of an innovation process. While the deals with the research foundations and with the venture cap company facilitated the innovation process, the IPO deal and the merger deal hindered it. Hence, on a general level, our findings are in accordance with previous literature that has shown how calculations and deals both facilitate and hinder the innovation process (Baraldi and Lind 2017; Nixon 1998). However, a detailed look at our empirical case shows that it is not obvious if a calculation or a deal hinders or facilitates the innovation process.

Third, different types of calculations shape and create certain types of deals. From our case, we can conclude that calculations have different features; some are more open (more inclusive, no time content and open for interpretation of solutions that fit into the calculation), while others are narrower (less inclusive, an explicit focus on time and with less room for interpretation of solutions that fit into the calculation). For example, in our case, we can see that open calculations (e.g., market share calculation) were successful in spurring scientific interest and creating attention among academic colleagues in the scientific community, possibly because it was open for interpretion of possible solutions. However, it was very hard for the researchers to create deals with such an open calculation, perhaps because it was harder to draw a credible calculable space around the innovation. With a narrower type of calculation it seems to be easier to create interest among the investment community and secure funding, probably because it creates a clearer calculable space and has a time horizon that fits the interest of these actors. For future research, we believe that discussing and researching *features of calculations* can potentially be of great importance. How certain features of economic calculations mobilise and direct innovation processes is interesting and needs to be explored further.

Notes

1. The nucleotides come in pairs (adenine with thymine and guanine with cytosine), which create a double helix. Nyrén's idea was to use the enzyme pyrophosphate to detect whether or not a base pair was incorporated in a DNA sequence (Nyrén 2007).
2. PCR stands for polymerase chain reaction.
3. Genetic variation among individuals is captured by studying SNPs. The idea at the time was that information about human variations of DNA sequences (SNPs) would facilitate the development of new drugs.
4. HealthCap has since invested in more than 90 companies. Of these, 35 were start-ups, like Pyrosequencing. HealthCap has exited more than 45 of these investments. The total committed capital currently exceeds EUR 900 million, making HealthCap one of Europe's largest Venture Capital firms within the life science segment.
5. www.healthcap.eu/the-funds/the-investment-objective

References

Abernethy, M.A. and Brownell, P. (1997), "Management control systems and research and development organizations: The role of accounting, behavioural and personnel controls," *Accounting, Organizations and Society*, Vol. 22, pp. 233–248.

Alenius, E., Lind, J. and Strömsten, T. (2015), "The role of open book accounting in a supplier-network: Creating and managing interdependence across company boundaries," *Industrial Marketing Management*, Vol. 45, pp. 195–206.

Baraldi, E. and Lind, J. (2017), "Value measuring and value appropriation in business networks," in: Håkansson, H. and Snehota, I. (eds.), *No Business is an Island: Making Sense of the Interactive Business World*. Bingley, UK: Emerald, pp. 47–66.

Baraldi, E. and Strömsten, T. (2009), "Controlling and combining resources in networks. From Uppsala to Stanford, and back again: The case of a biotech innovation," *Industrial Marketing Management*, Vol. 38, Issue 5, pp. 541–552.

Carlsson-Wall, M. and Kraus, K. (2015), "Opening the black box of the role of accounting practices in the fuzzy front-end of product innovation," *Industrial Marketing Management*, Vol. 45, pp. 184–194.

Carlsson-Wall, M., Kraus, K. and Lind, J. (2009), "Accounting and distributed product development," *IMP Journal*, Vol. 3, pp. 2–27.

Christner, C.L. and Strömsten, T. (2015), "Scientists, venture capitalists and stock exchange: The mediating role of accounting in product innovation," *Management Accounting Research*, Vol. 28, pp. 50–67.

Davila, T. (2000 May), "An empirical study on the drivers of management control systems' design in new product development," *Accounting, Organizations and Society*, Vol. 25, Issues 4–5, pp. 383–409.

Davila, T. (2005 April), "An exploratory study on the emergence of management control systems: Formalizing human resources in small growing firms," *Accounting, Organizations and Society*, Vol. 30, Issue 3, pp. 223–248.

Ditillo, A. (2004 April–May), "Dealing with uncertainty in knowledge-intensive firms: The role of management control systems as knowledge integration mechanisms," *Accounting, Organizations and Society*, Vol. 29, Issues 3–4, pp. 401–421.

Dubois, A. and Araujo, L. (2006), "The relationship between technical and organisational interfaces in product development," *The IMP Journal*, Vol. 1, pp. 28–51.

Ford, D., Gadde, L.-E., Håkansson, H., Lundgren, A., Snehota, I. and Turnbull, P. (1998), *Managing Business Relationships*. Chichester: Wiley.

Håkansson, H. (Ed.). (1989), *Corporate Technological Behaviour: Co-operation and Networks*. London: Routledge.

Håkansson, H. and Lind, J. (2004), "Accounting and network coordination," *Accounting, Organizations and Society*, Vol. 29, pp. 51–72.

Håkansson, H. and Olsen, P. I. (2015), "The roles of money and business deals in network structures," *Industrial Marketing Management*, Vol. 45, pp. 207–217.

Håkansson, H. and Waluszewski, A. (2002), *Managing Technological Development: IKEA, the Environment and Technology*. London: Routledge.

Hoholm, T. and Olsen, P. I. (2012), "The contrary forces of innovation—A conceptual model for studying networked innovation processes," *Industrial Marketing Management*, Vol. 41, pp. 344–356.

Hughes, T. P. (1983), *Networks of Power: Electric Supply Systems in the US, England and Germany, 1880–1930*. Baltimore: Johns Hopkins University.

Law, J. and Akrich, M. (1994), "On customers and costs: A story from public sector science." *Science in Context*, Vol. 7, Issue 3, pp. 539–561.

Lind, J. (2017), "The role of accounting for managing innovation processes when relationships matter," *IMP Journal*, Vol. 11, Issue 1.

Mennicken, A., Miller, P. and Samiolo, R. (2008), "Accounting for economic sociology." *Economic Sociology – The European Electronic Newsletter*, Vol. 10, Issue 1, pp. 3–7.

Miller, P. and O'leary, T. (2007), "Mediating instruments and making markets: Capital budgeting, science and the economy." *Accounting, Organizations and Society*, Vol. 32, Issues 7–8, pp. 701–734.

Moll, J. (2015), "Editorial: Special issue on innovation and product development," *Management Accounting Research*, Vol. 28, pp. 2–11.

Mouritsen, J., Hansen, A. and Hansen, C. Ø. (2009), "Short and long translations: Management accounting calculations and innovation management." *Accounting, Organizations and Society*, Vol. 34, Issues 6–7, pp. 738–754.

Nixon, B. (1998), "Research and development performance measurement: A case study," *Management Accounting Research*, Vol. 9, pp. 329–355.

Nyrén, P. (2007), "The History of Pyrosequencing®." In *Pyrosequencing® Protocols* (pp. 1–13). New York: Humana Press.

Olsen, P.-I. and Håkansson, H. (2017), "The roles of deals and business networks in innovation process," *IMP Journal*, Vol. 11, Issue 1.

Perna, A., Baraldi, E. and Waluszewski, A. (2015), "Is the value created necessarily associated with money? On the connections between an innovation process and its monetary dimension: The case of Solibro's thin-film solar cells," *Industrial Marketing Management*, Vol. 46, pp. 108–121.

Revellino, S. and Mouritsen, J. (2009), "The multiplicity of controls and the making of innovation." *European Accounting Review*, Vol. 18, Issue 2, pp. 341–369.

Rockness, H.O. and Shields, M. (1984), "Organizational control systems in research and development," *Accounting, Organizations and Society*, Vol. 9, Issue 2, pp. 165–177.
Rogers, E.M. (1962; 2003), *The Diffusion of Innovation*. New York: Free Press.
Ronaghi, M., Uhlén, M. and Nyren, P. (1998), "A sequencing method based on real-time pyrophosphate." *Science*, Vol. 281, Issue 5375, p. 363.
Strömsten, T. and Waluszewski, A. (2012), "Governance and resource interaction in networks. The role of venture capital in a biotech start-up," *Journal of Business Research*, Vol. 65, pp. 232–244.
Tomkins, C. (2001), "Interdependencies, trust and information in relationships, alliances and networks." *Accounting, Organizations and Society*, Vol. 26, Issue 2, pp. 161–191.
Wedin, T. (2001), Networks and demand. The use of electricity in an industrial process. Doctoral dissertation, Acta Universitatis Upsaliensis.
Von Hippel, E. (1986), "Lead users: A source of novel product concepts," *Management Science*. Vol. 7, Issue 37, pp. 791–805.

4 Venture Capital Systemic Synergies and Networked Management Control in Rapid Scaling of Innovative New Business Ventures

Per Ingvar Olsen

Introduction

In this chapter, the objective is to examine the roles of management control networks and systems in a domain of business that may be seen as an extreme case of networked organizing—the business of scaling innovative technology start-ups to global business activities through rapidly accelerated innovation processes. This activity is a relatively recent phenomenon which in many ways has changed much of the global economic landscape as well as the way we nowadays understand business innovations and internationalization processes differently than was the case with the traditional view of an expansion process characterized by relatively slow learning and gradual movement from local to regional to national to international industrial and marketing activities (Johanson and Vahlne, 1977, 2009).

The chapter builds on previous studies reported in the business network and accounting in networks literature and applies a management in network perspective (Håkansson, Kraus and Lind, 2010). It pulls from a study that has used a "follow the deals" research approach to analyze financial to social-material innovation process interactions. Pulling from this study, I will discuss how we may understand rapid scaling processes as outcomes of highly structured networked management control systems at and in between different levels of financial and entrepreneurial management.

Accelerated fast to scale innovation processes has to deal with large economic opportunities as well as extreme levels of risks in terms of a very broad range of things that may go seriously wrong when these processes are speeded up. The fundamental problem is essentially the knowledge gap identified by Galbraith (1973): "the difference between the amount of information required to perform a task and the amount of information already possessed by the organization." The necessity of acquiring hard-to-get information that is needed to succeed is essentially why such processes are usually stepwise and slow. The observation that a much larger number of such rapid processes are successful provides an interesting opportunity to investigate what makes this possible. That is: how can knowledge gap–related risks be more effectively managed and controlled to allow for a more rapid scaling process at lower risk levels? What management control systems are at work? What management control strategies are applied, and what management tools are being used?

Following Miller and O'Leary (2007) and Christner and Strömsten (2015), accounting tools can be understood as intermediating instruments that have the function of interacting and aligning activities in systemic ways in order to share and sustain practices between and across dispersed actors and activities. They thereby shape certain practices that move development processes along certain trajectories. These may become shared scaling models within the industry. Over time, this may generate a continuous, collective accumulation of experience process across a large number of actors by means of creating systemic standardizations and synergies.

As a point of departure, I suggest that the increasing number of such rapidly scaling innovative firms can be seen as rooted in a process of industrialization that has become a large and highly structured "scaling industry." This refers in particular to the private equity industry, within which the venture capital (VC) industry is the part that is particularly dedicated to investing into and managing rapid scaling processes. To understand how Galbraith's knowledge gap problem is being dealt with requires an understanding of how this industry works, how it is structured, how management challenges at various levels or nodes of activity are responded to, and what kinds of management governance systems, control approaches and tools are being used across the industry.

A fundamental understanding of economic development, progress and growth associates with economic theories that emphasize an evolutionary view of an economy which is basically about the ever-expanding frontiers of acquiring and exploiting new knowledge (Penrose, 1959). Such new knowledge is generally understood as resulting from the unique capacity of man to interact, develop and create in collaboration and rivalry with others. This development theory of the economy is different from, and concerns a different dimension of, real economies than what is in focus in the fundamentally exchange and trade (barter) oriented "neo-classical" economic tradition that came to dominate economics since the early 1950s. In the evolutionary view, growth and prosperity are driven by the increasing returns that result from knowledge advancements transformed into scalable innovative technologies, activities, businesses and industries that deliver new and better solutions to user needs. In the neo-classical view, prosperity rather results from the efficient allocation of existing resources between actors and activities and from adding of more capital in exchange for labor.

In real economies, these two dimensions interact as two kinds of interacting activities that are always there. The essence of what the VC industry does is to connect these two economic dimensions that are in between financial allocation systems and development projects at the frontiers of building new increasing return businesses and industries. All such new ventures develop within very specific niches of social-material activities, and the world of innovation is accordingly extremely heterogeneous.

The scaling industry provides financing, usually not from industrial companies or rich individuals but from the broad financial resource base of modern economies, primarily represented by a large number of institutional savings and investment funds. Managers of such investment funds usually have no real insight into any of the heterogeneous innovation projects they invest in. At this level, the VC industry represents a particular class of risk-return investment opportunities to broad investment portfolios, and the fundamental business of the VC industry critically depends on its attractiveness as an investment class for such institutional fund managers, which is the overall success rate of the industry.

The objective of this chapter is to discuss essential aspects of what it is that makes it possible to systematically speed up the scaling process in such start-ups in the face of Galbraith's fundamental knowledge gap problem. What characterizes the management structures and the management control systems at work? What kinds of management tools are being used, and how do they contribute to resolving the knowledge gap problem? To illustrate and discuss this topic, I will report from a study about a radical new medical technology within the area of heart surgery denoted transcatheter aortic valve implantation (TAVI) (Cribier, 2012). The ambition is to illuminate and analyze the inter-related processes of financing, knowledge mobilization and development work that characterize a highly demanding, accelerated innovation process in the area of medical technology.

The next part will discuss and position this work in relation to management control and accounting in network literature. Subsequently, I will also present core elements of the legal structures of the VC firm and its management control structures and tools as a background for this case study, which aims at further exploring and illuminating these practices. In part four, I will briefly explain the methodology applied before presenting the case study in part five. A unifying analysis will then be provided before a round up in the concluding discussion in part seven.

Theory

Galbraith's knowledge gap is a fundamental source of the high risk facing all innovative entrepreneurs. The need to learn through trial and error and network building processes is at the core of traditional understanding of business scaling and internationalization processes. Small- and medium-sized enterprises usually do not make it, and international scaling has typically been seen as a domain dominated by firms which are already large that can use their already considerable resources and extended market activities to take on additional activities (Freeman, 2007; Laine and Kock, 2000). The theory of scaling start-up firms accordingly saw this as a slow process of stepwise stabilization at different levels of expansion—to be able to learn how to operate as you go. This stepwise, incremental process-oriented theory became known as the Uppsala model (Johanson and Vahlne, 1977, 2003, 2009; Selnes and Sallis, 2003).

From observation of the new wave of rapidly scaling technology ventures, a different view was offered by the International New Venture and Born Globals literature (Autio, 2005; Knight and Cavusgil, 2004; Coviello and Jones, 2004; Peiris, Akoorie and Sinha, 2012). Various studies pointed at knowledge and networks as the most important variables and focused on the importance of the entrepreneurs' prior knowledge and networks to explain how the need for trial and error learning can be partially avoided. Typical of these studies is that they apply a perspective that focuses on the roles of the entrepreneurs and the innovative firms and the networks they interact with. However, many argue that there is a lack of understanding of how the needed knowledge and the networks are actually acquired by these entrepreneurial actors (Weerawardena et al., 2007; Freeman et al., 2010; Zahra, 2005; Keupp and Gassman, 2009; O-Gorman and Evers, 2011).

A different approach would be to move attention away from the entrepreneurs to focus instead on the networked systems that have emerged over the past few decades, which we may broadly identify as "the scaling industry." This assumes that the knowledge gap problem is solved at an industrial level of organizing, not at the level of individual entrepreneurs or start-up firms. Industrial organizing permits the aggregation of experience and knowledge across a large number of cases and actors so that relevant knowledge can be mobilized and applied by many at a rapid pace. A major share of the scaling industry is represented by the VC industry, which is a particular part of the broader private equity industry. My study builds on research within this approach, and more specifically on business networks, systems and management control and accounting in networks studies. In this perspective, the explanations will focus on identifying and explaining the emergence of collective synergies within an industrial development perspective that has made it possible to resolve much of the knowledge gap problem in interacted, systematic ways.

Interacting Large Financial Resources and Heterogeneous Social-Material Innovation Projects

Economic growth and prosperity is generally understood as depending on the ability to move resources out of decreasing return activities and into increasing return alternatives through innovation and industrial improvement or transformation processes—in particular through financial re-allocation. New increasing return businesses are what we see as the outcomes of successful and profitable innovation processes driven by new knowledge creation and complex, hard to achieve interaction and scaling processes. Any economic system that aims at generating growth and prosperity over time must accordingly find effective ways to interact efficient financial re-allocation processes with effective knowledge-driven new business development processes.

Business network research is rooted in an interactional process view of the economic landscape in which resources, actors and activities are related and interdependent, with numerous studies of how facilitating improvements in development and producing and using settings drive economic development processes (Håkansson, 1982; Johanson and Mattson, 1985; Ford, 1990; Axelsson and Easton, 1992; Håkansson and Waluszewski, 2007; Håkansson et al., 2009; Ford et al., 2011; Olsen, 2013). Increasing economic returns—in this perspective—is the outcome of new combinations of alignment of activities and resources, of adjustments across interfaces, development of skills, experiences and structures affecting the entire interaction networks. Hence, economic improvements are the outcome of collective, networked processes that develop into systemic, synergetic effects that become stabilized through the networked systems themselves. Established relationships and aligned interfaces are also important resources, as networked interactions in the economic system (landscape) are particularly important to actors facing variations, uncertainty and mobility, with constant need for strategic and operational initiatives and responses.

Established inter- and intra-organizational routines facilitate adoption and enactment of changes and new innovations in the various parts of the networks. Hence, the ability to deal with variability and change is improved by the establishment of experienced-based structures and routines. This is what is also denoted in the embeddedness of business processes that both direct and improve the adoptability of the new into complex networked structures, often spanning across multiple organizational borders.

Theories of management in networks acknowledge that management is also a relational, interactional process of mutual influencing in which no one is in complete control (Bakken, Håkansson and Olsen, 2013). Management control activities are accordingly closely related to the use of control approaches, systems and tools that are the outcomes of lasting interactional processes in extended networks that ensure that they are adapted to the needs of both close and distant actors in interdependent networks. When there is an approach, a system or a tool that works better for the many, there is systemic improvement that represents collective synergy.

Most business and industrial network studies in the IMP tradition have concentrated on studying marketing and industrial interaction processes—usually based on case studies. The early ARA model (actors, resources and activities) and the 4R model (four resources: organizational, social, technical and physical) have been applied and extended in multiple ways. However, only a few have been studying the role of financing. Among these, there is also a few who have focused on the roles of the VC industry, its management control systems and accounting and calculating tools based on business venturing case studies (Baraldi and Strömsten, 2009; Christner and Strömsten, 2015; Strömsten and Waluszewski, 2012). Substantial influence on these studies also comes from other research domains, such as accounting, management control and new business venturing research.

Financial resources are not explicitly part of the 4R model widely used in IMP case studies. However, in studies that are particularly interested in interactions between allocations of financial resources and social-material interaction projects, there is a need to explicitly include financial resources in the analytical model. One approach has been suggested by Håkansson and Olsen (2015) with the introduction of a "deal model" that defines "a deal" as an interaction between two sets of actors that are bringing financial resources into particular social-material interaction processes. A deal is accordingly a settlement of conditions between financial resources and social-material development processes associated with a given innovation project. This is essentially an F-ARA model (finance—actor-resource-activity). A first empirical application of the model is presented by Olsen and Håkansson (2017) in another study of a TAVI innovation process that occurred parallel to, as well as in relation to, the case I will present in this chapter.

Accounting in Networks

A number of empirical studies show that business relationships have become more organized than before, and that there is increased use of sophisticated management tools and accounting practices that reflects more networked business practices (Håkansson, Kraus and Lind, 2010, 3). Studies of management tools and accounting in network practices vary across the different kinds of networked activities, industries and relationships observed. Many of the empirical studies have concentrated on seller-to-buyer relationships, supply chain management and other industrial relationships in a broad range of normal businesses (ibid., 1–14). Other studies have focused on how the accounting activity itself has been used as a dynamic tool to reshape and develop new forms of business organizing that call for even more expanded networked management, governance and accounting tools (Ford and Håkansson, 2010; Mouritsen, Mahama and Chua, 2010).

In this chapter, I will apply these general insights to help analyze how a networked understanding of the use of accounting tools as intermediate objects related to deals can help us better understand what the systemic synergies in the scaling industry are made of.

The Roles of Management Control in Innovation Processes

Studies of entrepreneurship and innovation processes have typically concluded that such processes are fundamentally uncontrollable, messy and a trial and error of muddling through processes in which most are unsuccessful (Van de Ven et al., 1999; Tidd, Pavitt and Bessant, 1997). These findings also resonate with arguments in industrial network research (Håkansson and Waluszewski, 2002). The conclusions follow from a recognition of the knowledge gap problem, the problem of alignment of interest and the problem of re-combining of heterogeneous resources in highly interdependent networked development, producing and using settings. New innovation will have to connect in multiple ways to whatever is already crowding the business and user landscapes. Hence, to innovate successfully requires access to extended networks of potential connections in which each new innovative venture can be exposed to relevant, rapid testing of its explicit and implicit propositions to others. Management control of innovation processes must address and manage this complex task, and management control systems and accounting tools must somehow be useful in the pursuit of it.

Davila (2000) summarizes research on management control systems in product development and argues that management control plays a positive role by supplying information required to reduce uncertainty rather than reduce goal divergence problems traditionally seen as the core function of management control. Following Chenhall and Morris (1986), Gordon and Narayanan (1984) and Kaplan (1983), he argues that such information goes beyond the traditional control perspective focused on accounting numbers and costs and probability and budget measures to include a broader information set. This includes customer evaluations, product design issues and time-related measures. Management control systems are used to close the gap between "the information required to perform a task and the amount of information already possessed." This view is also consistent with Tushman and Nadler (1978), who argued that management control systems are effective tools to manage the uncertainty needed to reduce Galbraith's knowledge gap.

Research in product innovation in the 1990s identified three main types of information gaps: market uncertainty, technology uncertainty and project scope uncertainty (McGrath, 1995; Shenhar and Dvir, 1996; Von Hippel, 1988; Wheelwright and Clark, 1992). These three types of risk are core to innovation process management control systems. In addition to the uncertainty characterizing the project, the design of management control systems was found to depend on the strategies of engaged actors (Govindarajan and Gupta, 1985) as well as on the organizational structure surrounding the project (Bruns and Waterhouse, 1975). Of particular importance are control systems that ensure that the goals of owners are imposed on or otherwise reflected within the organization (Davila 2000; Davila, Foster and Gupta, 2003; Granlund and Taipleenmääki, 2003).

In innovation processes, this typically concerns owners such as the entrepreneurs, the financial investors who take ownership positions (angel capital and VC) and industrial investors who for some reason take an interest in the innovation project. Ownership of such companies is related to and based on the provision of different kinds of critically important resources where entrepreneurs obtain ownership control rights as suppliers of unique intellectual property (new technological knowledge), investors as suppliers of money and industrial investors as potential acquirers of the firm or as users of its output. Hence, ownership control is not homogeneous with respect to the resource that defines ownership, such as in most other owned enterprises. These companies accordingly have "multiple patronage" challenges among the owners with potentially high levels of conflict of interest. Hence, at the core of an effective management control system, there needs to be a system to align and manage the different ownership interests (Hansmann, 1996).

The Role of Accounting in Innovation Processes

Christner and Strömsten (2015) use the concept of mediating instruments (Miller and O'Leary, 2007) to analyze how accounting calculations participated in shaping particular trajectories of development in a detailed case study within the medical technology area (Pyrosequencing of DNA). They also introduced a longitudinal study design to this particular area of research by following the process through three different stages. Based on the study, they argued that different accounting calculation formats were used in the different stages that shaped the direction of the processes by linking certain scientific and economic ideas and certain actors in specific ways. This linking of domains and of economic ideas and formats substantially influenced and shaped the trajectory of the project's development process. As a consequence, they proposed a concept of calculative momentum to address the variable influential forces observed. Their arguments also pull from Mouritsen, Hansen and Hansen (2001, 2009), who showed how different accounting formats and calculations suggested different potential directions for product development processes. Hence, such instruments serve as evaluation tools for project development managers. As given instruments, they also possess considerable influence in themselves. This line of reasoning has roots back to Callon (1998), who applied a similar approach to studies of how scientific constructs and calculating formats are influential in the making of markets (Olsen, 2005).

Accounting formats and calculation can accordingly be seen as enablers of product innovation. They can be tools to reduce uncertainty and mediating objects to facilitate and structure dialog, interactions and alignments among actors engaged in interacting financial, technological, social and other activities in development processes (Håkansson and Lind, 2004; Jørgensen and Messner, 2009; Christner and Strömsten, 2015). They can also be shared tools that facilitate structured interactions by a large number of actors (Miller and O'Leary, 2007). Accounting tools may frame situations in similar ways that point at alternative courses of action, making certain trajectories more possible and attractive to actors that have different roles to play.

Forming Trajectories and Shared Roadmaps by Exploiting Established Systemic Synergies

Mouritsen, Hansen and Hansen (2009) argue, on the bases of three different case studies, that particular accounting tools may have both a direct impact on the forming of particular trajectories and serve as instruments to systematically address certain challenges of broader economic and strategic concerns to the company. Hence, they are core management control and evaluation tools.

Miller and O'Leary (2007) evaluate situations in which more extended interactions over time occur in relation to a shared "roadmap" that connects future images of where development should be heading with past and present actors and activities that play various roles in the development process. Such a "roadmap" spells out a broader image of a pattern of interrelated activities, decision points and overall guidelines shared among the actors. In the context of rapidly scaling technology ventures, such roadmaps may also be very useful. These can be interpreted as outcomes or effects of configurations of industrial structuring, management control systems and accounting tools that lead to preference for certain trajectories in light of broader strategic and economic concerns (Revellino and Mouritsen, 2009).

Research Questions and Contributions From the Study

In this study, I raise the question: What are the essences of the observed capability of the scaling industry to radically reduce and manage the risks and increase the speed of innovation processes? Can we explain what these systemic synergies are that may be exploited by the many actors within the industry? What roles do the deals and the associated intermediate accounting and calculating tools play? What structures, systems and tools of management control are used?

The study focuses on following the deals through the different stages and seeks to illustrate and analyze the industrial systems that interact in the processes of deal making through the scaling process. To analyze the industry, I distinguish among four commonly acknowledged levels of analysis that correspond to four interrelated levels of financial investment management: the institutional fund level, the VC firm level, the VC fund level and the entrepreneurial firm level. Each of these can be seen as a node in an extended managerial network at work in the industry, and each can be seen as a particular network on its own in more focused analysis of its particular management control and accounting practices.

This study contributes by analyzing the essential structures of the scaling industry and by identifying core mechanisms and systemic synergies. It argues that at the core, there is an extreme horizontal and vertical network system rooted in financial portfolio management and systemic syndications of investments and partnership building. This aggregates into what is in essence the "open corporate innovation model" of the VC industry.

Legal Structures and Management Control Systems in the Venture Capital Industry

Venture capital firms invest in entrepreneurial start-ups perceived as having high potential for rapid growth (Gompers and Lerner, 1999; Timmons and Bygrave, 1986). In situations when there is a dedicated user interest in the innovation with a capacity to pay for the innovation, start-ups may obtain a supplier contract to finance its development costs either through forward sales or debt financing. With no such contract, the entrepreneurial start-up will depend on equity financing by selling ownership control in exchange for funding. This is what VC firms offer. They are active owners who take board positions and actively engage as owners in developing the firms they invest in. Usually, they only invest in firms where they can expect to acquire dominant ownership control. This implies that the original entrepreneurs who established a firm based on the perceived value of the intellectual property they contributed will usually not control the firm after a VC company has effectively engaged in it.

There has been extensive research on the relationship between VC firms and start-ups (see Strömsten and Waluszewski, 2012 for a review). These, in particular, focus on what VC firms contribute to the innovation projects. They basically contribute with three critically important resources: 1) money; 2) knowledge and foresight based on experience; and 3) extended networks to financial, commercial and technological actors (Sahlman, 1990; Barney et al., 1996). They also contribute with their reputation, which is particularly useful to help start-ups overcome their "liability of newness." Hence, the value that a VC firm may contribute is closely dependent on its being part of multiple extended networks. In essence, it is a value network type of business in which the values it creates critically depends on its ability to connect the entrepreneurial start-up to others (Stabell and Fjeldstad, 1998).

Because VC firms take ownership control over the entrepreneurial start-up, they are also in a position to move in their own management control systems. Towards the managers of the start-up, these are generally based on principal-agent logics to prevent opportunistic behaviors by ensuring alignment of interest between the VC owners and the managers, who are usually offered share options or other incentive schemes based on shared ownership. However, equally important is the ability to use the VC company's business service networks; its accounting and auditing practices; its legal contracts, legal advisors and law firms; its networks with competent managers and management teams; and so on. Equally important is the ability to control the process of additional financing. Because VC firms usually acquire dominant ownership control no later than after the second round of investment, the fast-scaling entrepreneurial firms should primarily be seen as internal projects within the VC scaling industry, not as independent entrepreneurial firms controlled by the entrepreneurs.

How Then Are Venture Capital Companies Legally Structured?

Venture capital firms are private equity partnership organizations owned and operated by so-called general partners (GPs). Ownership and control are essentially based on a knowledge partnership arrangement similar to what we find in law firms and consultancy firms. These are managers in the company who raise money from limited partners (LPs), who are most often institutional investors. These are invited to invest money in particular funds of limited duration (usually 7–10 years). Each fund invests in a selection of entrepreneurial firms over the lifespan of the given fund. When the fund expires, there is a forced exit by the fund from all its investments. The fund is terminated, and the investment, along with the accumulated net result, is delivered back to the LPs. The limited timeframe is a guarantee offered by the GPs to the LPs to safeguard the LPs' investment in the face of potential opportunistic behavior by the GPs.

This legal structure forces each fund to carefully select and manage a limited portfolio of investments so as to exit from these investments with sufficient capital return for up to 10-year-long investments by the LPs before they receive any returns at all. Because some of the investments in a fund's portfolio typically fail and some only deliver modest results—and because nobody in advance is able to identify which will fail and which will succeed—for each entrepreneurial start-up, ex ante investment must be evaluated as a feasible, high-potential, fast-growth project able to also carry the weight of losses for the failing firms in the portfolio. Hence, the deal flow into a VC company and the evaluation processes they conduct to select the investment objects are extremely important.

Each fund is managed by a board of directors representing the VC firm and the LPs. A VC firm typically manages several funds with different profiles and start-termination dates, and each fund typically has investments from different LPs. The GPs do the fund raising and overlook activity and administer the different funds. They also do the work on behalf of the board of each fund by representing the VC firm and fund on the board of each of the portfolio firms. Each GP manages a small number of portfolio firms and is directly responsible for managing the strategy of the owners to develop each firm in order to reach a successful exit.

The internal deal between the GPs and the LPs is that the GPs receive a fixed payment per year for their management services, which are usually set to 2% of the given fund size. Over a period of 10 years, this accumulates to more than 20% of the fund. In addition, the GPs typically receive a share of the net profit calculated after the LPs have been returned their investment. This share is usually set at around 20% (Strömsten and Waluszewski, 2012). Hence, ex ante investment—the return on the investment—is at least less than minus 20%, which will also have to be re-gained before there is a net positive return for the LPs. In effect, each investment object must have a realistic opportunity to return at least 10 times the investment within 10 years to deserve being included in the portfolio of a VC fund.

All of this illustrates how the VC system is set up to accelerate the innovation scaling process in a standardized legal structure with distinct divisions of roles and responsibilities along with a highly incentivized reward system.

To manage the investment and scaling process, it is common to use a system of staged financing referred to as the A, B, C, D, and so on rounds of investments scheme, in which additional funding is provided when certain milestones are reached. Such milestones are critical events that signal to the investors that particular risks have been eliminated. This typically concerns technology risks, market risks and project scope risks (e.g., regulatory risks that may reduce the domain of use). The first rounds of investments are used to establish control, reduce risks and stage the organization for rapid scaling. During this part of the process, the use of money is usually moderate in order to be able to abort the project at a limited loss. However, when core milestones are met, there is typically a policy to "pour money in" to scale the operation fast, while, in parallel, the VC company intensifies its efforts to find and execute a profitable exit through an industrial sale or an initial public offering (IPO).

At the core of the management control system is the value assessment process of the entrepreneurial firm. Because risks are high, the initial valuation at the point of entry must be fairly low. This also ensures that ownership control can be acquired at a low cost before major investments are made in later investment rounds. When reaching certain milestones, risks are reduced, and value assessment increases. Later stage investors—if the company is successful—accordingly pay more per share and dilute existing shareholders less per dollar invested. Calculating the value of the firm at each stage is typically done by triangulating among different evaluation references, such as assessment of similar cases (like in the housing market), assessment of minimum target exit values and time to exit, internal rate of return requirement for the individual project as well as for the portfolio and so on.

Asymmetric information between existing shareholders and the new would potentially reduce the price at which others would like to enter and, to protect new investors, the VC industry generally practices various forms of preferred shares and anti-dilution clauses. Over several rounds of investments, this leads to a shareholder structure with a hierarchy of preferred classes of shares in which the entrepreneurs and the managers in the entrepreneurial firm hold common shares or common share options at the bottom end and the last-to-enter investor holds the most protected preferred shares at the top end. This system also causes the effect that none of the shareholders are able to exit without the consent of the last-to-enter investor. The system is also such that the last-to-enter investor has the right to re-gain his investment first with a minimum return to the investment, then the next to last and so on. When this is done all the way through, the remaining profit may be shared equally or according to other rules established in the consortium that may also prioritize entrepreneurs and shareholder managers. As a result, the entrepreneurs as well as the mangers of the entrepreneurial firm holding common stock or stock options will only be able to exit when the financial investors are also doing it, and they will only receive a profit if the total gain is large enough to pay for all the preferred stock arrangements. This causes the entrepreneurs and the managers to stay on board and work towards a fast and large exit opportunity, as a moderate financial return exit will give them nothing.

This high-pressure, fast-scaling system forces the innovation processes as far as possible out of the "learning by doing" mode and turns attention to "learning before doing" (Rosenberg, 1982). Hence, a critical need is to identify and recruit managers with more than sufficient experience and expertise in the specific context of operations relevant to each company in the portfolio.

Methods

How the wave of rapid and successful scaling of highly demanding entrepreneurial businesses has become possible has been researched from different approaches. Even though the role of VC is generally acknowledged as an important factor, this role still appears to be under-researched and under-articulated. Hence, the need for various kinds of studies to explore and to extend our knowledge about the industry and how it works is required. This chapter is based on a single case study, which is really not going into detailed, in-depth investigations but which attempts to illuminate some of the systemic and networked characteristics of how the industry and its management control systems work in relation to rapidly scaling cases. The ambition is to propose complementary theoretical propositions by means of analytical generalization.

The case study is part of a broader study of the development and application of TAVI in Scandinavian hospitals. An important part of this study has been to trace the pathways of technological innovation back to the inventors and to follow the innovation processes that came to shape and the way the technology vendors eventually came to interact with hospitals in Scandinavia to establish and develop their TAVI practices. The study identified two major innovation trajectories, one of which ended up in the California-based company Edwards Lifesciences and the second as a subsidiary of the large medical technology conglomerate Medtronic Inc., in the name of Medtronic CoreValve. The Edwards Lifesciences case is published by Mikhailova and Olsen (2016) and Olsen and Håkansson (2017). This chapter is based on the second TAVI innovation trajectory; that of Medtronic CoreValve.

The research on the innovation history of CoreValve emerged out of interviews with representatives of Medtronic CoreValve in Scandinavia and from interviews with practitioners at various university hospitals in Norway, Sweden and Denmark. These indicated that the ways TAVI were practiced at different hospitals appeared largely to depend on which technology supplier they worked with. To understand why these were substantially different, the research team started investigating the two different innovation processes through literature studies and through secondary open sources of information. It turned out that, in particular, the CoreValve case revealed what appeared to be a highly structured, high-intensity innovation process that was amazingly rapid and successful. This sparked off particular interest also in the innovation process model and the systemic, interactional mode of operation we discovered. In this way, the two innovation stories became not only complementary elements of a broader story about innovation and adaptation of new technologies in medical practice but also interesting innovation process studies in themselves. It is this "independent" story of the CoreValve innovation process that will be presented and discussed in this chapter.

To structure the data gathering process, I decided to follow the financial deals that were made through the process (Håkansson and Olsen, 2015, 2017). The model helped address the interfaces and the timing between the activities of the entrepreneurial firm and the financing activities of the VC firms that gradually engaged with CoreValve. In this case—because it turned out to be a rather clean VC case—data about the deals and the actors involved were available from the Crunchbase.com database. Based on these data, it was possible to trace connections to other deals to information about the investment partners in each round of investment and to individuals in core positions in the technology start-up companies. From there, I searched for additional information in the research literature—in particular, in the medical literature on TAVI—and in other open secondary information sources, such as press releases and business magazines, for additional information to put together the puzzle and check for inconsistencies and misunderstandings. We have not—so far—conducted any interviews with actors directly involved in the deal-making processes; hence, all data are taken from secondary sources.

To make sense of these observations, the study has been supported by literature studies of the VC industry to make more informed assessments of how the VC firms operated in this case. This complementary investigation made it much clearer that the CoreValve case was indeed a very typical example of a successful VC-driven "scaling to exit" innovation process. This gave me some confidence in raising my ambition to pull out theoretical implications and suggestions based on the case. Based on this, I have used an explorative grounded theory method in combination with insights from the accounting in networks literature to provide a first analysis of the networked organizing and management control systems and tools observed.

The Medtronic CoreValve TAVI Case

The case is about the development of TAVI, which from around 2007, emerged as a radical new minimally invasive technology and medical procedure to replace the aorta heart valve in otherwise inoperable high-risk patients with severe aortic stenosis. The condition is life threatening, and without treatment, life expectancy is less than 2 years. Recently, TAVI has also been permitted for operable medium-risk patients.

This part of the TAVI history starts with the French heart surgeon and inventor Jacques R. Seguin and his co-inventor George Boertlein. In December 2001, they established a French start-up company called CoreValve. My story ends in 2009 with the acquisition of the company by the large US medical technology conglomerate, Medtronic Inc. Additionally, I will give a brief presentation of some of what happened subsequently. The case presents the history of CoreValve through several rounds of financial investments and through several generations of rapid technological development. It traces the story forward through the first-in-human operation conducted in Germany in 2004 and the moving of CoreValve's HQ and core development activities from Paris and San Diego to Irvine, California. It also presents the interplay between the financing and the building of the core team that developed, scaled and brought the new technology and its auxiliary products to the market.

Seguin is a former professor of heart surgery at Paris University, who for years had been actively engaged in the patenting of new technologies in the area of heart surgery (patents.justia.com/inventor/jacques-r-seguin). In December 2001, he left the university and his practice to create CoreValve in collaboration with co-inventor George Boertlein and Dr. Med Jean-Claude Laborde, who became responsible for the laboratory experiments and the medical trials. The idea was to develop a technology that allowed for a heart valve replacement by using a catheter-based technique requiring only a minor access hole to the femoral artery to perform the procedure.

At the time, another company called Percutaneous Valves Technologies (PVT) located in New Jersey, US, was already engaged in developing a similar technology (Mikhailova and Olsen, 2016; Olsen and Håkansson, 2017). The establishing of CoreValve thereby represented the early start of a race to develop and to potentially dominate a new niche in the global medical technology industry. The initiative followed a strong international trend at the time towards minimally invasive medical technologies and an accelerating shift from traditional open surgery towards the use of interventional cardiology techniques to treat diseases in the cardiac system. With TAVI, interventional cardiology for the first time entered the highly prestigious area of structural heart diseases, a domain belonging to thorax surgeons.

Angel Capital Investment and the San Diego Relationship

The first round of financing was done by a group of angel capital investors in San Diego, California. The leader of the group was Rob Michiels who, from 1977 to 1989, had been a manager and vice president of the structural heart decease technology company, Edwards Labs, before becoming president of Interventional Technologies Inc. in San Diego. He then retired and started engaging in seed funding activities with a group of angel investors. In 2002, the group invested 1 million USD in CoreValve, while Michiels also was engaged as an advisor and consultant to the company. He also collected a small development team of medical technology engineers in San Diego, who worked with the Paris-based inventor group in France.

Between 2001 and 2004, the Paris and San Diego CoreValve teams progressively developed the first-generation valve, leading to the first-in-human procedure conducted at a heart center in Siegburg, Germany, by Laborde and

Dr. Eberhard Grube in 2004. This happened 2 years after a first-in-human TAVI operation had been done by PVT in Rouen, Paris, in 2002. Hence, at the time, PVT had a 2 years' lead in the race.

In 2004, Edwards Laboratories acquired PVT and moved the company to Irvine, California, where it mobilized substantial resources aiming to establish a dominant position in the expected future market for TAVI (Mikhailova and Olsen, 2016). For CoreValve and its investors, this meant that there was already a first mover in the field that had substantial resources and capabilities. This implied that it would be a demanding race both in terms of speed, financing and technological innovation and, on the other hand, that others would be using substantial resources and efforts to open the market by moving the new technology through demanding regulatory procedures. Other medical technology companies also started working with the new approach. Hence, this was a race in which speed to market would be very important for the second movers. It was also clear that there was a race to establish proprietary control through patenting. Because Edwards through the PVT acquisition had acquired a number of early TAVI patents, there was considerable risk of later patent infringement battles with Edwards.

The A Series Venture Capital Deal

One million USD was far too little for CoreValve to engage the expertise and development resources needed, and the company accordingly worked to raise more money in the VC market. In 2003, after PVT's first-in-human operation in Paris, the San Francisco based VC company Sofinnova Partners invested 5.5 million USD (4.5 mill Euros) in a first "A series" investment round through its European partner organization, Sofinnova Partners, in Paris.

Sofinnova Partners, established in 1972, is one of the early VC firms in Silicon Valley. It was involved in some of the early successes of the new financial industry at the time, such as Genentech. Over the years, the company has raised and invested 1.42 billion USD in scaling technology startups (www.Sofinnova.com, www.Sofinnova.fr). Through the CoreValve investment, Sofinnova took a position on the company board and engaged to move the company forward, recruit people and plan the further financing and ownership strategy.

This meant that the project could now be speeded up to reach the goal of the activities funded by the series A financing: to conduct a successful first-in-human procedure to demonstrate to the financial investors that the company's proprietary technology was indeed viable and that the company could potentially keep up on speed with PVT.

The company successfully did its first-in-human procedure in Germany the following year. However, broad survey-based feedback from the medical community showed that the device was too wide to be useful for most patients and had to be made substantially smaller.

Michiels recognized that to work more effectively on these very demanding developmental challenges and to compete with Edwards Lifesciences after the company acquired PVT in 2004, CoreValve would also have to move its activities to Irvine, south of Los Angeles. This is a birthplace and global center of the modern biomedical industry which also includes the heart valve industry.

> A lot of medical technologies (originate) with physicians all over the world, Michiels says, but only a few areas, including southern California, have the necessary concentration of biomedical engineers and facilities to turn these ideas into reality. That's why, while (the CoreValve system) was invented in France, it was brought to life here in Irvine.
>
> (*The Orange County Register*, March 8, 2007)

The company accordingly swopped its HQ from France to Irvine, where the new headquarters (HQ) opened on January 1, 2005. Michiels then took on the job of president and chief operating officer of the company and gathered a team of highly experienced senior employees to develop the technology, each with more than 20 years of experience in core positions within the heart valve and cardiac technology industry. The youngest was in his 50s. Among them were Stanley Komatsu, the former vice president for valve operations responsible for Edwards' tissue heart-valve manufacturing operations for 20 years. Edward J. Panneck Jr., a former vice president for catheter operations, had worked with Michiels in Interventional Technologies on catheter design for years. A third was Than Nguyen, a former leading engineer at Baxter Healthcare Corp. responsible for designing medical implants to treat cardiovascular diseases, who was now a consultant on designing and manufacturing such systems (*Business Wire,* September 7, 2004). The company thereby obtained access to a broad range of expertise and, through its extended industrial networks, to resources that could be mobilized to develop, test and get professional feedback on the development process.

To be inserted into the major artery, the stent with the artificial valve inside it had to be crimped to a much smaller size. CoreValve's technology was using a self-expandable material to avoid using a balloon technology used by PVT and Edwards. The device had to be crimped at a low temperature in advance of the procedure before opening up by itself as the temperature increased when inserted into the aorta. To further crimp the device, the team invented new ways of attaching the stent and the valve, which permitted a new design of the stent. The team eventually managed to crimp the device to less than 6 mm, which was smaller than that of Edwards, when presenting the first generation of CoreValve's "Revolving system," the combined technologies required to perform TAVI procedures. The smaller crimped size made CoreValve slightly more attractive to cardiologists, but the somewhat longer device turned out to have other challenges, such as a greater tendency for patients to need a pacemaker after the operation (Khawaja et al., 2011).

The B Series Venture Capital Deal

Following the company's first-in-human procedure, with the plan to move of the HQ to Irvine and the need to gather a highly professional development team, Sofinnova moved to organize another round of investment. It did so by inviting the large private equity investment company, Apax Partners, in New York and Paris, to lead the investment round based on their second opinion evaluation of CoreValve. This resulted in July 2005 in a "B series" investment of all together 24 million USD, which also included the Swedish VC company HealthCap in Stockholm. Apax Partners is a major private equity investment company in New York, funded in 1969, that has raised and invested around 20 billion USD over the years, mostly through later stage restructuring and buyout funds. HealthCap is a VC company established in 1996 that has raised 800 million USD and invested for the most part in scaling health care technology start-ups in Scandinavia, Europe and the US. Both VC firms got representation on the board of directors in CoreValve (www.crunchbase.com/Corevalve). The company thereby had the necessary financial resources to move rapidly forward with the development of the second and third generation of CoreValve's "Revalving System."

The added financing provided the basis for accelerating the project both technically and in relation to the regulatory procedures. A first target for the company was to achieve a CE Mark in Europe as a necessary requirement for starting commercial marketing of the product to European hospitals. The European regulatory requirements are less restrictive for medical technologies than the US Food and Drug Administration (FDA) regulations, which is why such technologies and products are first launched in Europe and in countries such as Canada and Australia before the trial procedures to achieve a first FDA approval for commercial sales are typically completed. CoreValve received its first CE Mark to market its Revalving System for use on high-risk inoperable patients in February 2007, which was more than half a year before its rival Edwards Laboratories also received its first CE mark in November 2007 (Mikhailova and Olsen, 2016).

By obtaining the CE Mark before Edwards, CoreValve had managed to close the time gap to the PVT–Edwards TAVI process in the European market—and could thereby start marketing in Europe to establish customer relationships with the most important university hospitals before its rival. This gave CoreValve a first mover advantage in Europe that to a substantial degree compensated for its smallness. However, with a much larger organization, Edwards also managed to initiate and carry through the more demanding FDA procedure, which eventually led Edwards to obtain a 3-year monopoly in the US market from 2011 to 2014. But no doubt, the ability of the small technology start-up company, CoreValve, to catch up with the much larger rival, Edwards Laboratories, was rather impressive.

With CE approval, CoreValve now had to organize and scale its international marketing and sales operations as well as build and manage manufacturing, logistics and demanding regulatory processes in the US as well as in a number of other nations. This required additional funding and hiring of marketing and sales people and building, primarily through outsourcing, a manufacturing and logistics operation. Now, the experience, networks and capacity of the Irvine-based senior team really became an important asset to the company, as many of the industrial and logistical resources and activities could be mobilized at a rapid pace by reaching out to trusted people they had been working with for years.

According to our informants at Copenhagen University Hospital (Rigshospitalet), the first person to contact them and start organizing collaboration on behalf of CoreValve after the CE approval in 2006 was a representative of HealthCap. Apparently, CoreValve at the time did not have a marketing organization—at least not one that stretched all the way to Scandinavia. In Copenhagen, the first TAVI procedure was done in late 2007.

The C Series Venture Capital Deal

The investors could now start planning the next move: to sell the company through an industrial exit. To manage this process, the company in early 2006 recruited a chief financial officer, J. C. MacRae, who had extensive experience with both IPOs and mergers and acquisitions in the industry. He came from a similar position in ActiveX Biosciences and, before that, he had also had senior management positions in ISTA Pharmaceuticals, Imagyn Medical Inc., InnerSpace Medical Inc., Retroperfusion Systems Inc. and VLI Corporation—all medical device manufacturers (Businesswire.com, March 1, 2006).

The company still had no revenues from sales and needed to expand rapidly over a wide frontier of activities. It thereby needed to use a lot more money. It accordingly had to mobilize for a third round of money raising. This time, yet another VC company was invited to lead the investment round, to conduct a second opinion evaluation of the company and the investment opportunity, negotiate a valuation assessment and organize a syndicated investment deal that included substantial follow-up investments from all the three already involved VC funds: Sofinnova, Apax and HealthCap. The new lead investor was the, by origin, Israeli-based VC firm, Maverick Capital, which had moved its HQ to Dallas, Texas. The company was established in 1993 and had over the years raised and invested 10 billion USD (Crunchbase.com).

The deal settled on a 33 million USD syndicated investment in March 2007, just 1 month after CoreValve had received its CE Mark approval to start marketing in Europe. At this point in time, a total of 64 million USD had been invested in the company by a group of angel investors and four international VC firms. The company could thereby aggressively build and scale its activities to reach a market breakthrough into a range of leading European hospitals and heart clinics.

Edwards Lifesciences was a major incumbent in the market for structural heart diseases with a complete domination of surgeons in its customer base. This motivated the company to put substantial effort into developing new TAVI procedures, technologies and marketing approaches that would also include surgeons as participants and users of TAVI products (Levin, 2010; Mikhailova and Olsen, 2016; Olsen and Håkansson, 2017). This situation did not apply to CoreValve, which, as a lean start-up company, concentrated on developing a technology and procedure to be used only by interventional cardiologists. This led the two companies to launch rather different marketing approaches towards the hospitals to sell rather similar technologies; where Edwards strongly advocated a surgery-cardiology team based at their customer health clinics, CoreValve approached only medical doctors who specialized in interventional cardiology.

Because of the high medical risks associated with the procedure, the challenging conditions of the very old patients and the lack of experience with the new procedure, substantial effort had to be put into organizing a system for training and supporting the new TAVI teams at each customer hospital. All of this had to be organized by the vendors. As the FDA procedures that Edwards engaged in moved forward, many of these precautions and systems were included in the regulatory requirements that also CoreValve would have to conform with in its later FDA processes. Hence, CoreValve also actively responded to and upgraded its activities as it learned what requirements were included by the FDA in its evaluations of Edwards' TAVI activities.

The Acquisition of CoreValve by Medtronic Inc.

With CoreValve's chief financial officer (CFO), J. J. MacRae, engaged in the company from early 2006, the board worked out strategies to seek a profitable exit for the owners of the company. According to the board member representing Sofinnova Partners, Antonine Papiernick, the company received several offers to acquire CoreValve from around a year before the company, finally in February 2009, settled on a deal with the large medical technology company Medtronic Inc. (*Financial Times*, www.ft.com/content/f4788f6e-01fe.11de-8199-000077b07658). Medtronic paid 700 million USD to acquire CoreValve plus performance-based milestone payments. CoreValve then became a fully owned subsidiary: Medtronic CoreValve LLC, headquartered in Irvine. The deal was one of the biggest exits for a VC-backed medical device company at the time (www.ft.com/content/f4788f6e-01fe-11de-8199-000077b07658). With a total financial investment of 64 million USD, it returned more than 700 million USD to its owners.

At the same time, Medtronic Inc. also acquired the Israel-based company, Ventor Technologies, for 325 million USD. This company had been developing TAVI technologies, along a strategy similar to that of Edwards, to develop a technology that gave the surgeons a role in the procedure. Jointly, these two acquisitions put Medtronic in a position to compete with Edwards on supporting different approaches to the operational procedure with the inclusion of surgeons who also represented a major part of Medtronic's customer base.

All together Medtronic paid more than 1 billion USD to get a position in an attractive new global niche market for TAVI devices. After a transition period of about 1 year when CoreValve's team continued working with the company, most of them left the company in 2010, while Medtronic mobilized to pull the company into the FDA procedure to improve the technology and to build the marketing and sales organization in Europe and elsewhere. In particular, it was critical for Medtronic to push for FDA approval to compete with Edwards in the US market, a goal the company managed to reach in early 2014, 3 years later than Edwards.

While starting commercial sales in 2007, the number of clinics doing TAVI procedures has expanded very rapidly, and the number of procedures reached an aggregated 50,000 procedures in 2011, 100,000 in 2012 and continued exponential growth in the years to follow. Until 2014 to 2015, the market was dominated by Edwards and Medtronic CoreValve, who shared most of the global market equally even though Edwards obtained an effective monopoly in the US from 2011 to 2014.

The race also sparked off a fierce battle over patent infringements with several court processes in both Europe and the US. Most of these have been settled in out-of-court settlements in which Medtronic accepted to pay compensations of more than 900 million USD to Edwards for infringing on early TAVI patents. Altogether, this implies that Medtronic has paid more in patent infringement compensations to Edwards than it paid to acquire CoreValve in 2009. Indeed, this is a substantial investment cost, which clearly illustrates the profitability associated with such a fast-growing medical technology niche market.

What Happened to the CoreValve Team After the Company Was Acquired by Medtronic?

Following the acquisition, Seguin, who had been chairman of the board of CoreValve, jointly with his close partner, Grube, have remained members of the board of Medtronic CoreValve. However, already in 2006, Seguin had started a new French company called STENTYS SA, based on his own patents, to develop different heart disease applications for the self-expandable stent technology that CoreValve had been using. The company, just like CoreValve, received its first VC funding from Sofinnova Partners (crunchbase.com). It received its first Conformité Européenne (CE) mark in 2010; moved its HQ to Princeton, NJ; and got introduced through an IPO at the EuroNext Paris stock exchange later the same year.

Michiels and the group of angel investors who first invested in CoreValve in December 2009 invested 750 000 USD in a company called CardiAQ

Valve Technologies Inc. Simultaneously, CardiAQ raised another 6.5 million USD from the seed capital investment fund Broadview Capital. CardiAQ was also located in Irvine and had developed a proprietary system for transcatheter mitral valve implantation (TMVI) that would permit physicians to do mitral heart valve replacement in a way rather similar to TAVI. In January 2011, Michiels moved from Medtronic CoreValve to become the CEO of CardiAQ Technologies, bringing with him the core members of the CoreValve team, such as MacRae, Lebarde, Komatsu, Panneck and Nguyen.

CardiAQ, in a B series investment round in November 2012, raised another 37.5 million USD from two other VC firms. In August 2015, Edwards Lifesciences acquired CardiAQ Technologies at a price of 400 million USD. At the time, CardiAQ had received a first CE approval in Europe and had got the first permission from the FDA to start early trials with 20 patients. Hence, CardiAQ Technologies was purchased at a somewhat lower price than CoreValve, but the company was clearly at an earlier development stage. From a financial investment of 45 million USD, CardiAQ returned 400 million in less than 6 years from the initial investment.

Lebarde continued as a member of the advisory board of Medtronic CoreValve and continued proctoring new TAVI teams for the company—a role in which he had been critically important to CoreValve. Eventually, in 2016, he started working with another medical technology start-up called 4Tech Inc. in Ireland, which had started working on the world's first transcatheter device for repair of the tricuspid heart valve (*Business Wire*, May 16, 2016).

MacRae only stayed with CardiAQ for a year, before moving on to become the CFO and vice president of Uptake Medical Corp., a Seattle-based leading developer of medical technologies for interventional emphysema therapy (Uptake Medical Corp, November 16, 2010).

Analysis: The Industrial Solution to the Knowledge Gap Problem in the Rapidly Scaling Technology Start-Up Process

The CoreValve case illustrates a rapid and successful scaling process of a radical new technology start-up from its local inception in France to its becoming a global industrial and marketing company headquartered in California as a subsidiary of a major incumbent firm less than 8 years later. Even though CoreValve was an independent start-up company established by French inventors, the developing and scaling process illustrates a number of features that illuminate how it emerged as part of a particular financial industry with a business model clearly targeting the scaling of this kind of start-up company. This financial industry was an absolutely critical part of what made it possible to mobilize and move the necessary resources, actors and activities to recombine them in the CoreValve company at the speed required to succeed in the race with Edwards Lifesciences. Essentially, this part of the process was about mobilizing money to acquire and combine the best knowledge, actors, networks and activities available to do the job at the place in the world where these resources were possible to find and acquire.

The case also illuminates how a group of experienced managers and angel investors may engage with the early entrepreneurs to complement the early team and thereby both expand its knowledge and networks as well as signal to the financial industry that this is a high-quality project that may offer a professional industrial partnership to VC investors. Eventually, this was the coming together of inventor, industrial and financial entrepreneurs in a unifying set-up.

Through these early interactions, knowledge, highly experienced actors and money started moving together. It was the interacting of the industrial management and angel investor group with the VC firms that essentially created this movability. The money was raised from a range of investors across the US, Europe and elsewhere through a system of syndicated investments using standardized formats and distributions of roles. The substantial financial investments in the company provided the basis for the recruiting and funding of a team of extremely experienced and specialized people with extended industrial networks.

This case study—in broad terms—confirms and illuminates the argument that what is at work here is a highly structured, networked industrial system based on shared industrial structures, financing and management systems, management control mechanisms and tools. The core of the industrial system is the ways that smaller shares of big money from across society's saving and investment systems are interacted with heterogeneous fast-to-scale entrepreneurial projects. In the CoreValve case, the French entrepreneurs were also highly experienced and remained on board the company despite others taking control. Hence, in this case, there was in effect an alignment of interests between those who owned on the basis of specific intellectural property rights (IPR) contributions and those who owned on the basis of capital investments and managerial capabilities.

The study also confirms the argument that this networked industry is based on a model of financing which requires that investors acquire sufficient ownership control to effectively manage the entrepreneurial start-up processes. This is the basis for moving in standardized management control systems, mechanisms and tools. It reveals the patterns of an open corporate innovation model—shared across the VC industry—that facilitates extended networked interactions across highly structured and aligned interfaces and by the use of similar managerial control systems and tools.

The "open corporate innovation model" reflects the observation that fast scaling of such firms happens within a corporate innovation system with powers of control at the level of what we may find inside industrial corporations. It also reflects that it is open in the sense that each project may partner with other VC firms in an industry with highly structured vertical managerial levels of operation and highly structured vertical network interaction modes. This provides both the discipline required to reach highly demanding targets and the flexibility to regroup in response to the heterogeneity challenges represented by the innovation projects. It is these shared structures and systems and the use of standardized managerial control and accounting and calculative tools that provided the backbone for the financial and innovation process management that made it possible to develop and scale CoreValve in such a short time and to exit from the ownership position with a very substantial economic payoff.

The fundamental structure is there to interact financial resources with heterogeneous innovation projects that can potentially be scaled at a rapid pace. Because of the high risk and the lengthy period from commitment of financial investments by the LPs to the harvesting of the fund 10 years later, risk and return management systems are multiple and highly sophisticated. They are managed through four different hierarchical levels of financial investment management:

1. *The level of large institutional savings and investment funds.* These are managed by standard portfolio management theory and models, in which financial opportunities are grouped into many different risk–return classes. Money is invested according to regulatory and strategic considerations across the different investment classes. The VC industry is one such class with high risk and subsequently high expected capital return requirements. The VC industry is in a competitive race to stay attractive to these institutional investors over time and as such has strong reasons to collaborate internally on developing a collective industrial system which is broadly effective.
2. *The level of the VC firm.* These are managed by GPs, who are essentially networkers in between financial partners and industrial competence resources that may be mobilized and interacted in concrete scaling of entrepreneurial firm cases. They raise money from institutional investors and provide management services in between the investors and the entrepreneurial firms. From their perspective, each fund is a syndicated investment that includes different institutional investors. With several funds in one VC company, this potentially gives the VC company a large financial network from which to find and combine financial partners to target different funds from different areas of innovation activities, such as health care innovations. This network also helps it identify and interact with large firms to orchestrate industrial exits.
3. *The level of each VC fund.* Portfolio management at this level is not similar to what is done by institutional investors but is rather a portfolio of entrepreneurial firms with similar, very high risk–return profiles. They rather have some kind of knowledge similarities that permit the GP networkers to exploit their industrial networks to attract and mobilize those who already know a lot about how to develop and scale a given case, such as illustrated by the roles of Michiels, MacRae and the other members of the CoreValve team. At this level, there is also a collective

model to organize syndicated investments with other VC firms or funds through the staged investment system used across the industry. These are core intermediating devices.

4. *The level of the entrepreneurial firm*. At this level, the financial management control system is based on the staged investment or milestone model and is focused on managing the financing to reduce risks; to demonstrate radical risk reductions through reaching core milestones; and, by staging the organization, to be able to rapidly advance to the next step if and when additional financing is invested. Hence, specific trajectories for each project are created by using commonly shared "roadmaps" with standardized, staged evaluation, decision and investment systems baked into the process.

At each of these levels, management control systems and mechanisms and the accounting and calculating tools used are different and particularly adjusted to the characteristics of the activity at each level, as well as to the power relations among the actors at the different levels. Hence, ownership to equity is structured through successive principal agent–based management control arrangements tailored to the kind of activity that takes place at each management level. Ownership of financial resources and of the investment objects is core to how this particular industrial system works.

At each of these levels, there are particular horizontal network systems. These provide opportunities to share and manage the high risks as well as network development by engaging in syndicated investments. Portfolio management of different kinds are combined with syndication of investment arrangements with particular management models and tools to orchestrate the various roles involved. In the CoreValve case, the use of shared syndicated investment models across the VC industry is striking.

The syndicated investment system is such that in each investment object, the first VC fund to invest will search for and propose another investment fund to take the lead in the following investment. By accepting this invitation, the new fund will do its own thorough due diligence investigation of the company; its patent portfolio, technology, regulatory and market development; its management team; its actual and potential markets; and so on. Based on this, it may propose a valuation of the company and a structure of a deal that would typically call for co-investments by the existing investor funds engaged in the given company. In this way, there will be a negotiation of the terms of the deal initiated by an external evaluation in which the inventors and the existing investors in the company are essentially at the same side of the negotiating table—to try maintaining alignment of interest between these different kinds of owners of the firm.

In such a structure, there appears to be at least three different ways that investment companies get involved in technology start-ups such as CoreValve. One is to be the first VC firm investor that moves in early and takes a position on the board which permits the investing company to establish ownership control through managing the further investment process. The second way is by being asked by the first investors to take a lead role in the next round of financing. The third way is by being asked by a lead investor to participate as an additional partner in the following syndicated investment. Successful investment firms obviously participate in all three ways, which implies that there is a variety of important relationships between these companies that emerge as a result of successive syndications. These permit them to manage their investment portfolios to reduce overall risks across more investment opportunities, exploit one another's competence and networks and participate in a global distribution of work that provides access to a very large resource and actor pool. Hence, an investment management firm will have greater benefit the more attractive it is to other investment firms as a partner to and initiator of such syndicated investments. In this way, the VC industry is highly networked and interacted and accordingly represents substantial investments in place. As illustrated in the CoreValve case, co-investors may also be called from the other side of the world, such as Swedish HealthCap, which may, for instance, have considerable valuable knowledge of and networks in Scandinavian and other European countries that in this case were useful in the early marketing phase.

The role of HealthCap is also discussed by Strömsten and Waluszewski (2012) in a different innovation case called "Pyrosequencing AB." This case is also discussed by Christner and Strömsten (2015). In their case, HealthCap invested as the only VC company through several rounds of investment and held several positions on the board of Pyrosequencing AB. Interesting to note is that HealthCap was established in 1996 and that its first Pyrosequencing investment was made in 1997, while its first investment in CoreValve was made in 2005. Different from in 1997, it was done as a co-investor in a syndicated model with much larger and more experienced investment firms. The absence of syndicated investments in the Pyrosequencing case may indicate that HealthCap at the time was a relatively unexperienced newcomer to the VC industry and as such had limed networks to other and more experienced VC firms. Hence, the CoreValve case may illustrate a more mature industrial investment practice than does the Pyrosequencing case.

The Industrial Networks and Serial Entrepreneurial Scale-Ups

A critical part of the "learning before doing" strategy and practice is to recruit a complementary team of highly experienced experts that fits the particular challenges of the start-up project. In this case, the recruiting process was kick-started by the angel investment group, which had relevant competence within the group. The CoreValve innovation process required a limited number of such actors with access to additional activities and resources that had to be extracted from their attachments to other activities and resources. The team accordingly needed substantial financial resources to be able to rapidly mobilize what was required to move the project forward.

These individuals are scarce and must be found and induced to take on such a job on short notice and with high intensity and demands. Such people are costly but very valuable to the investors. They are necessary to be able to plan and execute rapid development and scaling processes without unnecessary mistakes, conflicts and setbacks.

This implies that they will have to looked for in the largest, densest and most competent environments of the particular industry, among high-end management executives and engineers with present or former positions in leading companies and preferably with experience from similar kinds of scale-up processes. To move them, the financial investors will have to invest sufficient funding to both convince them of their financial commitments to the start-up company and of their ability to pay and secure the salaries as well as the incentive scheme within a realistic time span and plan.

These individuals also have extended networks with others. In the case of CoreValve, the management team was able to outsource most of the non-critical activities to others and to develop the technology and to establish manufacturing capacity, logistics, management systems and so on at a rapid pace by exploiting these many already established networks. Most of what they needed was already there and was accessible because of the more than 20 years of executive management experience each of them had.

Eventually, the entire process also depended on the availability of established medical technology corporations with global marketing operations and sufficient financial capacity to place competitive bids for the start-up company.

These requirements are essentially why new inventions that may develop anywhere in the world, such as in France, in practice will tend to circulate into the few places in the world where the relevant competences to rapidly scale the project are gathered. For biomedical technologies, Orange County in California is such a place—where the early transcatheter technology start-ups seem to have ended up almost side by side in the city of Irvine. The VC firms need to be there as well, but as we have seen, financial resources and ownership may be more distributed or rather composed in a broader way—for instance, to attract knowledge about particular domains of the global markets.

The case also illustrates how management teams may proceed to do serial-entrepreneurial projects by exploiting their experiences and networks to do projects that are relatively similar. Hence, domains of technology and practice may represent trajectories of technological developments over time. The less additional learning that needs to be explored in the next project the better. Even though Michiels and most of the team jointly moved on from Medtronic CoreValve to CardiAQ, the new project was done with different VC firms. MacRae continued going from project to project, specializing in the organizing of exit strategies. Finally, we also observe that Seguin went on to start a new company but in this case with the same first VC investor firm as in CoreValve and this time in France and by doing an IPO to maintain an independent company. There are many combinations, but the core management control systems, partnering models and accounting tools appear to be the same.

Conclusions

The study illustrates and confirms that the wave of rapidly scaling new ventures is rooted in a process of industrialization of what has become the VC scaling industry. Its business is to scale entrepreneurial start-ups. This industrialization is what essentially explains how the needed knowledge and the networks are actually acquired by the entrepreneurial actors (Weerawardena et al., 2007; Freeman et al., 2010; Zahra, 2005; Keupp and Gassman, 2009; Evers and O-Gorman, 2011). The answer is that it is not the original entrepreneurs who acquire knowledge and networks; rather, the entrepreneurs are acquired by those who already have the networks with knowledge and other resources needed. In this sense, the entrepreneurial role is shifted to a new kind of entrepreneurship more similar to "intrapreneurship," which is organized in flexible industrial and financial networks.

The VC industry has developed an open corporate innovation model shared across the industry that provides standardized "roadmaps" supported by industrial structures and systems, financial and management control systems and accounting and calculative formats and tools to support and discipline scaling processes. The sharing of these across the industry facilitates a system of flexible, networked collaboration to deal with the heterogeneity, variability, motion and uncertainties they are facing. The CoreValve case illuminates how these structured formats and tools shape the distribution of roles and the ways they interact with one another through the process—as mediating cross-boundary devices. The effects are substantial systemic synergies that improved the effectiveness and efficiencies of the entire scaling process.

A fundamental property of the model is that VC firms take ownership control over the entrepreneurial firms they invest in, so that ownership and management control are passed over from the entrepreneurs to the VC firms. This is the basis for moving in the industry's own management control systems and accounting tools as well as their professional service providers (e.g., accounting, auditing, lawyers) Hence, this is a form of systemic corporate innovation, not a clustering of individual entrepreneurial projects.

In the case study by Strömsten and Waluszewski (2012), they investigated how the fast-scaling policy of a VC company affected and constrained the networking processes of the entrepreneurial firm. In this study, the focus has been on investigating the networked characteristics of the VC industry itself to discuss how this system manages the challenges and risks involved in rapid scaling of heterogeneous entrepreneurial firms.

This study has contributed by illuminating the different layers of financial management control at work in the industry and the combination of syndicated investment systems, different kinds of portfolio management systems and their particular forms of management control and accounting and calculating tools used to discipline the actors and to speed up the innovation and scaling processes. The knowledge gap problem is resolved neither through learning by doing nor learning before doing. Rather, it is done by acquiring the knowledge and putting it to work in complementary, highly experienced expert teams with extended, already established, relationships with relevant actors, resources and activities that may be enrolled. The trick is to reduce the need for learning "before doing" and "by doing" as much as possible.

To resolve this problem, the industry has emerged as an extremely networked system, in which at each hierarchical level of investment management, the syndication and portfolio-based deal structures generate very extended networks across the VC industry as well as into the various industries, research communities and so on that belong to the heterogeneous world of innovation. The networked and flexible structure is what makes it possible to connect "ignorant money" to the world of scaling of heterogeneous entrepreneurial firms. The two different HealthCap cases discussed are perhaps good examples of different maturity levels in the VC industry with respect to the networking capacity of more or less experienced VC firms.

The financial and management control systems are specifically designed to deal with the challenges at each level of management, and the accounting tools used are accordingly very specific to their domain of use. The case in particular illustrates the system of networked, syndicated deal making in relation to the staged investment model which is again connected to the roadmap for targeted milestones that is at the core of how financing is directly interacting with the social-material innovation process at the level of innovation project management. This describes the particular mechanism which is at the center of the analytical deal model applied (Håkansson and Olsen, 2015).

This case study has not been able (so far) to go into more substantial depth when it comes to investigating and analyzing the use of the particular accounting and calculating tools. We have not had access to data about the valuation of CoreValve in the different rounds of investment, and we have not done interviews, observations or other close-to-the-actors research methods that might have given more insights into the actual use of the tools in practice and the assessments, controversies and settlements associated with their use. This has also made it impossible to learn about alternative trajectories for the CoreValve project that may have been discussed during the deal process. I believe such a deeper study of the CoreValve case would be interesting and would provide opportunities to dive a lot more into the details of management control and accounting in network practices in this case. So, this is a topic for further research.

References

Autio, E. (2005). Creative tension: The significance of Ben Oviatt's and Patricia McDougall's article 'Toward a theory of international new ventures'. *Journal of International Business Studies*, 36, pp 9–19.

Axelsson, B. and Easton, G. (eds) (1992). *Industrial Networks: A New View of Reality*. London: Routledge.

Bakken, T., Håkansson, H. and Olsen, P.I. (2013). Agency and economizing in interacted economies, *The IMP Journal*, 7(2), pp 1–6.

Baraldi, E. and Strömsten, T. (2009). Controlling and combining resources in networks. From Uppsala to Stanford, and back again: The case of a biotech innovation. *Industrial Marketing Management*, 38(5), pp 541–552.

Barney, J.B., Fiet, J.O., Busenitz, L.W. and Moesel, D.D. (1996). The subscription of bonding for monitoring in venture capitalist relations with high technology enterprises. *Journal of High Technology Management Research*, 7, pp 91–105.

Bruns, W.J. and Waterhouse, S. (1975). Budgeting control and organizational structure. *Journal of Accounting Research*, 13, pp 177–203.

BusinessWire (2004). CoreValve Establishes U.S. Operations, Hires Veteran Medical Device Management and Development Team. September 2007, https://www.businesswire.com/news/home/20040907005617

BusinessWire (2006). CoreValve names J. C. MacRae as Vice President of Finance and Chief Financial Officer. March 1, https://www.businesswire.com/news/home/20060301005070/

BusinessWire (2016). 4Tech and Dr. Jean-Claude Laborde Enter into Partnership to Accelerate 4Tech R&D and Clinical Development. May 16. https://www.businesswire.com/news/home/20160515005005

Callon, M. (1998). *The Laws of the Market*. Oxford: Blackwell.

Chenhall, R.H. and Morris, D. (1986). The impact of structure, environment, and interdependence on the perceived usefulness of management accounting systems. *The Accounting Review*, 61, pp 58–75.

Christner, H. and Strömsten, T. (2015). Scientists, venture capitalists and the stock exchange. The mediating role of accounting in product innovation. *Managing Accounting Research*, 28, pp 50–67.

Coviello, N.E. and Jones, M.V. (2004). Methodological issues in international entrepreneurship research. *Journal of Business Venturing*, 19, pp 485–508.

Cribier, A. (2012). Development of transcatheter aortic valve implantation (TAVI): A 20-year odyssey. *Archives of Cardiovascular Diseases*, 105, pp 146–152.

Crunchbase.com. https://www.crunchbase.com/organization/corevalve-2/funding_rounds/funding_rounds_list

Davila, T. (2000). An exploratory study on the emergence of management control systems: Formalizing human resources in small growing firms. *Accounting, Organizations and Society*, 30, pp 223–248.

Davila, T., Foster, G. and Gupta, M. (2003). Venture capital financing and growth of startup firms. *Journal of Business Venturing*, 18, pp 689–708.

Evers, N. and O'Gorman, C. (2011). Improvised internationalization in new ventures: The role of prior knowledge and networks. *Entrepreneurship & Regional Development*, 23(7–8), September 2011, pp 549–574.

Ford, D. (1990). *Understanding Business Markets*. San Diego: Academic Press.

Ford, D., Gadde, L.-E., Håkansson, H., Snehota, I. and Waluszewski, A. (2011). Analyzing business interaction. *The IMP Journal*, 4(1), pp 82–105.

Ford, D. and Håkansson, H. (2010). Accounting and inter-organisational issues. In H. Håkansson, K. Kraus and J. Lind (eds), *Accounting in Networks*. New York: Routledge.

Freeman, S. (2007). An integrated framework for de-internationalization strategies for smaller born globals. Exploiting the B2B knowledge network: New perspectives and core concepts. In: *23rd IMP Conference Proceedings*.

Freeman, S., Hutchings, K., Lazaris, M. and Zyngier, S. (2010). A model of rapid knowledge development: The smaller born-global firm. *International Business Review*, 19, pp 70–84.

Galbraith, J. (1973). *Designing Complex Organizations*. Reading, MA: Addison-Westly.

Gompers, P. and Lerner, J. (1999). *The Venture Capital Cycle*. Cambridge: The MIT Press.

Gordon, L.A. and Narayanan, V.K. (1984). Management accounting systems, perceived environmental uncertainty and organizational structure: An empirical investigation. *Accounting, Organizations and Society*, 9, pp 33–47.

Govindarajan, V. and Gupta, A.K. (1985). Linking control systems to business strategy: Impact on performance. *Accounting, Organizations and Society*, 10, pp 51–66.

Granlund, M. and Taipleenmääki, J. (2003). Management control and controllership in new economy firms—a life cycle perspective. *Management Accounting Research*, 19, pp 21–57.

Håkansson, H. (ed.) (1982). *International Marketing and Purchasing of Industrial Goods: An Interaction Approach*. New York: John Wiley & Sons.

Håkansson, H., Ford, D., Gadde, L.-E. and Snehota, I. (2009). *Business in Networks*. Chichester: John Wiley.

Håkansson, H., Kraus, K. and Lind, J. (2010). *Accounting in networks*. Routledge Studies in Accounting. New York and Oxon, UK: Routledge.

Håkansson, H. and Lind, J. (2004). Accounting and network coordination. *Accounting, Organizations and Society*, 29, pp 51–72.

Håkansson, H. and Olsen, P.I. (2015). The roles of money and business deals in networked structures. *Industrial Marketing Management*, 45, pp 207–2017.

Håkansson, H. and Waluszewski, A. (2002). *Managing Technological Development: IKEA, the Environment and Technology*. London and New York: Routledge.

Håkansson, H. and Waluszewski, A. (eds.) (2007). *Knowledge and Innovation in Business and Industry: The Importance of Using Others*. London: Routledge.

Hansmann, H. (1996). *The Ownership of Enterprise*. Cambridge, MA/London: The Belknap Press and Harvard University Press.

Johanson, J. and Mattson, L.-M. (1985). Marketing, investment and marketing investment in industrial networks. *International Journal of Research in Marketing*, 2(3), pp 185–195.

Johanson, J. and Vahlne, J.-E. (1977). The internationalization process of the firm: A model of knowledge development and increasing foreign market commitments. *Journal of International Business Studies*, 8, pp 23–32.

Johanson, J. and Vahlne, J.-E. (2003). Business relationship learning and commitment in the internationalization process. *Journal of International Entrepreneurship*, 1, pp 83–101.

Johanson, J. and Vahlne, J.-E. (2009). The Uppsala internationalization process model revisited: From liability of foreignness to liability of outsidership. *Journal of International Business Studies*, 40, pp 1411–1431.

Jørgensen, B. and Messner, M. (2009). Management control in new product development: The dynamics of managing flexibility and efficiency. *Journal of Management Accounting Research*, 21(1), pp 99–124.

Kaplan, R.S. (1983). Measuring manufacturing performance: A new challenge for manufacturing accounting research. *The Accounting Review*, 58, pp 686–705.

Keupp, M.M. and Gassmann, O. (2009). The past and the future of international entrepreneurship: A review and suggestions for developing the field. *Journal of Management*, 35, pp 600–633.

Khawaja, M.Z., Rajani, R., Cook, A., Khavandi, A., Moynagh, A., Chowdhary, S., Spence, M.S., Brown, S., Khan, S.Q., Walker, N., Trivedi, U., Hutchinson, N., De Belder, A.J., Moat, N., Blackman, D.J., Levy, R.D., Manoharan, G., Roberts, D., Khogali, S.S., Crean, P., Brecker, S.J., Baumbach, A., Mullen, M., Laborde, J.-C., Hildick-Smith, D. (2011). Permanent pacemaker insertion after CoreValve transcatheter aortic valve implantation incidence and contributing factors (the UK CoreValve Collaborative). *Circulation*, March, pp 951–960.

Knight, G.A. and Cavusgil, S.T. (2004). Innovation, organizational capabilities, and the born-global firm. *Journal of International Business Studies*, 35, pp 124–141.

Laine, A. and Kock, S. (2000). A process model of internationalization: New times demands new patterns. In: *Communication lors de la 16ème conférence de l'IMP*, University of Bath, School of Management.

Levin, S. (2010). Edwards: Transcatheter valve leader proves you can go home again. *Elsevier Business Intelligence*, 28.

McGrath, M.D. (1995). *Product Strategies for High-Technology Companies*. New York: Richard Irwin Inc.

Mikhailova, O. and Olsen, P.I. (2016). Internationalization of an academic invention through successive science-business networks: The case of TAVI. *Journal of International Entrepreneurship*, 14(3), pp 441–471.

Miller, P. and O'Leary, T. (2007). Accounting, hybrids and the management of risk. *Accounting, Organizations and Society*, 32(7/8), pp 701–734.

Mouritsen, J., Hansen, A. and Hansen, C.O. (2001). Inter-organizational controls and organizational competencies: Episodes around target cost management/functional analysis and open book accounting. *Management Accounting Research*, 12, pp 221–244.

Mouritsen, J., Hansen, A. and Hansen, C.O. (2009). Short and long translations: Management accounting calculations and innovation management. *Accounting, Organizations and Society*, 34(6/7), pp 738–754.

Mouritsen, J., Mahama, H. and Chua, W.F. (2010). Actor-network theory and the study of inter-organizatisational network-relations. In H. Håkansson, K. Kraus and J. Lind (eds), *Accounting in Networks*. New York: Routledge.

O-Gorman, C. and Evers, N. (2011). Network intermediaries in the internationalization of new firms in peripheral regions. *International Marketing Review*, 28(4), pp 340–364.

Olsen, P.I. (2005). The-re-formatting of electricity, and the making of a market. In B. Cszarniawska and T. Hernes (eds.), *Actor-Network Theory and Organizing*. Liber/Copenhagen: Business School Press.

Olsen, P.I. (2013). IMP theory in light of process- and systems theories. *The IMP Journal*, 7(3), pp 159–170.

Olsen, P.I. and Håkansson, H. (2017). The roles of deals and business networks in innovation processes, *The IMP Journal*, 11(1), pp 25–50.

Orange County Register (2007). How Rob Michiels and CoreValve got where they are today. March 8. https://www.ocregister.com/2007/03/08

Peiris, I.K., Akoorie, M.E. and Sinha, P. (2012). International entrepreneurship: A critical analysis of studies in the past two decades and future directions for research. *Journal of International Entrepreneurship*, 10, pp 279–324.

Penrose, E. (1959). *The Theory of the Growth of the Firm*. New York: John Wiley and Sons.

Revellino, S. and Mouritsen, J. (2009). The multiplicity of controls and the making of innovation. *European Accounting Review*, 18(2), pp 341–369.

Rosenberg, N. (1982). *Inside the black box. Technology and economics*. Cambridge, UK: Cambridge University Press.

Sahlman, W. (1990). The structure of governance of venture capital organizations. *Journal of Financial Economy*, 22, pp 473–621.

Selnes, F. and Sallis, J. (2003). Promoting relationship learning. *Journal of Marketing*, 67, pp 80–95.

Shenhar, A.J. and Dvir, D. (1996). Toward a typological theory of project management. *Research Policy*, 25, pp 607–632.

Stabell, C.B. and Fjeldstad, Ø.D. (1998). Configuring value for competitive advantages: On chains, shops and networks. *Strategic Management Journal*, 19(5), pp 413–437.

Strömsten, T. and Waluszewski, A. (2012). Governance and resource interaction in networks. The role of venture capital in a biotech start-up. *Journal of Business Research*, 65(2), pp 232–244.

Tidd, J., Pavitt, K. and Bessant, J. (1997). *Managing Innovation: Integrating Technological Markets and Organizational Change*. Chichester: Wiley.

Timmons, J.A. and Bygrave, W.D. (1986). Venture capital's role in financing innovation for economic growth. *Journal of Business Venturing*, 1, pp 161–176.

Tushman, M. and Nadler, D. (1978). Information processing as interacting concept in organizational design. *Academy of Management Review*, 3, pp 613–624.

Uptake Medical Corp (2010). News & Events. November 16. http://www.gbsventures.com.au/news-and-events/uptake-medical-technologies-emphysema-therapy-j-c-macrae-vice-president-and-chief-financial-officer

Van de Ven, A.H., Polley, D.E., Garud, R. and Venkataraman, S. (1999). *The Innovation Journey*. New York: Oxford University Press.

Von Hippel, E. (1988). *The Sources of Innovation*. New York: Oxford University Press.

Wheelwright, S.C. and Clark, K.B. (1992). *Revolutionizing Product Development: Quantum Leaps in Speed, Efficiency, and Quality*. New York: The Free Press.

Weerawardena, J., Mort, G.S., Liesch, P.W. and Knight, G. (2007). Conceptualizing accelerated internationalization in the born global firm: A dynamic capabilities perspective. *Journal of World Business*, 42, pp 294–306.

Zahra, S.A. (2005). A theory of international new ventures: A decade of research. *Journal of International Business Studies* 36, pp 20–28.

5 Fostering Corporate Innovation by Living Apart Together

Management Accounting Information Exchange in the Bosch Startup Platform

Marc Wouters and Michael Pelz

Introduction

"Hello, I'm looking for number 5, the Bosch startup platform." "Oh, that's here. With whom do you have a meeting?" "With Ms. Sauter." "Oh, just step inside and I'll take you to her." Approximately this conversation (originally in German) occurred when I was in the right street but couldn't find the entrance. Finally I saw an open door, somewhere at the back of a building, walked to it and spoke to a man inside. As we walked together to look for my meeting, I realized this obviously was not a normal Bosch site, with gates and stern-looking men behind a security desk, where a visitor must be announced, fill out a form, show a photo ID, get a badge and be collected by a host. My curiosity about the place grew even stronger.[1]

In this chapter, we present a descriptive case study of a corporate program that lets employees start new businesses as if they are independent startups, offering them the freedom to be entrepreneurs but at the same time allowing them to use resources of the corporation. Called the "startup corporation" (Davila & Epstein, 2014) or "inside-out" startup program (Weiblen & Chesbrough, 2015), this approach aims to combine the philosophy of the startup with the experience, resources, and network of an established company. From the perspective of the corporation, this process aims to support radical innovation that would otherwise be far less likely to happen successfully.

The case study pertains to the Bosch startup platform (BOSP). We focus on the corporate startup activities that aim to support Bosch's innovation—innovations that are less likely to happen within the "normal" Bosch organizational research and development (R&D) context. Thus, the "apart" in the title of this paper refers to the fact that people have moved to BOSP from the large corporate organization, Robert Bosch GmbH, but maintain an intimate relationship with Bosch (the "together" part). The case focuses on the exchange of information, in particular among the startups and the BOSP organization and between BOSP and the Bosch corporate organization.

Although some information about BOSP is publicly available on the internet, in the popular press and academic papers (e.g., Hank & Meck, 2015; Weiblen & Chesbrough, 2015), this chapter provides more detailed information and discussion based primarily on several interviews with various employees and the chief executive officer (CEO) of BOSP and on information gathered through a research assistant who spent several months full time on site. He talked with many people throughout the organization and could see examples of all the different kinds management accounting reports produced.

The "inside-out" startup program such as BOSP is one of the models Weiblen and Chesbrough (2015) describe for how large, established firms and startups can cooperate. Briefly addressing the other models is helpful to provide a better understanding of what is specific to the "inside-out" startup program, see Figure 5.1. The models are differentiated in Figure 5.1 along two dimensions: whether the corporation has equity in the startups and the direction of the information flow. Most of these models relate to acquiring external technology and information through the cooperation with startups. As mentioned, the focus of this chapter is on the inside-out startup program.

Traditionally, programs with equity involvement have dominated. *Corporate venturing* involves investing in startups to obtain access to external technology that is strategically important for the corporate organization, for example, because it can lead to disruptive innovations in the corporation's current markets. An example is the investment of Bosch in the startup SEEO in the US, which has a unique battery technology. This technology is strategically important in Bosch's traditional automotive business because electric cars will become a growing part of that business.

The *outside-in startup program* is a form of non–equity-based partnership. The goal is also to acquire new technology and innovations from startups, but the corporation does not have a significant equity investment in a startup it cooperates with. The corporate organization and the startup work together on the basis of a joint development agreement. This cooperation may also include a form of limited exclusivity for the corporate customer, in return for which it provides various kinds of support to startups, such as technological expertise or equipment, application knowledge, or access to potential customers.

		Direction of information flow	
		Obtaining external technology	Commercializing internal technology
Corporate equity investment	Yes	*Corporate venturing*	*Inside-out startup program* (the focus of this chapter)
	No	*Outside-in startup program*	*Startup platform program*

Figure 5.1 Models for startups and corporations to work together (adapted from Weiblen & Chesbrough, 2015).

The *startup platform program* is also based on offering support, and the goal is to spur complementary external innovation to promote and improve an existing corporate innovation. The corporate organization provides a technology platform, such as software development tools, which startups can use to build their products. These products then strengthen the corporate innovation. The startups and corporation thus work together on a common technology platform. Weiblen and Chesbrough (2015) describe the example of the software company SAP, which supplied free developer software licenses and access to a development system to startups, so these could build their own software products for the new database technology HANA. The startups' customers for these software products with applications for HANA then became customers of SAP. Thus, this model essentially also enables the corporate organization to tap into external ideas and innovations.[2]

Finally, the *inside-out startup program*, also called corporate incubation or corporate startup, works in the other direction. This program involves investing in new startups that aim to commercialize the corporation's internal technology in other markets because it does not fit the corporation's strategy (Davila & Epstein, 2014). This approach is an alternative for selling or licensing that technology to complete outsiders. We use the term *inside-out startup program* rather than *corporate incubation* because it more clearly describes that technology and people move from the corporation to the outside and become a startup, facilitated by the program the corporation puts in place for such transitions. Weiblen and Chesbrough (2015) discuss two important conditions for success of this kind of program. First, the startup should have more freedom than normal R&D projects in the corporate organization. While it should have the autonomy of a "normal" startup so that the law and all normal rules for doing business apply, it should not have to comply with additional corporate guidelines, influence, and standard procedures. Second, it should have the ability to access corporate resources, since the point is to create an advantage by combining the agility of a startup with the resources of a large corporation.

The inside-out startup program is the model for which Weiblen and Chesbrough (2015) provide the fewest examples, which reinforces the impression from the literature that the use of this program is still relatively rare.[3] Another article (Chesbrough, 2000) describes the operating model of the Lucent New Ventures Group (NVG) and its early successes. This model was created in 1997 to commercialize technologies emerging from Bell Laboratories that did not fit with any of Lucent's established business. Joining a venture sponsored by NVG provided the potential for greater rewards than commonly available through Bell Labs and imposed some modest amount of risk on employees but far less than in independent startups financed by venture capital.

Next we provide and discuss descriptive information about BOSP. We focus on the idea and organizational design of BOSP and on the exchange of management accounting information among different organizations.

The Case of the Bosch Startup Platform

The Robert Bosch startup GmbH is located in Ludwigsburg in Germany and was established in 2013 as a 100% subsidiary of the Robert Bosch GmbH. BOSP comprises seven startups (as of the end of 2016) located in Germany, Austria and the US, and it employs around 65 people in Germany, of which seven are the central BOSP team and the others are working at the startups.[4] The objective of BOSP is to create an entrepreneurial environment for corporate startups within the Bosch Group. BOSP provides support and resources to motivated founder teams and their corporate startup ideas. BOSP's vision is to establish an entrepreneurial atmosphere in which tomorrow's breakthrough innovations can be developed by Bosch corporate startups. On its website, BOSP is described as follows:

> We are the professional home for start-ups which develop new, sustainable and profitable business in new markets based on Bosch technology innovation. Our teams are focused on radical innovations that don't find their way to market through existing Bosch business divisions. Their challenge is to develop the right product, build a suitable business model and find the right customers in order to enter business fields where Bosch isn't active yet.

How Does It Work?

The Challenge of Radical Innovations

Why is developing radical innovations within Bosch difficult? Essentially, radical innovations make atypical demands on company resources. Suppose someone working in an R&D department within Bosch has an idea for developing a particular technology toward a new product or service offering. If this development fits into one of the company's current business areas, then the existing business processes work well. The result is an extension of the current product portfolio, which can be produced at the existing manufacturing sites and can be sold to customers Bosch is already doing business with. But radical innovations are more difficult for Bosch and many other corporate organizations. The eBike provides a good example. The electric bike idea was new in many ways because this product involved a larger number of customers (bike manufacturers) that each purchase a smaller number of units compared with Bosch's normal automotive customers. The engine power is much less than that for cars, and while the quality requirements are lower, the sales price is also lower. The project for developing the eBike was tried unsuccessfully in two business areas and became a winner only on the third attempt. While the eBike did become a success in the end, it could easily have failed. The innovation was too radical to easily fit the normal business processes with the rules, assets, and experience of people that are already in place.

Selecting and Supporting Startup Ideas

The objective of BOSP is to overcome this problem by providing a more suitable environment for radical innovations. Let's take the same starting point: someone working in an R&D department within Bosch learns about a particular technology and has an idea for developing that technology toward a new product or service offering. That person or a small team can propose this idea to BOSP, which then applies a selection process for applicants. The first step is a six-week preparation and selection program called the "grow program," which prepares the team for a pitch of the startup idea to the BOSP board. At the same time, the grow program provides information about the candidates to assess their suitability to become internal Bosch entrepreneurs at BOSP. A very important criterion is how fired up the candidates are about the idea and whether the individuals involved are actually ready to leave Bosch and move over to BOSP with the idea. Also, it's important that the candidates' focus extend beyond technology alone: "They should have an entrepreneurial—not a nerdy—way of thinking," is how someone at BOSP expressed it.

Founders so far have come from central R&D departments at Bosch for five of the seven BOSP startups (Deepfield Robotics, Zenoway that is the result of merger of an original BOSP startup and an external startup acquired by Bosch, and two more from German R&D departments, along with Mayfield Robotics from the US R&D department). Another startup came from the Bosch Software Innovations department. A further startup (Cerix) had already developed beyond the initial idea within the R&D department at a Bosch production site and became part of BOSP that provided the suitable environment for this initiative. Experience so far suggests that a team of at least two and preferably three founders makes for a stronger start.

Several criteria apply to the ideas that are presented. Suitable projects fit the strategic vision of Bosch—which is summarized by the slogan "invented for life" (or *Technik fürs Leben* in German)—are based on technology that Bosch owns, start a business that is new for Bosch, and are scalable and have the potential to become large enough to be interesting for such a large corporate organization as Bosch. Of around thirty ideas that are submitted to BOSP per year, about six are presented to the BOSP Board, and about two per year are accepted.

The founders move to the BOSP site and start developing the product, approaching customers and other business partners, experimenting with variations of the offering and adjusting it, selling to pilot customers, and expanding revenues from regular sales. The corporate startup founders not only move to BOSP in terms of location, but they also give up their jobs at Bosch and become employees of BOSP. There is no formal return guarantee if their startup fails; they will have to apply for a new position at Bosch, although rather than being treated as outside applicants, they will be more like applicants for internal job rotation. At BOSP, they basically retain their original salary and benefits (although BOSP is not part of Bosch's collective labor agreement in Germany), so the downside risk is limited. On the other hand, they have no stock in their startup and receive an annual bonus based solely on their startup's success, so the upside potential is also limited, too.[5] As a result, unlike an independent startup, this arrangement does not offer the high potential to become very rich—or lose it all. Bosch wants to tap into another kind of motivation: the opportunity to get the technology to work, to have more freedom to do something with their drive, to create something exciting.

BOSP is also set up to potentially work with external startups not owned by Bosch and to make available space and other services it provides to its own startups (for a fee). This is not happening yet, so this discussion is limited to the current situation of internal Bosch startups.

One of BOSP's startups, Deepfield Robotics, illustrates how startups can be quite different from the normal Bosch business in terms of product type or customer base. At the same time, its technology is "typical" for Bosch, and it needs to have the potential to become very large, which is also typical for the huge corporation that Bosch is. Deepfield Robotics describes itself on its home page as an "inspired team of engineers, software developers, robotics specialists and agricultural engineers (that) develops innovative solutions for the future of agriculture."[6] Deepfield Robotics differs markedly from the normal Bosch business because it is about to enter the market of agricultural technology, which is completely new to Bosch. The startup offers new technology-based agricultural products, such as a sensor to monitor asparagus fields via a smartphone app or a robot to extinguish weeds in fields. The products aim at a new customer base of farmers and strive for increasing their efficiency with technology. However, Deepfield Robotics is at the same time very typical for Bosch. The startup uses existing Bosch technology and patents for its products. For instance, the asparagus sensor box is a product Bosch previously developed for a non-agricultural application that has been adapted to agricultural use by the startup. The startup's business model is partly based on digitalization. Together with the asparagus sensor, farmers purchase a license for the corresponding smartphone app. This concept matches Bosch's strategy focus on digital business models and the Internet of Things, and it fits the "invented for life" slogan. Moreover, if the startup's technology achieves market success, it has the potential to be further extended, be scaled up, and become a large business. Future applications are already conceived, such as the monitoring of strawberry fields.

A Basic Rules Company

A key difference between BOSP and Bosch is that BOSP has fewer rules, resulting in less "bureaucracy" for people who want to be innovative. BOSP is what Bosch calls a "basic rules" company, which means that the only rules that apply ensure BOSP operates legally and complies with general Bosch rules for doing business, such as those regarding health and safety. However, other rules that are more detailed regarding the specific development and production situation do not apply. For example, Bosch's detailed stage-gate process does not allow people to continue working on a development project beyond a particular stage until the customer has signed off on all the specifications. The specs cannot be changed later in the process, and a stage that doesn't work out cannot be repeated. Such iterations would be considered failures in Bosch's normal R&D procedures and structures, which are intended for the regular innovation projects of Bosch. However, BOSP has different needs and can start working with customers on much more flexible basis. While expectations must be realistic, a fertile starting point can be the view that "we're not sure if it will work, but we have this idea." Regular customers do not usually expect that perspective from big Bosch and usually do not want it as part of their R&D processes.

Experimentation With Business Ideas

BOSP encourages experimentation. The point is to quickly find out whether an idea works rather than to achieve perfection in product development. The website proclaims: "We don't waste time making detailed plans too early. We focus on evidence-based progress in our teams—allowing them to keep focus and being able to communicate progress more effectively. This is why we don't play the crystal ball game." Experimentation can also mean discontinuing a startup, or one of the major projects of a startup, although that's much more difficult, as we will discuss later.

The startup Deepfield Robotics also serves a good illustration of BOSP's understanding of learning and experimentation with the customer. The startup's initial idea was to develop a robot for various agricultural applications. The founders had in mind a robot that is able to sow, harvest, and spray herbicides. One idea was that the robot should be able to harvest asparagus. The founders spoke to farmers about their ideas, including a farmer who specialized in asparagus. Through the conversation, the founders discovered that their potential customer was less interested in the robot than in monitoring the parameters of his field, such as the temperature, because these parameters mainly influence the growth of asparagus. He wanted to know which temperature the soil had so he could better decide which agricultural process needed to be carried out next (whether to wait, adjust the plastic cover on the fields, or start the harvest). On the basis of this insight, the startup changed its initial idea and started developing a sensor for asparagus fields combined with a smartphone app. The sensors would measure the temperature of the field and show the data on the app, which would give the farmer the information on his smartphone. Thus, Deepfield Robotics learned from communicating and experimenting with a potential customer and developed a new business model. As is typical of such experimentation, with hindsight, the new offering may look quite obvious, but beforehand, everyone had a different idea.

The startup mobikee provides another illustration of learning within BOSP. The startup's idea was to develop a single smartphone app with which users could find and use various mobility services in a city, such as car sharing, bike sharing, and scooter sharing. With the support of BOSP, mobikee could approach Bosch employees as potential customers to try the initial version of the app and to continuously test subsequent early versions of the app. mobikee gained two important insights from these trials. First, mobikee understood how it needed to change particular aspects of its maps, in particular, how the map showed for a vehicle if the location for dropping it off was flexible or not. Tests confirmed that customers understood the new depiction better. Second, mobikee understood how to improve the registration process for the application, more specifically, when and how to request payment information from potential new users.

Interorganizational Information Exchange

This section focuses on the interorganizational information exchange between the BOSP board, the investor boards, and the startups. However, first we will briefly also describe information exchange between BOSP and Bosch headquarters (HQ), although this, strictly speaking, should not be part of this section on *interorganizational* information exchange because both entities are organized within the same corporate hierarchy.

Information Exchange Between BOSP and Bosch Headquarters

For financial accounting consolidation purposes, BOSP is part of the normal accounting process. All financial BOSP data, such as monthly numbers on actual revenues and expenses, are basically available for Bosch HQ in the central accounting SAP database. Twice a year, BOSP must provide a report comprising its balance sheet, profit and loss account, and an analysis of the changes of assets. The report consists of year-to-date actual data and a forecast to the year's end. The profit and loss account shows the operative value contribution (OVC), which for BOSP is basically the same as EBIT. BOSP does not have to provide the extensive monthly business report required of most other units, which may include numbers on headcount, capacity utilization, cost of goods sold, production costs, and variance analysis, so here BOSP enjoys some special treatment.

As part of its huge R&D effort, Bosch provides BOSP with an annual budget of several million euros that BOSP can invest in its startups, and this budget is the allowable negative OVC result of BOSP. The request for the next year's budget is submitted in April and decided in June. Also important is that the startups generate revenues, which are another source of funding and which provide an indication the startups are developing viable business ideas for which real markets exist. This process differs considerably from how Bosch looks at its corporate venture capital department, which is evaluated on its return on investment. In addition, Bosch HQ makes occasional special requests for information, for example asking for a split of the purchases between German and non-German suppliers or for a list of long-term purchase contracts that BOSP might have.

Information About the Plans and Results of a Startup

The BOSP board reviews the initial proposals for new startups and the overall progress of the BOSP portfolio, which should be balanced in terms of startup maturity. In addition, every startup has its own investor board, which reviews that specific startup in more detail. In this section, we describe the different kinds of information that are produced. In the next section, we describe when this information is reported to the BOSP board and the investor boards.

One form of management accounting used consists of *a set of nonfinancial "readiness" key performance indicators (KPIs)*. The development process of a startup is defined in terms of nine milestones (after milestone 0, which is pre-discovery): 1–3 are discovery, 4–6 are incubation, and 7–9 are acceleration, also called "scaling." At each of the milestones, the maturity of the startup is measured on four key performance indicators: technology (readiness of technology), market (evidence for real customer interest), resources (availability of resources needed), and organization (awareness of the business aspects such as strategy and business processes) (the "TMRO" performance indicators). For each KPI, nine levels of maturity are described in general terms to be able to assess the level of a given startup at a particular point (so after completing a milestone). Roughly, the project should move from level 1 to 9 on these readiness KPIs when going from milestone 1 to 9. Very important for BOSP is a *balanced* development so that the project progresses on all four KPIs over time. Technology is often the driver, in the sense that technology provided the initial inspiration for the startup and is also what the founders know and like. However, technology is usually not the most difficult aspect to solve. Commonly, the investor board must push team members to go out and talk to customers.

The *financial project net present value calculation* covers the first six years of the startup in terms of cash flows, leading to a net present value (NPV) of the entire project. The initial project calculation needs to be approved by the BOSP board as part of the business plan. Later this calculation is updated with actuals and revised estimates (e.g., because of revised sales forecasts or new approved funding levels). The different versions of the calculation are retained, with comments about their assumptions, opportunities, and risks.

Moreover, there is a *cash flow report for the current and next calendar year*. This cash flow report contains data about two components of the cash flow: the *funding* that Bosch provides and the *cash inflows* (or revenues—the timing difference between these two concepts can be ignored) the startups generate. These components can be shown at different levels: for an individual startup or aggregated for BOSP as a whole. For both funding and cash inflows, the report includes four different kinds of numbers, namely current forecast, actual, plan, and approved:

- "Current forecast" represents the actual up to that point in the current year (year to date) plus the estimates for the remainder of the current year (e.g., based on purchase orders the startup has already placed).
- "Actual" refers to the realized cash flows of previous years.
- "Plan" for the next year represents the funding and cash inflow for that year as specified in the current version of the project calculation. (It may seem unusual that the plan column is still shown—after a target value has been fixed, most management control system would dismiss earlier numbers that may have been playing a role in the negotiations—but showing the plan number serves as a reminder that significantly less funding from Bosch was approved in 2016 than asked for based on earlier business plans.)
- "Approved" represents the allowed funding and targets cash inflows as decided by the BOSP board, which BOSP divides among the startups. After formal approval, these approved numbers become part of the updated project NPV calculations.

A special element of the cash flow report is the item "extra needed" for funding. Of the total funding provided to BOSP, a small part is kept centrally and not immediately allocated to the startups. If the total available budget for funding after the initial allocation creates particularly strong tensions for a particular startup, the startup may receive some additional funding in the form of two components: "approved" plus "extra needed."

Another report is the *actual cash outflow per milestone*. As soon as a purchase order is placed, the anticipated cash flow is included until (via "ordered" and "invoiced") it is actually paid. The purpose of this report is to keep track of actual spending so the founders know how much spending is left for the current milestone. The cash flow is also broken down by month for the current calendar year. This report also shows the planned cash outflow for the next two milestones.

Furthermore, the *operating plan for next 15 months* basically shows a much more detailed calculation of the cash flows and includes different components for the cash inflows and the cash outflows. The purpose is to let the startup founders think in more detail and in financial terms about their business. This tool is customized for the different startups.

Several observations can be made with respect to these reports. First, the management accounting information for the startups is all based on cash flows. For example, if a startup spent €500,000 on equipment that will be fully and linearly depreciated in five years, only this investment cash flow appears in the various reports mentioned earlier and not the resulting yearly depreciation expense of €100,000. That depreciation expense will be part of BOSP's OVC result, which is accrual based for consolidation purposes within Bosch but is not included in the management accounting information for startups described above. Similarly, if a startup sold equipment for €500,000 to a pilot customer and, as part of the deal, offered an extensive warranty, the full cash inflow of €500,000 is shown as the sales revenues. The resulting costs for providing the warranty will show up when costs for replacement parts, travel, and labor are incurred. Second, the various reports are produced at different times because these are used for different purposes, making connection of the numbers difficult. For example, one would expect that the cash outflow for a particular month is the same in the actual cash outflows per milestone report and in the operating plan for the next 15 months. However, the most recently produced report will include the most up-to-date numbers, which may not be consistent with an earlier produced report. Third, the terminology in the reports is a mix of cash flow and accrual terms. "Sales," "costs," "expenses," "earnings," and "cash flows" are used interchangeably, which can be quite confusing for the startup founders, who typically have no business background.

Reporting Information to the BOSP Board and the Investor Boards

In this section, we describe when the various reports are provided to the BOSP board and the investor boards. For the *initial proposal* (milestone 0), a startup team presents to the BOSP board a business plan based on Osterwalder's business canvas (Osterwalder, Pigneur, Bernarda, & Smith, 2014). This business plan includes the initial financial project NPV calculation with estimates about sales prices, sales volume, and costs. However, because uncertainty is great, these numbers will not become targets for which people are going to be held accountable. Their more important purpose is to see whether the team is thinking about such issues—whether the team members at least have thought through how the business plan could work, not just technically but also financially. The team should have a specific "hypothesis" for its business model. If the hypothesis is accepted, the team gets permission to spend a certain amount of money in the early milestones, but that amount is not really a budget, and as the team usually cannot spend much money usefully anyway, one team spending more and others less is not problematic. Should a startup not develop successfully, the project may be terminated, which would also have to be decided by the BOSP board. Similarly, the board decides on the timing of exits that are successful. To date, termination and exits have not occurred.

Each startup's investor board meets when the startup has completed a milestone for *reviewing and supporting the progress of a startup*. The investor board assesses how well the startup is progressing and decides on the cash flow budget for the next milestone. The team presents what it has achieved to its investor board and states (sometimes implicitly) which maturity levels the team has reached on the four KPIs. The controller reports how much money has been spent getting to the milestone. The team also presents its plans for the next milestone, and the controller presents how much money will be needed for that endeavor. The decision could also require repeating the same milestone. The startups have much freedom for what and how they present to their investor board. For example, there's much variation regarding the level of detail and how the information is structured and designed. These investor board meetings do not only to decide on further funding but also about helping the startup. The board and startup management talk about ideas, problems, and solutions, for example, who in the big Bosch corporation could help or how to get contacts to customers and other useful partners. The CEO of BOSP is not a formal member of these investor boards because the relationship between BOSP and the startups is not strictly hierarchical. In fact, within BOSP, the CEOs of two of the larger startups are also in the management board of BOSP.

Most financial information is prepared by BOSP's controlling staff because the startups do not have their own staff (they are currently still too small for that). The controller discusses the plans with a startup for how it wants to get to the next milestone and estimates the various kinds of costs that will be incurred. The investor board looks only at the total costs for the next milestone and at expected revenues (if already applicable) and number of staff. Actual expenses may differ from the budget, in mix or in total—that is considered alright—when that makes sense for the activities of the startup. For example, the plan might be to hire a software developer, and then attracting such an employee may not be possible, so the work is outsourced, changing the expenses. This approach also differs significantly from the regular R&D structures and processes of Bosch. On the basis of these plans, the financial project NPV calculation is updated.

Reviewing and planning for BOSP is the task of the BOSP board. This board meets three or four times a year to evaluate initial proposals and to assess the progress of the portfolio of BOSP's startups. The emphasis is on BOSP as a whole rather than on individual startups, although the board may discuss some of these specifically.

The BOSP board receives information about the readiness KPIs, based on the evaluations the investor boards have made for the startups. For each startup, the information is presented in a slide with a 2×2 matrix with some qualitative information for the four TMRO areas, a statement about the levels the startup has achieved for each area, and suggested actions (e.g., how many pilot customers the startup should try to get). These actions should reflect the emphasis for further, balanced development towards the next period, until the BOSP board meets again. The BOSP board also gets a slide showing a funnel with all startups shown on it, so the four TMRO areas are aggregated into one overall readiness score per startup. In addition, the BOSP board receives the cash flow report for the current and next calendar year for each startup as well as for BOSP as a whole.

Information, Expertise, and Other Resources That BOSP Provides to the Startups

While BOSP provides various general resources to startups, such as financing, work space (office, workshop), furniture, equipment, and accounting, the key point is to have access to resources within Bosch because that is potentially a unique advantage for these kinds of startup programs implemented by large corporations such as Bosch. Key examples in this case are:

- *Bosch technology*. The BOSP startups can use existing technology that Bosch owns, as in the Deepfield Robotics example that used an available sensor box (that wirelessly transmits the sensor data) to adapt for use in combination with the sensor in asparagus fields. Moreover, startups can ask for support of a Bosch R&D department to carry out development projects together.
- *Bosch production resources*. While small batches of a startup's product are produced manually in a first step, larger batches can be produced at one of Bosch's production sites.
- *Legal services*. For instance, a startup planning to extend its business internationally received expertise and support for writing contracts with international partners. This startup also had concerns about protection of data privacy and received advice from the legal department of Bosch, which turned to a specialized, external legal firm for this support. Bosch also takes care of all patents and other activities related to intellectual property (IP) for the startups. Because Bosch is the trustee of the startups' patents, anyone checking patent ownership sees not the name of a small, unknown startup but that of the huge Bosch corporation.
- *Human resource management systems and policies, such as for ongoing education*. Also, the startups can advertise their job openings to Bosch employees.
- *Startups can use the Bosch brand*. Startups can present themselves as a Bosch company and in some cases can also use the Bosch brand for their products and services.
- *Contacts with potential customers and other partners*. For example, one startup founder explained that Bosch's key account management was very helpful when the startup needed to get in touch with automotive manufacturers as potential customers. With the existing contacts of Bosch, the startup gained access to these manufacturers much more easily than a non-corporate startup that has no early relationship with the automotive industry.
- *Purchase contracts*. Startups can use the conditions in the existing Bosch purchasing contracts when they buy things.
- *Pilot customers*. Last, startups can draw on Bosch employees as potential pilot customers. One of BOSP's startups will soon launch the beta version of its smartphone application for Bosch employees before

approaching the whole market. In this way, employees will provide feedback for how to improve the product.

BOSP also offers mentors and partners in different stages of the startup development. In the phase of idea generation before a team becomes part of the BOSP organization, multiple internal and external mentors work with the teams of potential entrepreneurs to prepare them for their pitch. As soon as a startup is part of BOSP, it can choose Bosch-internal mentors (e.g., Bosch executives) and external mentors (e.g., former Bosch managers, such as the director of Bosch VC who recently retired, or professors for entrepreneurship). At an early stage, startups receive additional mentoring by BOSP employees, such as the BOSP CEO.

Some Diverse Experiences Thus Far

Getting Radical Innovations

Attracting projects for radical innovations and getting these started at BOSP is not an easy task. Often, the proposed startup ideas need to be rejected. Many concern incremental innovations that would advance existing Bosch businesses but are not radical enough to become part of BOSP. They are better situated in the Bosch departments where they originated. Others do not have enough growth potential to become interesting for Bosch.

Another reason for the slow growth of the number of startups is that motivating Bosch employees to take this step is difficult. The profile of an "average" employee at Bosch does not correspond with the profile of a "typical" entrepreneur. BOSP has concluded that employees consider the change from Bosch to BOSP a risk rather than an opportunity. From BOSP's point of view, this perspective is hard to understand since BOSP offers highly comparable working conditions and makes clear that it will take care of the startup founders and employees in the event of a startup failure (although exactly how this would unfold is still somewhat ambiguous because it has not happened yet).

A positive experience for BOSP concerns the fast progress toward commercialization of some of its startups. As an example, one startup developed faster than expected and grew within six months to a team with two founders, nine employees, and students doing paid internships at the company. Another startup, Deepfield Robotics, exemplifies the fast commercialization of ideas. The speed of changing initial ideas in experimenting with customers and creating new business models is exceptional from BOSP's point of view. BOSP considers these results as evidence that the way BOSP operates is effective.

Experimenting and Changing Course

The experiences so far have shown that measuring the startups' progress in financial terms and determining how much more money to invest (or whether to stop the venture) are still very difficult. Accurate predictions of revenues and of how much further funding is needed are highly uncertain. Assessment of readiness on the TMRO items can be quite vague. Additionally, while experimentation and learning are encouraged, knowing when to stop is tricky—how many iterations (i.e., redoing the same milestone) should be allowed? To date, no startup has been terminated, even though some startups' financial forecasts do not look promising, and reasons for continuing these ventures are not obvious.

Although experimentation, learning from it, and adjusting the business are taking place, some founders are challenged by the need to let go of the formal processes and extensive planning they were accustomed to as former Bosch employees. Additionally, some have difficulty letting go of their initial idea if results show that the idea might be not suitable for a startup business. BOSP seems to be challenged to make these would-be founders think like entrepreneurs in such a way that they actively learn and change their products according to the new insights they gain from learning and experimenting.

Working With Basic Rules

The basic rules seem to work well within BOSP, but matters become complicated if startups need access to Bosch resources outside BOSP. For instance, a startup for digital business models wanted to sell its service online using an external service provider to manage the subscriptions and the internal Bosch accounting system in SAP to receive payments from customers. In this scenario, systems would have to be connected to enable the transfer of data. Moreover, these transactions, which involved many new customers and selling subscriptions instead of tangible product, were quite different from existing Bosch transactions, requiring changes in several procedures in the Bosch SAP system and involving various Bosch departments to get approval for these changes. In all, this adjustment took over one year.

Tailoring of Management Accounting at BOSP

Another positive experience is that there are significant degrees of freedom for tailoring management accounting at BOSP. The controllers have flexibility to develop and try out new controlling practices that are suitable for the BOSP context. The Bosch strategy department has recognized this need and has asked about the experiences with the TMRO KPIs described earlier, which BOSP has implemented on the basis of a recent management book (Arteaga & Hyland, 2013). The strategy department now considers using these KPIs more widely within Bosch for tracking the progress of innovation projects, as they differ from the usual Bosch metrics. Such an exchange is positive because BOSP is also expected to contribute to entrepreneurial thinking at Bosch.

Management accounting jobs at BOSP are quite broad and less specialized than at Bosch itself. The management accountants at BOSP estimated that only about 20% of their work consists of conventional controlling tasks. For example, they do not have to report on a monthly basis to the Bosch HQ, as every other subsidiary has to do. The rest of the job consists of solving concrete problems for startups, such as finding more expert information and assistance within Bosch relating to taxation matters, legal issues, or planning product exhibitions. This role of the management accountants is also reflected by some of the founders, who appear to see controllers at BOSP as problem solvers and contact persons.[7]

Providing a Startup Environment

Some characteristics of BOSP are perceived as not yet fully compatible with a startup environment. BOSP requires a business forecast for the next six years, but founders have difficulty predicting the business development this far into the future. In addition, startups have to claim their financial needs for the following year very early—for example, in April or May 2016 for 2017.

Some startups are also challenged by Bosch's expectation that their business model will have to be able to yield very large revenues; otherwise it's not really interesting for a huge company such as Bosch. On the other hand, a startup's financial needs are minute in relation to the available budget of the Bosch organization. The difference between €1 million or €2 million of financing for a startup could be seen as insignificant in comparison with budgets for some large Bosch R&D projects, but the startups have to be very assertive in their attempts to achieve funding. This situation is sometimes perceived as a mismatch between the startup and the corporate incubator.

Another challenge is to create a true startup atmosphere that fits the context of a competitive marketplace for the new products and services these startups are working on. The startup employees are somehow still employees of a corporate company. The atmosphere is not too stressful, the pay and conditions are very good, and the founders have an employment contract for 40 hours per week. Some people felt that the pressured, busy startup atmosphere was absent, saying that the workplace was basically empty after 6 pm and on weekends.

Conclusions and Suggestions for Future Research

BOSP is an example of an inside-out startup program. It is a separate organization, fully owned by Bosch, which Bosch employees can move to and found a startup built on their business ideas. The objective is to support radical innovations for Bosch, which are much more difficult to bring to fruition with the normal Bosch business processes and organizational structure. In the previous sections, we described how BOSP works in areas such as selecting ideas, working with basic rules, experimenting with the startup offerings, and the interorganizational exchange of information for supporting such activities. As this study was intentionally descriptive, focusing on how BOSP is designed and how information is exchanged, an interesting follow up would be to pursue this case over a longer time and to have more interaction with the various stakeholders, such as Bosch management, the BOSP and investor boards, and all the startups. Davila and Epstein (2014) mention that the largest impact of corporate startup programs "lies in creating and growing markets that require the joining of diverse resources, knowledge, and networks" (p. 71), and the various startups within BOSP illustrate this nicely.

Weiblen and Chesbrough (2015) mention two important conditions for startup programs such as BOSP to work. First, the startups need sufficient *autonomy from corporate guidelines*, influence, and standard procedures. We have seen that BOSP and its startups have great freedom within the scope of the parent organization. This latitude pertains to various business processes and how management accounting is being done. BOSP did not have to produce detailed monthly reports for Bosch headquarters; it could focus on cash-flow-based instead of accrual-based financial metrics; and it could implement the TMRO nonfinancial metrics, which are not used elsewhere within Bosch. However, being part of Bosch meant the startups sometimes needed or wanted to interact with other Bosch entities that are not basic rules companies, and then the opportunities for doing things their own way were limited. Examples presented in this chapter related to the timeline for planning and budgeting within the Bosch planning and control methods and adjusting particular SAP procedures when payments needed to be processed by Bosch accounting departments. These constraints are inevitable because the freedom only applies to the inside-out startup program organization. The case illustrates that the issue of autonomy is more subtle than perhaps previously understood.

Second, Weiblen and Chesbrough (2015) discuss that startups must have sufficient *authority to access corporate resources* when needed. Similarly, Davila and Epstein (2014) mention that providing resources is important for corporate startups, as "these organizations combine tangible resources such as capital and access to suppliers and distribution channels with intangible ones such as brands, relationships, knowledge, and management" (p. 76). Another study (Gassmann & Becker, 2006) specifically focuses on the resource flow between startups and the parent incubator, and it differentiates between tangible and intangible resources flowing from the incubator to the startup.[8] Tangible resources comprise financial, physical (e.g., physical space, infrastructure and production facilities), and tangible knowledge resources (e.g., the use of databases or patents). Intangible resources comprise branding and knowledge (e.g., advice and coaching and contacts). The study includes many interesting examples of corporate incubators, and it provides a literature review and framework of resources that are important in corporate incubation, including resources that may flow back to the corporation. The results suggest that the corporate incubator is mainly associated with a physical resource flow, with less clear evidence on tangible and intangible knowledge. Our findings included several examples of resources and knowledge transfer to the BOSP startups.

The literature also mentions several important topics that may be more difficult to realize in practice. First, it is challenging to foster *balanced* experimentation in this context. Davila and Epstein (2014, p. 74) point out that experimentation and discovery are that a success factor for a corporate startup program. The program needs to move "from the concept of planning as a blueprint for execution to planning as a discovery path" (p. 74). This factor appears to be important for BOSP's corporate startup program as well because BOSP encourages experimentation and learning with potential customers, as exemplified by Deepfield Robotics and mobikee. However, Davila and Epstein (2014, p. 78) also explain that a corporate startup program must balance market forces (especially in capital markets and product markets) and company forces because "the innovation process needs the creativity of markets as well as the destruction that happens within them. One typical effect of lowering market forces within organizations is that projects with little promise can be kept alive for too long." BOSP has not terminated any startup so far, and BOSP management indicates that financial analysis of this decision is difficult. Also, some of the founders perceived that the available financing is distributed indiscriminately among all startups and question whether it might be better to stop the less promising startups. These perceptions suggest that it is difficult for BOSP to balance market and company forces in an optimal way. Our study suggests that there seems to be a delicate balance for inside-out startup programs between, on the one hand, stimulating experimentation, changing course, and looking for other opportunities and, on the other hand, effectively creating market pressures and, if needed, stopping startup investments. The difficult challenge is to foster *balanced* experimentation.

Second, Davila and Epstein (2014, p. 80) discuss that "in contrast to startups where the stimulus to create is embedded in the forces of markets, established companies need to design how their employees will use their creativity." In the case of BOSP, seven proposals were accepted for the corporate startup program, and relatively few new proposals for radical innovations have been submitted by Bosch employees. As mentioned earlier, BOSP sees obstacles to motivating Bosch employees to become entrepreneurs, persuading them to discard their normal working practices that focus mainly on incremental innovation and inducing them to think and learn like a founder. These perceptions suggest that BOSP has to find a better way to stimulate Bosch employees to use their creativity. This challenging situation at BOSP underlines that the important objective of creating a stimulus for employees to use creativity can be quite difficult to realize (Davila & Epstein, 2014).

In sum, the most import insights from this study are that providing corporate resources to startups, which is a key idea behind the inside-out startup program, actually worked in this case. Also, giving startups considerable freedom took place, but this was limited to the "sheltered" startup program within the corporate organization. It was found to be difficult is to stimulate people to come up with radical innovation and to actually go over to the startup organization; another difficult point was to foster balanced experimentation.

Ideas for Future Research

As mentioned in this chapter, one idea for future research is to follow this case of BOSP over a longer time and to have more interaction with the various stakeholders, such as Bosch management, the BOSP and investor boards, and all the startups. From primarily describing the processes and interorganizational management accounting, the focus of the study could move to more theoretically grounded questions. For example, exploration of the motivational aspects of the corporate startup would be interesting. Which factors are currently increasing or diminishing the motivation and the efforts of the founders? Given that this setting has less upside potential but also less downward risk, which kinds and levels of incentives would be most appropriate? The study of Chesbrough (2000) describes the incentives that are provided as part of the inside-out program of the Lucent New Ventures Group and compares them with incentives that to private venture capital firms provide to startup founders.

Another idea is to describe more examples of inside-out startup programs in depth because very few in-depth case studies have been done, even at a descriptive level. As mentioned earlier, Weiblen and Chesbrough (2015) offered the fewest examples of this type of collaboration between startups and corporate organizations, and we could also find only a few examples in public sources. Most startup programs are essentially outside-in.

Our examination also suggests several ideas for future research more focused on management accounting. First, more studies could address the exchange of management accounting information with respect to corporate startup programs and how this exchange influences the success of corporate startup programs. The literature on inside-out startup programs is remarkably silent on this subject.

Second, an interesting comparison would be that of the use of management accounting at BOSP and perhaps other inside-out startup programs to the use of information by private venture capital firms. The parent firm implementing an inside-out startup program—Bosch in this case—may learn from VC firms that already have a lot of information concerning selecting, coaching, monitoring, funding, and terminating startups. What information and methods do these firms use (e.g., De Clercq, Fried, Lehtonen, & Sapienza, 2006; Heinzelmann, 2016; Smith, 2005)? Corporate venture capital may also offer an interesting comparison (e.g., Napp & Minshall, 2011), not only to see which existing management accounting practices of experienced parties could be adopted but also to develop ideas on how these practices would have to be adapted to the context of inside-out startup-programs.

Third, future research could focus on developing management accounting methods that help to monitor the development of startups in financial terms. A key question is how the impact of market uncertainty and technical uncertainty on the financial value of the venture can be modeled (Wouters, Roorda, & Gal, 2011). Another question is how management accounting may help to foster balanced experimentation and strike a balance between flexibility (experimentation) and endlessly trying. Modeling this balance through the lens of real options may be appropriate, but transferring the concepts of financial options to the far less clearly defined context of flexibility and experimentation of new ventures may be strongly limited (Adner & Levinthal, 2004; McGrath, Ferrier, & Mendelow, 2004; Wouters, 2010). Moreover, the consideration of sunk costs in management accounting calculations is intriguing. What might be the effect on sensible, balanced experimentation if sunk costs are immediately "forgotten" and the decision on additional investments is based on only the future investments and financial value of the venture?

A final idea for future research is look at how experiences with corporate entrepreneurship and the insights these experiences have generated can be used elsewhere within corporations. Of course, corporations have different needs for incremental innovation, but some factors may still apply. For example, these startups may be good at working with customers and the customer's customers and learning from them how to improve their own offering, something large supplier firms may also want to become better at (Anderson & Wouters, 2013). Similarly, Bosch wants to stimulate a more entrepreneurial attitude throughout the organization: "Also in a startup, you should have a masterplan, but you have to accept that things turn out differently and you have to learn, sometimes painfully. We want to stimulate this attitude among our colleagues."[9]

Notes

1. We thank Mr. Florian Müller for his assistance with the research and management and employees at BOSP for their openness to participate in this research.
2. Although the term "platform" is used, the BOSP does not fall into this category.
3. We could identify only few examples of inside-out startup programs (e.g., Siemens' next47). Interestingly, most of these mentioned that they are not exclusive to corporate employees founding a startup based on a corporate technology (inside-out) but are also open to independent startups with an external technology who ask for support from the corporate organization (so outside-in), whereby the corporation may or may not have equity involvement.
4. The legal structure is a bit more complicated. For example, a separate legal entity exists in the US for Mayfield Robotics, and part of the startup Zenoway is located in Austria, where it legally belongs to another Bosch unit. These nuances are not important for this study.

5. BOSP plans to implement a bonus for all startup employees that depends on the duration of membership in the startup and the startup's exit performance. This policy would be very different from the financial incentives at Bosch, but BOSP would have the freedom to adopt it.
6. *Deepfield Robotics—Who we are.* www.deepfield-robotics.com/index-en.html (accessed 16 November 2016).
7. The following anecdote illustrates this perception of management accountants in the role of problem solvers. We participated in a meeting at BOSP with a startup founder, a management accountant, and a research assistant. The purpose was to test a new tool for evaluating a startup's market value. The founder was asked to provide numbers on expected revenues and costs for the 15 months and to enter these into the tool. The founder went smoothly through his operating plan and could easily provide several numbers. But when he was asked to specify the expected fixed costs, he paused. He said he had no idea, immediately turned to the management accountant, and casually asked her the help him with this. It seemed an open, friendly, and appreciated way of asking her to support him.
8. In that study, a corporate incubator is more than an inside-out startup program; rather, it provides resources to internal corporate ventures because the corporation wants to extract value from its portfolio of technologies. However, a corporate incubator also provides resources to independent (external) startups because the corporation wants to explore new technology for its core business.
9. Klaus Köster. *Interview mit Bosch-Macher—„Dass Projekte scheitern, gehört dazu."* Stuttgarter Nachrichten. www.stuttgarter-nachrichten.de/inhalt.interview-mit-bosch-macher-dass-projekte-scheitern-gehoert-dazu.6b8add8e-b747-45ce-8787-c44805f1e910.html (accessed 19 October 2016, translated from German).

References

Adner, R., & Levinthal, D. A. (2004). What is not a real option: Considering boundaries for the application of real options to business strategy. *Academy of Management Review*, *29*(1), 74–85. http://doi.org/10.5465/AMR.2004.11851715

Anderson, J. C., & Wouters, M. J. F. (2013). What you can learn from your customer's customer. *MIT Sloan Management Review*, *54*(2), 75–82.

Arteaga, R., & Hyland, J. (2013). *Pivot: How top entrepreneurs adapt and change course to find ultimate success*. Hoboken, NJ: John Wiley & Sons. http://doi.org/10.1002/9781118778852

Chesbrough, H. (2000). Designing corporate ventures in the shadow of private venture capital. *California Management Review*, 42(3), 31–49. http://doi.org/10.2307/41166041

Davila, A., & Epstein, M. (2014). *The information paradox: Why good businesses kill breakthroughs and how they can change*. San Francisco: Berret-Koehler Publishers.

De Clercq, D., Fried, V. H., Lehtonen, O., & Sapienza, H. J. (2006). An entrepreneur's guide to the venture capital galaxy. *Academy of Management Perspectives*, *20*(3), 90–112. http://doi.org/10.5465/AMP.2006.21903483

Gassmann, O., & Becker, B. (2006). Towards a resource-based view of corporate incubators. *International Journal of Innovation Management*, *10*(1), 19–45. http://doi.org/10.1142/S1363919606001387

Hank, R., & Meck, G. (2015, September 20). Geld wirkt demotivierend. *Frankfurter Allgemeinen Sonntagszeitung*.

Heinzelmann, R. (2016). Making up performance: the construction of "performance" in venture capital firms' portfolios. *Qualitative Research in Accounting & Management*, *13*(4), 445–471. http://doi.org/10.1108/QRAM-09-2015-0078

McGrath, R. G., Ferrier, W. J., & Mendelow, A. L. (2004). Real options as engines of choice and heterogeneity. *Academy of Management Review*, *29*(1), 86–101. http://doi.org/10.5465/AMR.2004.11851720

Napp, J. J., & Minshall, T. (2011). Corporate venture capital investments for enhancing innovation: Challenges and solutions. *Research-Technology Management*, *54*(2), 27–36. http://doi.org/10.5437/08953608X5402004

Osterwalder, A., Pigneur, Y., Bernarda, G., & Smith, A. (2014). *Value proposition design: How to create products and services customers want*. Hoboken, NJ: John Wiley & Sons.

Smith, J. A. (2005). Empirical study of a venture capital relationship. *Accounting, Auditing & Accountability Journal*, *18*(6), 756–783. http://doi.org/10.1108/09513570510627702

Weiblen, T., & Chesbrough, H. W. (2015). Engaging with startups to enhance corporate innovation. *California Management Review*, *57*(2), 66–90. http://doi.org/10.1525/cmr.2015.57.2.66

Wouters, M. J. F. (2010). Customer value propositions in the context of technology commercialization. *International Journal of Innovation Management*, *14*(6), 1099–1127. http://doi.org/10.1142/S1363919610003021

Wouters, M. J. F., Roorda, B., & Gal, R. (2011). Managing uncertainty during R&D projects: A case study. *Research-Technology Management*, *54*(2), 37–46. http://doi.org/10.5437/08953608X5402001

6 We Went Too Far, and We Learnt From It

Management Control in the Development of the Boeing Dreamliner

Jodie Moll and Fiona Harrigan

Introduction

Research and development (R&D) represents a series of high-value activities that play a critical role in the future competitiveness of an organisation (Bardhan, 2006; Emmanuel, Harris and Komakech, 2010; Nixon, 1998; Rilla and Squicciarini, 2011). Owing to the increasingly sophisticated and complex nature of modern technologies and the rising cost of R&D, it has become for many organisations unaffordable (Hagedoorn, Link and Vonortas, 2000). Recent advances in information and communication technologies have spurred many organisations in this situation to opt for an asset-light business model to leverage supplier's knowledge and to reduce the risks associated with innovation by sharing the upfront investment (Archibugi and Iammarino, 1999; Bardhan, 2006; Chesbrough, 2010; Gassman, Enkel and Chesbrough, 2010; Grimpe and Kaiser, 2010). In some cases, organisations choose to outsource R&D to locations outside of their host country under the assumption that this will help them reduce costs or address problems related to trying to attract a skilled workforce or technological assets (Rilla and Squicciarini, 2011). At issue for the managers working in these firms is how they can facilitate the coordination of R&D and the manufacture of integrated components when they outsource these tasks to suppliers. This chapter focuses on this issue. It provides an empirical examination of the management control systems (MCSs) that were designed to coordinate the development and manufacture of the Boeing 787 Dreamliner.

Our aim is in this chapter is to contribute to and extend the much less developed literature on accounting in networks. In recent years, researchers have made considerable progress towards understanding the roles accounting plays in inter-organisational arrangements, including those for R&D (Abernethy and Lillis, 2001; Dekker, 2004; Håkansson and Lind, 2004; Mouritsen and Thrane, 2006; van der Meer-Kooistra and Scapens, 2008, 2015). A striking feature of many of these studies is that they focus heavily on open book accounting practices that firms have developed and use to manage dyadic inter-organisational relationships. To date, there has been little consideration given to the wider set relationships that partnering firms are embedded in and to the indirect effects produced as a consequence of them (Caglio and Ditillo, 2008; Håkansson, Kraus, Lind and Strömsten, 2010). For instance, Håkansson et al. (2010) explain that a supplier's relationships with its vendors or suppliers produce indirect effects for others in the network.

Within the accounting literature, what we know about accounting and its role in managing R&D in complex networks is based on a study by Miller and O'Leary (2007). Miller and O'Leary studied the set of mediating instruments (Moore's Law and a technology roadmap) that the semiconductor industry uses to help those working in that industry to coordinate their R&D. The study reported in this chapter is, therefore, one of the first investigations to focus specifically on accounting for R&D in a complex network setting. It provides new insights into the obstacles or control problems that surface when managers are faced with designing MCS that coordinate the R&D activities of an integrated set of global firms.

In the next section, we describe the institutional exceptions framework developed by Orr and Scott (2008). We use this framework in the empirical parts of the chapter to understand the MCS that are used to facilitate management of the 787 value chain. Following that, we provide a detailed review of the 787 project before offering some concluding remarks and suggestions for future research.

The Institutional Exceptions Framework

Much of the existing literature on accounting in networks considers the transaction costs of outsourcing in terms of measuring the value of the products exchanged (Orr and Scott, 2008).[1] Yet Orr & Scott argue that global arrangements give rise to additional 'institutional transaction costs' (p. 21) that reduce the profitability of the organisational arrangement (see also Sydow, Schüßler and Müller-Seitz, 2016 for a discussion of transaction costs). Orr and Scott (2008) suggest that we can understand such transaction costs by considering *institutional exceptions*. An institutional exception is defined as "an occasion when a knowledge void about pertinent institutional elements interferes with task completion and requires troubleshooting" (Orr and Scott, 2008, p. 566). Their framework (see Figure 6.1), which has its roots in institutional theory (c.f. DiMaggio and Powell, 1983), is intended to understand the process by which institutional transaction costs occur and the decisions that firms take in responding to them.

The framework adopts a broad interpretation of institutions defining them as including local regulative institutions (i.e. laws and rules), normative frameworks (i.e. work practices) and cultural cognitive institutions (i.e. shared beliefs and mental models). It is an ignorance or lack of knowledge of the institutions embedded within partnering organizations that leads others working within a global network to incur transaction costs. Furthermore, we argue that the problem of institutional exceptions is likely to be

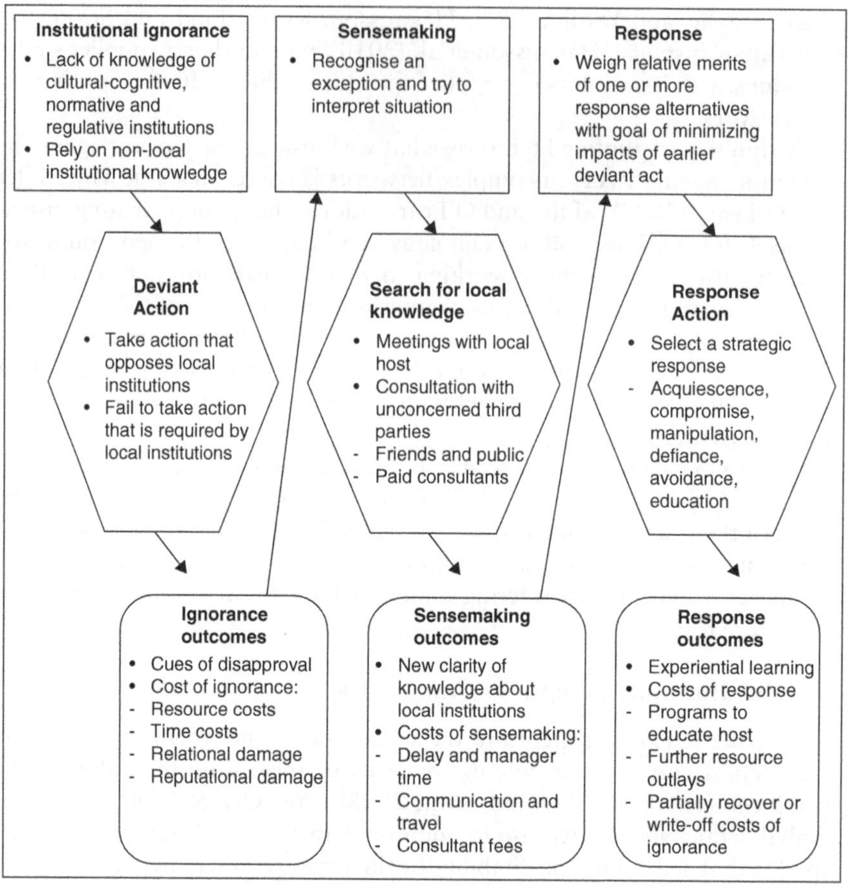

Figure 6.1 The Institutional Exceptions Framework, adapted from Orr and Scott (2008), p. 581.

exacerbated for a company that is part of several global value chains such as Boeing because it and the actions of the suppliers it partners with can also produce indirect effects on others embedded in the network (Håkansson et al., 2010; Lind and Thrane, 2010).

Once there is recognition of transaction costs, an organisation will try to remedy this ignorance by engaging in sense-making activities that help them to understand the local environment of the partnering organisation better. According to Orr and Scott (2008), the outcome of the sense-making activities is an organisational response, which can take many forms. In their model, they incorporate Oliver's (1991) typology of responses, which include acquiescence, compromise, manipulation, defiance, and avoidance. They also add education to that typology since many exceptions are unintended and may require some form of learning as part of the response.

In the next section, we introduce Boeing as a backdrop for the empirical discussion that follows.

Introduction to Boeing

Boeing is one of the world's leading aerospace companies, and it relies heavily on the revenues contributed by the Boeing Commercial Airplanes Group (BCAG) (i.e. 68% or $66,048,000 of the company aircraft revenue FY, 2015). The company has customers in more than 150 countries, and more than 70% of its sales are outside of the US (Boeing, 2005; Boeing.com). Worldwide it employs more than 160,000 people.

The institutional environment within which Boeing operates is complex. In the US, the Federal Aviation Administration (FAA) regulates production, quality systems, and continuing operating safety of all commercial aircraft. National aviation authorities administer similar requirements in each country in which Boeing operates. The aircraft must pass safety inspections in both the US and in Europe.[2]

Aside from these regulatory pressures, Boeing is subject to a wide range of expectations arising from its reliance on its 28,000-supply base, which operates in more than 50 countries (Boeing, 2011). More than 5,400 organisations are suppliers of the BCAG.[3] Each year the company purchases more than $28 billion in goods and services from suppliers.[4]

From Boeing's perspective, the customer base is turbulent. More than 30 airlines have filed for bankruptcy since 2008 (Boeing, 2009). Contracts for the sale of aircraft such as the 787 are typically fixed but contain clauses allowing an indexed price escalation (Boeing, 2009) to account for economic fluctuations that occur between the point of sale and time of delivery. Boeing also faces significant financial risk since purchase agreements with customers enable the customer to cancel or claim compensation when there is a delay in aircraft delivery.

We turn next to the 787 project.

The Dreamliner

In 2003, the development of the 787 was given the go-ahead by the Board of Directors based on projections of a demand for 3,500 aeroplanes over a 20-year period, contributing more than $400 billion to the company (Boeing, 2003). The 787 Dreamliner is a wide-body twin-engine jet airliner with a seating capacity between 242 and 330 depending on the model (787–8, 787–9, 787–10). For the first time, more than 50% of the aircraft body is a composite, making it lighter, fire resistant, and stronger and requiring significantly less maintenance[5] than aluminium (Norris, Thomas, Wagner and Forbes Smith, 2005, p. 50; see also Arkell, 2005; Norris, 2007). Owing to the composite components being constructed as single pieces, they are rivet-less, and this means that aircrafts require fewer parts.[6] This design is expected to make the operating costs of the aircraft and its maintenance more cost effective than existing models in service. For instance, Norris et al. (2005) suggest that the single largest cost an airline incurs with owning and maintaining an aircraft is when it requires heavy maintenance and is out of service for a significant period.

A combination of economic imperatives (i.e. intense global competition; price pressures; declining profit margins; and the emergence of aggressive new aircraft manufacturers from several countries, including Russia, China and Japan) and technical challenges forced the group to rethink how it should execute the project. It decided to outsource 70% of the design and manufacturing of critical components of the aircraft (Norris and Wagner, 2009).

This approach represented a significant change in how Boeing undertakes R&D. In other projects, Boeing had been an original-equipment manufacturer (Norris and Wagner, 2009). It purchased parts and services from a range of suppliers on an "arm's length" basis but kept the main design and manufacture of the aircraft in house. When it used suppliers, it was on a build-to-print basis (Hiltzik, 2011; Mecham 2007a; Pritchard and MacPherson, 2004, 2005).[7] To this end, the company did not rely on others for investment and bore the risk of unforeseen problems. For the 787, its role was to be a large-scale integrator.

Boeing also undertook the final assembly of the aircraft. Seventeen Tier 1 suppliers in 10 different countries, including Russia, Japan, China, the Republic of Korea, Australia, the United Kingdom, France, Germany, Sweden, and Canada, were chosen to be involved in the partnership (Boeing, 2005). The expectation was that a global partnership model would enable BCAG to reduce the development costs of the aircraft from the $12 billion spent on the 777 aircraft to $8 billion.[8] Also, suppliers would be able to work on the aircraft components simultaneously, and therefore Boeing expected that it would be able to reduce the aircraft time to market drastically. An aggressive schedule of 2008 was set for the first delivery.

The company Chairman President (McNerney, 2008) explained the impact that the 787 was to have on the aerospace industry in the following terms:

> the 787—as the first large jetliner with a composite fuselage and wing—is truly a game-changing aeroplane for airline economics, passenger comfort, fuel efficiency and (very importantly) environmental impact. The 787 program's global business model also represents a substantial advancement.

Currently, sales of the 787 Dreamliner family stand at 1,161. Demand for the aircraft follows aggressive sales tactics with reports that early buyers receive offers of up to a 25% discounts on the aircraft on its list price of $193.5 million (Isidore, 2011). Today, the average list price of the 787–8 aircraft is around US$239 million,[9] although some have suggested that it is common for Boeing to offer discounts of up to 45% on that list price (Gates,

2012). From a customer perspective, the 787 aircraft is more cost effective;[10] it provides a 15% reduction in operating expenses.

The natural starting point for our case is the formation of the global partnership. Next, we turn our attention to that process.

The Process of Global Partnering

The idea was that the 787 project would involve a global partnership requiring the major components of the aircraft to be designed in a virtual environment and built at one of the 135 supplier sites before being shipped to Boeing's Everett facility for final assembly. Each plane would take Boeing three days to assemble.

In choosing its partners, Boeing took a different and somewhat radical approach from its other projects. In the 787 project, suppliers were required to pay for the up-front non-recurring R&D costs related to the component that they are to produce (Nambisan and Sawhney, 2007). For instance, Alenia is reported to have spent upwards of $600 million developing the fuselage barrel (Pappalardo, 2007). Suppliers were also to make payments to Boeing to reimburse some of the costs incurred in designing and testing the aircraft (Boeing, 2009, p. 59). Consequently, financial status is one criterion used in selecting suppliers. Table 6.1 outlines the cost sharing payments that suppliers made to Boeing.

The intellectual property arrangement is such that Boeing retains substantial rights to some components (Boeing, 2009, p. 58). Other components are owned by suppliers or are held jointly between Boeing and a supplier (Nambisan and Sawhney, 2007). Partners are paid by Boeing once each aircraft receives its certification and the customer has taken delivery of it. As a result, suppliers bear some of the cost should there be delays in manufacturing. Suppliers benefit from this new business model since for the first time, they are to be involved in the after-market maintenance, and others are not able to compete to provide that service.

Boeing chooses to partner with many of the first-tier suppliers that have supplied parts on other projects. However, 30% more of the 787s components are to be outsourced to foreign suppliers than any other aircraft (Hiltzik, 2011). In some instances, the company chooses to partner with a foreign supplier as part of an industrial agreement with a non-US customer. In return for a contract for sale, Boeing chooses suppliers in the customer's host country (i.e. South Korea, Japan, China and Russia). This arrangement

Table 6.1 Partners' cost-sharing payments made to Boeing

Year	*2004*	*2005*	*2006*	*2007*	*2008*
Cost-sharing payments ($ millions)	205	611	160	130	50

Adapted from Boeing Annual Reports

is intended to incentivise those in the host country to purchase the Dreamliner knowing that they will indirectly be contributing towards helping their own local economy (Boeing, 2009, p. 42).

For the 787 project, Boeing selects the first-tier partners (Mitsubishi, Kawasaki, Fuji, Vought, Alenia, Rolls Royce, Dassault, Korean Air Lines Aerospace Division, among others) at concept development stage. For the first time, the Tier 1 suppliers are responsible for selecting sub-tier suppliers and for receiving and assembling the components before they send them to the Everett plant for final assembly (Pritchard and MacPherson, 2004). For instance, Hamilton Sundstrand, a systems supplier, is responsible for nine systems on the 787. That company manages the integration of those systems, overseeing verification testing and certification. Interestingly, some suppliers such as Vought are reported not to have an engineering department when Boeing selects them as a 787 partner (Domke, 2008).

A multi-tier global collaboration is expected to reduce the workforce that Boeing requires for the project from 5000 to 1,000 employees. Compared with other projects, the new arrangement is also to decrease the number of suppliers Boeing will contract with since Tier 1 suppliers choose their own supply base (Seil, 2006).

In the end, Boeing awards contracts to several of the suppliers it has partnered with on other projects contracts. It also forms new partnerships with companies such as Messier-Dowty, which it contracts to design, develop, and manufacture the landing gear (Norris et al., 2005). Because of the cost of certifying components, Boeing limits its contracts for some parts to two suppliers. This approach is intended to provide flexibility to the customer, but it is also designed to limit the cost of certifying the components used in the aircraft. For instance, Boeing awards both Rolls Royce and General Electric's GEX contracts to provide Engines.

Outsourcing the R&D of the 787 to far-flung companies adds to the complexity of Boeing's institutional environment, especially since many of suppliers on the 787 project benefit from government subsidies. Relying heavily on a global supply chain also means that each partner's ability to fulfil contractual arrangements is subject to volatility in foreign political and economic environments, which can result in delays or even stoppages of deliveries. Boeing[11] and its suppliers' workforces are also represented by 14 different US labour organisations and non-US labour organisations (Boeing, 2010, p. 13).[12]

The contracts with suppliers set out the expectations that Boeing has regarding the tasks that it is to carry out that are legally enforceable, but they are incomplete. MCS are designed to prevent the global partnership from malfunctioning by providing inter-organisational processes indicating how the collaboration should materialise.

Managing the Global Partnership

From the start, Boeing knows that the project's success will be determined by how well it coordinates the activities of its globally dispersed business partners (Seil, 2006). Boeing relies on a combination of formal and informal control systems to manage the project. While developing an innovative aircraft is a priority for the company since it is facing new entrants in the commercial aerospace industry, Boeing is mindful that the aircraft still needs to be affordable for its customers and they see software as being key to achieving that goal.

Dassault Systèmes is contracted to provide a virtual solution or as it was known within Boeing a "Global Collaboration Environment" (GCE). Product lifecycle management solutions application software is expected to provide wider visibility to the activities of its far-flung suppliers. That software is made accessible to all its Tier 1 partners.[13] The Product lifecycle management uses CATIA, an integrated suite of computer-aided design (CAD), and DELMIA, a computer-aided manufacturing (CAM) application. The CAD which allows a 3D view of the technology permits the engineers to look at parts and rotate them 360 degrees. The real-time connectivity that CATIA facilitates amongst the partners means that engineers designing a component can synchronise it with the components adjoining it (Bruno, 2005; Seil, 2006). This new approach is supposed to enable a more precise fit between the components, and it is expected to shorten the product development stage by allowing suppliers to make changes to manufacturing during design phases. DELMIA software aims to provide virtual planning and production. This software is used to enable the engineers to simulate the exact 787 manufacturing processes before building any tools or production facilities (Dassault, 2006).[14] The virtual environment accounts for the entire lifecycle of the 787 aircraft, including sales, after-sales service, and future derivative aircraft (Norris and Wagner, 2009). Boeing also provides a document (referred to as the Commonality Matrix) to its partners outlining the standards for business processes (Stackpole, 2007).

The less detailed design specifications that Boeing gave to partners means that aircraft designs are transitory since suppliers can be forced to refigure what had been previously considered to be an adequate design as a response to specification alterations made by other partners to the interdependent components. For instance, changes in design by one partner can increase the weight of the aircraft, forcing others in the partnership to look for other ways that they can keep the aircraft within the required specifications. To that end, the virtual solution can be understood as a boundary object because the software enables others to specify the extent of modifications that are possible such that the components fit together and meet the weight specifications of the aircraft in the final assembly. According to Dassault, this digital manufacturing environment "creates a 'loop back' between 787 design and manufacturing engineers, no matter where they are, eliminating the risk of committing to a design change only to discover it cannot be manufactured or that it requires costly changes to other components" (Dassault, 2006). It "avoids the costly late-stage errors that can occur with untested designs and production planning" (ibid.). From Boeing's perspective, while this design approach adds new ways of working for their staff, they consider it to be a sensible way to manage the project as it is unfolding because it enables them to monitor the status of their far-flung suppliers R&D activities. One main benefit of this 'virtual' design approach is that time changes in different sites around the world do not restrict the partner's progress (Arkell, 2005). The engineers can test the suitability of a larger number of designs within a shorter amount of time (Norris et al., 2005). The precision and standardisation of detail of each of the components that they can develop with the aid of the software are also considered to be useful for those expected to maintain the aircraft once it is in use.

The approach of developing an exact digital copy of the aircraft is radically different from prior R&D processes. Many engineers took much convincing that software is an effective substitute from the mock-ups that they traditionally built. The virtual environment is forcing significant changes to their R&D processes. For the 787 project, many of the Boeing staff are no longer involved in the R&D process. In comparison, in some supplier companies, such as Vought, R&D processes gain much more prominence. To overcome the disbelief on the part of the engineers, Boeing built a full-size proof of concept mock-up of the nose of the aircraft (Norris et al., 2005).

To complement the Dassault software that it introduced, Boeing establishes Life Cycle Product Teams (LCPTs). The aim of these teams is to ensure that the entire set of costs involved with manufacturing and maintaining the aircraft are considered when its partners compare the various design options. The LCPTs form a Partner Council to hold monthly or bi-monthly meetings to share progress and expertise. This council consists of executives from the major partners in the 787 project. The idea for the Council is modelled on practices used in the military side of Boeing's business. The LCPTs are considered to be essential for ensuring that design specifications keep to the promises made to customers. Like other projects, the key metrics that Boeing uses to assess the suitability of the aircraft's design include drag, weight, noise, schedule reliability, and development and build costs (Hale, 2006). However, the life cycle management approach demands that two new measures are added to the toolkit: maintenance costs and aeroplane availability (Hale, 2006).

Keeping track of the delivery of components to the Everett facility is important to Boeing since it can only store a small number of aircraft components at any one time. Lacking space makes the sequence of deliveries critical. To account for this, Boeing adopts a just-in-time (JIT) approach requiring a wider visibility across the entire supply chain activities so that it can track the delivery of the interdependent components.

Anticipating problems that might occur in managing the logistics of a global supply chain, Boeing decided to bring in a third-party intermediary, New Breed Logistics Inc., which has experience with managing out-of-sequence deliveries (Boeing, 2006; New Breed Inc, 2006). New Breed is to provide an interface between suppliers and the final assembly line (Norris and Wagner, 2009). They implement Exostar, a form of software developed by E2open, to provide transparency across the supplier's activities and allow them to coordinate and integrate planning schedules, issue and track purchase orders, exchange shipping information, and manage returns and inventory consumption (Smock, 2009).

Boeing also recognises that informal networks are a basis for which the partnership can fill gaps in the formal network (Noll, 2006). For instance, employees suggest that the partnership benefits from team members 'self-organising' (Seil, 2006). These informal networks are the result of some 260 engineers working for Mitsubishi, Kawasaki and Fuji being sent to the Everett plant to work alongside Boeing engineers in finalising the design of the 787 aircraft (Bowermaster, 2005).

The success of the project also relies on the informal networks that are used to provide oversight of the Tier 1 suppliers and the sub-tier suppliers, many who have the added problem of language barriers (Mecham, 2007a). For instance, Pat Russell, the former director of global supply at Vought Aircraft, explains that it uses global suppliers itself in countries such as Germany, Israel, and South Korea. His view is that such informal networks are critical to managing supply chains since "engineers, by their very nature, are not necessarily the strongest when it comes to communication skills" (cited in Moad, 2007).

In summary, the integrated information technology architecture that all partners have access to and the monitoring of decisions by the LCPTs are designed to act as substitutes for hierarchical forms of control that Boeing uses to manage R&D on other projects. These systems are intended to represent remote supplier events that others in the supply chain can act upon if required to ensure the aircraft is delivered on time and within budget. The LCPTs are also a substitute since they help to remind partners of the specifications that they are expected to work within when improving component designs. These controls are intended to transform Boeing's approach to producing new commercial aircraft by demonstrating the viability of the global partnership model for keeping the company at the cutting edge of innovation.

Despite its efforts to eradicate problems in the early stages of the project by providing a level of visibility to the partner's activities, the risk that Boeing would not be able to execute the project successfully remains high for four main reasons. First, the aircraft involves a highly complex design using unproven exotic materials. (Around 50% of its primary structure—the fuselage and wings—are made of composite material). Second, complete assemblies must be moved considerable distances and delivered in time for final assembly. The schedule for delivery of aircraft is critical because contracts have provisions in them enabling customers to either cancel their order or claim compensation. Third, the virtual design platform relies on partners updating changes to their own processes or components into the software in real time so that they are visible to other partners.[15] When partners do not document changes to components in sufficient detail, partnering organisations are unable to respond. Fourth, Boeing cannot easily track where inventories, especially the sub-tier supplier's ones, are or how well suppliers are executing against production plans. Boeing has contracts with far-flung suppliers, and they are expected to manage the sub-assemblies, which this means parts are to arrive at Boeing's final assembly plant, with Tier 1 suppliers having preassembled their mechanical, electric, and hydraulic capabilities (Mecham, 2007c). There is a possibility under this arrangement that Boeing could be unaware of production delays caused by Tier 2 and 3 suppliers and therefore would be unable to intervene with the schedule of deliveries to ensure that they would not be out of sequence. In simple terms, despite the virtual platform, the organisation is running the risk of ignorance about the supplier's activities or an 'information asymmetry problem' that would prevent them from properly managing the collaboration. As it turns out, what are to frustrate Boeing's efforts is a failure on their part to properly consider the extent to which the systems that they implement provide the level of visibility to the supplier's activities that is needed for deviations from the plans to be identified and dealt with in real time. Also, in monitoring the supplier's activities, no consideration is given to the Tier 2 or 3 supplier activities, since Boeing expects they will be managed by Tier 1 suppliers. Yet these turn out to be critical for the success of the project. Next, we consider these deviations.

The First Institutional Exception Is Recognised

Owing to the JIT approach that Boeing chose to use and its general attitude it should set the broader parameters of the project but leave it up to suppliers to innovate, it took until the start of the final assembly processes for the company to realise the extent to which its partnering firms practices (both manufacturing and the documentation of it) were incongruous and were contributing towards the malfunctioning of the global partnership model (Norris, 2007). The company annual reports provide evidence that Boeing is ignorant with regards to the deviations in its partner's work; as late as the fourth quarter of 2007, Boeing was still saying that the company expected to meet the 2008 delivery schedule (Bair, 2007; see also Mecham 2007b).

The final assembly of the aircraft in the Everett facility began on May 16, 2007. However, it did not go ahead as scheduled (Mecham, 2009a). Suppliers of the engines and instrumentation delivered late (Boeing, 2010; see also Mecham and Norris, 2008). Part of the problem was that the benefits of tapping into the expertise of suppliers did not materialise for several of the core components of the aircraft when suppliers chose to deviate from the plans, using inferior products which they had not adequately documented (Norris, 2007; Hiltzik, 2011). For instance, Boeing reported that there were defects in supplier (Alenia) components related to the horizontal stabiliser (Boeing, 2010, p. 7 & 27; see Mecham, 2011a; Norris, 2010a, b) and the fuselage (Gates, 2009) disrupting manufacturing process flows.

These problems were a surprise to Boeing, which was expecting for the assembly to go ahead as planned.

Also, reports suggest that components arrived at the Everett facility with marks or tapes on them showing where defects were present (Norris and Wagner, 2009). To meet delivery schedules and cost-driven milestones, several of the foreign suppliers performed work using temporary components, and these caused the structures to sag, making them ill-fitting for the aircraft (Norris and Wagner, 2009). The 2007 reveal of the aircraft also hints that suppliers such as Mitsubishi found it difficult to manage its own supply chains. When the components arrived at Everett, what was visible was that fasteners used to fit components together were either missing or that the supplier had used temporary fasteners. Fasteners represent only 3% of the aircraft. However, Boeing must replace these fasteners to complete the final assembly, and this significantly slows the final assembly. According to Norris and Wagner (2009, p. 132), this problem is difficult for Boeing to overcome because there is an industry-wide shortage in the fasteners because of an aero-space boom in the mid-2000s (see also Hughes 2011; Norris, 2007; Mecham, 2007c).

However, as Boeing was to find out the suppliers also had manufacturing documentation issues (Anselmo, 2008; Domke, 2008; Holzman and Shanhar, 2010; Thomas, 2008a; Mecham 2007a, c). It needs a detailed record of the most current configuration of the aircraft. Mecham (2007c) explains: "The documentation necessary to support work completed by suppliers before shipment wasn't matching the work remaining to be completed in Everett."

Partners developed documentation that was consistent with their local ways of doing things, and these do not permit Boeing to identify easily what changes are being made or to conduct any evaluation of them. For instance, in interviewing one of Boeing's engineers, Ostrower (2008) reported:

> Traceability to the source [of manufacturing] is something that is missing in this programme. When you receive a travel tag from a partner and it is written in Japanese with English subtitles it sure makes you wonder if something got lost in translation.

The very different ways that suppliers document their activities make it difficult for Boeing to reconcile the supplier processes with its own. It must perform the additional task of updating the aircraft manuals to ensure they represent the processes used to manufacture and assemble the components. It must identify and track the changes that suppliers have made that were off-plan or under-specified in the documentation that suppliers have issued to understand whether the changes are sound but also if they are likely to have an impact on interdependent components. It must verify that a detailed account of the manufacturing process has been recorded so that it provides a meaningful representation that can support decision making regarding the maintenance of the aircraft. The smallest details of a nut or bolt used to fit a component need to be documented; if they are missed, it can have catastrophic consequences. The Air Transport Association also requires detailed records. Complete and up-to-date documentation is necessary for a plane to become FAA certified and for Boeing to in the future avoid fines for providing incomplete work instructions.[16] The integrated architecture has been unable to predict these off-plan changes because the data and models that are fed into it are incorrect (Mecham, 2009b). According to Hamilton Sundstrand President David Hess, Boeing is partly to blame for the situation that unfolded. He explains:

> After key suppliers fell behind, "they [Boeing] panicked a little bit and rather than follow the logistics plan that they had planned on where everything gets delivered to the structure partners . . . they said, 'Everybody just send your stuff here. . . . So bang, tens of thousands of parts ended up on the factory floor without any documentation or traceability. They had to start putting a jigsaw puzzle together without any directions."
>
> (as cited in Anselmo, 2008)

It is important to note that while there are instances when the documentation issues are mainly problems of language barriers that occur when paperwork trails are written in the non-English languages of many of the suppliers (Norris and Wagner, 2009, p. 134), the instructions were also not in keeping with Boeing's own ways of documenting parts and instructions (Mecham, 2010). Since Boeing had concerns that translating that documentation may produce errors, it chose to verify and update the suppliers' documentation. That process is extremely time-consuming and costly, and it is to blame for much of the delay in the delivery of aircraft (Norris and Wagner 2009, p. 139).

In the end, any cost savings that should have materialised from the flexible software that Dassault designed were undermined by supplier behaviours. For instance, in 2008, Boeing is reported to have been penalised by its customers to the amount of $2.5 billion for late deliveries (McInnes, 2008), and in 2009, reports are that customers cancelled more than 60 orders. Boeing also ended up doing ten times more of the work than it had anticipated (Ray, 2010). However, reports are that the late delivery of aircraft had significant implications for some suppliers that signed risk and revenue partnership agreements with Boeing. Many faced cash flow problems (Greising and Johnsson, 2007). Boeing's management controls have proven to be ill-suited for integrating and coordinating the supplier's behaviours, and this means that some suppliers were penalised financially because of delays in the assembly of aircraft since payment is dependent on the delivery of aircraft to the customer (Mecham and Norris, 2011; Norris and Wagner, 2009; Zhao and Shenhar, 2011).

The inevitable slippages in the delivery of the aircraft that followed from these problems forced Boeing to reconsider whether the benefits of the global partnership model are materialising. Under the new management of Pat Shanahan, it was decided that Boeing should terminate some of the partnerships and reintegrate some of the manufacture and assembly of some of the components (Boeing, 2010, p. 5; see also Mecham 2011a). In 2009, it did this by purchasing Vought Aircraft Industries business in South Carolina (Mecham, 2008). As the principal supplier of fuselage sections, bringing the production of this component back in house was intended to improve the long-term competitiveness of the company and reduce the risk of production interruptions for Boeing customers (Weber, 2009). That same year, it also purchased Alenia North America's 50% ownership interest in Global Aeronautica, a fuselage manufacturer, making Boeing the sole owner of this company. A statement in the 2009 Annual Report (p. 4) summarises Boeing recognising these institutional exceptions and its initial response:

> We have also taken steps to reduce risk in our supply chain. We have brought certain work back inside Boeing, and we have increased visibility and coordination across all suppliers with new information technology tools. Through the purchase of Vought and Global Aeronautica facilities in North Charleston, South Carolina, and the establishment of a 787 final assembly facility there, we will also improve our long-term competitiveness and reduce the risk of production interruptions for our customers.

The transaction costs were, however, not limited to the opportunity cost of lost sales and damage to Boeing's reputation. They also involved significant investment in new MCS. The new MCS were expected to address the institutional ignorance among the partners and increase the visibility and coordination of their activities.

Towards a More Compatible Management Control System for the Global Partnership

A crucial development in the 787 project occurred in December 2008 when Boeing launched a Production Integration Centre (PIC) with the help of Blue Sky Integrated Technologies. According to James (2009), its purpose was threefold: (1) to monitor the activities of its counterparts, (2) to resolve problems, and (3) to keep advancing the project. Urgent changes were needed since the 787 accounted for some 40% of the total backlog of orders for BCAG (Boeing, 2009, p. 4).

The PIC is an office built to overlook the assembly of 787 aircraft. Its intended focus is to measure R&D success by tracking the suppliers including any threats to the delivery of quality products. Twenty-seven workstations and a ten-foot-high by forty-foot-long video wall are used to display a wide-range of supplier information from earthquakes and floods near factories to other human-made events such as labour union strikes and transportation issues (Norris and Wagner, 2009).[17] The idea is that the centre is to be modelled on the practices of other centres that also operate around the clock such as such as government emergency operations centres and NASA's Mission Control Centre. The software used in the centre is designed in house to provide more detailed information about its business partners' activities. A status report is prepared daily summarising the key issues facing the global supply chain. Ben Funston, the supplier management leader at the centre, explains the need for the PIC:

> On a legacy program, you can pretty much walk out into the Everett factory and kind of get a feel for how production's going. The reason isn't because that's an all inside make, but basically because we ship in a bunch of small sub-assemblies and we integrate it all here. The 787 program is totally different—a different business model. We still have a global footprint but those partners out there are doing all the design and integration and build. So by the time you get here to Everett you're receiving a few sections of fuselage and wings and we integrate it here. So we needed a tool to give us situational awareness into the production system, the ability to have early issue detection and real-time problem resolution.
>
> (cited in James, 2009)

A major innovation in this centre is an integrated production-view tool which can be used to provide further visibility to the remote supplier activities. Like many balanced scorecards which rely on colour coding to identify problem areas, this tool uses red to indicate when a supplier's manufacturing process is off plan by two days. Yellow is used to suggest that the manufacturing process is off plan by a day, and green means the component is on schedule and assembly is as per the plan. The tool also uses a magenta line to indicate where a component should be regarding its schedule and a blue one to show its progress (Creedy, 2010; James, 2009).

When the supplier is off schedule, other tools are brought in such as a Tandberg camera, which enables Boeing to observe in real time the supplier's activities. That camera is installed at every Tier 1 supplier site to allow teams that are globally dispersed to examine and resolve problems. The camera is also used by Boeing to conduct virtual inspections of the finished components before they are shipped to the Everett site (Creedy, 2010). Boeing also introduces the quality assurance system that it uses in other projects. This system had been abandoned on this project since it was considered to deviate from a lean philosophy. According to Norris and Wagner (2009, p. 140), this system allows senior personnel to inspect the quality of suppliers' work in batches and does not rely on the individual rejection approach that was part of Boeing's lean philosophy.

Boeing also decided to establish a Fastener Procurement Model (FPM) to centralise the procurement of fasteners for the 787. The FPM is expected to increase the volume of fasteners that it purchases to allow the company to negotiate more favourable prices. It also requires anyone using fasteners to make a daily record of inventory levels (Anupindi, 2011).

In December 2009, the company embarked on its first test flight. In total six planes were to undergo testing to become FAA certified. As part of the testing phase, Boeing wrote off three of the six planes that were being used to get the aircraft certified because of the extensive modifications that it had to make to the side of body (Boeing, 2010, p. 27). Also, an onboard fire occurred during testing of one of the planes, highlighting the need for further changes to the power distribution panels. The aircraft also required some updates to be made to the systems software (see, CNN Wire Staff, 2010; Thomas, 2008b). These problems forced Boeing to reclassify $2.7 billion from inventory to R&D expense (Boeing, 2010 p. 7 & 24) and forced it to delay the delivery of certain components in 2010 to reduce out-of-sequence work moving into final delivery (ibid. p. 27).

On October 26, 2011, 40 months late, Nippon Airways completed its first commercial flight of the 787 from Tokyo to Hong Kong (McCurry, 2011). By this time, many of Boeing's other customer's deliveries had been pushed back by more than three years.

Currently, Boeing produces ten 787 aircraft a month at two sites.[18] As production has been ramped up, institutional exceptions continue to surprise the organisation, and its response has been to increase oversight of the supply chain. For instance, because of two batteries overheating in its aircraft, the company held meetings with outside experts as well as suppliers, regulators, and customers to resolve the issue.[19] In response to these ongoing problems (see Mecham, 2011b), suppliers are now to be subjected to more intensive and regular performance monitoring, including reviews of production materials, schedules, and finances. Boeing has also begun to review how suppliers evaluate their own vendors (Kesmodel, 2011).

The high transaction costs of the 787 are also partly responsible for the introduction of a new company-wide initiative rolled out in 2012 across its supply chain called 'Partnering for Success'. This initiative is designed to provide more transparency to the supply chain to help reduce supplier costs. Those involved in this initiative have given Boeing access to their books and operations (Wilhelm, 2014). The initiative is intended to allow the partners to provide ideas for how costs can be cut across the value chain. To date, Boeing has reported that they could implement more than 1,900 ideas from the Partnering for Success initiative (Muilenburg, 2014). Dennis Muilenburg, vice chairman, president, and chief operating officer at Boeing, explains the program:

> And what we're looking at there, is a new way of engaging with our supply chain instead of doing it as individual program-by-program,

> airplane-by-airplane, negotiations and dialogue with our supply chain, let's do it at a company level. And what we're finding is huge opportunities for us to drive commonality of processes and complements across multiple platforms. We're finding efficiencies in how we do business. Many of our suppliers are gaining volume advantage as a result which turns into pricing advantage for Boeing. So it adds value to both companies. And those kind of win-win solutions we see accelerating.[20]

In summary, Boeing has learned that the combination of incomplete contracts and its inability to monitor the activities of its foreign suppliers and to rely on them to provide accurate and detailed information on their operations in a form consistent with Boeing logics and compliant with FAA regulation adds significant transaction costs to global projects. Boeing also incurred further transaction costs because of not paying sufficient attention to how the Tier 1 suppliers choose and manage their own supply chains. These costs came as a surprise to Boeing, and consequently, they must now sell a larger number of aircraft for the project to break even. Hiltzik (2011) sums up the situation:

> The next-generation airliner is billions of dollars over budget and about three years late . . . much of the blame belongs to the company's quantum leap in farming out the design and manufacture of crucial components to suppliers around the nation and in foreign countries such as Italy, Sweden, China, and South Korea. Boeing's dream was to save money. The reality is that it would have been cheaper to keep a lot of this work in-house.

Boeing's management does not deny that it made costly mistakes in its assumptions regarding what the global partnership would deliver. In reflecting on the history of the project the now former president and chief Executive Officer of Boeing Commercial Airplanes was to comment:

> On 787 programme quite frankly we reached too far. We started with some technologies that weren't mature enough. We came up with a model for the global supply chain that quite frankly we hadn't thought all the way through. And we learned from those mistakes . . . I think there are a lot of lessons on the 787. You could spend a lot of time here dissecting all of them. If I had to really boil down what took this program of on a path that got us in trouble. We started chasing a financial measure. . . . Return on net assets. We didn't want to make the investment that needed to be made. We asked our partners to make the investment and we created this wide, this supply chain all over the world. We have work with people that had never really done this kind of technology before and then we didn't provide the oversight that was necessary. In hindsight, we spent a lot more money in trying to recover than we ever

> would have spent if we tried to keep many of the key technologies closer to Boeing. What you are going to see in the future is we are going to do more inside than we did on the 787. I think the pendulum swung too far. My view is we need to know how to do every major system on the airplane better than our suppliers do. That doesn't mean we are going to do everything but we are going to do some of everything. I think that is one of the big lessons learned.[21]

Jim McNerney, the former president and chief executive officer of Boeing, offers a similar assessment of the project:

> You need more insistence on commonality of IT tools, and you need more insistence on [supply chain] integration. And we just booted it. And our only defence is that every industry I know boot that once and then they learn. And unfortunately, we paid billions upon billions in the learning process there.
>
> (as cited in Ostrower, 2011)

These conclusions are not surprising to several critics in the industry. As Tom McCarty, president of the Society of Engineering Employees in Aerospace, explains:

> Plane-making is best done by a group of engineers and builders working in close proximity without the distractions of language barriers, cultural differences and bureaucracy.[22]

Despite cost over-runs, Boeing reports that the 787 Dreamliner still has a three- to four-year lead in innovation and technology over its closest competitor (McNerney, 2011) and that Boeing has no intention of abandoning the global partnership and returning to its old ways of working. In an interview, McNerney commented:

> We are not going back to the old Boeing. This is a matter of rebalancing. We have to be global. We have to have global cooperation to make things. Most of the market over the next 20 years will be outside the United States. It is a big change. Twenty years ago most of the market was in the United States for commercial airplanes. Now, 80% will be outside. So partnerships outside the United States have to continue. But, I think we have learned some very difficult lessons on controlling both the original concept and the detailed design while still partnering with people outside the United States. It is more a matter of where we draw the line. We went too far. We've learned from it. Fortunately, we have an airplane that everyone wants.[23]
>
> (Bloomberg, March 11)

Concluding Discussion and Directions for Future Research

The study of the 787 Dreamliner is intended to deepen our understanding of the complexities involved in managing a network. To Boeing, the 787 is the first project in which the organisation transformed itself into a large-scale systems integrator. It partnered with a network of suppliers whose role was to carry out most of the R&D work. To Boeing managers, when the project commenced, the MCS provided only a high level of visibility to suppliers' activities. Table 6.2 lists the different control systems that Boeing implemented as the project unfolded.

The main concern of Boeing initially was the delivery schedule, not the partners' work activities or methods for recording and measuring their R&D progress. Boeing was, therefore, ignorant about any the deviations its partners had made from what the Dassault software showed. Also, it remained ignorant about the indirect effects caused by the Tier 1 suppliers not providing adequate oversight to their own supply chains. This ignorance caused financial setbacks for some suppliers, who followed the schedule and supplied their component on time but were only paid once aircraft was delivered to the customer.

The asset-light business model caused Boeing to incur significant transaction costs in the form of lost contracts, investments in new MCS (i.e. PIC,

Table 6.2 Summary of the control systems

Initial control system	*New controls added as a response to the first institutional exceptions*	*New controls added as a response to further institutional exceptions*
Product life-cycle management solutions (CAD, CAM)	Production integration centre—information on earthquakes, floods, labour union strikes, transportation issues and Integrated production view tool	Performance measures: production materials, schedules, finance, supplier evaluation of vendors
Performance measures (drag, weight, noise, schedule, reliability, development, build costs, maintenance cost, airplane availability)	Quality assurance system	"Partnering for Success"—open book accounting, cost reduction planning
Just-in-time approach	Fastener procurement model	
Exostar supply chain management	Daily status report on supply chain	
Commonality matrix standards		

FPM, and Partnering for Success), engineering travel to partner sites, and supply chain experts that were brought in to consult on the problems causing delays. Even today, Boeing continues to incur transaction costs related to this project in the form of the Partnering for Success Initiative. Boeing introduced this initiative in part because of the ongoing issues that it has faced in managing the 787 project, and it is designed to help Boeing and its partners to reduce their costs. The initiative requires that suppliers open their books to Boeing and make their work practices more transparent so that the network can collaborate to try to make the entire supply chain operations more cost effective.

From Boeing's perspective, it has little choice but to defy many of the supplier's ways of working because it needs to provide documentation that meet the requirements of the FAA. But it also tries to establish initiatives such as the Partnering for Success to promote education amongst those in the network so they can learn from each other about possible cost reduction options.

From the suppliers' perspectives, those that have partnered with Boeing on the 787 project have little choice but to acquiesce to the heightened monitoring of their activities given that Boeing has reversed some of its outsourcing decisions and reintegrated certain components. However, as we have indicated, it is also in the suppliers' interests to be more transparent so that their activities are not out of sync with others in the network. By syncing their delivery schedules, they may limit some of the indirect effects such as the longer payback period that some suppliers experienced because of the actions of others in the network.

The case of the 787 reveals that organisations may have grossly overestimated the power of MCS to facilitate the coordination of R&D and the manufacture of integrated components by a global supply chain. Companies that outsource their R&D activities to far-flung suppliers need to understand that cost savings may not materialise, even when MCS are relied upon to reconcile the local norms and customs of suppliers. Part of this problem stems from language issues, but it also can be traced to the indirect effects that occur from the embedding of the suppliers in such a complex network.

Because the rising cost of R&D makes it unaffordable for many firms to do in house, more empirical research on these kinds of complex inter-organisational arrangements is needed to gain a better appreciation of the types of MCS that can be developed to help alleviate concerns regarding institutional transaction costs. Calculations such as the total cost of ownership may, for instance, help firms to make smarter decisions regarding off-shore outsourcing, but more research needs to be done on the matter of how such calculations can capture the wide variety of institutional transaction costs that can arise from inter-organisational arrangements. To managers responsible for globally outsourced R&D, further research is also required to understand if certain MCSs can overcome some of the language issues.

Finally, further research must be sensitive towards the shifting attitudes away from asset-light business models. To this end, research should seek to understand more about the role of accounting in deciding which systems and capabilities the firm should re-shore and re-integrate.

Notes

1. For instance, the classical make-or-buy decision typically involves a comparison of the lower purchase price bid by suppliers against the internal production costs (see, Gietzmann, 1996).
2. In Europe, the European Joint Aviation authorities regulate the industry.
3. Tinseth, R. (2013).Our supply chain. *Randy's Journal: A Boeing Blog*. www.boeingblogs.com/randy/archives/2013/02/supply_chain.html
4. Boeing (undated). World Class Supplier Quality—Boeing 787 Updates. http://787updates.newairplane.com/787-Suppliers/World-Class-Supplier-Quality
5. According to Hughes (2011), the 787 will not require a major service for twelve years.
6. A single metal barrel on a traditional aircraft requires some 50,000 rivets (Norris et al., 2005).
7. This requires that parts are built per standard specifications.
8. Wayne, L. (2006). Boeing bets the house on its 787 Dreamliner. *New York Times* (May 7).
9. Boeing (undated). About Boeing Commercial Airplanes. www.boeing.com/company/about-bca/index.page#/prices
10. McCurry, J. (2011). Boeing 787 Dreamliner lands after first passenger flight. *The Guardian* (October 26).
11. Some 57,000 (36%) members of the Boeing workforce are represented by unions (Boeing, 2009).
12. Recognising and understanding the relationships with supplier workforce labor organizations is important for assessing potential work stoppages, which can cause the supply of components to be out of sequence, disrupting the final assembly and causing delays in the delivery of aircraft.
13. Dassault had been the supplier of software for Boeing since 2003, providing virtual design (CATIA) and collaboration technologies (ENOVIA) for the 777 aircraft.
14. Dassault reported that this was the first time a manufacturer had purchased its entire suite of software programmes.
15. Presentation by David Noll of the Boeing Company, 11th ICCRTS, September 28, 2006. www.dodccrp.org/events/11th_ICCRTS/html/presentations/038.pdf
16. For instance, Boeing is reported to be facing fines of some $1,050,000 for inadequate instructions for the 777 Oxygen Systems (see, Mecham, 2011c).
17. See also Jenks, M. (2010). Boeing 787—Challenges of Complex Global Systems," 2010 MIT SDM Systems Thinking Conference (October 21, 2010). https://sdm.mit.edu/systems_thinking_conference_2010/presentations/jenks.pdf
18. In 2009, Boeing decided that a second facility would be needed and it built a new facility in Charleston, South Carolina. That facility began its operations in 2012.
19. See McNerney Speech 2013 Address to Shareholders, Annual Meeting.
20. December 3, 2014, The Boeing Co. (BA) Credit Suisse Global Industrials Conference.
21. Albaugh, J. (2011). Albers Executive Speaker Series. *Seattle University* (January 20) (Podcast).

22. Peterson, K. (2011). A wing and a prayer: Outsourcing at Boeing. Special Report. *Reuters* (January 20). http://mobile.reuters.com.
23. McNerney says Boeing Dreamliner is model customers want. *Bloomberg* (March 11), Published on Youtube March 23, 2012. www.youtube.com/watch?v=X1N-M1VZ2s8

References

Abernethy, M. A., and Lillis, A. M. (2001). Interdependencies in organization design: A test in hospitals. *Journal of Management Accounting Research*, 13, 107–129.

Albaugh, J. (2011). *There Are No Shortcuts: Reflections on Leadership, Ethics, and Innovation*. Albers Executive Speaker Series. Seattle University (January 20, 2011), Seattle, WA.

Anselmo, J. (2008). 787 supplier blames logistics for Boeing's delays. *Aviation Week* (April 16).

Anupindi, R. (2011). Case study: Boeing's Dreamliner. *Financial Times* (October 10). Available at www.ft.com/content/a7d38332-ef70-11e0-941e-00144feab49a

Archibugi, D., and Iammarino, S. (1999). The policy implications of the globalisation of innovation. *Research Policy*, 28, 317–336.

Arkell, D. (2005). Exponential potential: Similarities between 777, 787 help airlines, passengers and Boeing. *Boeing Frontiers*, 4(5). Available at www.boeing.com/news/frontiers/archive/2005/september/staff.html

Bair, M. (2007). Building the dream: Boeing 787. *Aero Magazine* (Quarter 4), p. 3.

Bardhan, A. D. (2006). Managing globalization of R&D: Organizing for offshoring innovation. *Human Systems Management*, 25(2), 103–114.

Boeing. (2003). *Annual Report*. Available at http://investors.boeing.com/investors/financial-reports/default.aspx

Boeing. (2005). *Annual Report*. Available at http://investors.boeing.com/investors/financial-reports/default.aspx

Boeing. (2006). Boeing selects New Breed Logistics Inc. to manage logistics for 787 Dreamliner. *Media*. Available at www.boeing.com/news/releases/2006/q1/060223a_nr.html

Boeing. (2009). *Annual Report*. Available at http://investors.boeing.com/investors/financial-reports/default.aspx

Boeing. (2010). *Annual Report*. Available at http://investors.boeing.com/investors/financial-reports/default.aspx

Boeing. (2011). Boeing honors supplier performance excellence. *Media*. Available at http://boeing.mediaroom.com/index.php?s=43&item=1753

Bowermaster, D. (2005). Boeing, Japan say aerospace deals now official. *The Seattle Times* (May 26).

Bruno, M. (2005). Transoceanic innovation: Hawker de Havilland, a Boeing subsidiary and 787 supplier, embraces new tools and processes to link teammates worldwide. *Boeing Frontiers*, 4(6). Available at www.boeing.com/news/frontiers/archive/2005/october/i_ca3.html

Caglio, A., and Ditillo, A. (2008). A review and discussion of management control in inter-firm relationships: Achievements and future directions. *Accounting, Organizations and Society*, 33(7–8), 865–898.

Chesbrough, H. (2010). Business model innovation: Opportunities and barriers. *Long Range Planning*, 43, 354–363.

CNN Wire Staff. (2010). Boeing cancels Dreamliner test flights. (November 10). Available at http://money.cnn.com/2010/11/09/news/companies/boeing_dreamliner_emergency_landing/index.htm

Creedy, S. (2010). The Boeing 787 team that is living a dream. *The Australian* (April 23). Available at www.theaustralian.com.au/business/aviation/the-boeing-787-team-that-is-living-a-dream/story-e6frg95x-1225857133866

Dassault. (2006). *Future of Manufacturing on Display at Virtual Rollout Milestone* (December 6). Available at www.3ds.com/press-releases/single/boeing-simulates-and-manufactures-787-dreamliner-at-industry-first-event-with-3d-plm-from-dass/

Dekker, H. C. (2004). Control of inter-organizational relationships: Evidence on appropriation concerns and coordination requirements. *Accounting, Organizations and Society*, 29(1), 27–49.

DiMaggio, P. J., and Powell W. W. (1983). The iron cage revisited: Institutional isomorphism and collective rationality in organizational fields. *American Journal of Sociology*, 48(April), 147–160.

Domke, B. (2008). Boeing 787 lessons learnt. *Internal Presentation to Airbus* (October 20). Available at http://www.planebusiness.com/buzz/airbus2.pdf

Emmanuel, C., Harris, E., and Komakech, S. (2010). Towards a better understanding of capital investment decisions. *Journal of Accounting and Organizational Change*, 6(4), 477–504.

Gassman, O., Enkel, E., and Chesbrough, H. (2010). The future of open innovation. *R&D Management*, 40(3), 213–221.

Gates, D. (2012). Boeing raises list prices, especially for 787. *The Seattle Times* (August 7). Available at http://old.seattletimes.com/html/businesstechnology/2018866271_boeing08.html

Gates, D. (2009). Boeing stops work on 787 fuselages made in Italy to fix wrinkled skin. *Seattle Times* (August 14). Available at www.seattletimes.com/business/Boeing stops work on 787 fuselages made in Italy to fix wrinkled skin es-made-in-italy-to-fix-wrinkled-skin/

Gietzmann, M. B. (1996). Incomplete contracts and the make or buy decisions: Governance design and attainable flexibility. *Accounting, Organizations and Society*, 21(6), 611–626.

Greising, D., and Johnsson, J. (2007). Behind Boeing's 787 delays. *Chicago Tribune* (December 8).

Grimpe, C., and Kaiser, U. (2010). Balancing internal and external knowledge acquisition: The gains and pains from R&D outsourcing. *Journal of Management Studies*, 47(8), 1467–6486.

Hagedoorn, J., Link, A.N., and Vonortas, N. S. (2000). Research partnerships. *Research Policy*, 29, 567–586.

Hale, J. (2006). Boeing 787 from the ground up. *Aero Magazine* (Quarter 4). Available at www.boeing.com/commercial/aeromagazine/articles/qtr_4_06/AERO_Q406_article4.pdf

Hiltzik, M. (2011). 787 Dreamliner teaches Boeing costly lesson on outsourcing. *LA Times* (February 15). Available at http://articles.latimes.com/2011/feb/15/business/la-fi-hiltzik-20110215

Holzman, V., and Shanhar, A. (2010). The unfulfilled (or delayed) Dreamliner's dream: The case of the Boeing 787 Dreamliner. *The Henry Crown Institute of Business Research in Israel, Working Paper No 3/2010.*

Hughes, P. (2011). Boeing 787 Dreamliner: On board the plastic plane. *The Telegraph* (October 26).

Håkansson, H., and Lind, J. (2004). Accounting and network coordination. *Accounting, Organizations and Society*, 29(1), 51–72.

Håkansson, H., Kraus, K., Lind, J., and Strömsten, T. (2010). The industrial-network approach. In H. Håkansson, K. Kraus and J. Lind (Eds.), *Accounting in Networks*. New York: Routledge.

Isidore, C. (2011). Boeing's game changer finishes first flight. *CNNmoney* (October 26). Available at http://money.cnn.com/2011/10/25/news/companies/boeing_787_dreamliner/index.htm?iid=EAL

James, A. (2009). Boeing's 787 production is mission-controlled. *Seattle Post-Intelligencer*. www.seattlepi.com/business/article/Boeing-s-787-production-is-mission-controlled-1303651.php

Kesmodel, D. (2011). Boeing examines supply chain for weak links; as it prepares to boost product, jet maker steps up scrutiny of vendors' materials, finances and even tools. *Wall Street Journal* (December 30).

Lind, J., and Thrane, S. (2010). Towards accounting in network settings. In H. Håkansson, K. Kraus and J. Lind (Eds.), *Accounting in Networks*. Routledge Studies in Accounting. New York and Oxon, UK: Routledge.

McCurry, J. (2011). Boeing 787 Dreamliner lands after first passenger flight. *The Guardian* (October 26).

McInnes, I. (2008). *A 787 supply chain nightmare*. Available at www.aerospace-technology.com/features/feature1690/

McNerney, J. (2008). Address to shareholders. *Annual Meeting*, Chicago, IL (April 28). Available at www.boeing.com/media/speeches/

McNerney, J. (2011). Address to shareholders. *Annual Meeting*, Chicago, IL (May 2). Available at www.boeing.com/media/speeches/

McNerney, J. (2013). Address to shareholders. *Annual Meeting*, Chicago, IL (April 29). Available at www.boeing.com/media/speeches/

Mecham, M. (2007a). More oversight: Boeing emphasizes 787 production oversight. *Aviation Week* (November 19).

Mecham, M. (2007b). Boeing suppliers begin production of 787 shipsets for first ANA delivery. *Aviation Daily* (December 12).

Mecham, M. (2007c). Boeing faces "pretty tight" 787 delivery schedule. *Aviation Week* (September 9).

Mecham, M. (2008). Boeing buys Vought share of fuselage builder. *Aviation Week* (March 28).

Mecham, M. (2009a). Boeing resets clock on 787. *Aviation Week* (August 11).

Mecham, M. (2009b). Design issues starting to plague 787. *Aviation Week* (June 28).

Mecham, M. (2010). 787 deliveries may be pushed into 2011. *Aviation Week* (June 16).

Mecham, M. (2011a). Boeing shifts 787 stabilizer work. *Aviation Week* (June 29).

Mecham, M. (2011b). Supplier issues slow 787 progress again. *Aviation Week* (July 13).

Mecham, M. (2011c). Boeing fined for poorly written instructions on 777 oxygen systems. *Aviation Week* (June 28).

Mecham, M., and Norris, G. (2008). Suppliers raise risk of more 787 delays. *Aviation Week* (May 23).

Mecham, M., and Norris, G. (2011). Questions remain about Boeing 787 schedule. *Aviation Week* (January 24).

Miller, P., and O'Leary, T. (2007). Mediating instruments and making markets: Capital budgeting, science and the economy. *Accounting, Organizations and Society*, 32(7–8), 701–734.

Moad, J. (2007). Boeing's big supply chain wager. *Managing Automation* (Posted on July 23, 2007). Available at www.managingautomation.com/maonline/magazine/read/view/Boeings_Big_Supply_Chain_Wager_17760261

Mouritsen, J., and Thrane, S. (2006). Accounting, network complementarities and the development of inter-organisational relations. *Accounting, Organizations and Society*, 31(3), 241–275.

Muilenburg, D. (2014). Management discussion section. *The Boeing Co. (BA) Credit Suisse Global Industrials Conference* (December 3). Available at http://s2.q4cdn.com/661678649/files/doc_transcripts/Credit-Suisse-Transcript.pdf

Nambisan, S., and Sawhney, M. (2007). *The Global Brain: Your Roadmap for Innovating Faster and Smarter in a Networked World*. Upper Saddle River, NJ: Pearson Education.

New Breed Inc. (2006). *Boeing Selects New Breed to Provide Logistics Support for 787 Dreamliner Production*. Available at www.newbreed.com/nb_document.jsp?DocumentID=1

Nixon, B. (1998). Research and development performance measurement: A case study. *Management Accounting Research*, 9, 329–355.

Noll, D. (2006). Managing virtual networks on large scale projects. *Boeing Organization Effectiveness Consulting Group, Presentation, 11th ICCRTS Coalition Command and Control in the Networked Era* (September 28).

Norris, G. (2007). Restoring faith. *Aviation Week & Space Technology*, 167(21), 46–48.

Norris, G. (2010a). Boeing pushes first 787 delivery back to 2011. *Aviation Week* (August 27).

Norris, G. (2010b). Boeing extends 787 inspections to new areas. *Aviation Week* (August 13).

Norris, G., Thomas, G., Wagner, M., and Forbes Smith, C. (2005). *Boeing 787 Dreamliner-Flying Redefined*. Perth: Aerospace Technical Publications International Pvt Ltd.

Norris, G., and Wagner, M. (2009). *Boeing 787 Dreamliner*. Minneapolis: Zenith Press.

Oliver, C. (1991). Strategic responses to institutional processes. *Academy of Management Review*, 16(1), 145–159.

Orr, R. J., and Scott, W. R. (2008). Institutional exceptions on global projects: A process model. *Journal of International Business Studies*, 1–27.

Ostrower, J. (2008). One year on: The story of the 787. *Flight International* (May 5). Available at www.flightglobal.com/news/articles/one-year-on-the-story-of-the-787-223453/

Ostrower, J. (2011). Boeing aims at smooth ramp-up. *Flight International* (June 14). Available at www.flightglobal.com/articles/2011/06/14/357533/boeing-aims-at-smooth-ramp-up.html

Pappalardo, J. (2007). Alenia's gamble. *Air & Space* (July). Available at www.airspacemag.com/flight-today/alenias-gamble-18611587/?no-ist

Pritchard, D., and MacPherson, A. (2004). Outsourcing US commercial aircraft technology and innovation: Implications for the industry's long term design and build capability. *Canada-United States Trade Center Occasional Paper No. 29*. Canada-United States Trade Center, State University of New York, Buffalo, NY.

Pritchard, D., and MacPherson, A. (2005). Boeing's diffusion of commercial aircraft design and manufacturing technology to Japan: Surrendering the US Aircraft Industry for foreign financial support. *Canada-United States Trade Centre Occasional Paper No. 30*. Canada-United States Trade Center, State University of New York, Buffalo, NY.

Ray, S. (2010). Headaches still from Boeing 787 suppliers' parts. *Seattle Times* (May 20). Available at http://seattletimes.nwsource.com/html/businesstechnology/2011916380_boeing21.html

Rilla, N., and Squicciarini, M. (2011). R&D (re)location and offshore outsourcing: A management perspective. *International Journal of Management Reviews*, 1468–2370.

Seil, W. J. (2006). Sharing the dream: How the right tools and an inclusive culture supper the 787 global partner network. *Boeing Frontiers* (August 28–29).

Smock, D. (2009). What's causing huge delays for the Boeing 787 dreamliner? *Design News* (August 24). Available at www.designnews.com/document.asp?doc_id=228554

Stackpole, B. (2007). Boeing's global collaboration environment pioneers groundbreaking 787 Dreamliner development effort. *Design News* (May 15). Available at www.designnews.com/document.asp?doc_id=225598

Sydow, J., Schüßler, E., and Müller-Seitz G. (2016). *Managing Inter-organizational Relations: Debates and Cases*. London: Palgrave.

Thomas, G. (2008a). The dream and the nightmare. *Air Transport World* (December 34–40).

Thomas, G. (2008b). Rolls, Boeing, Airbus face new A380, 787 problems. *Air Transport World*, (December 9).

van der Meer-Kooistra, J., and Scapens, R. W. (2008). The governance of lateral relations between and within organisations. *Management Accounting Research*, 19(4), 365–384.

van der Meer-Kooistra, J., and Scapens, R. W. (2015). Governing product co-development projects: The role of minimal structures. *Management Accounting Research*, 28, 68–91.

Wayne, L. (2006). Boeing bets the house on its 787 Dreamliner. *New York Times* (May 7).

Weber, J. (2009). Boeing to reign in Dreamliner outsourcing. *Bloomberg Business Week* (January 16).

Wilhelm, S. (2014). As Boeing grows, aerospace supplier mergers and acquisitions accelerate. *Puget Sound Business Journal* (December 19). Available at www.bizjournals.com/seattle/news/2014/04/24/boeing-chief-price-pressure-on-suppliers-needed.html

Zhao, Y., and Shenhar, A. (2011). Why 787 slippages were inevitable. *Aviation Week & Space Technology*, 173(8), 58.

7 Accounting, Cross-Company Negotiations, and Time-Based Compromises

A Case Study of Product Innovation

Martin Carlsson-Wall and Kalle Kraus

Introduction

This chapter deals with accounting and product innovation. Product innovation has been put forward as highly critical for value creation on industrial markets in both the accounting (e.g., Davila and Wouters, 2004; Mouritsen et al., 2009; Van der Meer-Kooistra and Scapens, 2015) and marketing literatures (e.g., Håkansson and Waluszewski, 2002, 2007; Hoholm and Olsen, 2012; La Rocca and Snehota, 2014). Our findings build on an in-depth case study of ABB Robotics, a producer of industrial robots, and more specifically examine how accounting is involved in innovation conducted between Robotics and its close customers and suppliers.

Product innovation processes are characterised as interactive, non-hierarchical, and unpredictable (Dubois and Araujo, 2006). Owing to the complexity of integrating technologies, products can rarely be designed on the drawing board (Brusoni et al., 2001; Brady and Davies, 2004). This means there is a continuous need for re-designs to be made. In addition, research has shown that product innovation typically occur in close cooperation with customers and suppliers rather than within individual firms (Håkansson and Waluszewski, 2002). Therefore, it is not possible for managers in one company to dictate the decisions concerning the re-designs of all the other companies involved. Rather, product innovation typically involves *a series of compromises* when the company and its close customers and suppliers together try to handle the constant emergence of new tensions and opportunities (c.f., Dubois and Araujo, 2006).

From an accounting perspective, such a setting raises new and interesting research issues. One of these is to analyse the impact of accounting practices on innovation processes that integrate a large number of technologies across company borders. The fact that one company cannot fully dictate the conditions in most product innovation projects brings to the fore the roles of accounting in cross-company negotiation processes. This issue was brought up conceptually by Tomkins (2001) but has rarely been elaborated on in subsequent studies. Another issue concerns the role of accounting in an innovation process characterised by numerous re-designs as no company can predict the end result of the process. Accounting may be used for optimisation and the follow-up of pre-set goals, as documented in earlier studies (Carlsson-Wall and Kraus, 2015; Nixon, 1998; Jörgensen and Messner, 2009, 2010), but it may also be used to stimulate interaction between different companies, which will facilitate the collective process of finding mutually satisfactory compromises. Thus, studying product innovation begs the more specific question that we ask in this paper: *what is the role of accounting in the series of compromises that are made throughout the product innovation process?*

Case Analysis

The research setting and topic for this study is ABB Robotics (Robotics) and the innovation of robot systems. Robotics develops, manufactures, and sells robots and is one of the world's largest robot manufacturers. Its annual turnover is about 250 million Euros, and the company employs 600 people. All of the major functions of Robotics, such as product development, marketing, purchasing, and production, are located in Västerås, Sweden. The annual sales volume varies between 8,000 and 10,000 robots. An industrial robot is composed of two main parts, a robot (with its main components: motor, gear, arm), which actually performs the activities, and an industrial control system, which steers and controls the robot's actions. Robotics' customer and supplier relationships provide an additional level of complexity. Compromises are not only arrived at in relation to trade-offs for the individual product (the industrial control system or the robot), but these compromises also have to be analysed in relation to large framework contracts that Robotics signs with customers such as General Motors or suppliers like Motorola. Robotics therefore provides a research setting in which compromises during product innovation can be studied not only in relation to trade-offs between components within a single innovation project but also in relation to other products as well as customer and supplier relationships. Our case analysis draws primarily on semi-structured interviews but also includes direct observations and documents. In total, 49 people were interviewed, many of them several times, with the average duration of an interview being about one hour. The interviewees included the top management and people working within different parts of Robotics, such as, purchasing, development, quality, logistics, production, accounting, and sales.

The S4 Project: Accounting and Cross-Company Negotiations

S4, the development of a new industrial control system, is a large innovation project. A central customer in S4 is General Motors (GM). Being one of the largest automotive manufacturers in the world, GM provided both knowledge and credibility to Robotics. However, when S4 began, GM had not agreed to be the lead user. On the contrary, in the large and comprehensive framework contract with Robotics, GM had chosen an older industrial control system to avoid quality problems (called S3). From Robotics' perspective, this was unfortunate because the product cost of S3was much higher than the estimated product cost of S4. Robotics' staff therefore focused on convincing GM that a re-design was needed, i.e., that S4 should replace the old industrial control system. For instance, the salesmen tried to convince GM's purchasers that using S4 would require fewer training and service costs, and in parallel, Robotics' engineers emphasised to the GM engineers that the new functionality would enable GM to increase productivity in the factories. GM started to show interest, but initially did not make a decision to re-negotiate the framework contract and change from the old industrial control system to S4. The accounting quantifications of the savings in training and service costs provided by Robotics were not enough to convince GM.

However, the negotiations intensified when GM needed new functionality, which meant a need for increased computer memory requirements in the industrial control system. As one Robotics product manager explained:

> GM came back and said; "OK, we know we have a technical specification that is good enough to twist your arm and we know that this means that you are making customised adaptations for us. . . . What do you want to deliver to us?"

Intense negotiations relating to the cost and functionality started to take place between the purchasers and engineers from GM and the sales people, the engineers, and the product manager from Robotics. The engineers at Robotics emphasised that these negotiations and the interactions with GM staff were crucial for lowering its production costs. Table 7.1 demonstrates Robotics' different savings and the increases in cost broken down into individually significant items or functionalities. Several different components and reductions required specialised knowledge of different kinds. Engineers and

Table 7.1 Robotics' internal accounting calculations for the work-arounds

Function	*Cost savings (+)/cost increases (–)*
Replace flange disconnector with one of rotary type	$92,990
Replace servo power disconnector with one of rotary type	$187,000
Replace push buttons and lamp sockets with a cheaper brand	$4,300
Usage of less expensive connectors	$127,000
Cost reduction on other specific components	$150,00
Modifications of the mechanical units	$887,000
Replacing S3 with S4	$1,145,000
Total estimated cost savings	*$2,458,290*
Increased memory requirement	$-1,329,375
Total estimated cost increases	*$-1,329,375*
Net savings	**$1,128,915**

sales managers from Robotics, and engineers and purchasing managers from GM jointly discussed different types of solutions that gave a reasonable trade-off between cost and functionality when deciding on appropriate re-designs. Robotics called this process of seeking mutually satisfactory solutions to problems encountered doing 'work-arounds'; work-arounds provided an important means of attaining an accounting-driven cross-company negotiation about re-designs. Engineers and sales managers at Robotics explained that their internal accounting quantifications, i.e., the specified cost savings for each function and component, were vital for successful negotiations with GM because they enabled informed trade-offs to be made between technical requirements and the financial impact of these requirements.

With the prices in the frame contract as a background, the modifications were evaluated and prioritised. Sometimes technically well-functioning solutions were rejected because they were too expensive. Describing the cross-company negotiations about re-designs, a sales manager at Robotics explained:

> We had many tough discussions [with GM representatives]. These discussions ended up in lists of items to be traded . . . if you let go of this demand and use this component or feature instead, then we can deduct X dollars per robot and so on. It was quite successful.

As Table 7.1 illustrates, by replacing the push buttons with a cheaper brand, Robotics saved $4,300, and by using less expensive connectors, an additional $127,000 could be gained. A big difference was the switch from S3 to the new system, S4. As such, accounting quantifications formed the basis for how Robotics staff negotiated during the work-arounds and guided the compromises that were made between Robotics and GM during innovation. General Motors eventually accepted S4, and Robotics could then add the new functionality that GM wanted, i.e., a more expensive computer memory, which added total costs of $1,329,375.

Our findings from the S4 innovation project indicate that accounting served as an *anchor* that framed the compromises that were made between Robotics and GM during product innovation. In the work-arounds, accounting created consensus around prioritisations, gave focus to the joint problem solving, and facilitated and directed knowledge integration between Robotics and GM. As such, accounting sometimes formed the basis for rejecting technically well-functioning solutions because they were too expensive, but on other occasions, accounting formed the basis for searching for possible solutions that represented compromises between improved technological content and additional costs.

The S4B Project: Accounting, Re-designs and Time Pressure

A few years after the introduction of S4, customers had begun to ask for new functionality. However, Robotics had not finished the next platform, called

S5, and therefore it was necessary to make an extension of S4. This became the S4B project. In contrast to S4, S4B was not a planned project in Robotics' product management pipeline and, from the start, there was intense time pressure. The background to S4B was a large order from BMW. Despite having purchased S4, BMW was not completely satisfied and unexpectedly demanded a large re-design a few months before the order was about to start being delivered. As the project manager for S4B described the situation:

> BMW was offering us a very larger order, 4–5,000 robots, or at least many thousands of robots. However, BMW did not like S4. We therefore made a customisation for them. First prototypes, demonstration examples, just to show them something.

BMW's main concern was the physical size of S4. Instead of having a customer module outside the industrial control system, BMW wanted this module to be placed within the industrial control system so that everything would fit into one large cabinet. Even though Robotics understood the rationale behind this, the development department hesitated because a key feature in the next large generation project, i.e., S5, was the reduction in physical size. To spend engineering resources developing a larger industrial control system seemed like a strategic mistake. On the other hand, BMW was offering a very large order of 4,000 to 5,000 robots, and future sales were not as optimistic as they had been six months earlier. In parallel with the BMW order, Robotics' sales organisation in France had also received negative feedback about S4. In addition to extending the size, the two biggest customers, Peugeot and Renault, wanted to re-design the front of the system because it was inconvenient for access, and every minute of downtime was estimated to cost about $10,000. By changing the contacts and how the service personnel accessed the system, it was argued that quality problems could be solved much more rapidly.

Robotics faced a dilemma. BMW, Peugeot, and Renault could secure sales in the short term if Robotics could meet the customer requirements quickly. From a long-term perspective, however, these customer requirements were counterproductive to the launch of the S5, the next-generation project. The large automotive customers needed prototypes rapidly, and Robotics was under tough time pressure. Within Robotics, tensions increased between departments. On the one hand, key account managers wanted a quick go-ahead to ensure that they could win the large framework contracts with BMW, Renault, and Peugeot. In contrast, the product management department and the production team wanted a more detailed analysis to avoid future quality problems. As a compromise, it was decided that a new development project was needed because it would be too costly to do unique customisations for the three large customers. As a result, the intermediate solution, S4B, was formally started. Commenting on this, a product manager said:

> We had a sales organisation that ran customer projects and a product organisation that was responsible for products. Sales were much quicker and more flexible, did not optimise cost or quality. It was more a case of "We have an order, we have to fix it!" When several customers evidently wanted the same thing, we realised it was time to make a standard product of out of this.

The product manager explained that there was no time for detailed accounting calculations. In addition, the uncertainty and technical complexity made it difficult to know what financial data to use in the estimations. Instead Robotics relied on its previous experience of the costs for unique customisations conducted for large automotive customers, which showed them to be very costly. This meant that an innovation project, i.e., S4B, seemed reasonable also from a financial perspective.

When S4B was officially started, time was short for the development of prototypes, and an early problem was to find a suitable supplier. Most serial suppliers were fully engaged in developing S5, and it was difficult to find a supplier that was prepared or able to be responsible for the entire re-design. However, a new company called Design-Net had just been formed. Design-Net was a Swedish network of mechanical and engineering companies. By working together under one brand name, the goal was to attract larger industrial companies such as ABB and Ericsson. Through personal contacts within the ABB Group, Robotics and Design-Net started to negotiate. With the urgent time pressure, contract discussions progressed quickly. Based on the technical requirements laid down by BMW, the general outline was drafted over the phone and then written down in an e-mail. As the Design-Net owner recalled:

> It was damned simple, getting those contracts. They were based mostly on trust. I think that is important, and a strong Swedish tradition. When one does business with an American company . . . then it takes forever because they read everything literally. For us, Swedes, a contract is a base for continuous discussions.

Compared with S4, several new organisational and contract issues were tested in S4B. First, Design-Net was given the project management responsibility for the entire re-design. Previously, Robotics' suppliers had only been responsible for individual components. Second, since S4B was not initially perceived to be very risky, the contract was not very detailed. The majority of effort was spent on discussing the functional deliveries and the project cost, which was set at 7 million kronor (about 800,000 Euros). Describing the negotiations, the Design-Net owner continued:

> It started with . . . the sales department [at Robotics] said that if they wanted the BMW deal, they needed to re-design S4. But the purchasing

> manager initially said "We don't have any resources!" Then, someone came up with the idea that it could be outsourced. So I sold him a package.

Six months into the project, Robotics unexpectedly realised that S4B needed integration with S4. Developing S4B had become more complex because smaller re-designs required consultation with the parts suppliers for S4. At the same time, Robotics was under extreme time pressure to deliver prototypes of the S4B for BMW, Peugeot, and Renault. To strengthen integration with S4, Robotics convinced Design-Net to change the parts supplier. Instead of working with the local supplier, Design-Net started to work with Serial-P, which produced the cabinets for S4. The deadline for delivering prototypes to Peugeot and Renault was only two months away, and Design-Net and Serial-P had never worked together before. Several Robotics managers also noted that Design-Net seemed to spend project resources faster than expected. As one technical manager said:

> They never warned us, but you could just see it. We got weekly reports of how much money had been spent. You could see that this was never going to work. However, before the budget was spent, they always said "Don't worry," but then afterwards, they wanted more money.

As a consequence of the time pressure and the different views on conducting the re-design, unexpected cost increases occurred when Design-Net's re-design did not fit the production processes at Serial-P. In total, 200 to 300 different screw holes did not fit the cabinet that Serial-P was producing, and it was difficult to say who was responsible for the problem. Describing the problem with the wrong screws, the senior engineer at Design-Net argued that Serial-P was to blame. According to him, Serial-P was not used to working with the latest production methods. On the other hand, since Serial-P used the same production process for both S4 and S4B, they argued that Robotics was to blame. With the urgent need to satisfy Peugeot and Renault, both Robotics and Design-Net realised that the risk of delay in delivery to Peugeot and Renault would be extremely costly. As a consequence, they quickly agreed on a compromise in the form of a 50%–50% split of the cost of about 600,000 kronor (about 70,000 Euros). Reflecting on this sharing of unexpected cost increases, the D-Network owner said:

> Many times the customers [Peugeot, Renault] did not know how they wanted it . . . they innovated along the way. This led to discussions and sometimes Robotics did not want to pay for the additional work.

To summarise, we see that the start of S4B was a compromise that was arrived at because it would be too costly to make unique customisations for each of these three large customers. From the product management's perspective, the development of S4B was not an optimal solution, but since the key account managers wanted a go-ahead decision directly, it became a compromise. However, in contrast with the previously described S4 project, there was no time for detailed accounting calculations. Instead, Robotics relied on previous experience of the costs for unique customisations for its large automotive customers, which showed that they were very costly. This meant that the innovation project, S4B, seemed reasonable from a financial perspective. Our findings demonstrate how the time pressure, in the form of commitments to customer deadlines, in addition to the inherent technical complexity, affected the innovation process. In comparison with the S4 project (where detailed calculations were made), S4B was not planned and there was intense time pressure from the outset to deliver prototypes quickly to BMW, Peugeot, and Renault. Hence, adding an inter-organisational level to the analysis of innovation shows that the time pressure had to do with customer commitments. This impacted on the role of accounting in the innovation process. With urgent time pressure, in combination with technically complicated issues, there was no room for detailed calculations because it was considered that they would take too much time to perform. Instead, time-based compromises were made, relating the large estimated revenues of customer contracts to what were considered to be "reasonable costs." For example, in the selection of Design-Net, since the project cost of 7 million kronor was seen as reasonable in relation to the larger revenues of the frame contracts and time was short, no detailed calculations were made regarding the costs. A similar example was shown in the distribution of costs arising from the use of the wrong screws. Since the estimated revenues from Peugeot and Renault orders were so high and there was tight time pressure, a problem costing 600,000 kronor was not seen as a major reason to create unnecessary tensions with Serial-P. The compromise was to split the costs 50–50 between Robotics and Design-Net. In this way, accounting created consensus about the fact that a problem needed the full attention of all involved in the development and had to be solved quickly because it would be related to large estimated revenues from customer orders. The rough calculations of the potential revenues were considered to be enough to make the compromises worthwhile, so no detailed analyses were made on the costs side.

Conclusions

Based on an in-depth case study of ABB Robotics, a producer of industrial robots, this study has analysed how accounting is involved in innovation conducted between Robotics and its close customers and suppliers. Our findings contribute to the accounting-and-innovation literature (e.g., Carlsson-Wall and Kraus, 2015; Christner and Strömsten, 2015; Jörgensen and Messner, 2010; Moll, 2015) in a number of ways. First, the innovation process involves a series of compromises when the company and its close customers and suppliers together try to handle the constant emergence of new tensions, opportunities, and contradictions. This brings to the fore the roles of accounting in cross-company negotiation processes, an issue brought up conceptually by Tomkins (2001) but rarely elaborated on in subsequent studies. Our findings reveal intense negotiations relating to the cost and functionality that took place between the purchasers and engineers from General Motors and the sales people, the engineers, and the product manager from Robotics. Robotics' internal accounting quantifications, i.e., the specified cost savings for each function and component, were vital for successful negotiations with GM because they enabled informed trade-offs to be made between technical requirements and the financial effects of these requirements. As such, accounting not only guides negotiations and knowledge integration within companies as documented in prior research (e.g., Nixon, 1998; Jörgensen and Messner, 2009, 2010); it also served as an *anchor* that framed the compromises that were made between Robotics and GM. Accounting created consensus about prioritisations, gave focus to the joint problem solving, and facilitated and directed knowledge integration between the companies.

Second, we contribute by detailing the importance of time when analysing the roles of accounting in product innovation. The S4B project had not been planned and included in Robotics' product management pipeline, and there was intense time pressure right from the very beginning to deliver prototypes to BMW, Peugeot, and Renault. The urgent time pressure in combination with technically complicated issues meant that there was no room for detailed calculations to be made, so, instead, *time-based compromises* were made by relating the large estimated revenues of customer contracts to what were perceived to be "reasonable costs." When Design-Net was selected as the supplier, the project cost of 7 million kronor was perceived to be reasonable in relation to the larger revenues of the frame contracts, and no detailed calculations were made to analyse whether the estimated cost was realistic or not. Similarly, since the estimated revenues from Peugeot and Renault orders were so high and there was tight time pressure, costs of 600,000 kronor arising from the wrong screws being used were split 50–50 between Robotics and Design-Net without detailed analysis. With the time pressure that all of those concerned were operating under, accounting, in the form of rough calculations of potential revenues, created consensus about the fact that a problem needed full attention and influenced the compromises during innovation, but no detailed analyses were made on the costs side.

We suggest that our findings will be of value for the planning of future studies. There is a need for further research on the roles of accounting in product innovation, theorising how accounting is used in the ongoing cross-company negotiations, as well as theorising how time pressure impacts on the roles of accounting in these development processes. In terms of research design, our findings also highlight the importance of including project and inter-organisational levels of analysis to capture the full complexity of accounting issues and their impact on product innovation.

References

Brady, T., and Davies, A. (2004). Building project capabilities: From exploratory to exploitative learning. *Organization Studies*, 25, 1601–1621.

Brusoni, S., Prencipe, A., and Pavitt, K. (2001). Knowledge specialization, organizational coupling and the boundaries of the firm: Why do firms know more than they do? *Administrative Science Quarterly*, 46, 597–621.

Carlsson-Wall, M., and Kraus, K. (2015). Opening the black box of the role of accounting practices in the fuzzy front-end of product innovation. *Industrial Marketing Management*, 45, 184–194.

Christner, C.H., and Strömsten, T. (2015). Scientists, venture capitalists and the stock exchange: The mediating role of accounting in product innovation. *Management Accounting Research*, 28, 50–67.

Davila, A., and Wouters, M. (2004). Designing cost-competitive technology products through cost management. *Accounting Horizons*, 18, 13–26.

Dubois, A., and Araujo, L. (2006). The relationship between technical and organisational interfaces in product development. *The IMP Journal*, 1, 28–51.

Håkansson, H., and Waluszewski, A. (2002). *Managing technological development: IKEA, the environment and technology*. Routledge: London.

Håkansson, H., and Waluszewski, A. (2007). *Knowledge and innovation in business and industry: The importance of using others*. Routledge: London.

Hoholm, T., and Olsen, P.I. (2012). The contrary forces of innovation. A conceptual model for studying networked innovation processes. *Industrial Marketing Management*, 41, 344–356.

Jörgensen, B., and Messner, M. (2009). Management control in new product development: The dynamics of managing flexibility and efficiency. *Journal of Management Accounting Research*, 22, 99–124.

Jörgensen, B., and Messner, M. (2010). Accounting and strategising: A case study from new product development. *Accounting Organizations and Society*, 35, 184–204.

La Rocca, A., and Snehota, I. (2014). Relating in business networks: Innovation in practice. *Industrial Marketing Management*, 43, 441–447.

Moll, J. (2015). Editorial: Special issue on innovation and product development. *Management Accounting Research*, 28, 2–11.

Mouritsen, J., Hansen, A., and Hansen, C.Ø. (2009). Short and long translations: Management accounting calculations and innovation management. *Accounting, Organizations and Society*, 34, 738–754.

Nixon, B. (1998). Research and development performance measurement: A case study. *Management Accounting Research*, 3, 329–355.

Tomkins, C. (2001). Interdependencies, trust and information in relationships, alliances and networks. *Accounting, Organizations and Society*, 26, 161–191.

Van der Meer-Kooistra, J., and Scapens, R.W. (2015). Governing product co-development projects: The role of minimal structures. *Management Accounting Research*, 28, 68–91.

8 Developing Innovation via Tensions Between Focal Firms and Suppliers

The Role of Accounting in Creating Heterarchies Across Organisational Boundaries

Jan Mouritsen and Kim S. Hald

Introduction

This chapter considers accounting as an engine for the development of innovative capabilities in inter-organisational relations. This requires that accounting rather than being a mechanism that stabilises matters by fencing inter-organisational spaces into durable and possibly disciplinary relations becomes more of a 'performable space' (Busco and Quattrone, 2015; Quattrone, 2015). Such a space is more imaginative than accounting for fixed expectations and responsibilities (Puyou, Quattrone, McLean and Thrift, 2012). Innovative capabilities are ones that make it possible for inter-organisational relations to develop and thus transform the roles and aspirations held by the participating firms. This understanding of accounting emphasises its imaginary rather than controlling qualities and helps to disclose *new worlds* rather than primarily *territorialise existing* worlds. In this sense, accounting provides power to influence a firm's development of its products and processes (Revellino and Mouritsen, 2015). This, it does, by mediating heterarchical relations by which they introduce a certain sense of dissonance in organisational relations (Stark, 2009); such matters can be extended beyond the organisational boundary into the inter-organisational space. The role of accounting in this endeavour is that it not only describes relations between firms; it more importantly develops and helps enact such relations. With Muniesa (2014), it is possible to argue that accounting provokes the development of the economy, or more specifically, it is possible to argue that accounting helps provoke the development of innovation in inter-organisational settings.

To develop this point, the chapter discusses an instance when accounting helped provoke relations between a focal firm and its suppliers with a view to innovation. The case is surprising because the relevant accounting was not primarily a property of the focal firm but one which more precisely, via the intervention of both the focal firm and its suppliers, re-made not only accounting but also the separate organisations of the two sets of firms and of the relations between the firms.

The chapter argues that innovation is an effect of how accounting mediates relations between a focal firm and its suppliers. In particular, accounting helps develop the type of values that account for interactions between firms, and accounting develops the means by which not only who in the focal and supplier firms communicate with each other but also what they communicate about. Therefore, the development of accounting is a precursor to the development of organisational relations and in turn to the development of innovation. This happens because the language developed by accounting becomes an engine of relationships and since engagement involves transformation it functions through dissonance. Dissonance is the materiality out of which it is possible to imagine how new roles and ambitions can be created and in turn how innovation can become established (Stark, 2009).

Accounting's Re-constructive Potential

Paradoxically, even in supply chain- and network-oriented accounting research, the concern is often hierarchical (Hopwood, 1996). This means that the accounting mechanisms studied in inter-organisational relations are concerned with the problems of the focal firm. Much research has discussed the complex relations between focal and supply firms. Håkansson and Lind (Håkansson and Lind, 2004, 2006) have shown how such relations are constituted by many streams, including not only the product but also communication, information and negotiation. Likewise, research about internal and inter-organisational controls (Carlsson-Wall, Kraus and Lind, 2011; Dekker, 2016) identifies continuity between the focal firm's accounting and its extension into the inter-organisational space. This continuity reflects a general concern about the relative hierarchies or power relations between (a set of) firms (Frances and Garnsey, 1996; Seal, Berry and Cullen, 2004; Kraus and Strömsten, 2016), e.g. through open book accounting (Agndal and Nilsson, 2010; Alenius, Lind and Strömsten, 2015; Kajüter and Kulmala, 2005; Windolph and Moeller, 2012). Accounting tends to change random interactions into firm-like relationships in an attempt at coordinating already known and existing firms by accounting mechanisms that extend well beyond the firm (Håkansson and Lind, 2006). In this literature, production is distributed among firms in a perhaps ever-growing supply chain, but the focal firm remains a key actor (Håkansson and Lind, 2004; van der Meer-Kooistra and Scapens, 2008).

Much of this research extends beyond the mere description of the presence of accounting. It also provides a dynamic perspective of the effects of accounting (sometimes part of a wider governance structure) on the development of new and innovate operating relations. There is a dynamic implication of accounting on operational activities in which firms are enabled to develop new relations and find new forms of cooperation. These new forms of cooperation may sometimes involve understanding accounting not only as fixed structure but as a base that can be 'adapted' to by local additions

(Håkansson and Lind, 2004) or more generally as one set of controls that may be supplemented with other types of governance (van der Meer-Kooistra and Scapens, 2008). The general claim is here that there are dynamic business processes which a stable accounting cannot fathom, and additions and supplements have to be designed which can manoeuvre complex relations.

However, some papers seem to have paid even more explicit attention to accounting not as a base around which variations can play out but as changes in the central movement of accounting apparatuses providing them with radically new identity via a dynamic rendering of relations between a focal and supplier firms. For example, Chua and Mahama (2007) show that accounting actively co-constructs relations between a focal firm and a supplier by its ability to motivate, if not force, participating parties to redesign accounting in view of the very information that accounting produces. Accounting was not taken for granted, but by making it a mechanism for dialogue and debate between parties, it gained a performative power of the properties of the relationships. It helped re-negotiate relationships (and not primarily helped to enable a relationship) as it helped to make clear that effects were not as anticipated. This would re-organise relations between the parties in the sense that its framing produces some overflows that need re-framing. So, accounting is a force that re-forms the relationship rather than one that enables a relationship.

Likewise, Mouritsen, Hansen and Hansen (2001) show that accounting is fluid in the sense that certain aspects of its calculation can be given more or less weight over time and then influence the properties of the focal firm to fit the capabilities proposed from the supplier. In this case, accounting was a target costing procedure that was used to specify to suppliers how cost targets should be understood. However, by using this mechanism, a particular supplier started to ask new questions, and suddenly it became clear that a more interesting dialogue could be developed if it were based not on the target costs themselves but on the associated (non-financial) functional analysis. This motivated the focal firm to transform itself to become even more adept in managing outsourcing of development work than before. The change of accounting developed a set of relations which implied changing the capabilities of the participating firms.

These two examples pay attention to the surprising effects of accounting. Rather than understanding accounting as a device for stabilising relations, accounting may turn out to produce surprising effects. In a sense, these papers are early examples of a much more expansive agenda in which accounting may be considered a knowledge producing entity, or as Busco and Quattrone have proposed, it may be a 'performable space' (Busco and Quattrone, 2015; Quattrone, 2015) rather than only a territorialising mechanism (Miller and Power, 2013). The possibility of a performable space is that accounting makes it possible for many actors to have dialogue and communicate. Since accounting is a bad representation of the world (it is never a copy of it), its incompleteness forces people to make sense and add to it (Jordan and Messner, 2012; Mouritsen and Kreiner, 2016). The possibly creative force coming out of this may be heterarchical, i.e. the firm is moved from positions and values that can neither be ranked nor predicted in advance (Quattrone and Hopper, 2005; Stark, 2009). Therefore, it is important to research more precisely how innovative relationships establish themselves in inter-organisational relations. To this end, we draw on a study of HearingCorp's (pseudonym) relation to its strategic upstream suppliers.

Case Study: Accounting Mediating HearingCorp and Strategic Supplier

Method

Interactions between HearingCorp and its suppliers were followed over a period of 3 years. The field work included 38 interviews with members of HearingCorp and supplier organisations as well as participant observation in 40 meetings. Participation in meetings provided a platform from which the actors could be followed more carefully. Some of these meetings provided the opportunity to observe dialogue between the focal buying firm HearingCorp and its suppliers. Specifically, these meetings dealt with actors and activities involved with the construction of the involved inter-organisational accounting systems. Meetings and interviews were recorded. The physically presence of the researcher at the meetings further helped supplement recordings with field notes.

Data was collected and analysed using a three-step approach. Two of these stages were integrated in the data collection process while still being situated in the empirical field. First, the emergence of the observed management accounting system was observed. This was a process applying the principle of snowball sampling in which action and activity revealed from one interview and related to developments concerned with the management accounting system led to the identification of more actors and interview respondents that were involved in forming and shaping these developments. This initial tracing of history was also a tool to familiarise the researcher with the firm and with key actors in the empirical field. Second, the analytical process continued as a cycle between observations of field encounters, follow-up interviews and identification of new meetings or interviewees. With a focus on tracing calculation, information and numbers among the focal firm and suppliers, interaction that involved suppliers or related suppliers to re-design activities were of particular interest. Most of the dialogue from these meetings and interviews was transcribed and coded. Based on this initial analysis, individual positions and how the involved actors sought to legitimise their re-design plans or sought to problematise already in place accounting inscriptions were identified. Third, and after all data collection had stopped, we removed ourselves from the empirical field. This helped us to establish a distance to the field that was needed to establish overview of the data collected. At this the final stage of analysis, we looked for common themes and relations between variables that could help trace calculation, information and numbers among the focal firm and suppliers. We marked all involved accounts of the developments that had been observed while submerged in the empirical field. We then grouped these accounts in themes that could help us explain roles played by the focal and supplier firms and how these could be thought of as linked to the observed re-presentations of the accounting inscription.

Empirical Findings

The empirical account shows how an existing accounting system, the SC-Scorecard, was challenged by strategic suppliers because of its inability to re-present performance that linked suppliers to innovations. Also, there was a challenge in the existing accounting mechanism to relate suppliers to the product development function. Therefore, suppliers objected, and this led to the emergence of a new and mainly non-financial accounting system (the SP-System) that enabled the production of a stronger innovative space.

HearingCorp and the SC-Scorecard

HearingCorp developed, manufactured and sold advanced hearing aids. According to product development engineer's miniaturisation, artificial intelligence, microphones, transducers and microchip capacity were central in ambitions to win new market shares. There was a continuous flow of product introductions and new products with short life cycles. Innovations were therefore central to all activities and relations in the supply chain. Competition increasingly was suggested as requiring ability to innovate, develop and deliver new products to the market faster than competitors and strategic suppliers played a critical part in this ambition.

To cope with these challenges, accounting was call upon, and a supply chain balanced scorecard (SC-Scorecard) was developed. It included a focus on supply operations and was supposed to be able to provide answers to "all" or most aspects of supply chain performance and supplier relations. This was a grand ambition and it was global in the sense that it reached all corners of the focal firm's Enterprise Resource Planning System (ERP). SC-Scorecard displayed a series of financial and non-financial top-level performance indicators (Figure 8.1). For each perspective, a clock hand indicated if current performance was above target (green), on target (yellow) or under target (red). Clicking on each of the perspectives, there was opportunity to drill down into performance details.

With SC-Scorecard, HearingCorp's managers could simulate scenarios and calculate consequences. It packed a model of the supply chain via several interlinked Excel sheets, and it was structured in the balanced scorecard's four perspectives. It presented itself as an opportunity to manage at

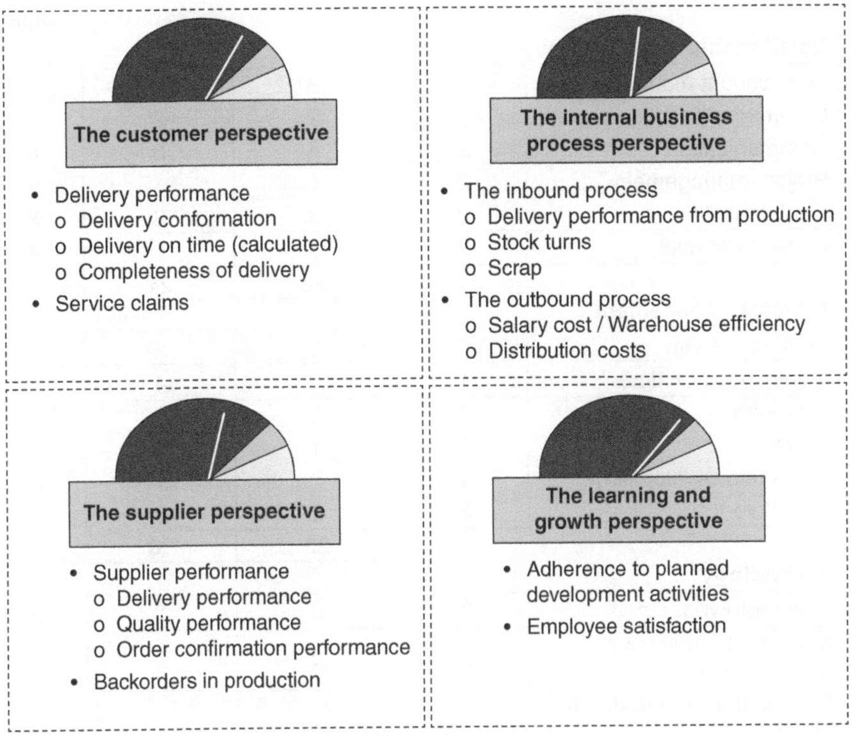

Figure 8.1 The SC-Scorecard.

a distance. However, measures concerned with innovation was strangely absent, and SC-Scorecard stabilised relations and failed to provide a space for innovations.

The New Supplier Performance System

The new supplier performance system (SP-System) was highly related to HearingCorp's important innovative suppliers. Although the SC-Scorecard already included a concern for supplier performance, the important innovative strategic suppliers refused the performance presentations included. They requested additional measures which would focus more on their competencies in driving innovation and technology. Compared with SC-Scorecard, the SP-System was "a much more in-depth evaluation" of the supplier capabilities rather than only of its transactions. It was arranged in five dimensions (see Figure 8.2).

The product delivery and quality measures that were included were almost identical to the ones that were already part of the supplier perspective in the SC-Scorecard. However, three completely new performance dimensions were

Performance Indicators	Importance	Expectations	Performance	Action Plan
Relationship Management				
Key account management	2	3	3	
Commitment	2	2	2	
Communication	2	4	3	X
Project management	2	1	1	
Confidentiality	2	3	2	X
Code of conduct	2	3	1	X
		32	**24**	
General Management				
Professionalism	3	2	2	
Inquiry reaction time	1	3	4	
New ideas	2	2	2	
IT-set-up	1	1	2	
Economic development	1	2	1	X
Proactive	3	2	3	
		22	**26**	
Technology				
Fast prototypes	2	3	1	X
Master and prove new technologies	2	2	2	
Master simulations/virtual prototyping	2	2	4	
Responsibility/new components	2	3	1	X
		20	**16**	
Delivery				
Delivery on time	2	2	2	
Order confirmation	3	2	2	
Spontaneous part deliveries	1	2	2	
Invoicing	3	2	2	
		18	**18**	
Quality				
Measurement capability	3	2	1	X
Process control capability	3	3	3	
Inspection procedures	2	3	2	X
Quality report (QR)	3	4	3	X
Answers to QR	2	2	4	
		37	**33**	
		129	**117**	

Figure 8.2 The new supplier performance system (SP-System).

included, and this extended the re-presentation of performance to include a concern for innovations and the ability to innovate. All of the measures here were subjective evaluations of suppliers' technological and managerial competencies. Most important, strategic suppliers' technological competencies were now included in this new and extended assessment. The measures had been included on specific request from suppliers themselves. Performance measures that were entirely focused on the competencies that were needed to engage with HearingCorp in product development projects were included.

Also, the "relationship management" dimension was new. It was a performance dimension concerned with the supplier capabilities and commitment to a strong and enduring relationship which was considered strategically important. The ability to manage key accounts and a detailed assessment of the supplier's commitment and communication in the relationship was included as performance measures in this dimension. The "general management" dimension included performance measures such as levels of supplier professionalism and an evaluation of the supplier's economic development and stability.

Re-presenting and Re-relating via the Intervention of Strategic Supplier

The SP-System differed from the SC-Scorecard because strategic suppliers objected to the Scorecard's inability to account for component innovations and technology cooperation. They wished to forge stronger relations with the product development function, and the current accounting system mainly enabled relations with the commercially focused procurement department. A record from the field highlights how one of the strategic suppliers had requested performance information:

> Our ISO9000 certification requires us to collect structured feedback from our key customers. Nearly all of our customers provide us with such performance feedback. How can we know exactly how we perform if we do not get these kinds of data from our customers we ask ourselves.

Strategic suppliers were important to HearingCorp, and their request to access performance feedback led to new practices on continuous supplier evaluations. However, because SC-Scorecard happened via ERP and because the transaction records stored in ERP were not able to distinguish much between different types of suppliers, all suppliers were re-presented simply as general "suppliers." For all suppliers, supplier performance was therefore assessed and defined as ability to confirm to product quality requirements, to deliver performance and to order confirmation performance (see Figure 8.1). Following the uniform re-presentation of suppliers, updates on these measures were distributed by e-mail to all suppliers, both innovative/strategic and capacity/commodity suppliers, on monthly intervals.

However, an encounter observed in the field illustrates how a manager at a strategic supplier objected to the re-presentations and suggested component innovations and technology cooperation to be valuable and to be included in the supplier evaluation:

> We do not see ourselves as solely delivering products and components to your factories. Where we create the most value to you is via our component innovations and technology cooperation and early involvement in your product development. Why are these activities not measured as part of your evaluations?

Field notes and transcripts from another encounter highlight how strategic suppliers increasingly expressed dissatisfaction and concern. The lack of their involvement and the performance measures re-presenting their performance were contested. One key account manager at a strategic supplier commented:

> It would have been nice to have been involved somehow in the project that recently defined the parameters for our performance. We have done that with other of our customers and it has worked fine. The measures that currently define our performance are in our opinion much too superficial.
>
> [Field note: The key account manager was visibly angry and highly upset]
>
> Where have these subjects [performance measures] as I call them, come from? Have they come from a meeting within HearingCorp and does it mean that these are the areas that we need to concentrate on? Or do they derive from a book which suggests that one ought to concentrate on these areas?
>
> [Field note: This was stated in a serious tone while he was looking directly into the eyes of HearingCorp's procurement manager]

According to the strategic suppliers, measures inscribed in SC-Scorecard did not make the value created in the relationship with HearingCorp visible, as they focused on relations with procurement rather than with product development. This was a new proposition of what the relationship was all about compared with the one portrayed in SC-Scorecard. Value captured from suppliers in the relationship, as Ulaga (2003) suggests, can be arranged in a number of different value dimensions or relationship value drivers, among these "supplier knowhow." The SC-Scorecard did not provide such information, and to strategic suppliers, this presented itself as a major problem. This assumed them to be capacity or commodity suppliers rather than knowledge suppliers. They therefore insisted on a new form of evaluation based on the

SP-System. One illustration observed as an encounter between a strategic supplier and HearingCorp highlights concerted concern about the origins of numbers—how numbers took their form. A key account manager at a strategic supplier commented anxiously:

> Where are you going to get inputs for the evaluation from? Because most information is going to be subjective. . . . Is it the case that you are going to send out a questionnaire?

And when informed that an internal databased was opened for everyone to supply event-based supplier evaluation information, thus becoming the mechanism from where to generate performance information, the same supplier representative commented rather annoyed:

> Okay, so everybody within the company can actually place a comment on any subject in there at any point in time? Do not take this the wrong way but that's the wrong way to do it, because people putting in comments are not necessarily involved in the areas where they comment and therefore do not know the details on how we are performing in that area. You [the strategic purchaser] are not involved in the technology [cooperation] and therefore do not know the details on how we are performing in that area.

There was a dual concern. The first concern was that the database constructed to collect cases of "positive or negative encounters" with suppliers, and that acted as organisational memory, could not be controlled. Inputs into this database could be registered at any time and by any employee in HearingCorp, and according to suppliers, this presented itself as a problem. No one knew if the person registering was really well informed about supplier capabilities and thus capable of providing input into the performance evaluation. Even the strategic purchaser, the one responsible for the relationship with the strategic supplier, was deemed incompetent in performing the assessment. The second major concern was that the SC-Scorecard did not link strategic suppliers with HearingCorp's product development engineers. The new accounting system, however, would enable strategic suppliers to move its relationship with HearingCorp away from the commercially oriented procurement department to the innovation-focused product development function. Strategic suppliers considered the product development functions as particularly knowledgeable evaluators.

These field encounters illustrate how suppliers were concerned not only with the performance measures of the involved accounting systems but also with the organisational relations they forged when in use. Following supplier objections to the use and potential misuse of the database, where the validity of performance knowledge was put into question, the database was discarded. Instead an annual supplier assessment took place during which all departments in HearingCorp that interacted with the supplier participated, and this included the product development function. Not only did this develop a relationship between strategic suppliers and product development; it also surprisingly strengthened the power of procurement, which made this an opportunity to liaise more with product development. The procurement manager noted that increasing demands for speed of innovation, and new product development required integration of procurement with product development:

> Compared with a few years ago, today we are much more visible to the product development function. But we need to be even more visible to them. Therefore we must continue to find ways through which we can integrate their and our activities.

The procurement manager saw the SP-System as a strategic asset that could relate it to product development, something that the SC-Scorecard had been unable to do. The procedure demanded that the two entities participated in meetings which would align their perceptions of the supplier's performance. This was an opportunity to interact and to build stronger bonds with product development.

Developing a New Language Concerned With Innovation

The new accounting system (SP) transformed the roles and aspirations held by the involved organisational entities. It was a compromise which held the procurement department, the product development function and strategic suppliers in a relationship that required interaction (see Figure 8.3).

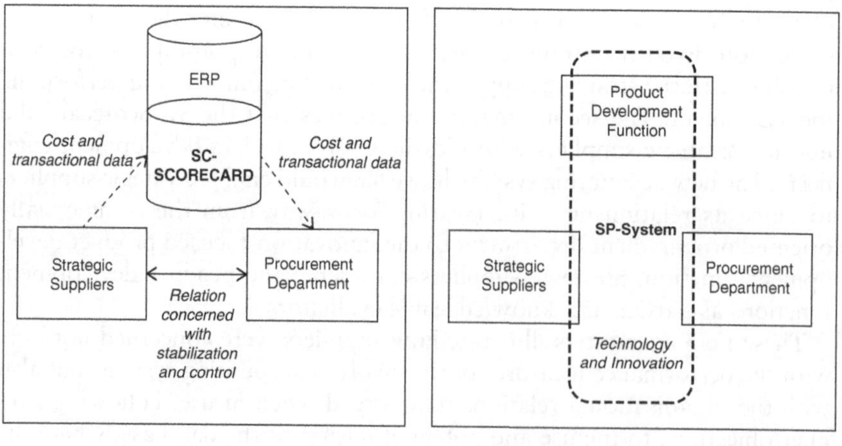

Figure 8.3 From stabilisation and control to a performative space focused on technology and innovation.

It developed a more powerful performable space and made it possible for strategic supplier and the procurement department to connect and communicate much more forcefully with the product development function. The new accounting mechanism thus influenced the relations among HearingCorp's procurement function, product development function and strategic suppliers and helped develop a new language concerned more with technology and innovation than with cost and commercial and transactional performance.

The new subjective assessment procedure fostered compromises. At annual meetings, supplier performance could be explained and negotiated internally across functions and with suppliers. It developed an ability to discuss innovations and improvement. The SP-System thus enabled actors to produce propositions about relations and capabilities the supplier should invest in. The new accounting system also fostered dialogue, leading to propositions on how involved actors should change to foster more value to be captured from suppliers. The relationships among the procurement department, the product development function and strategic suppliers built on an annual assessment process in which incidents could be raised and which led to a conceptualisation of the relationship between HearingCorp and strategic suppliers as one about capability and innovation. Accounting in this situation changed to an entity that was concerned with how suppliers could provide innovations and increased relationship value more than how it performed in the short term. Now HearingCorp did not command accounting; neither did suppliers, it was a co-construction situated between the involved organisations and organisational entities. Accounting was now outside ERP but inside the processes of collaboration which were already established.

Discussion: The Role of Accounting in Developing Inter-organisational Heterarchies

The case of HearingCorp illustrates how accounting is not only a matter of the activities of the focal firm but also of other firms participating in enacting the supply chain relation. It takes advantage of other research which has detailed the role of accounting and governance in relation to the complexities of inter-organisational cooperation about innovation. For example, Håkansson and Lind (2004) details how relations between Ericsson and its suppliers were organised by a complex form of accounting which at its base was structurally fixed and yet at its edges would be supplemented to cater for the precise coordination requirements of the specific relation. Yet the case of HearingCorp also raises an additional and different concern, namely, the more radical one in which accounting is an object between a focal firm and suppliers which is not only enabling of an existing quality of a relation but also—and perhaps more importantly—a mechanism that transforms the relationships between suppliers and the focal firm. This includes the production of new topologies of power, and it includes the production of structurally different, not previously visible, organisational connections between the focal and supplier firms.

First, accounting is an object of interest not only to the focal firm but also to peripheral firms. The peripheral firm may not accept the role ascribed to it by accounting and propose a form of 'counter-accounting'. This happens because accounting is not a representation that copies the world in a miniature picture but a re-presentation which actively engages in editing and formulating relations between firms; it is a 'performable space' (Busco, Quattrone and Riccaboni, 2007; Busco and Quattrone, 2015) which makes it possible to imagine new relations. Accounting provides visibility that drives debate and search; accounting is here both a source of experimentation which makes it possible to make new sense of the world via interpretive flexibility and a source of power which insists on being interpreted and thus problematises the world (Mouritsen and Kreiner, 2016). By doing this, it performs a type of 'symbolic violence' in which it forces participants to speak its language (Oakes, Townley and Cooper, 1998). At least, this is the version of accounting preferred by much research on inter-organisational relations. The case of HearingCorp offers additions to this explanation because here accounting is not able to hold the periphery in its designated space.

Instead, in the case, the periphery raised another voice in an attempt to *become* strategic. That is, suppliers propose new accounting to establish a new role for themselves. This is strategy not in the usual sense in which suppliers are strategic because of the focal firm's strategy. This is strategic in the sense that it is a proposition from the periphery to become strategic around issues and possibilities that the focal firm may not have imagined or envisaged before. This is a role in which suppliers insist that they are more than their established transactions because they have information, knowledge and capabilities that may not be recognised by the focal firm. Transactions point towards a present situation of on-going supply chains action while capabilities points towards the innovation in relations, i.e. innovation in the pattern of interaction between focal firm and suppliers. As the case shows, it is an *advantage for the supplier* to bring its own version of the accounting system forward, and this propose how a different type of accounting could work. It is not enough to be against the present system; it is necessary to bring an alternative: an accounting system has to be challenged by another accounting system. This is a sense in which one type of accounting competes for relevance with a different one (Mouritsen, Hansen and Hansen, 2009). This materialises the possibilities of a new language of the relations between firms. In a sense, this is a trial of strength about the best way to understand the subject matter involved in supply relations. It is by re-presenting the language and visualisation of accounting that new motives and orientations can be developed. (New) Accounting is here a mechanism that challenges (old) accounting and in turn problematises relations. In this sense, accounting re-problematises what the relation is about. In the case of HearingCorp, accounting problematises whether the relation is about subcontracting transactions or of developing something via the relation. This is an innovative movement.

Second, change of accounting is associated with subsequent changes in relations. This is not so surprising; it is more surprising that these changes are as much internal as external. They are even much more in place at the focal firm than at the supplier. This is surprising. For the relation to work 'well', the supplier requested to work with other entities within the focal firm than what was proposed in the original accounting design (Mouritsen, Hansen and Hansen, 2001). This theme is different from the research that shows how accounting (and governance) is supplemented with variation to repair and enable complex, yet stable, relations. The transformation found in HearingCorp disrupts the focal firm so that relations originally related from the procurement department were to be conducted by the research and development (R&D) department. So, new relations form between the focal and the supplier firm. But more also: new relations form between functions within the focal firm. Procurement and R&D suddenly stand in an operative relation as they *together* create the connection to the supplier. This common task also changes the identity and power of the different functions. Procurement and R&D change their relations to each other.

Third the case suggests that interest in innovation adds emphasis to a new object of accounting such as intellectual capital rather that an accounting concerned with coordination of flows. The point about intellectual capital is that it does not coordinate existing worlds but helps develop new worlds (Spinosa, Flores and Dreyfus, 1997). Intellectual capital is concerned with framing competence rather than efficiency (Mouritsen and Larsen, 2005; Mouritsen, Larsen and Bukh, 2001; Mouritsen and Thrane, 2006). It is concerned not with supply relations as such but with the conditions for such relations to become something. This may be implicit in other research on inter-organisational accounting and governance, but the case of HearingCorp notes that this may be a different type of accounting than that normally associated with inter-organisational relations (yet see Mouritsen and Thrane, 2006). It is a radical transformation more than a supplementary addition to the accounting infrastructure because it cannot be found in the typical representation of transactions. It is a new condition of possibility for other things to happen, things that may not even be thought out in the present point in time. Rather than modelling the relation as a coordination task, intellectual capital models the capabilities of possible relevance to other possible worlds, to other possible supply relations. Therefore, intellectual capital is accumulated but with only little orientation to a particular supplier relation. Instead of predicting the future, it develops capabilities for futures to be imagined and discovered. It is a procedure for tinkering with the future more than a mechanism for predicting it.

Such a condition is conducive to innovation. As the case shows, the focal firm could mobilise resources it never knew it had access to, and the supplier firm could mobilise knowledge that would otherwise have been lost 'on hold' and therefore be without consequence. The effect of such intellectual capital accounting is its possible transformative effects on the qualities of relations and *then* on their operational quantities. This is the condition for innovation.

Conclusion

This chapter reflects on the dynamics of supply chain relations and understands accounting as an engine for this. As an engine, accounting provides force or power but does not determine relations. Instead, accounting first is a performable space which has to be made a resource for interpretation. Second, it is also performative since it produces problematisation. This problematisation then becomes the means from which interpretive flexibility emerges. Because of this conditioned character of interpretation, accounting provides power. The case shows how moving from one type of accounting to another changes modes of problematisation. This change makes it possible to engage with new issues and problems.

This change also harks back on the focal firm: here relations between entities are put into question because of the change in modes of problematisation. Therefore, the internal mode of organisation is an effect of the external problematisation of accounting as it is provided by the supplier's intervention. The changes coming out of this produce innovation not because of a direct relationship between new knowledge and innovation but because new accounting forces entities to change even if they may not want to. This is the heterarchical influence that discovers new knowledge and new aspirations that may not be easy to rank but which produce transformations and dynamics in relations. The effects cannot be predicted but emerge as new relational processes.

References

Agndal, H. and Nilsson, U. (2010) 'Different open book accounting practices for different purchasing strategies', *Management Accounting Research*, 21(3), 147–166.

Alenius, E., Lind, J. and Strömsten, T. (2015) 'The role of open book accounting in a supplier network: Creating and managing interdependencies across company boundaries', *Industrial Marketing Management*, 45, 195–206.

Busco, C. and Quattrone, P. (2015) 'Exploring how the balanced scorecard engages and unfolds: Articulating the visual power of accounting inscriptions', *Contemporary Accounting Research*, 32(3), 1236–1262.

Busco, C., Quattrone, P. and Riccaboni, A. (2007) 'Management accounting: Issues in interpreting its nature and change', *Management Accounting Research*, 18(2), 125–149.

Carlsson-Wall, M., Kraus, K. and Lind, J. (2011) 'The interdependencies of intra- and inter-organisational controls and work practices—The case of domestic care of the elderly', *Management Accounting Research*, 22(4), 313–329.

Chua, W. F. and Mahama, H. (2007) 'The effect of network ties on accounting controls in a supply alliance: Field study evidence', *Contemporary Accounting Research*, 24(1), 47–86.

Dekker, H. C. (2016) 'On the boundaries between intrafirm and interfirm management accounting research', *Management Accounting Research*, 31, 86–99.

Frances, J. and Garnsey, E. (1996) 'Supermarkets and suppliers in the United Kingdom: System integration, information and control', *Accounting, Organizations and Society*, 21(6), 591–610.

Håkansson, H. and Lind, J. (2004) 'Accounting and network coordination', *Accounting, Organizations and Society*, 29(1), 51–72.

Håkansson, H. and Lind, J. (2006) 'Accounting in an interorganizational setting', in *Handbooks of management accounting research*. Oxford, UK: Elsevier, pp. 885–902.

Hopwood, A. G. (1996) 'Looking across rather than up and down: On the need to explore the lateral processing of information', *Accounting, Organizations and Society*, 21(6), 589–590.

Jordan, S. and Messner, M. (2012) 'Enabling control and the problem of incomplete performance indicators', *Accounting, Organizations and Society*, 37(8), 544–564.

Kajüter, P. and Kulmala, H. I. (2005) 'Open-book accounting in networks: Potential achievements and reasons for failures', *Management Accounting Research*, 16(2), 179–204.

Kraus, K. and Strömsten, T. (2016) 'Internal/inter-firm control dynamics and power—A case study of the Ericsson-Vodafone relationship', *Management Accounting Research*, 33, 61–72.

Miller, P. B. and Power, M. (2013) 'Accounting, organizing and economizing: Connecting accounting research and organization theory', *Academy of Management Annals*, 7(1), 555–603.

Mouritsen, J., Hansen, A. and Hansen, C. Ø. (2001) 'Inter-organizational controls and organizational competencies: Episodes around target cost management/functional analysis and open book accounting', *Management Accounting Research*, 12(2), 221–244.

Mouritsen, J., Hansen, A. and Hansen, C. Ø. (2009) 'Short and long translations: Management accounting calculations and innovation management', *Accounting, Organizations and Society*, 34(6/7), 738–754.

Mouritsen, J. and Kreiner, K. (2016) 'Accounting, decisions and promises', *Accounting, Organizations and Society*, 49(1), 21–31.

Mouritsen, J. and Larsen, H. T. (2005) 'The 2nd wave of knowledge management: The management control of knowledge resources through intellectual capital information', *Management Accounting Research*, 16(3), 371–394.

Mouritsen, J., Larsen, H. T. and Bukh, P. N. D. (2001) 'Intellectual capital and the "capable firm": Narrating, visualising and numbering for managing knowledge', *Accounting, Organizations and Society*, 26(7–8), 735–762.

Mouritsen, J. and Thrane, S. (2006) 'Accounting, network complementarities and the development of inter-organisational relations', *Accounting, Organizations and Society*, 31(3), 241–275.

Muniesa, F. (2014) *The provoked economy: Economic reality and the performative turn*. New York: Routledge.

Oakes, L., Townley, B. and Cooper, D. J. (1998) 'Business planning as paedagogy: Language and control in a changing institutional field', *Administrative Science Quarterly*, 43(2), 241–275.

Puyou, F., Quattrone, P., McLean, C. and Thrift, N. (2012) *Imagining organizations: Performative imagery in business and beyond*. New York, NY: Routledge.

Quattrone, P. (2015) 'Value in the age of doubt: Accounting as a Maieutic Machine', in M. Kornberger, L. Justesen, A. K. Madsen and J. Mouritsen (eds) *Making things valuable*. Oxford: Oxford University Press, pp. 38–61.

Quattrone, P. and Hopper, T. (2005) 'A "time—Space odyssey": Management control systems in two multinational organisations', *Accounting, Organizations and Society*, 30(7–8), 735–764.

Revellino, S. and Mouritsen, J. (2015) 'Accounting as an engine: The performativity of calculative practices and the dynamics of innovation', *Management Accounting Research*, 28, 31–49.

Seal, W., Berry, A. and Cullen, J. (2004) 'Disembedding the supply chain: Institutionalized reflexivity and inter-firm accounting', *Accounting, Organizations and Society*, 29(1), 73–92.

Spinosa, C., Flores, F. and Dreyfus, H. L. (1997) *Disclosing new worlds: Entrepreneurship, democratic action and the cultivation of solidarity*. Cambridge, MA: MIT Press.

Stark, D. (2009) *The sense of dissonance: Accounts of worth in economic life*. Princeton, NJ: Princeton University Press.

Ulaga, W. (2003) 'Capturing value creation in business relationships: A customer perspective', *Industrial Marketing Management*, 32(8), 677–693.

van der Meer-Kooistra, J. and Scapens, R. W. (2008) 'The governance of lateral relations between and within organisations', *Management Accounting Research*, 19(4), 365–384.

Windolph, M. and Moeller, K. (2012) 'Open-book accounting: Reason for failure of inter-firm cooperation?', *Management Accounting Research*, 23(1), 47–60.

9 Combining Differentiated Knowledge for Innovation across Organizations

The Role of Accounting and Management Controls

Angelo Ditillo and Ariela Caglio

Introduction

The management accounting literature has largely been interested in investigating the inter-organizational relationships between partners that operate along the value chain. The majority of contributions concentrate their attention on upstream vertical (supplier) and, to a lesser extent, downstream vertical (buyer) relations (Caglio & Ditillo, 2008). Much less attention has been dedicated to direct horizontal (industry insider) relations; i.e., competitors; and/or indirect horizontal (industry outsider) relations, i.e., complementors aimed at innovation.[1] This is a critical limitation in the literature given that these forms of collaboration can be characterized by different forms of ownership arrangements (Das & Teng, 1998, 2001), contractual agreements (Grandori & Soda, 1995), and governance structures (Caglio & Ditillo, 2008). Because of these potential differences, it is doubtful that the conclusions reached by extant contributions with reference to other forms of collaboration can be easily and automatically extended to inter-organizational relationships that aim to produce innovative solutions and/or that these conclusions are comprehensive. There may be relevant differences that produce or exacerbate control problems, and there may be control mechanisms that are ineffective because they are detrimental to innovation efforts (Bedford, 2015). Moreover, additional mechanisms may be needed to address specific issues that are unique to these forms of inter-organizational relationships. For example, in innovative initiatives, it may be more problematic to evaluate the effort and contribution of each party to the final output, which makes the issue of how to define the value appropriations of each partner particularly difficult. In addition, given that knowledge resources are provided and jointly used by each party, severe knowledge appropriation concerns may emerge and affect the management of the relationship. At the same time, rules and procedures may introduce constraints that may stifle individuals' creativity, which is functional to developing innovative solutions. Thus, the question arises regarding the suitability of these controls in contexts where idea generation and development represent the core of the relationship. As a result, we currently know very little about the control of horizontal inter-organizational agreements between firms that engage in a joint pursuit of innovation (the only notable exception being van der Meer-Kooistra & Scapens, 2015).[2] In this chapter, we aim to illustrate some specifics of these agreements and explain the role that accounting and, more generally, management controls have in their management.

Innovation Inter-organizational Relations, Management Control, and Accounting[3]

Various studies have maintained that firms decide to activate agreements with other firms to develop innovative solutions because inter-firm relations spur the innovativeness and learning of the organizations involved (e.g., Hagedoorn & Duysters, 2002; Lee, Lee & Pennings, 2001; Feller, Parhankangas, Smeds & Jaatinen, 2013; van der Meer-Kooistra & Scapens, 2015). One key argument for this conclusion is that inter-organizational arrangements are needed to gain power and control over critical resources, which cannot all be internally generated (Cummings, 1984). Despite this advantage, however, inter-organizational agreements oriented towards innovation are characterized by complexities related to exchanging and integrating knowledge and skills to generate innovative solutions and require the mobilization of tacit, non-routine, and highly uncertain knowledge management processes (Anand & Khanna, 2000).

The perspectives adopted so far to study inter-organizational relationships have largely focused on the possibility that firms that develop a relationship have incentives to cheat and free-ride in order to pursue their interests at the expense of the objectives of the collective effort; therefore, it is necessary to apply mechanisms to align their intentions (cooperation and value appropriation problems). Moreover, these perspectives have concentrated on the need for firms in relationships to split the tasks, define the way to perform inter-organizational activities, establish each one's contribution within the relationship, and determine the degree of mutual satisfaction to be achieved. The corresponding interdependencies need coordination and joint actions across organizational boundaries to preserve the match between partners' interfaces (coordination problems) (Dekker, 2004; Caglio & Ditillo, 2008). On the contrary, very little attention has been dedicated to the processes of knowledge generation, integration, and transfer, which are crucial for understanding the management of innovation in inter-organizational relationships. To incorporate these elements into the analysis, we could ask the following question: if we removed conflict from interests and coordination complexity, would we still need controls to manage inter-organizational relationships to innovate (Grandori, 2001)? The answer is complex and multifaceted because we would still need mechanisms that support the management of relevant knowledge and that possess the superior characteristic of allowing access to one another's knowledge but simultaneously avoiding knowledge misappropriation by the counterparts (knowledge appropriation problems) (Caglio & Ditillo, 2008).

These situations have been described in the organizational literature as contexts where the critical problem is governing collective action (Olson, 1965; Grandori, 1997). In these cases, the management of the relationship is complicated by the need to jointly use differentiated knowledge to generate a specific solution—developing a new product or service—thus activating intensive interdependence.[4] In addition, the uncertainty derives not from a high number of actors and activities with their related interconnections but from the inexistence of the knowledge to solve new problems. Control is much more problematic because the collaborating partners do not have reciprocal visibility on inputs or, often, outputs because they lack the specific technical knowledge to interpret them. Thus, adaptation is required to coordinate the collaboration (Grandori, 1997). Moreover, it is necessary to adopt organizational routines and mechanisms that contribute to activating the flow of knowledge from one firm to the other and to integrating different sub-sets of it. These routines and mechanisms consist of, for example, the use of intermediaries to support knowledge transfer. This is possible up to a certain extent where the reciprocal understanding is still occurring. Beyond a certain degree, the focus on designing the interfaces between the various outputs that have to be combined, and the transfer of these outputs replaces the transfer of knowledge in the coordination of the collaboration (Grandori, 2001; Ditillo, 2004; Ditillo, 2012; Ditillo, 2016). In this case, the collaboration is managed through peer-based interaction (Grandori, 1997; Ouchi & Bolton, 1988): information sharing and communication are essential in the management of the relationship (Ditillo, 2016).

While the management and management accounting literature share these preliminary conclusions on the governance of inter-organizational relationships oriented towards innovation, the key issue is related to the specific control mechanisms adopted and to the potential role that accounting may play in these contexts. Looking at existing papers that focus on the possible contribution of accounting to the management of these relationships, one may have the following expectations:

- Some authors have suggested that established accounting methods may play a key role in the formation of relationships during the contractual phase, rather than in its execution (Håkansson & Lind, 2004). Accounting is a key input in estimating the value generated, in evaluating the potential alternative contributions of each party and their financial implications, and in defining the rules for managing value appropriation concerns. It is used in contracts to monitor and report on contingencies or to track contract performance over time (Watts & Zimmerman, 1986; Richardson & Kilfoyle, 2009). Financial numbers define the boundaries for the project, although they could be changed or revised according to specific pre-defined rules if the collaborating parties agree (van der Meer-Kooistra & Scapens, 2015).
- They have also argued that there is a lack of joint accounting systems in collaborations between firms. For example, with reference to

inter-organizational relationships and networks, leveraging on Tomkins' (2001) contribution, Håkansson and Lind (2004) argued that collective accounting information, e.g., inter-organizational budgets and cost behaviour analyses, is not used in the relationship, and Richardson and Kilfoyle (2009) argued that "accounting information was not used to replace market prices to coordinate activities and accounting was not used primarily as a means to reduce opportunism between parties. [. . .] accounting may be reduced or absent in network governance structures" (p. 954). Given the specific nature of innovation inter-organizational relationships, in which contributions (inputs) and intermediate outcomes (outputs) are difficult to observe and assess, the above conclusions are expected to be even stronger, and accounting appears to play only a marginal role.

- It also maintained that the lack of accounting between collaborating partners does not eliminate the need for accounting within the parties. This is because each party could gain by improving the efficiency of its activities independently of the decisions made by other members of the relationship. In fact, if one party could maintain the revenue that could be gained from the inter-organizational relationship while reducing the costs of the solutions proposed with the collaboration, it would retain all the financial gains through operating efficiencies (Richardson & Kilfoyle, 2009). This is more so for innovative activities in which many elements, functionalities, and details of the solutions proposed are subject to design decisions and can therefore be rethought and remodelled in order to minimize costs. In other words, accounting is not about routine activities; rather, it is used to evaluate unique issues—the creation of features in new systems (Håkansson & Lind, 2004).

The Customer Care and Billing System Project: The Case Study[5]

Our empirical analysis is focused on a software development process and, specifically, on a project about the production and customization of existing software for the billing and customer care activities of a mobile operator's telecommunication division.[6] Different companies are involved in the development of this Customer Care and Billing System (CC&BS), as represented in Figure 9.1, which also illustrates the main actors who took part in the project in boundary-spanning roles.

Specifically, the customer is Tel.Co, a start-up GSM operator based in a Middle Eastern country. The other companies are potential competitors, but they work together as complementors on the project. In particular, ITS is the reference for Tel.Co and the focal actor, and it was asked to develop a customized software solution based on the CC&BS standard product provided by RGT. RGT was responsible for making all the kernel changes, and ITS was in charge of customizing the existing version of the CC&BS with

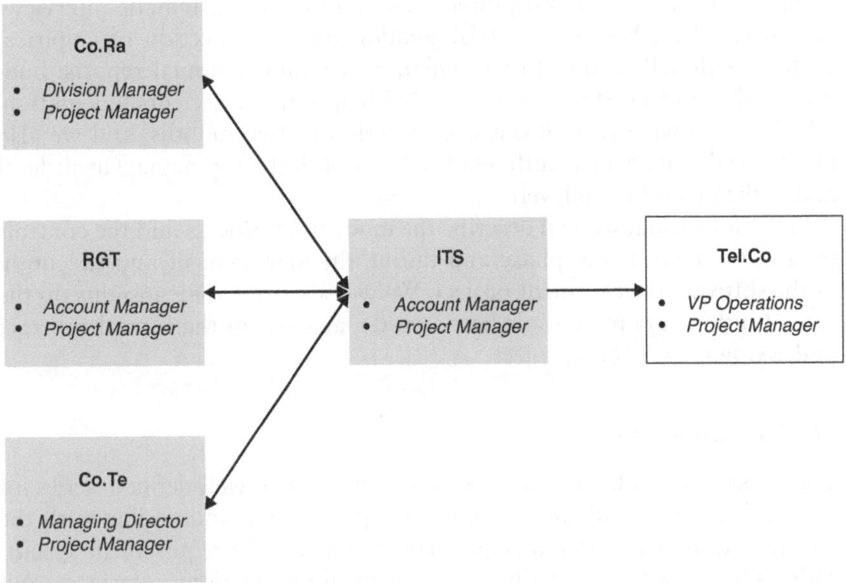

Figure 9.1 The companies involved in the project.

non-kernel modifications developed for Tel.Co. Therefore, ITS had to collaborate with RGT to propose custom modifications based on the requirements of Tel.Co. The innovation content of the project was related to these custom changes, which were defined jointly by the two software companies to redesign the CC&BS interfaces and to introduce specific functionalities in the existing product based on the novel needs of Tel.Co. In this respect, ITS also had to develop new software to allow the product by RGT to interface to a number of external systems employed by Tel.Co. In addition, ITS managed a number of staff, i.e., configuration analysts, from two additional companies: Co.Te, an expert computer support company specialized in customer service, and Co.Ra, a Middle-Eastern information technology services company. This choice was motivated by the fact that the customer was a company based in a Middle Eastern country and was aimed at constraining the project costs as well as at providing the basis for local support for the software product in the long term.

Our unit of analysis is the project, which is characterized by complex interactions at both the intra- and inter-organizational levels among different firms and teams collaborating to develop a new product. It is with reference to the project that ideas are converted into software applications using the differentiated knowledge and competences of different actors in these networked settings. This is also the most useful unit of analysis to understand the ultimate problems of coordination and knowledge integration at both the intra- and inter-organizational levels.

The chief financial officer was the initial contact with the firm. A combination of document analysis, direct observation, and systematic interviewing provided methodological triangulation for the collection of empirical evidence (Modell, 2009). In particular, we examined annual reports, budgets, and reporting statements along with specific project documentation. Observations were carried out over a period of two months, and we also interviewed managers at different levels (at both the top management level and at the project team level).

In the following, we will describe the innovation process and the controls used in the contracting phase and during the management and execution of the software development project. We will also give some insights on the role of different control tools based on the analysis of the formal contract underlying the CC&BS project.

The Innovation Process

The process of software development involved a well-defined series of phases, beginning with the requirement specification and ending with the testing and implementation stages. The first step—the requirement specification phase—served to define the set of required functions, interfaces, and performance outcomes for the software product. The second phase, i.e., the design phase, aimed at detailing the overall hardware-software architecture, the control and data structures, and the data users' manuals and test plans. The software development phase consisted of the actual development of the lines of code and their transformation into an executable programme. The testing and implementation phases aimed to prove that the software was in line with the customer's requirements.

ITS and RGT were involved together from the very first phases, as RGT made all the kernel changes to the product, while ITS made all the non-kernel changes. Co.Te also participated in the development of the system and focused on the payment part. Co.Ra contributed to the project especially in the last phases, during the delivery, testing, and implementation of the new product, when all the pieces of the software developed by the other three companies had to be put together.

At the beginning, it was established that the project had to be finished by the end of October of the same year. However, given all the requirements presented by the customer, it was not possible to meet the initial deadline. To solve time problems, the delivery strategy used by ITS was to provide the deliverables over three sub-phases to best meet Tel.Co's needs. First, a basic product was delivered; it consisted only of minimum customer administration and network interface functionality, and it intended to support Tel.Co's friendly user trial. This was followed by a system comprising the essential functionalities necessary to support live operations. Finally, the remaining software elements were supplied in a third release. The strategy adopted for the project implementation was based on ITS's previous experience in

CC&BS implementations. It is important to mention that although software development processes are described as apparently linear, they are iterative in nature (Ditillo, 2004, 2012).

The most crucial aspects of the project were inter-firm interdependencies and tight time constraints. To manage such constraints, ITS's project manager and the client's project manager met regularly on a weekly basis via telephone conference calls and on a bi-monthly basis in person. At these meetings, the ITS project manager updated the Tel.Co project manager on the status of the project, and the client project manager updated the ITS project manager on the status of its performance with regard to the client obligations. The two project managers jointly set the agenda of the bi-monthly meetings a week ahead of each meeting, and they agreed on the agenda for the weekly meetings before the meetings. The ITS project manager recorded the meetings and issued a report no later than two days after each meeting. One face-to-face meeting each month was also held to review the monthly progress report. These meetings were attended by the two project managers and a representative of the line management of both ITS and Tel.Co.

To solve potential tensions, the technical director of ITS was also involved in and had a direct responsibility for this project, which was considered very large and quite high risk for ITS. Interestingly, he described the software development process as "conceptual innovation and then a non-innovative process control to create the solution." He also added that one thing they were famous for was their innovative approach: "a unique selling point for [ITS] is our ability to create from nothing a system which reacts to the client's needs." As a way to prevent problems, he established a peer review system, whose aim was to "bring in some seasoned people to talk with the line of business, to talk with the sales community, who typically understand the aspirations of the customer most closely and the project, and the technical community, who actually are going to do it and make sure we all understand what the customer is trying to achieve, the nature of the contract we have." He also explained that they collocated the different teams in the same place so that there was a lot of informal communication: "the tension that they can have in terms of business delivery [. . .] is always a difficult one, but we encourage people to get together regularly to have an appraisal, a review."

The Contracting Phase

The most important tools used in the contracting phase of the project are the project plan, the GANTT chart, and the Quotation Management Summary (QMS). These tools, as illustrated in the following, have a complementary role.

The *project plan* defines the general framework for the project. It aims at describing what must be done to achieve the project objectives and puts the corresponding activities into context. First, the project plan includes a *description of the project* that outlines the status of the project plan (e.g., whether it is definitive or not, when the definitive version must be issued) and some related information (e.g., the timetable for all of the documents that must be issued). Second, it comprises the *specific objectives* of the project, its *success factors*, and a 'risk register' covering the activities and deliverables of the project and the constraints under which the project must operate. The risk register defines the likelihood of occurrence of each risk, the impact on the overall schedule, and time and cost implications. It also describes the containment actions to be taken to avoid these risks as well as the contingency plans should the risks occur. Project risks are reviewed on a regular basis, at least monthly, with the client project manager. The tool for implementing this review is the project status report (which will be described in the following). Risks become inactive over time, and new risks are added to the list as they are identified. Third, the project plan shows the *deliverables* with the corresponding *deadlines*, what has to be executed first, and the *interdependencies* between the activities of the project. The last are monitored and reported on a regular basis (weekly) through a project status report for the client project manager and ITS line management. Fourth, the project plan carefully describes the overall approach to delivering the CC&BS, which is a *lifecycle approach* consisting of the following phases:

- Planning phase: This phase entails the production of a detailed project plan, a quality plan and a documentation plan.
- Environmental set-up phase: The major activities in this phase occur early in the project lifecycle to permit development and site installations to begin.
- Analysis phase: The primary objective of this phase is to capture the client's specific requirements with respect to the interfaces and customizations to be described in the contract. This phase is complete when the client agrees with the specifications.
- Design phase: This phase aims at translating the client's specifications into technical specifications, describing the design activities to be implemented to satisfy the functional requirements.
- Actual development phase: The objective of this phase is to make the modifications to the existing product based on the technical specifications. This phase is complete when the associated code and unit test specifications are reviewed and signed off internally and when all the required modifications have been coded and unit tested.
- System test phase: The approach to system test is based on progressively integrating the codes required for the modifications into the core product. It is meant to validate the integrity of data flows through the systems and to ensure that defects or features of the core product are identified and appropriate action is taken.
- Integration phase: The integration testing of interfaces to external systems is carried out at the customer's office by using live interfaces to external systems. This validates the end-to-end flows of data.

- Acceptance phase: An acceptance test plan is generated by defining the detailed approach for performing the acceptance tests. The aim of this phase is to ensure the client that the system is able to support its business processes and operations in addition to the basic purpose of demonstrating compliance with its specification.
- Configuration phase: This phase begins early in the project to facilitate the development of a suitable agreed configuration in time for the first delivery of the product.
- Training phase: This phase runs through the earlier stages of the project to deliver training timed to support the first delivery of the product.

The project plan also defines and illustrates the structure of the project team, which is organized as shown in Figure 9.2. The chart also highlights the presence of actors in charge of integration tasks along the different phases of the project (i.e., system test manager, integration manager, acceptance test manager).

The *GANTT chart* is used for coordination purposes. It is linked to the project plan as it reflects and better specifies the activities of the project lifecycle. This chart is used to keep under control the times and deadlines of the different tasks as well as the completion of the project milestones. The GANTT chart fosters integration within the project by defining *when* the different actors will have to participate in the project and *which contributions* they are expected to deliver in the development of the final solution. As explained by the delivery manager of the CC&BS project, the GANTT chart is a more detailed translation of the project plan in terms of time, phases, and actors, and it is prepared by the project manager. The time estimates for the different activities are the result of past experience on previous projects and of a gap analysis based on the customization requirements defined by Tel.Co. In the work breakdown structure of the GANTT, the following information is included: code, task name, man days, start, finish, % of work done, to go, and resources (names of workers).

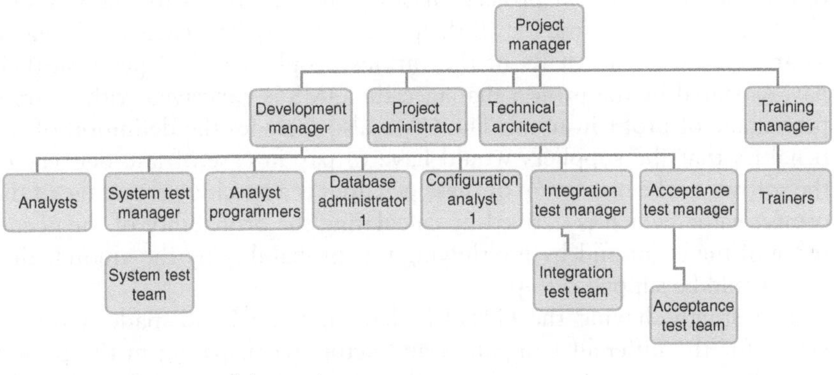

Figure 9.2 Structure of the project team.

This information is updated continuously in accordance with the modifications that occur in the project. In fact, every week, the developers must prepare a time sheet, and the delivery manager produces a report that includes the following items: task, place resource initials, primary name, work breakdown structure, to date/days, days this week, new forecast end date, to go, and last week to go.

This information not only keeps the project plan updated but also allows the delivery manager to analyse all the activities of the teams involved in the project as well as manage the resulting interdependencies. Basically, the delivery manager monitors time. In his words, the project is "time critical" because the various phases are executed in parallel by the different actors, and there are many interdependencies among the different firms involved in the project. Through the comparison of the GANTT chart and the weekly reports, it is always possible to understand who is responsible for the mistakes and the delays in the project. The results of the different actors participating in the software development are thus observable. In this sense, having specified the type and timing of the involvement of the different teams, it is not necessary to exchange any additional information regarding the contents of the specific activities and tasks required from them; i.e., it is not necessary to exchange and share knowledge-specific information. Information about time becomes the common denominator for interaction and the only type of information needed to support the software development process.

Together with the GANTT chart, the QMS sets the foundation for applying output controls to the project. The QMS, which is a sort of financial plan that describes the different elements that determine the price and includes other accounting-based information, provides a framework that can be used at a later stage to verify that the contributions to the project of all the counterparts are in line with expectations. The QMS is based on different mark-ups for the various elements of price: a mark-up for labour, a mark-up for materials, and a mark-up for other expenses. Travel expenses are billed periodically to the client. The foundation of the QMS is represented by the unit cost rate (UCR), which is applied to the hours charged to the client throughout the different project phases (hence the link with the GANTT chart, specifying the time for all the project phases). The UCR is calculated as an average of the UCRs of the various people, which depend on their pay. As stated by the project manager, the QMS is conceived with a target percentage of profit in mind. The QMS also includes the definition of the penalties that the suppliers would have to pay in case of late delivery of the software. The maximum of these penalties is a specific percentage of the project value, which is derived by calculating the probability of the occurrence of the event and by multiplying this probability by the amount that they would be supposed to pay.

Interestingly, having the GANTT chart and the QMS made it unnecessary for the different companies and actors participating in the project to exchange information regarding the contents of the specific tasks. The project was not where the actors integrated their respective knowledge and competences but was rather a background structure to make sure that their actions were coordinated (through the GANTT chart) and that the outcome was in line with their contributions (through the QSM).

The Project Execution Phase

During the project execution phase, the most important coordination and integration tools or levers used are the following:

- *Routine, formal meetings*: The acceptance test manager talks to the project team every day: "I find what they have been doing and if they have any problems, questions, technical. . . . I arrange for either find themselves the answer or I find the answer for them." In his words, he knows what is happening on a day-by-day basis during the acceptance test phase: "We have regular meetings, and I think every Tuesday, the progress is reported back, and the project manager or the delivery manager would be present." These routine meetings are presented as a strength of the project management philosophy at ITS: the acceptance test manager maintains that if team members have a problem, "they tell me immediately . . . so that we can solve it." Some people from Tel. Co are also involved in these formal meetings because the aim of the acceptance test and of the formal meetings is to prove that what ITS has delivered works and matches with what Tel.Co has required. In fact, as agreed in the contract, Tel.Co pays ITS after signing the acceptance test. Given that there are frequent formal meetings involving all the relevant actors on the project, for the acceptance test activity coordination, no additional formal reports are needed. In addition, during this phase, there is a clear link with the project plan (the GANTT chart), based on which it is possible to define a work breakdown structure for all the people involved in the acceptance tests. In fact, all the members of the development team are assigned work packages. The due dates are based on the plan that has been defined in the GANTT for the acceptance testing so that the acceptance test manager can rely on this chart to split the activity into the packages and efforts to be delegated to different team members. In defining the breakdown structure, there is a continuous interaction with the developers, as the acceptance test manager verifies with them whether the work packages and the due dates are realistic. In the end, splitting the acceptance testing activity into small tasks makes it possible for all the people involved in the project, at both intra- and inter-organizational levels, to always identify who is responsible for each work activity and to track the progress within each work package. In this way, "you can see how far you have got . . . and if something has to be delayed or you think it will be delayed, and maybe you must work harder."

- *Procedures and rule-based tools*: During the acceptance test phase, an acceptance test design document is produced for each of the release phases that describes the individual acceptance tests. This constitutes the basis for the acceptance test specifications, which are the formal acceptance rules for the system. The primary objective of the acceptance test is to demonstrate to the client that the system meets its specifications and is thus ready to go live. The result of the acceptance tests is measured against an agreed set of acceptance criteria to determine whether it is possible to proceed to the next phase of the project. According to the rules, site acceptance testing is complete when all criteria, as defined in the acceptance test plan, have been satisfied or the time limit for testing, as defined in the contract, has been reached. During the System test phase, there are strict pre-defined rules and procedures. For each test undertaken, the activities are recorded in a *spread sheet* that includes the following information: the name of the test, when it started, when it was completed, if it failed, and the number of errors found. There is also a daily monitoring of the errors, which are categorized in terms of the degree of importance. The tracking and statistics of tests and errors are communicated to the team in 15-minute daily meetings, in which both testers and developers participate. A daily report of outstanding issues and actions taken is prepared and shared through these meetings.
- *Reporting tools:* The *project status report* is the main reporting document used during project execution. It is a report prepared by the project manager to transfer information about the progress of the project's activities to all the involved actors. It is written in two different forms, one for the client and another for ITS. The former does not include all the detailed information linked to the way in which the project is actually managed, but apart from that, the two versions are quite similar. In the first part of the project status report, the project manager includes a general overview with the specifications of the exceptions to the plan, the major issues and risks (a detail of this is included in the risk register), the matters needing management action or awareness, the client status, and the contract status. This is usually written in a discursive, descriptive way. The project status report also includes other, more quantitative financial reports, such as the *financial status report*, which takes into consideration all the accounting and financial aspects of the project. It includes details about the contract price, the provisions, the estimated cost, the billings, and the payments. This is one of the most important documents for the project manager and is a means of control and communication for ITS, as it also presents the contract margin percentage, calculated as a ratio between the contract price and the total costs. The project status report also incorporates some other quantitative reports, such as the financial trend chart, the cash flow chart and the ledger reconciliation form. The last helps in reconciling the information collected at the project level with that of ITS UK.

Some Insights from the Formal Contract

The contract clearly states that ITS shall establish a *project plan* covering all scheduled activities to be accomplished by the project. This plan will be shared with the client and used as a basis for controlling and monitoring progress on the project. The plan will be updated following significant changes in the project, and progress against the plan will be reported monthly in the monthly status report to be submitted to the client.

The contract also specifies that ITS will issue a *monthly status report* covering at a minimum the following topics:

- overall status relative to schedule;
- objectives accomplished;
- risk management status;
- potential delays that could affect the schedule by at least two weeks and plans to get back on schedule;
- objectives planned for the next month; and
- updated action items list.

At the same time, the client will issue a monthly status report advising ITS of its progress in performing the client obligations.

It is also formally stated in the contract that ITS's project manager and the client's project manager shall *meet regularly* on a weekly basis via conference calls and on a bi-monthly basis in person. During these meetings, the ITS project manager will update the client project manager on the status of the project, and the client project manager will update the ITS project manager on the status of its performance in terms of the client obligations.

In addition, the contract is used to formally identify some of the most important characteristics of the controls to be used to coordinate the activities of the project at both the intra- and inter-organizational levels. It is especially detailed in outlining the features and aims of the *project plan*. In particular, the contract specifies that the project plan will define the project deliverables, the work breakdown structure for the project, the project risk register, and the project organization. It will be supported by a GANTT chart, in which the work breakdown structure will specify the project lifecycle and the individual phases of the project, including the inputs and outputs for each phase.

The contract also indicates the use of other control levers:

- the quality plan, defining the standards to be adopted in the project and the approval processes to be followed;
- the configuration plan, detailing the work to be done to gather relevant information from the client and to input this into the BSCS to define the system configuration for the client's operational use;
- the training plan, describing the courses to be developed and delivered to the client's staff (in terms of course objectives, syllabus, course duration,

number of trainees, training material to be provided, and equipment and facilities required from the client); and

- the acceptance test plan, indicating the approach and procedures (in terms of test specifications, timetable, responsibilities).

Discussion

Innovation is often achieved by means of the combinations of existing knowledge belonging to different organizations. Collaborating firms complement their own knowledge endowments with those possessed by their partners to introduce new solutions on the market. To this end, the knowledge of each collaborating entity should be incorporated into the joint project. This incorporation, however, can be problematic and can be carried out in many different ways, by means of processes of socialization, externalization, internalization, and combination (Nonaka & Takeuchi, 1995). Different control mechanisms can be utilized to support these processes. To date, the literature has focused to a great extent on the organizational economics and organizational theory variables to identify the control mechanisms that are most suitable to the various inter-organizational relationships. However, when the collaboration between firms is about innovation, one important variable, which has been neglected so far but appears to play a key role in this choice, is the type of knowledge that is combined by partner organizations. In the case analysed, the collaborating parties provide knowledge that is characterized by differences in technical specialties and, correspondingly, different cognitive orientations. These are reflected in differences in terms of language, the perception of relevant information in the frameworks and practices used, and the focus on various types of results. Therefore, our case illustrates an inter-organizational relationship characterized by knowledge differentiation, which is expected to generate problems in communication and in the evaluation of decisions and events (Grandori, 2001; Ditillo, 2012). Evidence shows that these relationships are managed by means of a high level of formalization of the interaction between the parties. In particular, first, the parties focus on output control so that they avoid the exchange of knowledge that the counterparts would find difficult to understand and apply. Parties share the outputs after specifying in advance the interfaces that allow the combination of each of their contributions and then converge gradually to a final solution. In our case, the QMS sets the foundation for result controls within the project. Being a financial plan and describing all the different elements that determine the final price, it provides a framework to translate the contributions of all the counterparts to the project into a common language, i.e., accounting information, and to verify that it is in line with expectations. The financial status report is then used to continuously monitor and communicate all the accounting and financial aspects of the project (price, provisions, costs, billings, and payments). Second, because of the difficulties of transferring knowledge, the interaction between parties cannot be left to intermediaries to support exchanges; rather, it requires face-to-face discussions incorporated in systematic and regular formal meetings between the relevant individuals of the collaborating parties. For example, during the acceptance test phase, which is particularly delicate in terms of knowledge transfer, frequent formal meetings involving all the relevant actors on the project are used for the acceptance test activities' coordination and control. These meetings are also used for identifying the work breakdown structure: there is a nonstop interaction with the developers, as the acceptance test manager verifies with them whether the work packages and the due dates are realistic. The case also suggests that it is important to define various formal teams that have related roles and accountabilities and take care of managing and monitoring the different phases of the product development, as illustrated in Figure 9.1. Third, one important outcome measure is represented by project completion time, which is a central dimension to monitor the effectiveness of joint solution development. This is because "product development time captures both the benefits and costs of sharing knowledge" across organizations (Hansen, 1999). Time is then the key aspect to achieve the coordination of activities ex-ante, and it is a core aspect of performance evaluation ex-post. For example, a GANTT chart is developed for coordination purposes. It is linked to the project plan, as it reflects and better specifies the activities of the project lifecycle, and it is used to keep under control the times and deadlines of the different tasks as well as the completion of the project milestones. The GANTT chart fosters integration within the project by defining when the different actors will have to participate in the project and which contributions they are expected to deliver for the development of the final solution. Fourth, for these reasons, contracts and formal procedures represent key mechanisms to regulate transactions. Contracts define technical specifications of intermediate and final outputs that each party have to produce as well as the interfaces to guarantee an effective integration with those of the counterparts. However, these interfaces are defined not as precise expectations of what has to be achieved but rather as acceptance criteria that guarantee the sufficient level of flexibility that innovation implies. By analysing the contract, we found that it represents a crucial means to support and manage the relationships at both intra- and at inter-organizational levels, as it defines the obligations, in terms of communication and reporting, of the different suppliers and teams participating in the project and of the client. We also understood that there are fundamental links with the control levers and tools described in the previous sections. Finally, accounting plays a key role in the contract phase to define ex-ante the criteria to manage value appropriation concerns, through the QMS and the financial status report. In this respect, time is the key dimension to translate individuals' contributions and activities into accounting-based results, which are essential for pricing decisions, estimating each party's contribution, and sharing the value generated. Moreover, with the 'risk register', accounting also plays a fundamental role in the execution phase in risk management, given that it allows for estimating the financial implications of unexpected contingencies, with the related impact in terms of value appropriation between parties.

Conclusions

This study has focused on the control mechanisms adopted by firms that collaborate on innovative activities. It has noted that traditional variables used to explain the adoption of inter-organizational controls (i.e., uncertainty, asset specificity, interdependence) are not sufficient to understand control configurations in innovation partnerships. These variables need to be complemented by another key variable, i.e., the characteristics of the knowledge provided by the parties involved in innovation. Our contribution and case study concentrate on one specific case, that in which the knowledge provided by the different parties is characterized by technical differentiation. One important distinctive aspect of our findings is that the interaction between the partner firms in such a case is characterized by a high level of formalization. Contracts, articulated inter-organizational charts, formal procedures, and accounting performance measures based on time represent key elements of management control systems. These conclusions contrast the achievements reported in extant literature on how to manage innovation activities in intra- and inter-firm contexts. Existing contributions on inter-firm agreements aimed at innovation, in fact, have tended to emphasize more the informal dimension of control by means of social peer-based interaction (Grandori, 1997; Ouchi & Bolton, 1988) as well as information sharing and intensive communication among the parties (Ditillo, 2016). Our results show a different picture and recall the importance of formal management control systems, which are not detrimental to innovation but rather are tools to create a space in which to orient innovation endeavours.

With this contribution, we hope that our study may represent a stimulus for future investigations on alternative forms of collaboration that are focused on innovation, based on different features of the knowledge provided by the different parties and characterized by various degrees of differentiation and uncertainty (Ditillo, 2012).

Notes

1. For this classification of inter-organizational agreements, see De Wit and Meyer (2010). According to these authors, upstream vertical (supplier) relations are relationships between a firm and the providers of production factors such as land, capital, materials, labour, and technology; downstream vertical (buyer) relations are relationships a firm has with its clients, i.e., actual users of the product or services or intermediaries trading the output; direct horizontal (industry insider) relations are relationships between a firm and other industry incumbents, i.e., competitors that produce similar goods or services; indirect horizontal (industry outsider) relations are relationships between a firm and a company outside the

industry, producers of complementary goods or services (e.g., hardware manufacturers with software developers).

2. There are, however, contributions that have focused on accounting and innovation (e.g., Davila and Oyon, 2009; Revellino and Mouritsen, 2009; Christner and Strömsten, 2015). Others have concentrated on horizontal relationships between competitors (e.g., Mouritsen and Thrane, 2006); still others have studied upstream and downstream vertical relations oriented towards innovation (e.g., Revellino and Mouritsen, 2015; Carlsson-Wall and Kraus, 2015).
3. Management accounting systems refer to the systematic use of practices that focus on outputs defined in monetary terms to achieve specific goals. Management control systems represent a broader concept that encompasses management accounting systems and also other controls, such as clan controls and informal personal and social controls (Chenhall, 2003).
4. Intensive interdependence occurs in cases of joint application of differentiated professional know-how to a common problem or transformation process, as exemplified by a medical team in a surgical intervention (Thompson, 1967; Grandori, 1997).
5. The case has been anonymized for confidentiality reasons.
6. See Ditillo 2008 and 2012. This case study has been re-analyzed more recently with the aim of teasing out novel insights on the role of accounting and management controls in innovation across organizations.

References

Anand, B. N., & Khanna, T. (2000). Do firms learn to create value? The case of alliances. *Strategic Management Journal*, *21*(3), 295–315.

Caglio, A., & Ditillo, A. (2008). A review and discussion of management control in inter-firm relationships: Achievements and future directions. *Accounting, Organizations and Society*, *33*(7), 865–898.

Carlsson-Wall, M., & Kraus, K. (2015). Opening the black box of the role of accounting practices in the fuzzy front-end of product innovation. *Industrial Marketing Management*, *45*, 184–194.

Chenhall, R. H. (2003). Management control systems design within its organizational context: Findings from contingency-based research and directions for the future. *Accounting, Organizations and Society*, *28*(2), 127–168.

Christner, C. H., & Strömsten, T. (2015). Scientists, venture capitalists and the stock exchange: The mediating role of accounting in product innovation. *Management Accounting Research*, *28*, 50–67.

Cummings, T. G. (1984). Transorganizational development. In B. M. Staw & L. L. Cummings (Eds.), *Research in organizational behavior 6* (pp. 367–422). Greenwich, CT: JAI-Press.

Das, T. K., & Teng, B. S. (1998). Between trust and control: Developing confidence in partner cooperation in alliances. *Academy of Management Review*, *23*(3), 491–512.

Das, T. K., & Teng, B. S. (2001). Trust, control, and risk in strategic alliances: An integrated framework. *Organization Studies*, *22*(2), 251–283.

Davila, A., & Oyon, D. (2009). Introduction to the special section on accounting, innovation and entrepreneurship. *European Accounting Review*, *18*(2), 277–280.

Dekker, H. C. (2004). Control of inter-organizational relationships: Evidence on appropriation concerns and coordination requirements. *Accounting, Organizations and Society*, *29*(1), 27–49.

De Wit, B., & Meyer, R. (2010). *Strategy: Process, content, context*. Cheriton House, North Way, Andover, UK: Cengage Learning EMEA.
Ditillo, A. (2004). Dealing with uncertainty in knowledge-intensive firms: The role of management control systems as knowledge integration mechanisms. *Accounting, Organizations and Society*, *29*(3), 401–421.
Ditillo, A. (2012). Designing management control systems to foster knowledge transfer in knowledge-intensive firms: A network-based approach. *European Accounting Review*, *21*(3), 425–450.
Ditillo, A. (2016). Discussion of Collaborative performance management in interfirm relationships. *Journal of Management Accounting Research*, *28*(3), 49–54.
Feller, J., Parhankangas, A., Smeds, R., & Jaatinen, M. (2013). How companies learn to collaborate: Emergence of improved inter-organizational processes in R&D alliances. *Organization Studies*, *34*(3), 313–343.
Grandori, A. (1997). An organizational assessment of interfirm coordination modes. *Organization Studies*, *18*(6), 897–925.
Grandori, A. (2001). Neither hierarchy nor identity: Knowledge-governance mechanisms and the theory of the firm. *Journal of Management and Governance*, *5*(3–4), 381–399.
Grandori, A., & Soda, G. (1995). Inter-firm networks: Antecedents, mechanisms and forms. *Organization Studies*, *16*(2), 183–214.
Hagedoorn, J., & Duysters, G. (2002). External sources of innovative capabilities: The preference for strategic alliances or mergers and acquisitions. *Journal of Management Studies*, *39*, 167–188.
Håkansson, H., & Lind, J. (2004). Accounting and network coordination. *Accounting, Organizations and Society*, *29*(1), 51–72.
Hansen, M. T. (1999). The search-transfer problem: The role of weak ties in sharing knowledge across organization subunits. Administrative Science Quarterly, 44, 82–111.
Lee, C., Lee, K., & Pennings, J. M. (2001). Internal capabilities, external networks, and performance: A study on technology-based ventures. *Strategic Management Journal*, *22*(6–7), 615–640.
Modell, S. (2009). In defence of triangulation: A critical realist approach to mixed methods research in management accounting. *Management Accounting Research*, *20*(3), 208–221.
Mouritsen, J., & Thrane, S. (2006). Accounting, network complementarities and the development of inter-organisational relations. *Accounting, Organizations and Society*, *31*(3), 241–275.
Nonaka, I., & Takeuchi, H. (1995). *The knowledge-creating company: How Japanese companies create the dynamics of innovation*. Oxford: Oxford University Press.
Olson, M. (1965). *The logic of collective action: Public goods and the theory of groups*. Cambridge, MA: Harvard University Press.
Ouchi, W. G., & Bolton, M. K. (1988). The logic of joint research and development. *California Management Review*, *30*(3), 9–33.
Revellino, S., & Mouritsen, J. (2009). The multiplicity of controls and the making of innovation. *European Accounting Review*, *18*(2), 341–369.
Revellino, S., & Mouritsen, J. (2015). Accounting as an engine: The performativity of calculative practices and the dynamics of innovation. *Management Accounting Research*, *28*, 31–49.

Richardson, A. J., & Kilfoyle, E. (2009). Accounting in markets, hierarchies and networks: The role of accounting in the transnational governance of postal transactions. *Accounting, Organizations and Society*, *34*(8), 939–956.

Thompson, J. D. (1967). *Organizations in action: Social science bases of administrative theory*. Piscataway, NJ: Transaction Publishers.

Tomkins, C. (2001). Interdependencies, trust and information in relationships, alliances and networks. *Accounting, Organizations and Society*, *26*(2), 161–191.

van der Meer-Kooistra, J., & Scapens, R. W. (2015). Governing product co-development projects: The role of minimal structures. *Management Accounting Research*, *28*, 68–91.

Watts, R. L., & Zimmerman J. L. (1986). *Positive ccounting Theory*. Upper Saddle River, NJ: Prentice-Hall.

10 Supplier-Initiated Open Book Accounting

Using Accounting Information to Initiate Changes in a Services Supply Chain

Sander van Triest and Jacco Blom

Introduction

In this chapter, we present a case of a supplier that initiated an open book accounting arrangement with its largest buyer to enact changes in the relationship. The supplier delivered bread and pastry products to its buyers, who operate restaurants and eating facilities. Logistics services were a key part of the supplier offerings: the supplier offered over 500 different products of which 70% were sourced from third-party suppliers to some 2,000 customer locations, and since food has a limited shelf life, these locations needed to be serviced multiple times per week. The supplier offered to open its books to its major buyer, a catering firm which managed restaurant locations for its clients. The open book process led to a more intensive relationship, whereby the buyer agreed to adaptations in its processes to achieve savings in the logistics costs. Furthermore, the buyer and the supplier cooperated in the development of new service offerings for the customers of the buyer's clients. The returns from the relationship improved for both parties: the buyer achieved savings through lower purchase prices and reduced logistics costs, while the supplier obtained efficiency gains on increased transaction volumes.

We analyze this case to understand the role of the open book information in changing the relationship and to understand why the supplier chose this specific approach to get the buyer to accept changes in the relationship activities. To do so, we first briefly discuss the literature on open book accounting and on services, before describing the case and proceeding with the discussion.

Theoretical Perspectives

Open Book Accounting, Power and Trust

Open book accounting refers to the exchange of proprietary cost information in an interorganizational relationship (Caglio and Ditillo, 2012). The literature identifies three mechanisms through which open book information may be used in relationships. First, the information can be used for interorganizational cost management: optimizing production activities over the whole buyer–supplier relationship, which may include adjustment of activities at the supplier in the product development stage or by changing existing production activities (Cooper and Slagmulder, 2004; Dubois, 2003). Second, the buyer can help the supplier realize lower raw material costs by offering support in the supplier's selection of second-tier suppliers as well as in its price negotiations with the second-tier suppliers (Romano and Formentini, 2012). Third, the buyer can use the open book information to pressure the supplier into accepting lower prices, either directly (Free, 2008; Romano and Formentini, 2012) or by using it in its relations with other suppliers to press for price reductions there, which undercuts the competitive position of the supplier in the open book relationship (Cooper and Yoshikawa, 1994; Alenius, Lind and Strömsten, 2015).

Empirical results from the literature suggest that the benefits of open book accounting accrue mainly to the buyer (Windolph and Möller, 2012: 57), and the initiative to implement open book accounting almost always arises with the buyer. Typically, the buyer is the more powerful party in the open book relationships described in the literature. Within a supplier–buyer relationship, power arises from the relative importance of the relationship volume to each party's activities, from the availability of other suppliers or buyers as a source of relationship volume, from contractual arrangements, and from relationship-specific investments (Milgrom and Roberts, 1992). In a transaction-oriented environment, if a buyer represents a larger share of supplier sales and the supplier's offerings can also be obtained from other parties, the buyer will be more powerful (Provan and Gassenheimer, 1994). By opening up the books, the supplier reduces the information asymmetry to the benefit of the buyer, giving the buyer the opportunity to use this information in negotiating for lower prices, or passing the information on to other suppliers to erode the focal supplier's competitive position. Thus, all formal agreements around open book accounting discussed in the literature help to protect the supplier's position: a target profitability for the supplier, rules for the sharing of cost savings, or agreements on expected volumes together with a compensation mechanism for a shortfall in volume (Dekker, 2003; Kajüter and Kulmala, 2005; Agndal and Nilsson, 2008).

Furthermore, the literature suggests that successful open book accounting requires the supplier to have substantial goodwill trust in the buyer in order to open its books: the supplier has to believe that the buyer will not use the information from the open book process to demand even lower prices (Carr and Ng, 1995: 360; Mouritsen, Hansen and Hansen, 2001: 225; Tomkins, 2001: 182; Dekker, 2003: 22; Kajüter and Kulmala, 2005: 200; Agndal and Nilsson, 2008: 164; Windolph and Möller, 2012: 58). Trust involves expectations with respect to future behavior of the other, trusted party. These expectations are based on the trusted party's trustworthiness (Mayer, Davis and Schoorman, 1995). The literature identifies two sources of trustworthiness: a calculative and a relational source (Poppo, Zhou and Li, 2016). If a party's trustworthiness arises from a calculative source, the trusting party believes that it is in the other party's self-interest to be trustworthy: the trusting party believes that the negative consequences of behaving opportunistically by the other party are larger than the potential benefits for this other party. Calculative trust is forward-looking, involving an ongoing assessment by the trusting party of whether it pays to cooperate for the trusted party (Poppo et al., 2016). On the other hand, if a party's trustworthiness is based on relational sources, this means the trusting party expects that the other party will act according to behavioral norms regardless of economic incentives (e.g., Coletti, Sedatole and Towry, 2005). Relational trustworthiness arises from shared values which have been shown to hold in past interactions: it is the result of past behavior (Poppo et al., 2016).

Services and Innovation

There is no universally accepted definition of services. As an indication, van der Valk and Axelsson (2015) identify 50 classifications of services within the purchasing literature alone. However, a common theme in the literature is that services involve supplier activities in addition to tangible products. As a result, several characteristics can be identified that are more applicable to services than to manufactured goods and that impact the management of services and the relationship with the customer purchasing the service (Subramony and Pugh, 2015). For example, since services involve supplier activities, they have an intangible component, which implies that they can only be evaluated completely by the customer after purchasing and consuming the service. This intangible component likewise makes performance measurement in the service generation process difficult and leads to heterogeneity in the service. Furthermore, the customer is often actively involved in generating the services. Finally, as a result of the intangibility and the customer involvement, services cannot be stored, which means that unused capacity is lost (e.g., Parasuraman, Zeithaml and Berry, 1985; Lovelock and Gummesson, 2004). Thus, quality assurance, performance measurement, and volume or demand management are managerial challenges in a service environment; they result from the intangible nature and from the role of the customer in the service process (Sampson and Froehle, 2006).

Given the key characteristic of customer involvement, innovation in services often focuses on the supplier–buyer interaction rather than on product and process characteristics, and innovation requires exchange of knowledge between the service firm and the client (Miles, 2006: 435). At the same time, high levels of interaction imply that 'conventional' sources of innovation, especially research and development (R&D) activities, seem less applicable to a services setting. Using survey data from Germany, Hipp and Grupp (2005) find that technology-focused R&D plays a less substantial role in services, with only 30% of services firms reporting R&D expenses compared with 55% of manufacturing firms. Rather, innovation expenditure in services firms is concentrated in investment in physical machines and resources and in employee training. For example, Grawe (2009) suggests that innovation in logistics services results from applying new technology such as containerization, identification chips (RFID), or electronic data interchange (EDI) platforms rather than developing new technologies as such. Much innovation in services is incremental, consisting of changes in the service process in response to individual users' needs (Sundbo, 1997). The difference between customization and innovation is not clear-cut in a service setting (Hipp and Grupp, 2005; Miles, 2006), but developing new (different) guidelines or rules on how to tackle customers' problems and needs which are transferrable to other settings can be viewed as an innovative activity, even while there is no new tangible technology.

Case: The Bakery and the Caterer

We investigate a case in which a supplier aimed to change the relationship with its largest buyer in a services supply chain. This supplier is a bakery, which we will denote BreadCo. It is located in the Netherlands, and it delivers bread and pastry in the Dutch foodservices market. The foodservices market provides customers with meals, snacks, and drinks for immediate consumption. BreadCo's customers include company caterers, health and care institutions, firms and organizations with in-house catering activities, and restaurants and hotels. At the time of the case events, revenues were in the range of 10 to 20 million euros, and the number of staff was some 200. We discuss the open book process between BreadCo and its largest customer, a caterer we call CaterOne. The timeline of this open book process is presented in Figure 10.1. The case is drawn from interviews with BreadCo management; access to internal company databases with information on unit sales, sales revenues, orders, employees, transport itineraries, deliveries, and so on, as well as the internal company accounts; access to all relevant email conversations of BreadCo management with the caterer and the consultancy firm that advised the caterer; and company presentations and written agreements. This includes the open book arrangement as it was implemented and the open book accounting information that was provided to the caterer during the relationship. We do not have direct information from the buyer. However, we want to know why the supplier voluntarily opened its books, how it realized adaptations in the service delivery process, and how it achieved a financial return from this. In this respect, the supplier's perceptions of the buyer's intentions and expected behavior are more salient than the buyer's own view on this (Caglio and Ditillo, 2008: 884).

BreadCo's Supply Chain in the Catering Market

BreadCo delivered over 500 different types of mostly fresh bread products to 2,000 locations. Since many food products have a very limited shelf life (a few days or even a single day), a catering location typically receives deliveries several times per week. BreadCo's supply chain involved raw materials suppliers for its own bakeries, third-party suppliers that delivered finished products, distributor companies, and customers. Although BreadCo had production facilities, it purchased some 70% of its supplies directly from third parties. It had one main site, where most of the production was concentrated and where logistics activities took place, and three smaller sites which mainly carried out logistics activities but where some specialty production facilities were located. In the logistics facilities, the items a customer ordered were gathered from the inventory, collected in crates and trolleys, and made ready for transportation; this step is called 'picking an order'. Coordination and scheduling of production and logistics were done at the main site. The production planning and the ordering of third-party products was based on sales estimates, since lead times were too long to wait for customer orders. BreadCo delivered to customer locations directly. Logistics activities were carried out by BreadCo's transportation department with a vehicle fleet that was owned by the firm. No third-party logistics firms were involved in the supply chain, except for two specialized foodservices distributors that were mainly used to service locations with very small order sizes: the two distributors serviced 30% of the locations, which together accounted for only 7% of sales volume.

Market Characteristics

Every organization providing a catering function was a potential customer for BreadCo. This included company restaurants and canteens, prisons, health care institutions and nursing homes, pubs and small restaurants, and schools. BreadCo's customers ranged from individual organizations with one restaurant location, to large hotel chains and catering firms having many locations. In the foodservices market, it is common for multi-location customers such as hotel chains to have agreements with more than one supplier for the same product category (such as bread), allowing their locations to choose among them. Although customers can organize their catering function themselves, many organizations turn to professional caterers to provide foodservices. The two largest customers of BreadCo belonged to this group of professional catering companies.

BreadCo management identified three categories of competitors. First, there was one major bakery chain that offered approximately the same product range. However, its supply chain was very different: it had over 100 small production sites, where bread was baked in a traditional way (so-called craft bakers). These production sites were able to offer regional products, which is important in the bread market and in the food market in general. Second, local bakeries were competitors, since they can (and do) supply bread and pastry to individual locations. Third, a number of industrial and wholesale bakeries supplied directly to organizations that accept a small range of bread products. These bakeries were specialized in high-volume production of a small range of products. Except for the first company, these competitors could not match BreadCo's offerings in full. BreadCo offered a broad range of products, and it had the required logistics capacity and quality to deliver the products on time.

Pricing and Cost Structure of BreadCo's Activities

In 2003, BreadCo started with a project to improve its costing information. There was no costing system in place, yet the firm's activities were diverse enough to warrant investigation into the cost structure. The costing project resulted in a new costing system involving direct costs and three indirect cost pools: transport costs, order acceptance costs, and general costs.

The *direct costs* were the cost of goods sold of a single product. This could be either the purchase price of a third-party product or the unit cost of producing the product by BreadCo itself.

The *transport costs* involved the costs of the transportation department. These costs included all logistics costs except for the picking costs at the logistics sites which were included in the general cost pool (see below). Transport costs were allocated using two standard rates, one for delivering to customer locations, and one for delivering to the foodservice distributors. The second rate was substantially lower, but customers who were supplied by the distributors would also be charged for the distributor costs.

Order administration costs represented the costs of the accepting and administering an order. They were allocated using four rates, depending on the mode of ordering. The least expensive way of ordering was by modem, followed by faxed orders, telephone calls from customers, and finally telephone calls to customers. Regular customers were called if their orders had not arrived by the day's deadline; often, it turned out that they had forgotten to place an order.

The third indirect cost pool of *general costs* consisted of all remaining costs: head office costs, sales force costs, housing, and picking costs. These costs were allocated through a fixed charge on each product. This fixed charge was a standard amount in euros per unit rather than a surcharge dependent on the level of the direct costs.

The structure of the costing system is summarized in Table 10.1. The net unit cost follows from the product cost (the cost of goods sold), to which a charge for the general costs of € 0.90 is added. Depending on the logistics and ordering choices of the customer, charges are added for delivery and for order acceptance. Thus, the total costs incurred for a customer faxing an order of three products costing € 4.00 each, to be delivered at the customer location are € 38.98. The total bill for the customer depends on the profit margin of the product.

Starting in 2006, the new costing system was used as the basis for pricing. Until 2004, product pricing of BreadCo was based on a list price for each product but with a large variety of separate agreements with different customer involving discounts, bonuses, and rebates. Typically, customers

Table 10.1 Structure of the new pricing system

Product price	
Product cost	X
General costs	0.90
Net unit cost	X + 0.90
Profit margin	P
Selling price	X + 0.90 + P
Charges	
Logistics	
—delivery to customer location	22.96
—delivery to distributor	7.49
Order administration costs	
—by modem	0.44
—by fax	1.32
—customer phones	1.71
—customer is phoned	2.20

Numbers have been changed for confidentiality reasons, but the relative magnitude has been preserved.

received standard discounts on the weekly bill and additional discounts with percentages increasing in volume. The two big catering companies also received discounts and rebates. In the end, differences in structure, amount, and timing of discounts and rebates existed for almost every individual customer. Under the new pricing system, the net unit cost is the basis for the net selling price that BreadCo wanted to receive for each product: this selling price equaled the net unit cost plus the target profit margin for that product. All customers were informed on the structure of the logistics and order administration costs, so that they knew what a delivery costs and what the cheapest way of ordering is.

The Open Book Process With CaterOne

Charging customers separately for customer- or order-specific activities is not exceptional, although it can be interpreted as a 'light' form of open book accounting, since it increases the customers' knowledge of the supplier's cost structure. However, BreadCo went a step further with the two big caterers it supplies. It offered to open its books completely, including disclosure of its profit margins. Both caterers entered into negotiations; we describe the process with the largest one, since this was completed first. This caterer (which we will call CaterOne) was responsible for more than a quarter of BreadCo's sales volume and at the time was its largest customer. Essentially, CaterOne was offered complete costing information: BreadCo truly opened its books, ultimately allowing CaterOne to audit its costing system. The time line of the open book process is presented in Figure 10.1.

Initiation phase

- 2003/04: improvement of BreadCo's costing system.
- 2004: main customers are informed on introduction of new pricing system, with separate charges for transport and ordering activities.
- November 2004: proposal to CaterOne: old prices plus 2% raise, or new pricing system with open books.
- December 2004: CaterOne hires a professional procurement firm, for now accepts old prices plus 2%.
- January 2005: procurement firm starts negotiations with BreadCo.

Negotiations phase

- January – June 2005: exchange of information on structuring of relationship, pricing systems, competitors, open book arrangements.
- March 2005: BreadCo offers 2% discount on 2005 prices if new pricing system is accepted for 2006.
- July 2005: procurement firm advises CaterOne to use BreadCo as single supplier of bread products.
- August 2005: draft agreement on new pricing system and open book accounting for the period September 2005 – September 2007, sharing of efficiency gains etc.

Implementation phase

- September – December 2005: renewal of pastry range; initiation of 'open book tracker'; discussion on price increase over 2006; working out details of draft agreement.
- January 2006: CaterOne starts replacing its current bread supplier with BreadCo for its locations.
- 2007: joint development of new service concept for CaterOne.
- End 2007: extension of open book agreement.

Figure 10.1 Time line of open book process between BreadCo and CaterOne.

Initiation Phase

During 2004, BreadCo informed its major customers on the changes in the pricing system. It entered into discussions with CaterOne to change the nature of their relationship. In November 2004, BreadCo offered two choices with respect to the pricing structure: the old pricing agreements (including discounts and rebates) with a 2% price increase across the board in 2005 or a new pricing agreement based on BreadCo's actual costs. The latter proposal was structured as follows:

- all products were priced at their unit cost plus the charge for general costs. No additional profit margin was added by BreadCo. In terms of Table 10.1, all products were priced at € X + 0.90;
- CaterOne could decide what margin it wanted from its customers. BreadCo would charge the end customers for its own unit cost plus the margin for CaterOne, and would refund this margin to CaterOne;

- transport and order administration costs were charged separately;
- BreadCo and CaterOne would cooperate in searching for cost reductions at all stages of the supply chain, so including the activities that led to the product surcharge of € 0.90; and
- the profit margin per product (P in Table 10.1) would be eliminated only if CaterOne increased the number of customer locations that are serviced by BreadCo.

CaterOne was not able to discuss the new pricing agreement in detail, partly because it was about to outsource its purchasing activities to a specialized professional procurement company that was going to tackle CaterOne's purchasing at a European level. Therefore, at first, the option of using the old pricing system plus a 2% increase was accepted. The procurement firm entered into discussion with BreadCo in January 2005, and together they quickly reached an understanding on implementing the open book agreement proposed by BreadCo. In March 2005, CaterOne received a 2% discount over the 2005 prices in return for the promise to accept the open book pricing structure.

During the first half of 2005, the procurement firm and BreadCo discussed opportunities to achieve cost reductions throughout the supply chain. Four main issues were discussed: delivery times, transport movements, the surcharge added to the product costs by BreadCo, and product costs as such (cost of goods sold).

DELIVERY TIMES

Customer locations requested delivery at certain time intervals. This complicated the scheduling of deliveries and often led to extra waiting time if the customer location was not ready to receive its order. Together with the procurement company, BreadCo developed a new transport pricing structure for CaterOne's customer locations. The procurement company suggested working with increased delivery windows, sometimes by providing BreadCo with extra access possibilities to customer locations (through keys or keycards) but more often by reassessing the current delivery arrangements: was it really necessary to use the existing delivery windows? Based on this suggestion, BreadCo developed a new transport pricing structure for CaterOne's customer locations. A location that requests delivery in a one-hour time window pays € 28.50, a three-hour time window has a transport charge of € 20.00, and a longer window costs € 17.50. This compares with an existing transport charge of € 22.96, as shown in Table 10.1.

TRANSPORT MOVEMENTS

The procurement firm wanted to achieve a reduction in the number of deliveries per week at the customer locations of CaterOne. However, end customers wanted to offer fresh bread to their patrons each day. To counter this problem, BreadCo developed a baking bag concept, whereby the bread is delivered in bags which can be heated (in the bag) in ovens. The unbaked bread can be stored for three days, thus enabling a longer delivery interval while still offering fresh bread. The baking bag technique was not new from a technological perspective, but until then it was not part of the offering to customers. The fresh bread was highly valued by the end customers who consumed the bread.

SURCHARGE

The open book proposal called for CaterOne to increase its purchase volume with BreadCo. An increase in volume would lead to more efficient processes at BreadCo and thus to efficiency gains. Although BreadCo initially wanted to keep the efficiency gains itself, it was an obvious issue to be raised during the negotiations by the procurement firm. In the end, a volume-related reduction of the surcharge to be paid by CaterOne was agreed upon. The maximum reduction would be achieved when CaterOne's sales volume more than doubled. This reduction was € 0.10, on the surcharge of € 0.90 per product.

PRODUCT COSTS

CaterOne was allowed to choose the suppliers of all products its end customers buy, so including BreadCo's self-produced items. However, the cost structure of BreadCo's production facilities was not disclosed. Price reductions would be obtained by CaterOne if it increased the volume from BreadCo's self-produced items, as well as from two large suppliers of BreadCo. A typical agreement offered a discount of up to 4% if the sales volume increased threefold. Furthermore, CaterOne was allowed to enter into negotiations with the suppliers directly.

The required volume increase for discounts on product prices and on the surcharge may seem high, given that CaterOne already was BreadCo's largest customer. However, CaterOne was not the end customer but part of a supply chain. CaterOne serviced a great number of customer locations, which could choose between BreadCo and its major competitor, the bakery with a large number of production locations. This implies that there was substantial room for volume growth if these locations switched to BreadCo as their bread and pastry supplier.

Although the negotiations went relatively smoothly with the procurement firm and with CaterOne's head office, the operational department of CaterOne was less enthusiastic: it would rather continue buying from the main competitor. This was because there was serious doubt about the quality of BreadCo's pastry products. For example, the temperature was not always right, or mistakes were made during transport. BreadCo was not aware of these issues, and it undertook measures to correct them, e.g., by changing the packaging as well as the product range.

Implementation Phase

Starting in January 2006, CaterOne transferred a number of end locations per week to BreadCo's customer base. However, CaterOne did not want BreadCo to send invoices based on the new pricing system to the customer locations, and the locations were invoiced by BreadCo using the old pricing system. The difference in sales revenue with the new pricing system was paid to CaterOne, which thus received all savings on the logistics and order costs. As a result, the customer locations did not get any incentive to change their behavior.

To facilitate the new relationship between BreadCo and CaterOne, an 'open book tracker' was developed by both parties (see Figure 10.2). The tracker reported relevant variables in the relationship on a monthly basis, such as sales volumes per location and per product and the realized discounts on product costs and the surcharge, as well as non-financial information such as the number of complaints from customer locations. In February 2006, CaterOne performed a first audit of BreadCo's books. At this audit, the open book tracker was discussed, and the calculation of the surcharge covering the general costs was explained. Furthermore, the auditors toured the facilities to gain more understanding of BreadCo's operations, as well as BreadCo's administrative processes. A subsequent audit focused on the purchase prices paid to third-party suppliers and the cost of BreadCo's own production.

As part of the relationship development, BreadCo and CaterOne started working together on developing a new concept for customer locations.

- Sales and discounts invoiced to end customers according to old pricing system
- Sales information as it should be invoiced according to the new pricing system
- Sales volume at BreadCo's production facilities and at the two major external suppliers
- Result for CaterOne: difference between old and new pricing system, discount on surcharge, savings on procurement costs (discounts on BreadCo's in-house production and for supplies from the two major external suppliers)
- Product sales of customer locations
- Complaints of customer locations, sorted by cause
- Number of customer locations sorted by delivery windows
- Number of customer locations sorted by ordering method (modem, fax etc.)

Figure 10.2 Contents of the 'open book tracker'. All information relates to CaterOne and its customer locations.

BreadCo developed several types of bread for this concept and helped in developing a new way of presenting bread to the end clients at the locations and optimizing procedures with respect to preparing and serving bread products. Although BreadCo had advised various customers on their operations in the past, this was the first time it cooperated with a customer in new service development from the start. A pilot was started mid-2007, and it was rolled out to several hundred locations in 2008. Another example of the development of the relationship was the introduction of a biweekly meeting between CaterOne and BreadCo. In these meetings, operational issues were discussed, such as the transfer of more locations to BreadCo, as well as any existing problems.

During the first year of the open book relationship, it proved difficult for CaterOne to achieve its volume goals. It did not succeed in switching all its locations to BreadCo: at the start of the process, BreadCo supplied approximately 50% of CaterOne locations, and at the end of the first year, this had increased to approximately 75%. As a result, CaterOne did not get the maximum discounts that the contract included, but it did pay lower prices, obtaining a substantial gain from the agreement.

Extension of the Agreement

During 2007, CaterOne agreed to an extension of the open book arrangement. The renewed contract, running for three years, included separate agreements on indexing of the logistics and general (surcharge) costs. The new price levels implied that CaterOne would receive a larger share of the efficiency gains. The renewed contract differed with respect to the operational aspects on one important point: there were no separate charges for the three delivery windows which were identified in the original contract. The three rates caused extra administration activities and led to discussions on where exactly a one-hour window ended but did not have much impact on operations. On the instigation of BreadCo, in the new contract, all deliveries to CaterOne were charged at the standard rate that all other customers paid.

Furthermore, the new contract included a profit-sharing arrangement between CaterOne and BreadCo rather than much lower surcharges. Under this arrangement, CaterOne would not receive any profit share in the first year and would receive a steadily increasing share in the following years. BreadCo pressed for this arrangement because during 2007, the managing director (who already had a minority stake) had bought the firm from the previous owner. The profit-sharing arrangement improved BreadCo's cash flows, which were needed to finance the acquisition.

Returns From the Open Book Process

The implementation of the open book arrangements and the changes in the relationship activities resulted in financial improvements for both the buyer and the supplier. The elimination of the profit margin for CaterOne implied a direct reduction in costs. Additionally, CaterOne had the possibility of obtaining volume discounts on the surcharge, as well as on the supplies bought from several large suppliers. BreadCo management estimated that the savings for CaterOne due to lower prices would be up to 10% if CaterOne succeeded in meeting the volume targets. For BreadCo, the returns needed to come from efficiency gains once the volume started increasing. The surcharge for the general costs was based on activity levels at the start of the open book process. Since the capacity in terms of buildings, picking facilities, and management had ample room for growth and consisted largely of fixed costs, the surcharge over any extra volume contributed almost in full to BreadCo profit. This increase in efficiency was not an immediate gain; rather, it was dependent upon the realization of the extra volume. At the end of the first year, the efficiency gains were substantial enough to offset the price reduction according to BreadCo management. Because of the efficiency gains from the increasing volume and the changes in the logistics processes, BreadCo achieved a comparable profit margin as it had before introducing the process, but this margin was earned on a larger volume, thus increasing the overall profit.

At the renewal of the agreement, BreadCo realized two changes that further increased the financial return of the relationship. The elimination of the three-tier logistics charge with lower costs for longer delivery windows increased the revenues from the logistics charges, reduced the costs of interaction with the locations, and enabled a further increase in the efficiency of the logistics processes. The change towards a profit-sharing agreement rather than a reduction in price levels improved BreadCo's financial position by delaying cash outflows.

Case Analysis

Innovation in the Relationship

The changes in the relationship between BreadCo and CaterOne can be categorized into three groups: changes in BreadCo's activities, changes in CaterOne's activities, and changes in the management of the relationship.

The changes in BreadCo's activities related mostly to the logistics activities, and there were no changes in the tangible production processes. Although there were some adjustments in the product offerings, notably the bread in baking bags, the changes in the pastry offerings, and new bread types for the new service concept developed jointly with CaterOne, these did not require new production technologies. The products that were supplied by BreadCo were non-specific to CaterOne and did not require complicated technology to produce or contain specialized parts. Thus, in the production process of the bread and pastry, there was little room for interorganizational cost management. Relative to the typical open book accounting setting, in which interorganizational cost management in product design and process technologies often leads to substantial capital outlays (e.g., Kajüter and Kulmala, 2005, Dekker, 2003), BreadCo did not need to invest in new equipment, hire new personnel with different capabilities, or re-train its employees. The logistics aspect of its services changed in that the delivery frequency was reduced, but the nature of the activities itself remained similar: picking the orders and transporting them to the customer locations. BreadCo was able to perform all logistics with its current logistics assets (truck and warehouse facilities); the efficiency gains from the reduced delivery frequencies opened up possibilities to target different markets.

As with the activities of BreadCo, changes in CaterOne's activities did not involve substantial tangible investments. The baking bag concept required standard kitchen equipment which was available in any professional kitchen. However, locations had to adjust the procedures regarding the delivery of BreadCo's products: the lower frequency implied that they needed to plan more carefully, while the increase in delivery windows (resulting in an uncertain timing of the delivery at the location) complicated staffing at the locations. Furthermore, the transfer of locations to BreadCo from a different bread supplier implied that these locations had to adjust to BreadCo's way of working. Thus, where in many open book cases, changes are implemented at the supplier's operations, here the buyer needed to adjust its operations to a larger extent.

The biggest changes in the relationship were not at the individual relationship parties but at the relationship level. At the most basic level, the transaction volume in the relationship increased by half in the first year of the open book arrangement. More important, while the relationship remained very transaction focused due to nature of the products, there was in an increase in operational coordination and coordination to enable efficiency gains and improvements. The open book tracker (see Figure 10.2) offered CaterOne detailed operational and financial information regarding the activities in the relationship, which was discussed in biweekly meetings. This changed the dynamic of the relationship according to the managing director of BreadCo:

> If you work together in analyzing the processes, you can coordinate them much better. . . . We now have regular meetings with [CaterOne headquarters]. We used to put one of our people at CaterOne, and he would be active at the operational level. Now, we are managing this much more from above: every two weeks, we discuss white spots [i.e. locations that have not yet been transferred to BreadCo], complaints, actions, it is really much more organized from above. . . . It used to be that, if they had a problem they would solve this through changing suppliers. Now, we discuss where the problem comes from.

Similarly, the development of the new service concept was the result of an increased interaction in the relationship according to BreadCo's managing director:

> They [CaterOne] have been working on a concept where customers cut their own bread, with a salad bar, and olive oils and dips, and we have developed several large flat breads that are easier to cut in one time. . . . And we have helped them think about how to make this easier for the customer. They wanted customers to cut the bread in triangles, and that's not easy, so we suggested to put some markers on the cutting boards. These are all very simple things of course but important if you want such a concept to work.

The service innovation described above did not require new production techniques (the different bread shapes did not require new baking equipment) but involved a new way of servicing the end customer. Even if these new ways were 'very simple', as BreadCo's managing director indicated, they represented a different service offering to the end client. This is typical for innovation in services, which often focuses on the supplier–buyer interaction rather than on product and process characteristics (Miles, 2006: 435). Indeed, overall the open book information did not result in new tangible products or other changes in the production activities of the supplier, nor of the buyer. However, by changing the delivery frequency and by changes in the buyer's procedures such as the use of baking bags, the supplier succeeded in improving both the volume and the efficiency of the activities in the relationship. Thus, while the direct impact of the open book accounting information was limited with regard to cost management activities in the relationship, the innovation in the logistics procedures, increased interaction in relationship management, and co-development of new service concepts resulted in a volume increase of 50% with the supplier's largest customer. This is a quite substantial change, even more so since there were no relationship-specific products or investments to drive this change.

Hipp and Grupp (2005: 523) find that technology-based research and development activities play 'only a minor role in services as compared to manufacturing'. Rather, because services typically require close interaction between service providers and customers, innovative activities are oriented to the adaption of the services to the user's need (Hipp and Grupp, 2005: 525). Here, the new logistics procedures reduced buyer costs, while the improved communication and cooperation enabled BreadCo to react to CaterOne's issues and problems rather than seeing a location simply switch suppliers if it was unsatisfied. Furthermore, the case illustrates how the key characteristic of customer interaction may impact innovation in services: to realize an adaptation in the service process, the customer may also have to adjust its activities. It would not have been possible for BreadCo to achieve the efficiency gains without changes at the customer locations.

The Role of Open Book Information in Realizing Innovation and Change

Much of the open book accounting literature focuses on manufacturing settings where the buyer initiates an open book process with its suppliers to engage in interorganizational cost management, with most of the benefits of cost reductions accruing to the buyer (e.g., Windolph and Möller, 2012). Typically, the buyer is the stronger party, and it has to reassure the supplier that it can be trusted to not take advantage of the open book information at the cost of the supplier (e.g., Tomkins, 2001). In the current case, the open book process was initiated by the supplier. The supplier aimed to realize changes in the relationship, but since it was the smaller party and its offerings were low on specificity, it had little leverage in convincing the buyer to agree to innovations in the relationship activities. Furthermore, within the services supply chain setting, these innovations required changes in the buyer's processes rather than changes in raw materials or components at the supplier's side of the relationship. As a result, in the current case, it was the supplier which tried to create trustworthiness with the buyer, and the buyer had to agree to changes in its processes. The managing director of BreadCo explained that the offering of the open book information was a means of creating trustworthiness:

> Trust is very important. . . . You see this in the management information we give them. We give them information they did not have before. That is very valuable to them. . . . They know that they pay an honest price because they have more insight, that is trust. It is all about convincing your buyer.

Through opening the books, BreadCo wanted to show that it was a trustworthy partner: the buyer could establish for itself that it paid an 'honest' (fair) price. BreadCo used transparency as a means of generating trustworthiness with the buyer. This was needed because BreadCo aimed to change the nature of the relationship into one with more interaction and cooperation, but CaterOne did not have any prior experience regarding the intended changes to warrant trusting behavior (Tomkins, 2001). Therefore, BreadCo could not rely on relational sources of trustworthiness, and it needed other ways of getting the buyer to agree to process adaptations. According to BreadCo's managing director, the changes could not have been achieved through pricing changes and targeted discounts:

> [Interviewer: Would it have been possible to achieve the changes using the existing pricing system?] No . . . if you are transparent, it makes the conversation much easier. If you keep everything vague, people will think you are holding something back.

CaterOne did not make much use of the open book information as such: it did not change its operations beyond the initial adaptations, nor did it enter into negotiations with BreadCo's third-party suppliers, even though it was offered this possibility according to the contract. However, BreadCo's management explained that any direct contact between CaterOne and the third-party suppliers would probably not lead to a better result for CaterOne: although CaterOne was BreadCo's largest client, representing 25% of sales volume, this also implied that BreadCo's purchase volume with its owns suppliers would be much larger than CaterOne would generate as an individual customer. Since there was no opportunity for inter-organizational cost management at the product level between CaterOne and the third-party suppliers, extending the relationship activities to BreadCo's suppliers was not useful for CaterOne (Dubois, 2003).

The importance of getting the buyer to accept changes in the relationship is also illustrated by the role of the procurement firm which was brought in by the international headquarters of CaterOne. The procurement firm entered the process after BreadCo first proposed the new system to CaterOne. According to BreadCo management, the procurement firm increased the speed of implementation because it brought a fresh view to the situation and was not hindered by existing relationships with other suppliers or attachment to established operating procedures:

> We were lucky that they had a restructuring at their headquarters. Instead of an independent purchaser at the Dutch headquarters, we got to deal with a worldwide purchasing firm that was brought in and wanted to change the purchasing policy radically. That was a big advantage! You have someone that knows nothing about Dutch habits, there are no vested interests, they are independent. With an organization with a purchaser that's been there for ten years . . . he thinks "That's way too much work, I only have a couple of years to go."

Thus, the adaptations in the relationship activities were facilitated by the absence of relational trust as a result of the severing of existing ties (e.g., Tomkins, 2001). Any existing relational trustworthiness that BreadCo had created with CaterOne was less important than the arguments for change. At the same time, since BreadCo already was a major supplier, CaterOne had experience with the capabilities of BreadCo in terms of product quality and delivery reliability, while alternative suppliers remained available for CaterOne. Indeed, although CaterOne agreed to a profit-sharing arrangement at the contract extension and thus took on a more vulnerable position than when it had simply pressed for lower prices, it did succeed in getting a larger share of the returns:

> At the negotiations for the new contract we had to give in on our share of the gains. Because I had bought the firm [from the previous owner], my negotiation position was less favorable.

Overall, while the open book arrangement resulted in a more intensive relationship, the buyer's attitude remained focused on financial gains. Thus, the suggestion from the literature that open book arrangements require high levels of trust does not seem to be validated by this case. The open book information was successful in getting the buyer to agree to changes in the relationship, but otherwise the relationship did not show a 'trust-based pattern' with non-specific contracts and an absence of bargaining power asymmetry (van der Meer-Kooistra and Vosselman, 2000). Indeed, at the extension of the open book arrangement, the contract became more detailed in certain aspects according to BreadCo's managing director:

> A downside of the first agreement was that it only covered two pages. They used to come in with people from [their head office] who all had their own interpretation of these two pages. . . . That led to a lot of disputes. We saw what was going wrong here, and that was too few descriptions, so we now drew up a contract with many examples: how do you calculate this or that item? what does it contain exactly?

The importance of detailed descriptions in the contract is another example of the impact of services characteristics: services are heterogeneous acts which complicates performance measurement and control. In the case setting, this is further complicated by the transactional nature of the services, which means that there are many discrete instances of the services. In the business services outsourcing settings of e.g., van der Meer-Kooistra and Vosselman (2000) and Langfield-Smith and Smith (2003), performance measurement and control is also difficult, but these relationships involved high levels of specificity leading to long-term commitments. CaterOne on the other hand had other sourcing options and kept on using them during the open book arrangement. Furthermore, it was not difficult for the buyer to switch suppliers because of low levels of product and asset specificity. In fact, this happened after the extension of the contract that provided the end point of the case. When this contract period ended, the buyer terminated the contract and switched to a different supplier who offered a lower price level. This was during the height of the 'Great Recession' of 2008–2012 when buyers were in an even stronger position, and it ultimately culminated in BreadCo's bankruptcy since it was not able to replace CaterOne's business.

Conclusion

The case we have presented concerns a services supply chain in which the supplier wanted to change the relationship: it wanted to increase the volume with the buyer and cooperate in the management of the relationship and the development of new services. Although the supplier produced a part of its offerings, the nature of the products, and the large share of third-party products implied that nature of the supplier's offerings was best characterized as a logistics service. Logistics services involve customer interaction, and to achieve changes in the relationship, it was required that the buyer would agree to adjust its operations. The supplier used open book information as a tool to convince the buyer to do this and create the starting point for innovating in the supply chain. As with many services, the nature of the innovations was rather simple, but upon implementation, the relationship volume increased substantially. Because services involve activities in addition to tangible products, cooperation at the relationship level rather than at the product or transaction level can also make a difference for the services supplier: the offering of detailed information through the open book tracker facilitated a better monitoring of the quality of the supplier's services for the buyer.

The pattern which emerges from the case is different from that of regular open book accounting, in which powerful buyers initiate open book accounting, and try to reassure the suppliers through contractual and relationship mechanisms that opening the books will not harm the suppliers (Kajüter and Kulmala, 2005). Although the powerful party in this case was also the buyer, the open book information was offered unconditionally by the supplier on the supplier's initiative. The opening of the books was the starting point for developing the relationship: The supplier wanted to create a partnership, with higher levels of relationship volume and cooperation. This entailed the creation of trustworthiness with the buyer, which needed to agree to changes in the relationship. The opening of the books helped in this by demonstrating that price levels were fair, which enabled a focus on operational improvement and development rather than a discussion regarding appropriation of returns for every individual item. Thus, the direction in which trustworthiness and trust 'flow' are different in supplier-initiated open book accounting (e.g., Dekker, 2003). We suggest that this is caused by the services character of the relationship in combination with the fact that the supplier wanted to achieve innovations in the relationship. Because of the importance of customer interaction in services, realizing changes—and thus realizing innovation—requires more than a one-time technological adjustment at the buyer; the buyer also has to agree to changes in its ongoing operations. The opening of the books was one additional way to convince the buyer to agree to this.

References

Agndal, H. and Nilsson, U. (2008) Supply chain decision-making supported by an open books policy, *International Journal of Production Economics*, 116(1), pp. 154–167.

Alenius, E., Lind, J. and Strömsten, T. (2015) The role of open book accounting in a supplier network: Creating and managing interdependencies across company boundaries, *Industrial Marketing Management*, 45, pp. 195–206.

Caglio, A. and Ditillo, A. (2008) A review and discussion of management control in inter-firm relationships: Achievements and future directions, *Accounting, Organizations and Society*, 33(7–8), pp. 865–898.

Caglio, A. and Ditillo, A. (2012) Opening the black box of management accounting information exchanges in buyer—Supplier relationships, *Management Accounting Research*, 23(2), pp. 61–78.

Carr, C. and Ng, J. (1995) Total cost control: Nissan and its U.K. supplier partnerships, *Management Accounting Research*, 6(4), pp. 347–365.

Coletti, A. L., Sedatole, K. L. and Towry, K. L. (2005) The effect of control systems on trust and cooperation in collaborative environments, *The Accounting Review*, 80(2), pp. 477–500.

Cooper, R. and Slagmulder, R. (2004) Interorganizational cost management and relational context, *Accounting, Organizations and Society*, 29(1), pp. 1–26.

Cooper, R. and Yoshikawa, T. (1994) Inter-organizational cost management systems: The case of the Tokyo-Yokohama-Kamakura supplier chain, *International Journal of Production Economics*, 37(1), pp. 51–62.

Dekker, H. C. (2003) Value chain analysis in interfirm relationships: A field study, *Management Accounting Research*, 14(1), pp. 1–23.

Dubois, A. (2003) Strategic cost management across boundaries of firms, *Industrial Marketing Management*, 32(5), pp. 365–374.

Free, C. (2008) Walking the talk? Supply chain accounting and trust among UK supermarkets and suppliers, *Accounting, Organizations and Society*, 33(6), pp. 629–662.

Grawe, S. J. (2009) Logistics innovation: A literature-based conceptual framework. *International Journal of Logistics Management*, 20(3), pp. 360–377.

Hipp, C. and Grupp, H. (2005) Innovation in the service sector: The demand for service-specific innovation measurement concepts and typologies, *Research Policy*, 34, pp. 517–535.

Kajüter, P. and Kulmala, H. I. (2005) Open-book accounting in networks: Potential achievements and reasons for failures, *Management Accounting Research*, 16(2), pp. 179–204.

Langfield-Smith, K. and Smith, D. (2003) Management control systems and trust in outsourcing relationships, *Management Accounting Research*, 14(3), pp. 281–307.

Lovelock, C. and Gummesson, E. (2004) Whither services marketing? In search of a new paradigm and fresh perspectives, *Journal of Service Research*, 7(1), pp. 20–41.

Mayer, R. C., Davis, J. H. and Schoorman, F. D. (1995) An integrative model of organizational trust, *Academy of Management Review*, 20(3), pp. 709–734.

Miles, I. (2006) Innovation in services, in: Fagerberg, J. and Mowery, D. C. (Eds.), *The Oxford Handbook of Innovation* (Oxford: Oxford University Press), pp. 433–458.

Milgrom, P. and Roberts, J. (1992) *Economics, Organization and Management* (Englewood Cliffs, NJ: Prentice-Hall).

Mouritsen, J., Hansen, A. and Hansen, C. O. (2001) Inter-organizational controls and organizational competencies: Episodes around target cost management/functional analysis and open book accounting, *Management Accounting Research*, 12(2), pp. 221–244.

Parasuraman, A., Zeithaml, V. A. and Berry, L. L. (1985) A conceptual model of service quality and its implications for future research, *Journal of Marketing*, 49(4), pp. 41–50.

Poppo, L., Zhou, K. Z. and Li, J. J. (2016) When can you trust 'trust'? Calculative trust, relational trust, and supplier performance, *Strategic Management Journal*, 37, pp. 724–741.

Provan, K. G. and Gassenheimer, J. B. (1994) Supplier commitment in relational contract exchanges with buyers: A study of interorganizational dependence and exercised power, *Journal of Management Studies*, 31(1), pp. 55–67.

Romano, P. and Formentini, M. (2012) Designing and implementing open book accounting in buyer—Supplier dyads: A framework for supplier selection and motivation, *International Journal of Production Economics*, 137(1), pp. 68–83.

Sampson, S. E. and Froehle, C. M. (2006) Foundations and implications of a proposed unified services theory, *Production and Operations Management*, 15(2), pp. 329–343.

Subramony, M. and Pugh, S. D. (2015) Services management research: Review, integration, and future directions, *Journal of Management*, 41(1), pp. 349–373.

Sundbo, J. (1997) Management of innovation in services, *Service Industries Journal*, 17(3), pp. 432–455.

Tomkins, C. (2001) Interdependencies, trust and information in relationships, alliances and networks, *Accounting, Organizations and Society*, 26(2), pp. 161–191.

van der Meer-Kooistra, J. and Vosselman, E. G. J. (2000) Management control of interfirm transactional relationships: The case of industrial renovation and maintenance, *Accounting, Organizations and Society*, 25(1), pp. 51–77.

van der Valk, W. and Axelsson, B. (2015) Towards a managerially useful approach to classifying services, *Journal of Purchasing and Supply Management*, 21(2), pp. 113–124.

Windolph, M. and Möller, K. (2012) Open-book accounting: Reason for failure of inter-firm cooperation? *Management Accounting Research*, 23(1), pp. 47–60.

11 Accounting and Networking

Anna Dubois and Lars-Erik Gadde

Introduction

During recent decades, the domain of accounting has been extended to increasingly consider issues outside the boundary of an organisation (Tomkins, 2001; Caglio and Ditillo, 2008; Håkansson et al., 2010a). One of these expansions was reported by Roslender and Hart (2002), who pointed to the emergence of a new sub-discipline within management accounting identified as 'accounting for strategic positioning'. The main mission of this supplementary accounting field is to embrace the harnessing of accounting information in support of the pursuit of the strategic position of a firm. Another extension regards the steadily increasing attention to accounting and cost management in inter-organisational settings (e.g. Seal et al., 1999; Dekker, 2003, 2004; Lind and Thrane, 2010).

In this chapter, we build on a combination of these developments by exploring the features and consequences related to accounting and inter-organisational strategising—one of three aspects of strategic management accounting distinguished by Carlsson-Wall et al. (2015). This aspect emphasises how accounting information can play a role in the strategic actions of firms. Investigation of these issues in inter-organisational settings requires a framing of these conditions. The framing applied in this chapter is derived from the industrial network approach—one of the schools of thought shown appropriate for analysis of inter-organisational cost management (Håkansson et al., 2010b). The authors claim that organisations are "continuously struggling to use their experience and knowledge of the networks as well as their relationships with others to improve their position" (ibid., p. 276). These efforts are recognised as 'networking'.

Networking involves identifying the scope for action, influencing others, and using the company's own resources in combination with those of the business partners. Networking includes numerous continuous, minor undertakings, as well as more strategic and long-term directed actions. According to the networking model presented in Håkansson et al. (2009), 'networking' actions are based on the 'network pictures' of managers and lead to particular 'network outcomes'. A network picture represents a manager's perception of the features of the network in which the firm is embedded and forms the basis for analysis and action. In turn, these actions result in certain outcomes for the firms in the network, both individually and collectively. In this way, the interplay among networking, network pictures, and network outcomes have strategic implications, thus affecting the positioning and behaviour of a firm.

The aim of the chapter is to analyse the role of accounting in the networking ambitions of firms. Such investigation should shed some further light on the connection between accounting and strategising in the terms of Carlsson-Wall et al. (2015). Particular emphasis is directed towards understanding how management accounting and accounting information can be used in networking to provide desired outcomes.

Empirical Setting and Outline of the Chapter

In the exploration of the interplay between accounting and networking, we rely on an empirical study that was previously used for analysis of strategic cost management (Dubois, 2003). This case study investigated the ambitions of a firm to rationalise its purchasing and supply costs for goods related to maintenance, repair, and operations (MRO items). These efforts were based on re-structuring of the supplier base of the firm, as well as changes of the features of the relationships with individual suppliers, with subsequent network effects. The case study was undertaken in the early 2000s. At that time, the networking framing was not yet developed, implying that the study included no systematic mapping of the managers' network pictures. Therefore, the analysis in this chapter centres on the interplay among accounting information, networking, and network outcome.

In the following section, we describe the situation of the buying firm before restructuring. These features obviously had an impact on the network pictures residing in the firm. However, the description of the situation of the firm represents our interpretation of these conditions rather than the actual perceptions of managers. The chapter continues with a narrative regarding the networking actions undertaken and the associated network outcomes. This is followed by analysis of the case and discussion of the findings in relation to other studies dealing with restructuring of a firm's supplier base. The chapter proceeds with examination of the interplay between networking and accounting information and concludes with implications regarding further research on inter-organisational cost management and the role of accounting in strategising.

The Situation of the Buying Firm Before Restructuring

The case study involves the Swedish subsidiary of a large multinational company. The specific interest in this chapter is directed towards the local service unit (LSU) at one of the company's plants in Sweden. This organisation was responsible for providing various services to the five business units (BUs) that were active at the plant. One of these services regarded procurement of MRO items, which was carried out also in relation to four workshops (WSs) conducting technical service activities within LSU (Figure 11.1). Seven buyers were involved in the purchasing team together with representatives of other functions. The WSs accounted for 80% of the time LSU spent on purchasing, while the BUs represented the remaining 20%.

At the time when the case study was conducted, cost management in general was focused on direct costs, while indirect costs were more or less neglected (Monczka and Morgan, 2000). The authors claimed that most companies were only at 'the tip of the iceberg' in terms of actual practices to improve performance through reduction of indirect costs. In particular, they claimed that firms were not looking at where costs resided and were lacking knowledge of cost drivers. Regarding opportunities for improvements, several authors advocated procurement of MRO goods as one of the areas where opportunities to reduce costs across corporate boundaries were most evident (e.g. Bechtel and Patterson, 1997; Le Sueur and Dale, 1998).

The rationalisation project was initiated because BU managers recognised a need to scrutinise the costs of using the services of LSU, which were perceived too high. The first analysis of the purchasing costs revealed the substantial indirect costs associated with MRO purchases. While the direct purchasing costs for this category amounted to MSEK 40, the indirect costs were estimated to be MSEK 32. The indirect costs thus corresponded to 80% of directs costs, which was substantially more than for purchases of other goods. These figures indicated a rationalisation potential in the procurement of MRO items.

The further analysis showed that LSU received more than 33,000 deliveries per year, indicating an average volume of around SEK 1000. The number of invoices amounted to about 40,000 per year. These figures are explained by

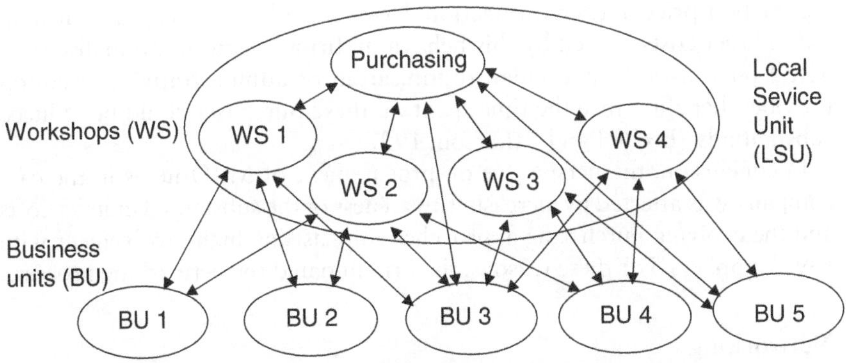

Figure 11.1 Connections between local service unit (LSU), its four workshops (WSs), and the five business units (BUs).

the characteristics of MRO purchasing in general and representative of many companies at the time (Gadde and Håkansson, 2001). The supplier base included more than 10,000 firms, many of which had not been used for several years. LSU's operations involved a huge number of internal cost centres, of which 500 were permanent; 1800 were project based and thus temporary.

The size of the supplier base is partly explained by contemporary recommendations in the purchasing literature to avoid dependence on individual suppliers. Through arm's-length relationships, buying firms were assumed to enable optimisation of the financial conditions in each business transaction by playing off suppliers through competitive tendering and moving from one vendor to the other when conditions changed. Through this multiple sourcing approach, adversarial relationships were common, since short-term orders were simply placed with the supplier offering the lowest price (Goffin et al., 1997). Such behaviour resulted in low involvement in relation to individual vendors in a huge supplier base. The direct costs for purchasing are assumed to be low when several suppliers compete for an order. On the other hand, this approach generates other costs that can be substantial. The case study illustrated that LSU secured its supply by stocking nearly 10,000 products in their 37 inventories. Such indirect effects in terms of supplier handling costs and other administrative arrangements are typical of multiple sourcing (Gadde and Håkansson, 2001).

In the late 1900s, the arm's-length approach to suppliers was supplemented by an alternative purchasing strategy that received increasing attention. This approach was based on extended involvement with a reduced number of suppliers. Strategies based on high involvement build on joint undertakings of buyer and supplier in terms of coordination of activities, adaptations of resources, and interaction among individuals (Gadde and Snehota, 2000). Since these actions are resource demanding, reduction of the supplier base is required (Cousins, 1999). Regarding MRO procurement, Bechtel and Patterson (1997) concluded that some firms had begun to modify their buying behaviour. Previously, the main attention had been directed towards obtaining the best price in each transaction. However, when realising the substantial indirect costs caused by this behaviour, firms began to rationalise their MRO purchases. In particular, routinisation of administrative procedures provided benefits since the time spent on these purchases could be reduced substantially (Bechtel and Patterson, 1997).

In conclusion, the perspective on procurement of MRO items in the case company was affected by increasing awareness of the substantial indirect costs and the evolving purchasing approaches emphasising high involvement with fewer suppliers. For these reasons, the firm initiated the networking process.

Networking

The networking actions of the firm are described with regard to the internal analysis and preparation, the identification and appointment of key suppliers, and the inter-firm reorganising undertaken.

Internal Analysis and Preparation

The first assignment of the appointed project group was to analyse where the indirect costs resided. This action was in line with recommendations by Monczka and Morgan (2000) and Kulmala et al. (2002), who claimed that facts rather than intuition would create a better base for defining opportunities for improvements with regard to supplier base rationalisation. The authors argued that reliable cost information would enable concentration on the fundamental issues, through clarifying the present state, as well as providing opportunities for evaluation of potential consequences of various actions. In this phase, LSU turned to the principles of traditional ABC analysis as suggested by, for example, Cooper and Kaplan (1988). Since LSU's primary concern related to the supply side of their operations, they stopped at what is labelled 'activity cost analysis', in which "the value chain is decomposed into strategically relevant activities" (Dekker, 2003, p. 7). The results of the monitoring of the indirect costs are presented in Table 11.1.

Second, LSU started to look for the drivers behind these indirect costs along the lines recommended by Shank and Govindarajan (1993). The analysis revealed a complex cost driver pattern. For example, the large number of internal cost centres obviously impacted negatively on administrative costs. At the same time, they were considered necessary for attaining a fair distribution of costs among the BUs. In relation to indirect costs in general, the cost centres caused several effects. They required internal transactions for products kept in stock and demanded separate orders and invoices for other products. The number of internal transactions was difficult to estimate, but according to a separate study, the total number of internal and external transactions of less than SEK 100 amounted to around 60,000 per year.

The responsibility for the cost centres was distributed among many people in the organisation. Not surprisingly, these managers were particularly concerned with the costs for which they were responsible, so they put a great deal of effort into identifying the cheapest source for each purchase. This behaviour was found to be the most important explanation for the large supplier base, which in turn had an impact on the number of products, deliveries, and invoices.

The significance of cost driver analysis in supply management has been pointed out by, for example, Monczka and Morgan (2000) and Ellram and

Table 11.1 Distribution of indirect costs on activities

Activities	*Costs (MSEK)*
Supplier handling costs	8
Costs for orders and call-offs	4.5
Goods receiving costs	4
Invoice handling and payments	7
Inventory costs	8.5
TOTAL COSTS	32

Stanley (2008) to identify how processes, activities, and decisions actually create costs in supply chains. Owing to prevailing interdependencies among the cost drivers in this case, it was difficult to attribute clear-cut relations to the five main types of costs for the activities identified in the process mapping in Table 11.1. After intense discussions, the project team agreed on the main cost drivers for the five activities as presented in Table 11.2.

The first conclusion of the project group was that the size of the supplier base was the overall cost driver. The number of suppliers directly affected the supplier handling costs and indirectly had an effect on all the other cost drivers. The second conclusion was that as long as the huge number of suppliers remained, it would be impossible to deal with the other cost drivers, such as transactions, deliveries, invoices, and the number of products. Thus, while reducing the number of suppliers would entail a direct impact on the supplier handling costs, the other cost drivers would be less affected. Dubois (2003) concluded that internal efforts to reduce cost can only take the firm to a certain point of improvement. After that, there are no additional cost rationalisations to be obtained in house, implying that further reductions require support from suppliers.

Such cooperation could only be realised with a reduced number of suppliers. The collaborative relationships with suppliers, necessary for these efforts, required a shift away from the prevailing strategy based on price pressure in individual transactions. Such transformation to improve in terms of strategic cost management was recommended by Monczka and Morgan (2000), who suggested buying firms to establish cross-enterprise strategies and share the results with business partners.

Research on purchasing in general provides massive support for increasing attention to enhancing the relationships with a reduced supplier base (Gadde and Håkansson, 2001; Cousins and Spekman, 2003). Similarly, as illustrated by Dubois (2003), MRO procurement evolved in the direction towards decreasing numbers of suppliers through centralisation of purchasing responsibilities. For example, at Whirlpool, each manufacturing division used to purchase the MRO goods they needed, although there were commonalities both among what the divisions purchased and the suppliers they used. Then Whirlpool reorganised its purchasing activities and consolidated its MRO purchases with national and regional suppliers. The

Table 11.2 Activities and cost drivers

Activity	*Main cost driver*
Supplier handling	Number of suppliers
Orders and call-offs	Number of external transactions
Goods receiving	Number of deliveries
Invoicing and payment	Number of invoices
Inventory	Number of products and total transactions

purchasing director commented that relationships with the right suppliers helped Whirlpool minimise its risk, be competitive, and set new expectations for performance. John Deere was another company that had rationalised MRO procurement. Deere had reduced the supplier base to attain significant improvements in service and technical support at its plants. After developing a category strategy, Deere appointed one supplier to be responsible for each group of items. Successful implementation of this approach required that the suppliers selected would be delivering the equivalent, if not better, service than the previous supplier had been providing (Dubois, 2003).

Category Groups and Key Suppliers

Reducing the number of suppliers turned out to be quite a complicated matter since the variety of products and suppliers was substantial. The first step in the implementation process was to define a limited number of category groups with as wide assortments as possible. The product range in each group was supposed to be possible to buy from one and the same supplier, who would then become a single source, rewarded with a three-year contract. Deciding what to include in each category group was an onerous task owing to the firm-internal demands and the fragmented structure of suppliers among which purchase volumes were to be distributed. Therefore, both internal stakeholders and suppliers had to be involved in these decisions. At the end of the process, five category groups were established. Together they represented a total procurement value of MSEK 15, included several thousands of suppliers, and more than 10,000 invoices. For each category, five to ten 'regular' suppliers had been used frequently, while one hundred to one thousand had been used occasionally.

The second implementation step was to ask three to five suppliers in each group for quotations. What specific MRO items to include became a matter of discussion between LSU and individual suppliers, since the vendors' assortments were both overlapping and diverse. For these reasons, it was difficult to make straightforward comparisons between quotations. A typical supplier covered around 80% of the requested assortment in a category, while the rest was not currently part of the product range. Several suppliers offered to add some of the remaining items in the assortment, while for others, they suggested replacement with alternative items.

On this basis, five key suppliers were selected as the single sources for each of the category groups. These five suppliers—all of which were distributors and already active as LSU suppliers—offered what was perceived to be the best conditions. In some cases, they agreed to cooperate with other suppliers—also sometimes their competitors—to supplement the assortment in the category. On several occasions, the suppliers proposed expansion of the requested product range on the basis of their knowledge of LSU's MRO needs. Also, the internal stakeholders that were involved adjusted their demands to better match what could be offered by the key suppliers. In addition, the key suppliers demonstrated willingness to make various adjustments to the demands of LSU, including participation in the category teams that were established. These teams were set up as a means of organising the collaboration between the buying firm (including also internal users) and the key suppliers as efficiently and effectively as possible to enable continuous joint improvements through collaboration.

Inter-Firm Reorganising

The category teams searched for actions to reduce the influence of the cost drivers. The most significant indirect cost—supplier handling costs—was reduced 'automatically' through the appointment of key suppliers. Moreover, both LSU and the suppliers were able to reduce other costs since LSU's previous buying behaviour was costly for both sides. However, there was an obvious trade-off between the cost savings gained through the reduction of the supplier base and the increasing costs for handling the relationships with the key suppliers. Regarding other cost drivers, the teams identified three general areas for rationalisation efforts. The first was to move some activities to suppliers since these firms were able to conduct them more efficiently than LSU. The second was to improve the joint performance through increasing buyer–supplier interaction and coordination. The third area concerned identification and analysis of internal costs (for both parties) that could be reduced through joint adjustments.

Inventories accounted for a substantial share of the indirect costs. The key suppliers now guaranteed frequent deliveries from stocks kept close to the plant. For this reason, LSU's internal inventories could be reduced to a minimum and even eliminated for parts of the assortment. Suppliers also took on waste management since their trucks could be used for returning goods. One of the category groups included technically critical parts that had to be traceable in case of accidents. Since these components had previously been purchased from several sources, LSU had to handle the specific certificates required, which resulted in quite high administrative costs. Now, the key supplier was in charge of the handling of the certificates, an activity they already conducted for other customers. By moving inventories, waste management, and certificate handling from LSU to the key suppliers, the scale of the operations increased and, consequently, the joint performance was improved.

The number of deliveries and transactions appeared as significant cost drivers. Transport costs were included in the price offered, implying that internal buyers considered transport to be 'free'. Of the suppliers' total cost, transport accounted for a proportion between 2% and 15%, depending on the volume. When LSU concentrated its purchases to the key suppliers, the costs per transport was distributed over larger volumes. The resulting cost reduction then could be shared by the parties. The administration costs for LSU were driven by the number of orders and the number of suppliers.

Through the single sourcing approach, the effects of both could be reduced. This arrangement also enabled simplification of order routines, which resulted in lower costs for both firms. Extranet solutions were developed to rationalise administration for some items. Others became included in consignment inventories set up at the plant by some of the suppliers. Hence, increasing buyer–supplier coordination through relationship-specific investments changed the cost structure, implying that costs previously driven by the number of orders and customers were transformed into relationship costs that were partly fixed.

Finally, some joint adjustments reduced internal costs for both buyer and supplier. Physical handling could be made more efficient through marking goods with (joint) bar codes and by investing in equipment to facilitate identification of goods. These changes also reduced the number of errors in the process, which were quite common in the previous arrangement. Extranet communication and adjusted routines enabled simplification of invoice administration and payments, including distribution of costs across LSU's cost centres. Regarding assortment decisions, cost drivers of both buyer and supplier could be taken into consideration. In some cases, the buyer's decisions were influenced by requirements of other customers of the suppliers. In some situations, the influence was in the other direction.

Network Outcomes

Effects for Buyer and Suppliers

The immediate financial effects of concentrating the purchases to the five key suppliers turned out to be extensive. First, prices were decreased as a direct consequence of the cost reductions enabled for the suppliers. The cost structure of a distributor is different from LSU's. For distributors, the main cost driver is the number of order lines, which makes the sales volume per order line a key issue. In addition, the turnover rate of the assortment is crucial to the distributor's financial outcome. Both these factors were positively affected by LSU's decision to single source the items in the category groups organised by the key suppliers. The effects on the price paid by LSU owing to these rationalisations landed in reductions in the interval of 7% to 15%. The price negotiations were based on transparent, open book principles and relied on shared benefits.

Second, when the supplier base was restructured, LSU became one of the most important business partners to the five distributors. In this way, LSU changed from being one of many customers to one that was given priority. With this new position, LSU was stimulated by suppliers to engage in closer collaboration and adjustments to reduce costs further. Examples of such efforts involved transfer of activities, inter-organisational coordination, and joint adjustments that improved performance considerably. The financial effects of this restructuring are difficult to estimate and were never assessed 'in total' by LSU. Rather than speculating about these consequences, we bring up some central issues in the discussion of the results. There we relate our findings to other studies in which cost management enabling joint adjustments within relationships were applied.

Effects in the Wider Network

Network outcomes were observed also in relation to the business partners of LSU and the key suppliers. Such effects regarded the key suppliers' other customers and suppliers, as well as LSU's other suppliers and its customers (the internal users). As pointed out earlier, all key suppliers were distributors and important to LSU in two ways. First, they contributed to enhanced efficiency because they specialised on purchasing and distribution. Second, they provided access to their own suppliers and the resources of these firms. In some cases, discussions were required with producers of technically advanced products. Before the reorganising, LSU staff tended to spend time on meetings with current and potential suppliers of new products. These contacts were now handled by the key suppliers since these firms were well aware of the needs of LSU. To fulfil this role, the key suppliers had to interact with internal users, which further extended their knowledge of LSU's context. Furthermore, when a new product was taken on in the previous arrangement, LSU was often forced to deal with a new supplier, thus increasing the indirect costs. In the new situation, the number of suppliers remained the same, and the cost consequences turned out differently because of the features of the key suppliers' cost structures.

The connections between the focal relationship and the suppliers' other customers were significant as well. The economies of scale for the bundle of customers increase when they exploit a supplier's resources in the same way. Therefore, enhanced similarities among the customers' needs, for example, in terms of assortment, geographical location, and service requirements, impacted substantially on a supplier's ability to be more efficient in purchasing and distribution than any of its customers.

There are important links between the key suppliers to develop further. Before the reorganising, there were no connections among the various suppliers with regard to their business with LSU. Each firm in the large supplier base was handled individually and through a low-involvement approach. As for now, the new collaborative situation with high-involvement relationships to five suppliers provides new opportunities. By stimulating collaboration among the key suppliers, it would be possible to improve performance even further.

Finally, the relationships between LSU and the key suppliers were connected also to the customers of LSU (i.e. the internal users). Once these users became involved in the discussions with key suppliers, new areas for adjustments and improvements were identified. Moreover, since the internal users now were engaged in category teams, analysis of the consequences of various actions could be reviewed in a wider context. In particular, the financial consequences could be assessed in light of both the buyer's and the supplier's cost structures.

Case Analysis

At the outset, LSU acted according to its role as a service provider to the BUs that were considered 'internal customers', the needs of which were satisfied at almost any cost. Over time, this approach resulted in an enormous number of product items, invoices, deliveries, and suppliers. When the substantial indirect costs following from this way of handling purchases were recognised, LSU started to consider alternative approaches to work in relation to both internal users and suppliers. Moreover, contemporary assumptions of the benefits residing in independence and avoidance of close relationships were challenged. Alternative theoretical models and conceptualisations advocating the benefits of high-involvement and close collaboration received increasing attention. By working together with suppliers on the basis of the common resources on the two sides of the relationship, new opportunities for cost reductions (and revenue improvements) were identified. In addition, successful examples from reorganising of MRO supply through this approach were made available in business magazines and through consultants.

These factors in combination made LSU launch the analysis and mapping of the nature of the indirect costs, the drivers of these costs, and the categorisation of MRO goods. The decisions concerning the appropriate supplier structure for these commodity groups were clearly affected by the changing view of relationship involvement. Network outcomes then appeared in the ways that could be expected on the basis of previous experiences of supplier base reduction in other contexts.

The main change and learning point for managers regarded what should be the relevant unit of analysis in the evaluation of efficient behaviour. Previously, the main attention was directed towards efficiency in individual transactions. After the reorganisation of supply, this scope was extended in two dimensions. First, the buying firm began to consider each transaction in a series of transactions since MRO items are purchased frequently. LSU implemented measures to reduce the long-term costs of doing business with one and the same supplier. As long as individual transactions were focused, the objects of these transactions were perceived as more or less given. Transactions in low-involvement relationships have to build on standardised products since buyers strive to maintain the option of switching among suppliers. Consequently, internal and indirect purchasing costs were also considered as fixed or (probably more likely) not considered at all.

Once the high-involvement relationships with key suppliers were established, the unit of analysis shifted. The relationships with suppliers became more or less fixed, and the objects of exchange no longer needed to be standardised. The content of the exchange with the appointed suppliers was affected through the buyer–supplier interaction. This interaction enabled joint consideration of the cost structures of both firms when deciding the features of what should be exchanged and how transactions should be organised. The analysis of the economic consequences of various supply options turned out differently when the cost structures of both firms were considered. Therefore, to benefit from joint efforts, the interacting firms extended their analyses in the time dimension. The short-term focus on single transactions was replaced by efforts to improve long-term performance. Obtaining these effects required changes in the interpretation of the buyer's own role, as well as the roles of suppliers and high-involvement relationships.

As the collaborative relationships evolved, LSU initiated the second extension of the unit of analysis. The items exchanged in the relationship with an individual supplier are used in combination with supplies from other vendors. When one supplier integrates activities that were previously distributed among several actors, substantial cost reductions could be exploited. The effects of buying assortments rather than single items provided similar benefits as the reliance on sourcing systems rather than individual components in assembly operations. This extension of the unit of analysis in the space dimension relates to a broadened perspective of what one supplier can offer. When single transactions are in focus, the potential contributions of individual suppliers are considered 'givens', while if relationships are perceived as 'givens', the scope of the supplier's activities and efforts can be widened.

Extension of the unit of analysis in the two dimensions provided the buyer with substantial opportunities for rationalisation. However, as shown in the earlier discussion of network outcomes in the wider network, this modification made it necessary to expand the analysis beyond the dyadic relationship. The costs in the relationship became driven not only by firm internal activities and joint undertakings of the two but also by how the focal relationship was connected to the rest of the network.

Strategising Through Reducing the Supplier Base

In this section, we relate our findings to other studies concerned with the role of purchasing management efforts to improve business strategy through reduction of the supplier base. This way of advancing company performance in general, and purchasing in particular, received great interest at the time when LSU started its reorganising. For example, Cousins (1999) concluded that extensive supply base reduction strategies had been witnessed in a wide range of firms in different sectors. Goffin et al. (1997) showed the benefits that buying firms can attain through closer relationships with reduced numbers of suppliers. The main effect observed in the latter study was that once the supplier base is reduced, the buyer is provided with resources to develop closer relationships with the remaining suppliers.

However, supplier base rationalisation and increasing supplier involvement is no panacea. Cousins (1999) found that some buying firms tend to expect benefits to flourish only because relationships are close. Similar concerns are expressed by Villena et al. (2015). Goffin et al. (1997) also warn firms for uncritical implementation of supplier base reduction. They claim that this approach should not be undertaken as an 'isolated' action but be part of a well thought out strategy for supply chain management improvements, such as reduction of inventories or other cost savings. Furthermore, Cousins (1999) concluded that supplier base rationalisation has not always generated the rewards that were first envisaged. One reason for these shortcomings was 'a haphazard approach', exemplified by the fact that unsuccessful firms were not aware of their actual costs of doing business. Another reason behind the problems in supplier base rationalisation seems to be that firms perceived a lack of research and literature pertaining to the drivers, processes, and benefits of this approach (Ogden, 2006). Sarkar and Mohaptra (2006) share this view by claiming that models of supplier base reduction are rare despite the overwhelming importance of this strategic issue.

The literature review conducted for this study identified two papers suggesting role models for dealing with implementation of supplier base rationalisation. First, Smart and Dudas (2007) studied the striving for strategic cost management in a large organisation aiming at realising synergies in their MRO purchases by combining volumes from the variousbusiness units. The first step in the process concerned analysis of data on the company's spending to identify items suited for centralised purchasing. This was followed by selection of the business units whose purchases were most relevant in relation to the grouping of items. After that, appropriate strategies for the various product groups were determined followed by shortlisting of potential vendors and selection of supplier(s). Finally, the cost consequences of the volume aggregation at selected suppliers were monitored and adequate adjustments undertaken.

Second, Ogden and Carter (2008) developed a processual approach for cost rationalisation through supplier base reduction. The main steps in this process included establishing of cross-functional teams, developing commodity sourcing strategy, identifying potential suppliers, selecting supplier(s), and implementing changes. This approach is quite similar to the one suggested by Smart and Dudas (2007), and both correspond well with LSU's reorganising of its supply base. The main differential is that LSU's approach emphasises the importance of interaction with suppliers, while the two other are more internally focused.

Karjalainen (2011) explored the role of centralised purchasing in supplier base rationalisation. The study showed the substantial cost benefits that are obtainable through exploiting potential synergies from centralisation. These benefits are derived from increasing economies of scale through aggregation of volumes. Moreover, economies of information and learning stem from internal sharing of the knowledge about suppliers, new technologies, and various applications. Furthermore, centralised purchasing may offer 'process economies'. These advantages can be attained through the establishing of a common way of working, showing worldwide one and the same line of conduct toward suppliers, for example, with regard to benchmarking procedures, joint training and development, and tendering procedures. Such specialisation and standardisation are supposed to lead to reduced administrative duplication (Karjalainen, 2011).

Networking and Accounting Information

The main contribution of this chapter is the finding that accounting information can play a significant role in the networking activities of firms. The strategic cost management framework developed by Shank and Govindarajan (1993) distinguished among three important aspects, all of which appeared vital in this case study. First, value chain analysis involves detailed scrutinising of the links between activities to determine the options for cost reduction. In our case, the activity analysis for allocation of indirect costs was crucial for identification of what networking actions to initiate. Second, strategic positioning analysis examines the role of cost management in supporting the organisation's value to their clients. In the LSU case, this issue regards the value provided to the internal users. The third element is cost driver analysis, considering how processes, activities, and decisions create costs. For LSU, this investigation revealed the size of the supplier base to be the most important driver of indirect costs with subsequent consequences for networking and network outcomes.

In this way, the case study also provides an illustration of 'accounting for indirect effects', pointed out as one of three significant opportunities offered by accounting information (Håkansson et al., 2010b). These effects regard not only the indirect costs. In line with Carlsson-Wall et al. (2015), indirect benefits were identified in LSU's relationships with suppliers. Moreover, the chapter exemplifies 'accounting for prioritisation'—the second opportunity assumed to be provided through accounting by Håkansson et al. (2010b). The accounting information retrieved in the case was useful for deciding what business partners to rely on as key suppliers, which in turn made the buying firm a prioritised partner to these suppliers. Finally, the study clearly demonstrates the features of the third aspect identified by Håkansson et al. (2010b)—'accounting for networking'—by describing and analysing the buying firm's networking actions. In this way, the study represents a contribution to strategic management accounting, since previous research on implementation is scarce, making Andersen and Dekker (2010) request further research on performance outcome.

In agreement with the findings by Dekker (2003), this study shows that substantial effects may be obtainable when costs are managed in cooperation with business partners. In a similar vein, Carlsson-Wall et al. (2015) concluded that close inter-organisational relationships were core in the strategy of the buying firm in their study. The intense discussions between LSU and the suppliers enhanced the buyer–supplier interaction and stimulated the exchange of information required for the integration of cost data across the supply chain. This finding is in line with the study of Dekker (2003).

One particular problem in the implementation of inter-firm arrangements concerns the distribution of the benefits that are generated through the combined efforts of several organisations. For example, Kulmala (2004) identified considerable disagreements on the way value is shared. Baraldi and Lind (2016) bring up three significant issues in this respect: creation, measuring, and appropriation. They conclude that a common situation is that the outcomes for various stakeholders do not reflect their contributions. The significance of the appropriation problem is pointed out also by Caglio and Ditillo (2008), arguing that companies must ensure that the value of the joint output is perceived by the parties to be clearly and fairly distributed. One reason for problems and potential conflicts in this respect seems related to the fact that firms are not measuring and managing their relationships in a mutually beneficial way (Cousins, 1999). The measurement problems are substantial because of the complexities of these inter-organisational arrangements (Tomkins, 2001). In a similar vein, Mouritsen (1999) concluded that, in principle, it is impossible to come up with an accounting calculation that would sort out and evaluate all pros and cons. Particularly intriguing in this respect is the evaluation of 'hard-to-quantify' factors (Kumar and Eickhoff, 2005).

To overcome these problems, Seal et al. (1999) conclude that a crucial role for management accounting is to define, investigate, and measure not only the costs of relationships; the potential benefits must also be scrutinised, a claim shared by Cullen and Meira (2010). Such expansion requires broadening of performance measures to include non-financial issues. This argument turns the focus to cross-organisational teams as a central component for more appropriate evaluation and analysis. Such teams need insight in the management accounting principles and procedures of both firms. Mainstream inter-organisational cost management is constrained by the fact that the focus is almost entirely on the buying firm (Caglio and Ditillo, 2008). Agndal and Nilsson (2009) show the benefits of taking the supplier's management accounting into consideration since this aspect was found more important than recognised by previous research.

In a similar vein, this case study illustrates the advantages of conducting the cost analysis jointly with suppliers rather than just applying an 'external perspective on the own operations' (Dekker, 2003). Finally, our findings support previous conclusions that strategy is not something that exist prior to accounting. Rather, strategy and accounting tend to evolve in tandem as claimed by Carlsson-Wall et al. (2015).

Implications for Further Research

This chapter aimed at exploring the role of accounting in the networking actions of firms. The previous section showed the significance of accounting information for networking and network outcomes. However, one dimension of the networking model in Håkansson et al. (2009) is missing in this study: the mangers' network pictures. Therefore, further research is needed to investigate the relationship between accounting information and the network pictures of the managers involved in networking. These perceptions of the features of the business landscape can be assumed to be substantially impacted by accounting information and vice versa. Such studies would thus enable investigation of the interplay between accounting information on the one hand, and network pictures, networking, and network outcomes on the other (Figure 11.2).

This study examined the short-term effects of the networking actions of the buying firm. Longitudinal research would enable analysis of the long-term effects of networking. In relation to the case in this chapter, the focus would then be redirected from one aspect of strategic cost management to another—from 'accounting and strategising' towards 'strategic management accounting in close inter-organisational relationships' (Carlsson-Wall et al., 2015). In addition, through longitudinal studies, it would be possible to analyse how the network outcome affects both network pictures and accounting information and thus also future networking. For these reasons, we subscribe to previous recommendations of more longitudinal studies (Dekker, 2004) to capture dynamic effects (Carlsson-Wall et al., 2015).

Finally, further research needs to be devoted to extended inter-organisational arrangements. This study showed that the changes undertaken in specific buyer–supplier relationships impact on other firms connected to the two. Also, Andersen and Dekker (2010) argue for a shift of analytical focus from dyadic relationships to network configurations. This approach would make it possible to trace indirect linkages in the network to further reduce costs and improve benefits (Håkansson et al., 2010b). Such research would be resource demanding with regard to data collection and analysis and require the deep-probing case studies recommended by Carlsson-Wall et al. (2015) and Håkansson and Lind (2004).

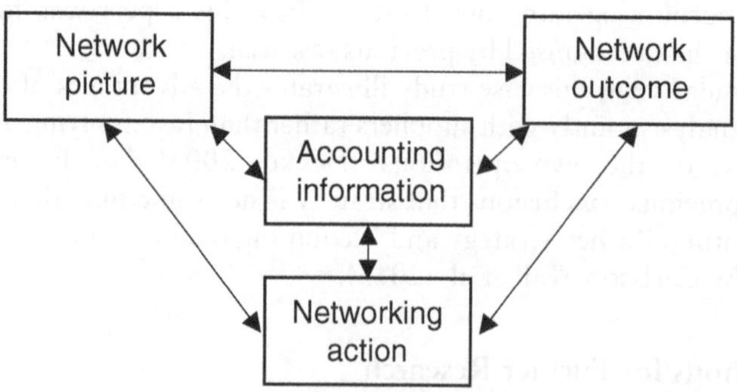

Figure 11.2 The interplay between accounting information and networking.

Further research that takes the above aspects into consideration will be able to contribute substantially to expanding the knowledge base regarding inter-organisational cost management and the role of accounting in firms' strategising. In the words of Langfeld-Smith (2008, p. 224), such studies would enhance the "understanding how management accounting practices come to the attention of organizational actors and how they are implemented and developed."

References

Agndal, H. and Nilsson, U. (2009). Interorganizational cost management in the exchange process. *Management Accounting Research*, 20(2), 85–101.

Andersen, S. and Dekker, H. (2010). Accounting in networks—The transaction cost economics perspective. In Håkansson, H., Kraus, K. and Lind, J. (Eds.), *Accounting in Networks*. London: Routledge, pp. 235–268.

Baraldi, E. and Lind, J. (2016). Value measuring and value appropriation. Paper presented at the *IMP Symposium: Making Sense of the Interactive World*, Uppsala, May 31–June 2.

Bechtel, C. and Patterson, J. (1997). MRO-partnerships: A case study. *International Journal of Purchasing and Materials Management*, 33(2), 18–23.

Caglio, A. and Ditillo, A. (2008). A review and discussion of management control in inter-firm relationships. *Accounting, Organizations and Society*, 33(7), 865–898.

Carlsson-Wall, M., Kraus, K. and Lind, J. (2015). Strategic management accounting in close inter-organisational relationships. *Accounting and Business Research*, 45(1), 27–54.

Cooper, R. and Kaplan, R. (1988). Measure costs right—make the right decision. *Harvard Business Review*, 66(5), 96–103.

Cousins, P. (1999) Supply base rationalization: Myth or reality? *European Journal of Purchasing & Supply Management*, 5(3–4), 143–155.

Cousins, P. and Spekman, R. (2003). Strategic supply and the management of inter- and intra-organizational relationships. *Journal of Purchasing & Supply Management*, 9(1), 9–29.

Cullen, J. and Meira, J. (2010). Inter-organizational accounting in dyadic settings. In Håkansson, H., Kraus, K. and Lind, J. (Eds.), *Accounting in Networks*. London: Routledge, pp. 35–59.

Dekker, H. (2003). Value chain analysis in interfirm relationships: A field study. *Management Accounting Research*, 14(1), 1–23.

Dekker, H. (2004). Control of inter-organizational relationships: Evidence on appropriation, concerns and coordination requirements. *Accounting, Organizations and Society*, 29(1), 27–49.

Dubois, A. (2003). Strategic cost management across boundaries of firms. *Industrial Marketing Management*, 32(5), 365–374.

Ellram, L. and Stanley, L. (2008). Integrating strategic cost management with a 3DCE environment: Strategies, practices, and benefits. *Journal of Purchasing & Supply Management*, 14(3), 180–191.

Gadde, L.-E. and Håkansson, H. (2001). *Supply Network Strategies*. Chichester: Wiley.

Gadde, L.-E. and Snehota, I. (2000). Making the most of supplier relationships. *Industrial Marketing Management*, 29(4), 305–316.

Goffin, K., Szwejczewski, C. and New, C (1997). Managing suppliers: When fewer can mean more. *International Journal of Physical Distribution & Logistics Management*, 27(7), 422–436.

Håkansson, H., Ford, D., Gadde, L.-E., Snehota, I. and Waluszewski, A. (2009). *Business in Networks*. Chichester: Wiley.

Håkansson, H. and Lind, J. (2004). Accounting and network coordination. *Accounting, Organizations and Society*, 29(1), 51–72.

Håkansson, H., Kraus, K. and Lind, J. (Eds.) (2010a). *Accounting in Networks*. London: Routledge.

Håkansson, H., Kraus, K., Lind, J. and Strömsten, T. (2010b). Accounting in networks—The industrial network approach. In Håkansson, H., Kraus, K. and Lind, J. (Eds.), *Accounting in Networks*. London: Routledge, pp. 269–291.

Karjalainen, K. (2011). Estimating the cost effects of purchasing centralization—Empirical evidence from framework agreements in the public sector. *Journal of Purchasing & Supply Management*, 17(2), 87–97.

Kulmala, H. (2004). Developing cost management in customer–supplier relationships: Three case studies. *Journal of Purchasing & Supply Management*, 10(2), 65–77.

Kulmala, H., Paranko, J. and Uusi-Rauva, E. (2002). The role of cost management in network relationships. *International Journal of Production Economics*, 79(1), 33–43.

Kumar, S. and Eickhoff, J. (2005). Outsourcing, when and how should it be done? *Information Knowledge System Management*, 5(4), 245–259.

Langfeld-Smith, K. (2008). Strategic management accounting: How far have we come in 25 years? *Accounting, Auditing and Accountability Journal*, 21(2), 204–228.

Le Sueur, M. and Dale, B. (1998). The procurement of maintenance, repair and operating supplies: A study of the key problems. *European Journal of Purchasing & Supply Management*, 4(4), 247–255.

Lind, J. and Thrane, S. (2010). Towards accounting in network settings. In Håkansson, H., Kraus, K. and Lind, J. (Eds.), *Accounting in networks*. London: Routledge, pp. 60–79.

Monczka, R. and Morgan, J. (2000). Competitive supply strategy. *Purchasing*, 128(1), 48–59.

Mouritsen, J. (1999). The flexible firm: Strategies for a subcontractor's management control. *Accounting, Organizations and Society*, 24(1), 31–55.

Ogden, J. (2006). Supply base reduction: An empirical study of critical success factors. *Journal of Supply Chain Management*, 42(4), 29–39.

Ogden. J. and Carter, P. (2008). The supply base reduction process: An empirical investigation. *The International Journal of Logistics Management*, 19(1), 5–28.

Roslender, R. and Hart, S. (2002). Integrating management accounting and marketing in the pursuit of competitive advantage: The case for strategic management accounting. *Critical Perspectives on Accounting*, 13(2), 255–277.

Sarkar, A. and Mohaptra, P. (2006). Evaluation of supplier capability and performance: A method for supply base reduction. *Journal of Purchasing & Supply Management*, 12(3), 148–163.

Seal, W., Cullen, J., Dunlop, A., Berry, T. and Ahmed, M. (1999). Enacting a European supply chain: A case study on the role of management accounting. *Management Accounting Research*, 10(3), 303–322.

Shank, J. and Govindarajan, V. (1993). *Strategic Cost Management: The New Tool for Competitive Advantage*. New York: The Free Press.

Smart, A. and Dudas, A. (2007). Developing a decision-making framework for implementing purchasing synergy: A case study. *International Journal of Physical Distribution & Logistics Management*, 37(1), 64–89.

Tomkins, C. (2001). Interdependencies, trust and information in relationships, alliances and networks. *Accounting, Organizations and Society*, 26(2), 161–191.

Villena, V., Choi, T. and Revilla, E. (2015). Managing the dark side of close buyer-supplier relationships. *Supply Chain Management Review*, 19(6), 50–55.

12 What's Successful?

Accounting for the Outcome of Governmental Innovation Policy

Jens Eklinder-Frick and Alexandra Waluszewski

Introduction

'Metrics' is 'the new black,' at least when it comes to measurements of the outcome of innovation policy support within the EU with England, Netherlands, Norway and Sweden in the forefront (Widmalm, 2013). Furthermore, the production of metrics is based on a rather specific understanding of innovation, as expressed in the contemporary EU and OECD policy regime. Innovation is assumed to have a) a distinct source in research, which b) through policy orchestration can be directed and transferred to market actors, which c) when made commercially available will transform knowledge advancements to innovations corresponding to societal and market needs, without intervening with established social and material structures (Slaughter and Leslie, 1997; Eklund, 2013; Waluszewski, 2011).

Behind this 'disentangled' (Eklund and Waluszewski, 2015) interpretation of the innovation process, a necessity can be traced. EU legislation, based on neo-liberal market ideas, does not allow individual member states to 'favour' domestic companies, for example, through public procurement acting as supporting customers for new technologies. Instead, the main policy mean is interventions in research and commercialisation of research advances to previously identified needs (Slaughter and Leslie, 1997; Högselius, 2010; Waluszewski, 2011). Since path dependencies within the business landscape are assumed away, the embedding of knowledge advances corresponding to market needs is considered a smooth and friction-free process. The companies and organisations that populate the market are assumed to independently decide which knowledge advances to absorb and transform into innovations (Waluszewski et al., 2017). This makes the role of innovation policy clear-cut: to provide the market with commercialised research results. As Högselius (2010, p. 271) puts it: 'With the good conditions in place, the free market is then expected to do the rest.'

A rather different understanding of the phenomenon of innovation is outlined in 'entangled approaches'—that is, empirically based process-oriented studies with the acknowledgement of the impact of 'investments in place' as a common denominator (Utterback and Abernathy, 1975; Rosenberg,

1982; Hughes, 1987; von Hippel, 1978; Håkansson, 1989; Håkansson and Waluszewski, 2002). In the main inspiring source of this study, the IMP research tradition (Håkansson et al., 2009), specific interest is directed to the interdependencies created by exchange interactions over time, in which social and material resources are related in intricate patterns across company borders. This implies that any potential innovation faces a number of related investments in place on the providing and the using sides of the exchange interface. The reactions from the actors representing them will have a great impact on the innovation journey, on its ability to get ahead and on the direction it takes (Håkansson and Waluszewski, 2002; Håkansson et al., 2009, Baraldi et al., 2011).

The innovation process is further complicated by the different characteristics of the value creation of the settings responsible for its *development*, its *production* and its *use* (Håkansson and Waluszewski, 2002, 2007). In short, besides being developed in a public research or in a private research and development (R&D) milieu, a successful innovation must also become embedded into a setting responsible for its production, including supply, logistics and marketing activities. Furthermore, it has to be embedded into a user setting in which it has to be related to a number of products or services already in use. A specific challenge is that all these settings are characterised by different social and material investments in place, to which the new has to be related and therefore must be able to contribute value in rather different economic logics (Håkansson and Waluszewski, 2007; Utterback and Abernathy, 1975). For example, a resource that appears as a valuable contribution in a public or private developing setting may appear as much more cumbersome when related to social and material investments in place in the setting where it is going to be industrialised and produced, i.e. in the setting where it is going to be taken into widespread use. (The different characteristics of the developing, producing and using settings will be discussed more thoroughly in the later research design section.)

To summarise, when investigating the accounting of the outcome of innovation policy support, it is important to consider what perspectives of the innovation process it rests on. The perspective that dominates the policy sphere can be characterised as 'disentangled,' that is, a successful innovation journey is assumed to be the result of the new solution's relative performance itself. The view outlined in empirically based process-oriented studies can be characterised as 'entangled,' that is, a successful innovation journey is seen as dependent on the consequences of the new for investments in place in the producing and using settings (Eklund and Waluszewski, 2015).

The aim of this chapter is to shed light on a governmental innovation agency's accounting for the outcome of innovation policy support. Hence, an overall research question can be formulated as follows: What aspects are taken as accounts for a successful outcome of governmental innovation policy support, and furthermore, what presupposition concerning the innovation process do they rely on?

The research question is investigated through an empirical study concerning financial and non-financial accounting (Lind, 2017) presented by a governmental innovation agency as indications of successful innovation investments. The focal agency is the Swedish Innovation Agency, Vinnova, which was established in 2000 with the innovation system paradigm as legitimation and a role model (Eklund, 2007; Widmalm, 2013). The study focuses on Vinnova's innovation support in one specific and highly prioritised industry and region — the Uppsala life science region. Besides hosting one of Sweden's largest universities, the Uppsala region, with its close ties to Stockholm, hosts 60% of the jobs within Sweden's Life Science industry.[1] The life science sector is one of Vinnova's five prioritised innovation areas and the Uppsala region was subsequently among the first three regions to be awarded Vinnova's most extensive policy support programme, the Vinnväxt programme. This programme remains to date Vinnova's largest investment in the life science industry (Vinnova, 2016/03).

The chapter is organised as follows. In the next section, we give a short overview of the study's theoretical and methodological point of departure. Thereafter, we present the mission of the focal innovation agency in general, its engagement in the Uppsala Life Science setting in particular and how the outcome of its innovation engagement is accounted for. In the concluding discussion, we summarise the seven different aspects that Vinnova is accounting for regarding its innovation support and juxtapose Vinnova's presupposition concerning the innovation process.

Theoretical Underpinnings

The theoretical underpinning of this chapter is the IMP approach (for an overview, see Håkansson et al., 2009), This approach recognises the direct and indirect interactions occurring in the business landscape, creating imprints on social as well as material resources exchanged, resulting in complex interdependencies spanning time and space. In turn, this makes contextual reactions critical for the direction and outcome of any attempt to create change (Håkansson and Waluszewski, 2002). As mentioned earlier, for a new product or service to survive the innovation journey, it has to be valuable in the setting where it is developed and in settings where it is taken into large-scale production and wide-spread use. In all three of these settings, the innovation must have direct and indirect interfaces with a number of social and material 'investments in place' (Håkansson and Waluszewski, 2002, 2007; Utterback and Abernathy, 1975). Hence, the value of the innovation is not a result of its intrinsic characteristics but what it can add to related resources.

The embedding process is further complicated by the fact that the using, producing and developing settings are characterised by different economic rationalities and by different types of investments in place (Håkansson and Waluszewski, 2007; Baraldi et al., 2011; Perna et al., 2015). In the *using setting*, the value of the new depends on whether it will clash with, or increase the benefits of, established material and immaterial investments, such as existing products and users' installed production systems. In the *producing setting*, the key economic question is how to use established facility systems as efficiently as possible, i.e. investments in place responsible for supply, production, logistics, marketing and services. For a potential innovation to become embedded, it has to add value to these investments. In the *developing setting*, which may include both R&D units of companies that are closely related to commercial production and use, and academic research, which is far more distanced from any direct producing and using settings, the value of new solutions is determined in relation to how much they contribute in relation to ongoing development paths (Håkansson and Waluszewski, 2007, pp. 153–154; Baraldi et al., 2011). The more distant a developing setting is from a producing and using setting, the weaker the connections are to commercial producing and using settings. This implies that the traditional academic research setting, where the development work is related to scientific paths, norms and institutions (Rider and Waluszewski, 2015) is, at least from a short-term perspective, a particularly challenging source of innovation. Any new solution stemming directly from academic research will carry minimal imprints of earlier investments in producing and using settings compared with a developing setting closer to producers or users (Håkansson and Waluszewski, 2007, 2013).

Methodology

In the investigation of the focal governmental innovation agency, Vinnova's financial and non-financial accounting for the outcome of innovation policy support was guided by the notion of different economic logics of creation of new resource interfaces in a *developing, producing and using setting*, (Håkansson and Waluszewski, 2007; Perna et al., 2015) as described earlier. In this study, the notion of different economic logics of resource interfaces in a developing, producing and using setting was implicitly used in the identification of a) the governmental innovation agency's understanding of critical interfaces in the innovation process and b) the governmental agency's identification of indicators of the outcome of innovation policy support.

With this as a guide, we undertook data collection based on primary and secondary data focused on what resource interfaces, in what settings that were acknowledged in the governmental policy agency's non-financial and financial accounting for the outcome of innovation support. The primary data consists of 23 interviews with respondents engaged in some of *Vinnova's* main innovation support programmes (where one of the main ones is named 'VinnVäxt'), with respondents engaged in innovation agencies supported by Vinnova. The latter are a) '*STUNS*', (an Uppsala-based organisation aimed at supporting collaboration between academia and industry in what's identified as the 'the Uppsala innovation system'); b) *Uppsala Innovation Centre*

(UIC) owned by Uppsala University and Vinnova, Uppsala University Innovation and Uppsala Berzelii Centre owned by Uppsala University; and c) the Vinnova-supported cluster organisation, *Uppsala BIO*, along with Uppsala BIO's and Vinnova's innovation programme *BIO-X*.

The secondary data consists of three main Vinnova reports (2014/02, 2014/07, 2016/03), in which evaluation and accounting for the outcome of innovation support investments is presented. Furthermore, it consists of annual reports of funded programmes and initiatives handed in to Vinnova and the official financial statements of the involved organisations, as well as the financial reports that the organisations publish in various marketing materials.

Empirical Study: An Innovation Agency's Accounting for the Outcome of Innovation Policy Support

Swedish membership in the European Union in 1994 placed a restriction on the ability to facilitate technological development and industrial renewal through policy engagement. In 2000, a number of sectorial support-oriented agencies, engaged in direct involvement in specific industrial sectors, were merged into the governmental innovation agency Vinnova (Eklund, 2007; Högselius, 2010). In line with the basic ideas of the national innovation thinking it was resting on, a main Vinnova task became to bridge knowledge advances made in the public knowledge-producing setting with market actors. The deepest message of the innovation thinking adopted by Vinnova was, as expressed by Widmalm (2013, p. 39), that the production and dissemination of innovative ideas can and 'must be managed' through policy orchestration. Or, as put by the innovation agency: 'Our mission is to promote sustainable growth by improving the conditions for innovation, as well as funding needs-driven research.'[2]

Hence, the main mission of Vinnova became to support knowledge transfer from academic research to private firms based on the assumption that they will transform knowledge advances to innovation corresponding to economic and societal needs. The activities of Vinnova involve a) funding research; b) funding company-driven development projects; and c) jointly managed long-term projects, something that includes interaction with other research financiers and innovation-promoting organisations. Vinnova invests about SEK 2.7 billion annually in various initiatives and presents its vision as follows:

> Vinnova's vision is for Sweden to be a world-leading country in research and innovation, an attractive place in which to invest and conduct business. We promote collaborations between companies, universities, research institutes and the public sector. We do this by stimulating a greater use of research, by making long-term investment in strong research and innovation milieus and by developing catalytic meeting places.[3]

Vinnova's Innovation Support of the Life Science Industry

On a national level, Vinnova funds different programmes that in turn funnel the innovation investments down to regional projects and initiatives, and the innovation support is designed as follows:

- *Innovation test beds* are set up to work as contact agencies in which companies can gain access to clinical environments within hospitals and laboratories to test their inventions. The test beds also offer the universities and hospitals the ability to catch the ideas for technical developments that the clinical staff or researchers develop (Vinnova, 2014/07).
- *Innovation offices* are setup in cooperation with universities to support researchers to develop research advances to innovations. The innovation offices support the securing of initial funding and advise how to proceed in the innovation process (Näringsdepartimentet, 2014).
- '*Winn Excellence*' and *Berzelii programmes* are set up in academic environments to help academics find collaborators from the industry to develop new technology.
- *Incubator programmes* fund incubators and coach start-up firms in their initial phase of forming companies and finding their markets.
- *Vinnväxt* is a programme that supports growth in regions that have a strong position within a specific industry. The programme is constituted as a competition where the winning regions will secure ten years of funding of 4 to 10 million SEK per year. The goal is to ensure that the selected regions will foster internationally recognised innovation milieus (Vinnova, 2016/08).

In the Uppsala region, all of the programmes mentioned are present in the following shape:

- Uppsala Akademiska; The Uppsala University Hospital, has a *test bed programme* labelled *Innovation Akademiska*.
- Uppsala University has an *innovation office* called *Uppsala University Innovation* and a Berzelii programme called *Uppsala Berzelii Centre*.
- The Vinnova Incubator programme funds the UIC, which is host to several start-ups focused on the life science industry.
- Uppsala BIO, established in 2003, was among the first initiatives to be awarded Vinnväxt funding to support the Uppsala region in developing a life science industry milieu (Vinnova, 2016/03). Uppsala BIO is a 'cluster initiative' whose goal it is to 'bring together academy, industry, healthcare, and local authorities in a common strategy and plan of action in order to strengthen the life science sector's competitiveness' (uppsalabio.com).'[4]

In Figure 12.1, the studied innovation programmes and initiatives within the Uppsala life science industry are depicted as well as their mutual relationships and their reported fiscal information.

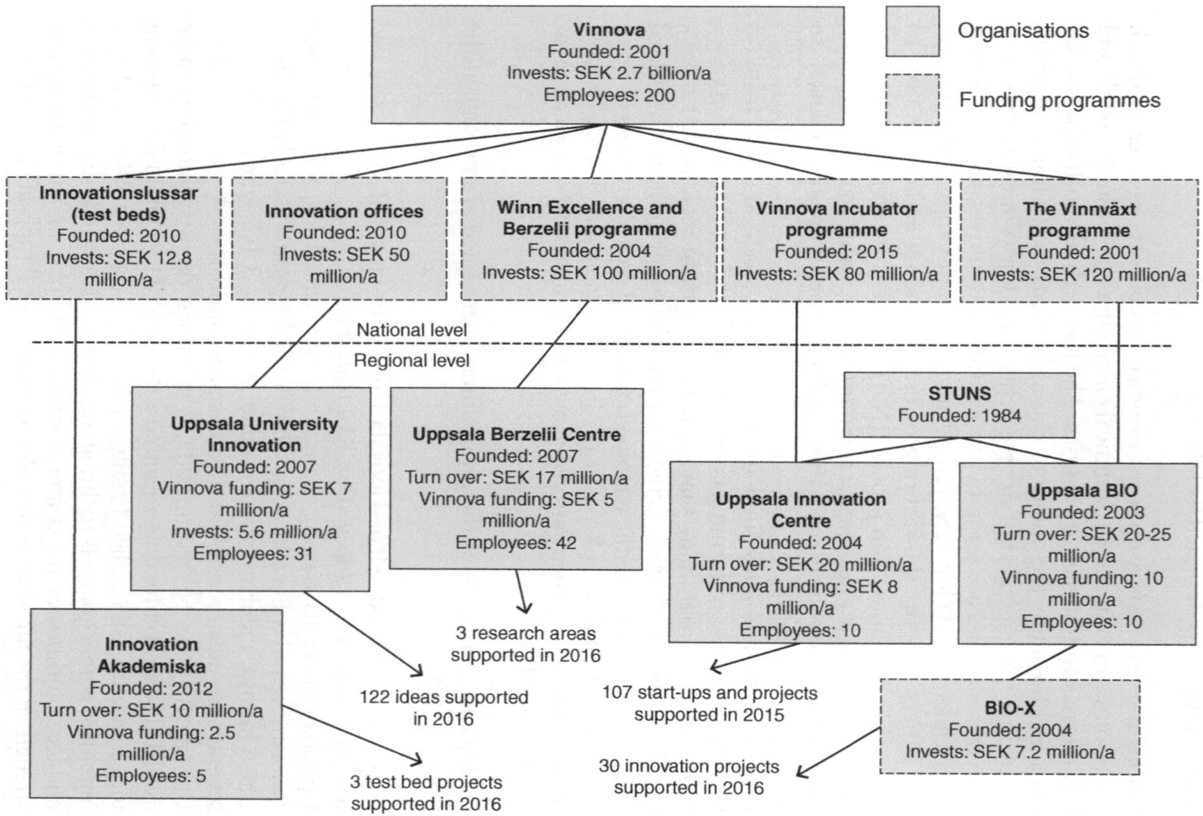

Figure 12.1 The governmental innovation agency Vinnova and its life science innovation support in the Uppsala region.

Vinnova's Accounting for the Outcome of Its Innovation Support

Vinnova's accounting for innovation support outcome is mainly concentrated on activities carried out in the *developing setting* of the innovation journey, and it is mainly based on non-financial accounting. Vinnova's most frequently used non-financial indicators for successful outcomes of its innovation support are the *number of patents* and the *number of academic publications* that the supported projects have resulted in, with the first mentioned as the perhaps most important.

Accounting for the number of patents is a key issue for managers of projects funded by Vinnova, who underline that this is perhaps the most important evaluation task. In one of its reports, Vinnova argues that 'patents and licences can be very important for the dissemination of knowledge, especially in knowledge intensive industries' (Vinnova, 2014/09). Support for this statement is gained from innovation studies by scholars such as Breznitz and Feldman (2010), Gregorio and Shane (2003), and Mueller (2006) (Vinnova, 2014/09).

What's absent in the Vinnova reports is a critical discussion of the relationship between patents and regional innovation effects. Actually, there is only one report that includes any comparison between the number of patents reported by Vinnova-funded projects and the numbers of the overall population within the same industry sector (Vinnova, 2016/03). This report did not find any significant effect of the policy support in terms of increased patent activity: 'when it comes to the patent activity among the participating companies it is level with the industry sector at large, the program has thus not had any effect on patent registry' (Vinnova, 2016/03).[5]

Furthermore, only one Vinnova report shows an accounting of the revenue generated from the patent activity emanating from supported projects. The revenue generated from direct support to individual small and medium-sized enterprises (SMEs) between 2007 and 2010 is presented in Vinnova (2015/05). Of the 55 firms that took part in the evaluation, 14 firms (25%) had applied for patent registration. Of these 14 firms, only four firms reported any revenue connected to these patents, which was estimated to total 57 million SEK in year 2010. However, one individual company represented 40 million SEK of this total amount. Hence, both the number of patents and the estimated revenue of these patents was heavily skewed in favour of only very few companies (Vinnova, 2015/05).

Accounting for number of publications is used as an important indicator of the outcome of Vinnova's innovation policy support when academic partners are involved, although the discussion of the relationship between numbers of publications and successful innovation ventures is absent. A high number of patents is simply, as one of Vinnova's project leaders expressed it, an essential part of being 'excellent'. For example, the 'effect analysis' of the Vinnväxt programmes reports that the researchers involved showed a higher publication rate than their peers. However, the collaboration did not result in a higher degree of co-authorship among the involved researchers. It thus seems that the Vinnova-funded projects attracted publication-prone scientists or spurred the involved researchers to increase the publication rate but did not foster a higher degree of cooperation among the researchers involved. Last but not least, the 'effect analysis' does not take into account if and how the publications contributed to specific innovation efforts.

Accounting for employment increase is used as another indicator of successful outcome of innovation support to funded companies. This figure is also used by the supported incubators as an indication of the success of related start-up companies. However, only the Vinnova report (Vinnova, 2016/03) puts this in relation to a control group of companies within the same sector of industry. According to this report, all but two of the 12 projects that were funded within the Vinnväxt initiative showed higher growth of employment than the control group, indicating that the Vinnova funding did have an effect on employment increase (Vinnova, 2016/03). Another Vinnova report (Vinnova, 2015/05), accounting for the effect the Vinnova funding of R&D projects had on SMEs, also showed that the number of employees rose following Vinnova funding.

However, when looking at the figures on the company level instead of the cluster initiative level, it became apparent that the rise in employment figures was highly skewed. A few of the funded SMEs had such high figures in employment increase that those few companies accounted for the increase of the entire population. The report also claimed that this skewness was not surprising, and prior research had highlighted that such skewness is a problem in similar effect accounting (Vinnova, 2015/05). The very same report also attempted to single out the number of people that were recruited in direct connection to the new innovation project that Vinnova funded.

Of the 59 that received funding, 22 companies had innovations 'on the market' five years after they received the Vinnova funding, that is, launched products or services. However, the reports do not say anything about the use of these innovations, that is, if a stable user setting of paying customers had been established and if the sales can carry the costs of the producing side.

Instead, the Vinnova report shows these 22 companies employed 67 people as a direct result of the Vinnova-funded innovation. However, these 67 new employees only amounted to 15% of the 22 companies' total employment during that time. Thus, because the employment numbers are highly skewed, it seems important to trace the number of new employees to the direct innovations projects that Vinnova funds and not only measure the amount of rise in employees on an aggregated cluster or company level. Also, the number of employees hired as a direct result of the Vinnova-funded innovations only signify a small number of the employees in those companies (Vinnova, 2015/05). Moreover, the rise in employees as a direct result of Vinnova funding could be seen as an input effect and not as an output effect or a result. A Vinnova report claimed that the Vinnova funds are often directly used to recruit new competence, and it is thus not the commercialisation of the innovations that supports the rise of employment; it is the Vinnova funding itself (Vinnova, 2016/03).

Accounting for additional investments is used by Vinnova as an indicator of success. For example, when accounting for the effects of the investments in Uppsala BIO, Vinnova reports (Vinnova, 2016/03) that besides the direct funding that Uppsala BIO received from Vinnova, Uppsala BIO managed to attract an additional 43 million SEK. The report mentions the sources of these additional investments as coming from other Vinnova-funded programmes, from academic institutions such as Uppsala University and the Karolinska Institute, as well as from the development funds put up by the Uppsala municipality.

Thus, all of the examples of 'additional' investments attracted by Uppsala BIO are made by other publicly funded institutions. When it comes to support to the academic actors involved in the Vinnväxt programme, the same accounting logic is followed. Two of the involved universities have received additional funding from the Swedish government's strategic research council, and that is reported as a success factor. In fact, *only 4% of the additional funding* received by the projects included in Vinnväxt *are from private sources* such as investments from industry, private persons or private foundations. The other reported additional funding comes from public money (Vinnova, 2016/03).

Thus, it seems as if most of the additional investments are in fact coming from the same public source as the initial Vinnova funding. However, Vinnova reports refer to studies conducted in Finland[6] and Germany,[7] where public investments are claimed to complement and heighten the companies' own willingness to invest in R&D projects (Vinnova, 2015/05). But these claims are purely based on other studies and the source of investments is not reported or defined any further in that Vinnova report.

Accounting for return on public investment is also used by Vinnova as an indicator of successful innovation policy investments. Put briefly, the one-time investment of Vinnova, viewed in relation to the beneficiary companies' tax and fee payments over a three-year period, is an often used metric by Vinnova in its effect analysis. The most detailed description of the accounting for 'return of public investment' can be traced back to a Vinnova report on 'theory and methods for choosing indicators for incubators' (Vinnova, 2005/02). This report suggests following the accounting of:

> [. . .] tax revenues that indicate that the society is getting their money back from the investments made in the incubator operations, which can be measured on a single company level as their company revenue tax, their total payroll tax, their employees withholding tax and their total sales tax (VAT).
>
> (Vinnova, 2005/02, p. 49)

This way of accounting for return on public investments is also used by Vinnova-funded organisations. Or as expressed by one of the managers of the Uppsala Innovation Centre UIC:

> The numbers are fantastic! Last year we could report a return of 13.1 times the money. That is an incredible figure! Few investments in the stock market will give you such a pay back. Sure, it is not a figure that will capture how the individual companies are developing for me as an investor; however, if you can pay taxes there is something happening within the company.

The use of the return on public investment measurement is defended in a rapport by Vinnova (Vinnova, 2015/05) with the claim that prior studies show that R&D investments, in general, generate a higher economic value than the cost of those investments (the report cites OECD, 2015; Baumol, 2002; Cameron, 1998; Yrlö, 2005). Also, the value generated to the public on such investments is generally several times higher than the private return of such investments (Vinnova report cites, Wolff, 1997). Thus, Vinnova rests its use of the return on public investments measurement on the notion that R&D investments are generally believed to generate pay offs for society at large. However, prior Vinnova reports question the validity of such measurements (Bager-Sjögren and Norrman, 2007; Broström et al., 2007). The main arguments from these reports are firstly 'that the accounting builds upon the validity of the assumption that the economic information about firm performance is equal to the performance of the project applied for' (Bager-Sjögren and Norrman, 2007) and that 'the investment is made in the development of a single product, but the following evaluation is made on the development of that whole company' (Broström et al., 2007).

A related challenge, acknowledged in a Vinnova report (Vinnova, 2015/05), is that a significant part of the Vinnova-funded projects has not been further developed within the same companies that received the initial funding. Thus, the Vinnova report claimed these changes in the dynamics of companies and in the ownership of innovation projects cause serious problems in tracing the long-term benefits associated with public fundings. Thus, the Vinnova report (Vinnova, 2015/05) concluded it was very likely that the value creation from the Vinnova-funded innovations would end up in other companies than those that received the initial funding.

To evaluate the soundness in putting Vinnova funding of a particular innovation project in relation to the total amount of tax and fees paid by the companies, the Vinnova report asked the beneficiary companies to estimate how much of their revenue could be traced to the innovation funded by Vinnova. The report concluded that among the companies that had innovations funded by Vinnova 'on the market for more than five years,' the revenue from those innovations did not amount to more than 10% of those companies' total revenue. Moreover, less than 30% of the funded innovation had generated enough revenue to cover its initial investments after five years. Thus, the Vinnova report concluded that it is a sound hypothesis that Vinnova funding contributed to an average of 10% of the beneficiary companies' total monetary gains five years after that company received Vinnova funding (Vinnova, 2015/05). That said, even if the Vinnova investments only contributed to an estimated 10% of SME's total value creation when those investments are made in general SMEs, investments made in start-up firms might have a higher impact. Using return of public investments when measuring the impact on companies connected to incubators might thus be more apt. However, measuring the impact on a single innovation project level will still capture the return on investments in a better way than to aggregate that measurement on a company level.

Finally, there are voices within Vinnova that express a more careful way of evaluating the use of return on public investments as a measurement of success. As one of the managers expressed it:

> We can never report to our minister of finance that the funding Vinnova invests ends up in that specific taxation reimbursement five years later. If we have 200 companies that, over a three-year period, received 300 million crowns in investments, what we can see is the direct outcome in the form of what they put on the market and what kind of employment opportunities they offered. But those results have to do with a lot of other things in the world and in the business ecosystem. We can only look at the overall picture.

Accounting for Project Members

The project members and their 'accumulated competence' is another important aspect in Vinnova's assessment of successfully funded projects. A general goal of Vinnova is actually, as expressed by one of their managers, to 'build new knowledge and people.' This is also reflected in the annual reports that funded projects deliver to Vinnova, including reports regarding the number and type of meetings organised, as well as a description of who attended these meetings in regards to their industry, academic or public organisation affiliation (Vinnova, 2013/05, 2010/01).

Searching for success factors in the team composition and its mutual learning is often explicitly contributed to the innovation systems approach (Vinnova, 2014/03, 2016/01, 2016/03, 2009/20). This entails that policy investments should not only fund individual projects, but those investments should also foster the collaboration among the region's public, academic and private spheres. The underlying assumption is the idea of a 'triple helix', that is, the presupposition that organised interaction among the state, industry and academia is a distinct mean to create regional knowledge diffusion and innovation (Vinnova, 2016/02, 2015/03, 2016/01).

A Vinnova report (Vinnova, 2015/05) describes this notion by claiming that all Vinnova frameworks for effect analysis should be based upon a 'conclusive systems perspective,' which includes a wide variety of methods for evaluating the effects of policy investments. The Vinnova report cites Edler et al. (2011), who describe the systems approach as a holistic approach.

> .... Holistic approach, combining formative and summative elements.... It combines the efficiency approach . . . on a project level . . . with the measurement of goal attainment, effectiveness and a range of impact dimensions. Being holistic also means to understand and measure the programme logic, thus the approach focuses on the integration of all types of additionality in its analysis.

The focus on capturing the effects of Vinnova funding on a systemic level is warranted (Vinnova, 2016/03) by citing the proposition from the Swedish government.

> Changes in industry development and competitiveness should best be understood from a perspective where the individual company is seen as being a part of a conclusive system, including all the companies, organisations and other actors that the company interacts with. Policy for business development should thus, to a large extent, view the individual company as only a part of a holistic system—innovation system or cluster.
>
> (*Proposition, 2001/02*: 4)

Such a systemic perspective in conducting the effect evaluation put the focus on 'who' is involved in the funded projects, in which a mix of public, private and academic actors is explicitly preferred (Vinnova, 2014/02). Also, this puts a focus on the number of activities conducted and who attends these activities. For instance, a Vinnova report (Vinnova, 2016/03) presents findings generated from a company questionnaire that concludes that 40% of the companies participated in seminars, industry gatherings and other types of strategic networking activities, while 21% participated in organised gatherings to form contacts with financiers, suppliers, collaborators or customers. Fifty percent of the companies claim that these meetings generated some sort of new collaboration. These figures are used as indicators that the funded projects had been successful and that the focus has been put on building networks and strengthening the local innovation system (Vinnova, 2016/03). One of the cornerstones in the argument that creating collaboration is in itself an indicator of success is the dissemination of knowledge. The Vinnova report (Vinnova, 2015/05, p. 17) claims

> This turns knowledge into a public good, that in turn becomes the building blocks for new combinations and innovative solutions. Imitation and further development of new products and processes will thus not be burdened by new development costs to develop the building blocks needed to innovate.

Besides measuring the number of meetings, seminars and industry gatherings, more qualitative measurements are also used to capture the holistic system's effects that Vinnova funding generates. Often the participants in the Vinnova-funded projects get to answer questions regarding whether their participation generated any new knowledge or helped them to incorporate any new organisational processes (Vinnova, 2016/1, 2014/02). Generally, the participants' subjective feelings towards the funded projects are interpreted as an indication of learning, in which a general positive outlook upon the projects is interpreted as an indicator for learning and knowledge dissemination (Vinnova, 2014/06). A Vinnova report claims that 'even if we don't find any significant difference between the companies that received funding and those that did not in terms of important measurements such as rate of survival, changes in turn over and so forth, a policy-supported R&D project can still be beneficial since innovation can spread to other companies' (Vinnova, 2015/05). This notion is referred to as 'spill-over' effects in some of Vinnova's publications (Vinnova, 2015/05, 2009/20, 2008/12). A Vinnova report concluded that even if they do not try to measure spill-over effects, they estimate that the spill-over effects that other companies will benefit from amount to at least double the value in immaterial assets of what the directly funded companies enjoy (Vinnova, 2015/05).

Accounting for Value in Selection

Vinnova funded programmes also have to account for the projects reviewed in the funding selection. For example, a programme manager claims: 'We look at 200 to 250 business ideas per year, which is fantastic. Those are the kind of figures they (Vinnova) are interested in.' A high number of evaluated projects are considered as a success indicator, or as expressed by one Vinnova manager: 'If you look at our projects (Vinnova), we have a very high competition rate for the funding, which at least in theory should lead to better projects.'

The general raison d'être of the Vinnväxt programme was explained in a Vinnova report (Vinnova, 2016/03). It was highlighted as being of great significance for the programme that only the very best regions would be awarded funding. The benefits of such competition were also highlighted throughout the report (Vinnova, 2016/03). Actually, this selection mechanism was believed to be so strong that it would make choosing control groups when comparing Vinnova-funded companies with non-chosen companies problematic. The report (Vinnova, 2015/05) criticises a report conducted by Samuelsson and Söderblom (2012) that compared the companies funded within the Vinnova programmes Forska & Väx and VIN NU since:

> The last phase of the evaluation and the selection process conducted by Vinnova will entail the projects with the highest potential for growth to be actively chosen. Putting the non-chosen companies in a control group

> to be compared with the chosen companies will thus imply an inherent selection bias.
>
> (Vinnova, 2015/05)

Thus, it is a generally held belief within Vinnova reports that competition within the selection process will generate more successful innovation projects. Therefore, the number of competing projects for each funding awarded is often reported and becomes a measurement of success in itself.

Accounting for Innovations in Use

A general definition of innovation is that a new product, process or service has been put into widespread use (Håkansson and Waluszewski, 2002). In Vinnova's accounting for successful innovations, established use is labelled 'implemented solutions' (Vinnova, 2014/07). However, it is difficult to find a distinct definition of 'implemented solutions,' something that is also acknowledged by the managers at Vinnova. One manager describes it as follows:

> That is taking it further than commercialisation. When we are looking at if something is commercialised, we are not looking at if something is used in our healthcare. If it is implemented it does not mean that it is sold somewhere else, it means that it is used and implemented right here. What it does not say, which is the difficult part here, is how much it is implemented; if it is only used by a small number of patients in Uppsala or if it is used by several thousands of patients all over Sweden. . . . So in that sense I guess implemented can mean just about anything.

Another manager concluded:

> What constitutes an innovation? We count how many products are on the market, or the potential of having a product on the market within a few years: A product based on research results from our centre.

Thus, there seems to be some confusion regarding what constitutes an innovation or an implemented solution. Sometimes the latter term is used to refer to something that is introduced to the market and sometimes as something that is being tested in a clinical environment (in regards to the life science sector). The difference is often not stated in relation to such figures within the reports collected by Vinnova (Vinnova, 2017/02).

In the Vinnova report evaluating the Vinnväxt program, some companies replied to a survey conducted by Vinnova (Vinnova, 2016/03). The survey states that 22 of 49 companies had introduced a product on the market as a result of the support they received from Vinnväxt. However, the report states that only 18 of the 22 products introduced to the market reported any sales.

Thus, introducing a product on the market and actually selling that product is measured as two different things.

In a Vinnova report measuring the 'health economic' effects of Vinnova funding, a framework for defining the implementation of a new inventions is suggested (Vinnova, 2014/06). The report differs among (1) an established product, (2) a product in an early phase of market diffusion, (3) a product being used in clinical trials, (4) knowledge that likely will result in a commercial product in the future, (5) knowledge that will open up new research opportunities in the future and (6) knowledge that will not likely contribute to a commercial product or future research. The report suggested that only products in steps 1 and 2 could possibly signify any actual health benefits for society at large. Of the 19 projects included in the report, only two projects could show such benefits four years after they received funding (Vinnova, 2014/06).

In sum, the definition of innovation goes from a project being in the idea stages of its innovation journey to its being an established product on the market; thus, there is no real common understanding of what measuring an innovation constitutes (Vinnova, 2017/02). Different words are used in different reports, and different definitions are sometimes used regarding the same concept. Therefore, the differences between innovation and implemented solutions are not conclusive.

Analysis and Concluding Discussion

The aim of this chapter has been to shed light on the aspects that are considered as accounting for a successful outcome of governmental innovation policy support and the presuppositions of the innovation process they rest on.

The empirical investigation of the accounting used by our focal policy actor, the Swedish innovation agency Vinnova, has shown that the innovation agency *identifies seven different aspects* as indications of the success of regional innovation support. Besides revealing why and how Vinnova is using this accounting, the empirical investigation also shed light over the internal discussion concerning pros and cons of the seven different aspects accounted for. Hence, the chapter has shown that Vinnova is trying to catch the value of the supported innovations through the use of different more or less 'objective' variables. These variables include accounting for a number of mainly non-financial aspects, such as number of patents, publications and employees and of financial aspects, such as the supported projects or firms' turnover and revenue. However, the chapter has also shown that within the policy agency, there is an awareness that the accounting does not reflect the result of the supported innovation projects in a proper way. The dissatisfaction especially concerned the lack of the ability to take the cross-border aspects of the funded innovation projects into account and the recognised experience that they often travel across organisational and geographical borders. The measurements used are thus considered to be too indirect to fully catch the outcome of investments made in specific innovation projects since the outcomes are often sought on a more aggregated level.

Table 12.1 gives an overview of the seven aspects and what they reveal of an innovation project, first in Vinnova's formal perspective and second in an interactive perspective (as discussed in the theoretical and methodological tools presented earlier).

First, a specific challenge of Vinnova and its accounting for innovation success has to be recognised. Vinnova most often supports innovation projects that are in a very early phase of development. Hence, most of Vinnova's supported activities take place in an academic or business development setting, where the latter is often represented by academic spin-offs and SMEs. This implies that Vinnova's accounting for innovation success is mainly made in a developing setting, while the most important interfaces for the survival and benefits of the innovation, the producer–user interfaces, are yet to be established. However, instead of giving attention to the challenge of accounting for the outcome of future benefits in interfaces that do not exist yet, the innovation agency is instead using the aspects accounted for as indications of future commercial benefits. Furthermore, the accounting is used as indications of aggregated social benefits, described in terms of knowledge 'spill-over' effects and the establishment of 'regional innovation milieu.'

None of the identified seven aspects accounted for can catch the pros and cons of the interface between the innovation the financed project is assumed to result in and other related social and material resources in the producer and user setting.

Hence, the choice of accounted aspects can also be regarded as an illustration of the concept of innovation that Vinnova is operating from. Although based on a systemic perspective, it is evident that the systemic aspects are considered from a high level of abstraction, where the basic challenge is to bridge the knowledge development taking place in an academic setting with the 'market' (Eklund, 2007; Waluszewski, 2011). The fact that the policy activities are concentrated in the developing setting (Håkansson and Waluszewski, 2007) is not problematised but rests on the idea that if the supported innovation activities result in a new commercial solution with better relative performance than existing ones, it will be transformed to a successful innovation. Hence, the contextual aspects of the producer and user setting are not taken into account.

When the interactive aspects of the producing and the using settings of the innovation are ignored, aspects inherent the developing setting become the focus, and such a perspective also affects what is being accounted for. The use of such indirect variables in turn causes problems of catching the pros and cons of supported innovation projects. It is thus apt to view the difficulty that actually is expressed in the Vinnova reports as an indication that the agency is trying to account for something that it is still struggling to define. If the accounting is focused on the developing setting, the settings where innovation attempts are realised, that is, large-scale producer and user

Table 12.1 An overview of sevens aspects of innovation accounted for

Accounting	*Seven aspects of innovation accounted for by Vinnova*	
	Indications in Vinnova's perspective	*Indications in an interactive perspective*
Patents and publications	Patents and publications indicate a commercial value in themselves, that is, an *indication of a future market success; implicitly a success in a producing as well as in a using setting regardless of investments in place in these settings.*	Patents represent *a cost in a developing and/or in a producing setting.* Patents *can generate value in a developing setting* in terms of facilitating the attraction of research funding. Patents *can generate value in a producing setting* if sold to another commercial actor. Patents *can generate value in a producer and user setting* if transformed to a product, process or service embedded in producer–user interfaces beneficial for both sides of the exchange interface, *that is, in relation to investments in place on both sides of the exchange interface.*
Employment increase	Accounting for employment increase in firms established by or financed through supported projects *is considered an indication of increased regional or local innovation activities.*	Employment increase in firms established by or financed through supported projects is considered an *indication of increasing activities in a developing and producing setting.* Employment increase *can be an indication of a successful mobilising venture capital.* *However, employment increase does not say anything of the ability to launch and embed a new product, process or service in a producer–user interface that is economically beneficial for both sides of the exchange interface.*
Additional investments	All additional investment made by the funded projects are considered *indications of commercial value.*	Additional investments can be indications that the funded projects have resulted in an innovation of commercial value in established producer–user interfaces. *However, it can also be an indication that the funded project or company has been successful in attracting other public or private funding.*
Return on public investment	Tax reimbursements on a company or regional level are used as *indications that a financed innovation project is creating commercial value.*	Tax reimbursement on a company level *does not reveal if the specific financed innovation project is embedded into commercially beneficial producer–user interfaces.*
Project members	Knowledge dissemination among project members, within organisational borders, is considered an *indication of regional value creation.*	Knowledge dissemination can contribute to value creation if it is transformed to new products, processes or services embedded into producer–user interfaces.
Value in selection	The higher numbers of projects in selection, *the more likely the chosen innovation projects will result in commercial value.*	The number of projects in selection does not reveal the most important aspect of an innovation to create benefits; *the reaction from investments in place when in a producing and using setting.*
Innovation in use	Limited usage of innovative solutions *indicate such solutions commercial value.*	*An innovation's commercial value is dependent on the direct and indirect consequences for related investments in place.*

interfaces, will be left out of the analysis. Vinnova is thus doomed to 'tie themselves up in knots' when trying to account for something the agency is conceptually vague about.

Notes

1. www2.vinnova.se/sv/Arkiv/20100924-Stockholm-Uppsalaregionen-life-science/ (2017-08-03).
2. www2.vinnova.se/en/About-Vinnova/ (2017-06-18).
3. www.vinnova.se/en/About-Vinnova/ (2017-03-21).
4. Together with its members, Uppsala BIO initiated a specific innovation agency in 2004 called BIO-X, devoted to support the development of new life science–based product proposals with funding and expert advice (bio-x.nu). The close collaboration between BIO-X and UIC is secured by the fact that they have a common owner in the shape of a regional foundation called STUNS. This foundation was established in 1984 to support the regional collaboration among the local universities, the businesses and the public in the field of the beckoning life science industry (STUNS, 2016).
5. The report compared the projects included within the Vinnväxt programme (of which Uppsala BIO is a part) between 2003 and 2008 to the general population of companies and could not find any significant rise in patent activity from the investments.
6. Espoo. Viljamaa, K., Piirainen, K., Kotiranta, A., Karhunen, H., and Huovari, J. (2013). *Impact of Tekes' Activities on Productivity and Renewal.* Helsinki: Ramböll.
7. Espoo. Ebersberger, B. (2005). *The Impact of Public R&D funding*, Karlsruhe: Fraunhofer ISI and VTT Technology Studies.

References

Bager-Sjögren, L., and Norrman, C. (2007). Public support to innovative ventures: Does it have any impact. *ITPS, Working Paper R200:010.*

Baraldi, E., Gregori, G. L., and Perna, A. (2011). Network evolution and the embedding of complex technical solutions: The case of the Leaf House network. *Industrial Marketing Management*, 40(6), 838–852.

Baumol, W. (2002). *The Free-Market Innovation Machine: Analyzing the Growth Miracle of Capitalism.* Princeton, NJ: Princeton University Press.

Breznitz, S. M., and Feldman, M. P. (2010). The engaged university. *The Journal of Technology Transfer*, 37(2), 139–157.

Broström, A., Anaya-Carlsson, K., Deiaco, E., and Scheffer, F. (2007). Vad kan Staten lära av en effektanalys av sådfinansieringsprogrammet. *SISTER, Arbets rapport 2007:62.* ISSN 1650–3821.

Cameron, G. (1998). *Innovation and Growth: A Survey of the Empirical Evidence.* Oxford: Nuffield College.

Edler, J., Berger, M., Dinnges, M., and Gök, A. (2011). The practice of evaluating in innovation policy in Europé. *Manchester Busines School Working Paper No. 626.*

Eklund, M. (2007). *Adoption of the Innovation System Concept in Sweden.* Doctoral Thesis, The Department of Economic History, Uppsala University.

Eklund, M. (2013). Science policy in a socially embedded economy. In Rider, S, Hasselberg, Y., and Waluszewski, A. (eds.), *Transformations in Research, Higher*

Education and the Academic Market: The Breakdown of Scientific Thought. Dordrecht: Springer Science and Business Media.

Eklund, M., and Waluszewski, A. (2015). The diversity of systemic innovation thinking: The theoretical underpinnings of NIS and IMP and the different assessment of an industry. *The IMP Journal*, 9(1), 26–45.

Gregorio, D. D., and Shane, S. (2003). Why do some universities generate more start-ups than others? *Research Policy*, 32(2), 209–227.

Håkansson, H. (1989). *Corporate Technological Behaviour: Co-operation and Networks*. London: Routledge.

Håkansson, H., Ford, D., Gadde, L.-E., Snehota, I., and Waluszewski, A. (2009). *Business in Networks*. Chichester: John Wiley and Sons.

Håkansson, H., and Waluszewski, A. (2002). *Managing Technological Development: IKEA, the Environment and Technology*. London: Routledge.

Håkansson, H., and Waluszewski, A. (eds.) (2007). *Knowledge and Innovation in Business and Industry: The Importance of Using Others*. London and New York: Routledge.

Håkansson, H., and Waluszewski, A. (2013). A never ending story—Interaction patterns and economic development. *Journal of Industrial Marketing Management*, 42(3), 443–454.

Högselius, P. (2010). Lost in translation? Science, technology and the state since the 1970s. In Lundin, P., Stenlås, N., and Gribbe, J. (eds.), *Science for Welfare and Warfare: Technology and State Initiative in Cold War Sweden*. Sagamore Beach: Science and History Publications.

Hughes, T. (1987). The evolution of large technological systems. In Bijker, W. E., Hughes, T. P. and Pinch, T. J. (eds.), *The Social Construction of Technological Systems*. Cambridge, MA and London: MIT Press, pp. 51–82.

Lind, J. (2017). The role of accounting for managing innovation processes when relationships matter. *IMP Journal*, 11(1), 7–24.

Mueller, P. (2006). Exploring the knowledge filter: How entrepreneurship and university–industry relationships drive economic growth. *Research Policy*, 35(1), 499–508.

Näringsdepartimentet (2014). *Utvärdering av innovationskontor till Utbildningsdepartementets fördelning av medel till innovationskontor vid universitet och högskolor*. Darienr 2014-06382. Stockholm: Näringsdepartimentet.

OECD (2015). The impact of R&D investment on economic performance: A review of the economic evidence. *Working Party of National Experts on Science and Technology Indicators*, 22 April 2015, Paris.

Perna, A., Baraldi, E., and Waluszewski, A. (2015). Is the value created necessarily associated with money? On the connections between an innovation process and its monetary dimension: The case of Solibro's thin-film solar cells. *Industrial Marketing Management*, 46, 108–121.

Proposition 2001/02:4 (2001). *En politik för tillväxt och livskraft i hela landet*. Stockholm: Sveriges Regering.

Rider, S., and Waluszewski, A. (2015). Crowding out knowledge: Efficiency, innovation and higher education. In Peters, M., Paraskeva, J. M., and Besley, T. (eds.), *The Global Financial Crisis and Educational Restructuring* (Global Studies in Education). New York: Peter Lang, pp. 235–248.

Rosenberg, N. (1982). *Inside the Black Box: Technology and Economics*. Cambridge: Cambridge University Press.

Samuelsson, M., and Söderblom, A. (2012). *Statlig finansiering och dess påverkan på innovativa småföretag—En beskrivande studie av VINN NU programmet*. Stockholm: Handelshögskolan.

Slaughter, S., and Leslie, L. (1997). *Academic Capitalism: Politics, Policies and the Entrepreneurial University*. Baltimore and London: Johns Hopkins University Press.

STUNS (2016). Verksamheter och fokusområden 2015–2016. *STUNS—Stiftelsen för samverkan mellan universiteten i Uppsala, näringsliv och samhälle*, Uppsala.

Utterback, J. M., and Abernathy, W. J. (1975). A dynamic model of process and product innovation. *Omega, The International Journal of Management Science*, 3(6), 639–653.

Vinnova (2005/02). *Teori och metoder för val av indikatorer för inkubatorer*. (Eds.) Löfsten, H., and Lindelöf, P. Stockholm: Vinnova, Swedish Governmental Agency for Innovation Systems.

Vinnova (2008/12). *A Benchmarking Study of the Swedish and British Life Science Innovation Systems: Comparison of Policies and Funding*. (Ed.) Bergqvist, H. Stockholm: Vinnova, Swedish Governmental Agency for Innovation Systems.

Vinnova (2009/20). *Analysis of Chain-linked Effects of Public Policy—Effects on Research and Industry in Swedish Life Sciences Within Innovative Food and Medical Technology*. (Eds.) Laage-Hellman, J., McKelvey, M., and Johansson, M. Stockholm: Vinnova, Swedish Governmental Agency for Innovation Systems.

Vinnova (2010/01). *Uppsala BIO lägesrapport till Vinnova*. Diarienr 2010–01193. Stockholm: Vinnova, Swedish Governmental Agency for Innovation Systems.

Vinnova (2013/05). *BIO-X slutrapport till Vinnova*. Diarienr 2013-05066. Stockholm: Vinnova, Swedish Governmental Agency for Innovation Systems.

Vinnova (2014/02). *Results From 18 VINN Excellence Centres Reported in 2012—Compilation of the Survey Results*. (Eds.) Anaya-Carlsson, K., and Lundberg, M. Vinnova, Stockholm: Swedish Governmental Agency for Innovation Systems.

Vinnova (2014/03). *Global Trends With Local Effects—The Swedish Life Science Industry 1998–2012*. (Ed.) Sandström, A. Stockholm: Vinnova, Swedish Governmental Agency for Innovation Systems.

Vinnova (2014/06). *Hälsoekonomisk effektanalys—av forskning inom programmet Innovationer för framtidens hälsa*. (Eds.) Eriksson, T., Roback, K., Lundqvist, M., Levin, L. Å., and Carlsson, P. Stockholm: Vinnova, Swedish Governmental Agency for Innovation Systems.

Vinnova (2014/07). *Slutvärdering Innovationsslussar inom hälso och sjukvården*. (Eds.) Fröberg, M., Henriksson, J., and Zingmark, A. Stockholm: Ramböll.

Vinnova (2014/09). *Universitets och högskolors samverkansmönster och dess effekter*. (Eds.) Perez Vico, E., Fernqvist, N., Hellsmark, H., Molnar, S., and Hellström, T. Stockholm: Vinnova, Swedish Governmental Agency for Innovation Systems.

Vinnova (2015/03). *Långsiktig utveckling av Svenska lärosätes samverkan med det omgivande samhället—Effekter av forsknings- och innvationsfinansiärers insatser*. (Eds.) Åström, T., Melin, G., Fridholm, T., Terrell, M. M., Stålfors, S., Ärenman, E., Henningsson, K., Londell Assbring, M., Arnold, E., and Danell, R. Stockholm: Technopolis Group.

Vinnova (2015/05) *FoU-program för Små och Medelstora Företag—Metodologiskt ramverk för effektanalyser*. Stockholm: Vinnova, Swedish Governmental Agency for Innovation Systems.

Vinnova (2016/01). *Vinnväxt—ett innovativt program i takt med tiden*. (Ed.) Nilsson, J. Stockholm: Vinnova, Swedish Governmental Agency for Innovation Systems.

Vinnova (2016/02). *Third Evaluation of Berzelii Centres—Exselent, UPSC and Uppsala Berzelii.* (Ed.) O'Kane, M. Stockholm: Vinnova, Swedish Governmental Agency for Innovation Systems.

Vinnova (2016/03) *Effektanalys av Vinnväxt programmet—Analys av effekter och nytta.* (Ed.) Kontigo, A. B. Stockholm: Vinnova, Swedish Governmental Agency for Innovation Systems.

Vinnova (2016/08). *Vinnväxt—A Programme Renewing and Moving Sweden Ahead.* Stockholm: Vinnova, Swedish Governmental Agency for Innovation Systems.

Vinnova (2017/02). *Testbäddar inom hälso- och sjukvård och äldreomsorg—Portföljutvärdering av Vinnovas program.* (Ed.) Kontigo, A. B. Stockholm: Cederberg, Kempinsky, Lindblom and Östlund.

von Hippel, E. (1978). Successful industrial products from customer ideas—Presentation of a new customer-active paradigm with evidence and implications. *Journal of Marketing*, 42(1), 39–49.

Waluszewski, A. (2011). Rethinking innovation policy. *The IMP Journal*, 5(3), 140–156.

Waluszewski, A., Baraldi, E., and Perna, A. (2017). The role of policy in innovation: The challenging distribution of social, material and monetary benefits. *IMP Journal*, 11(1).

Widmalm, S. (2013). Innovation and control: Performative research policy in Sweden. In Rider, S. et al. (eds.), *Transformations in Research, Higher Education and the Academic Market: The Breakdown of Scientific Thought.* Dordrecht: Springer Verlag, pp. 39–52.

Wolff, E. (1997). Spillovers, linkages and technical change. *Economic Systems Research*, 9(1), 9–23.

Yrlö, A. (2005). Impact of public R&D financing on private R&D does financial constraint matter? *ENERPRI Working Paper No. 30.*

13 The Governance of Collaborative Product Development

Jeltje van der Meer-Kooistra and Robert W. Scapens

Introduction

In recent years, the speed at which new technologies have been developing and existing technologies changing, together with the increasing international competition in high-tech industries, has led to changes in the business models used to organise and manage product innovation. Increasingly, new products draw on diverse and complex technologies, such as electronics, mechatronics, software engineering, and so on, all of which are unlikely to be available within even a very large organisation, either because they are outside the core competences of the particular organisation, or because the development of small specialist organisations make it more cost-effective for a large organisation to collaborate with such smaller organisations when developing new products. In this new form of new product development, knowledge flows across organisational boundaries. As management accounting and control researchers, we are especially interested in the governance of organisations which engage in such collaborative product development.

In this chapter, we will discuss two cases in which a number of independent companies collaborated in the development of an innovative product, and here the term *collaborative product development* seems very appropriate. Both cases were located in the southern part of the Netherlands and, as well as various companies, both also involved the local development agency, BOM.[1] These two cases will be described in this chapter. However, it is relevant to note that prior to these projects, BOM commissioned a report exploring the nature and benefits of collaborative product development (see Loeh et al., 2007). In collaborative product development, there is a limited number of key suppliers who are allocated significant responsibilities in relation to the new product development. These key suppliers are involved early in the product development process and are expected to share their extensive specialist knowledge and to take a leading role in respect of specific technologies, thereby creating many synergies in the product development process.

New business models are emerging for such collaborative product development. Whereas in traditional forms of subcontracting, the original equipment manufacturer (OEM) is the primary risk taker and adopts a hierarchical command and control approach, in collaborative product development, the parties (the OEM and the various suppliers) are equal and usually share both the rewards and the risks. Furthermore, in collaborative product development, the suppliers may have opportunities to build intellectual property (IP), while in traditional forms of subcontracting, they have little opportunity to build IP.

In this chapter, we focus specifically on developing new marketable products. In such cases, the 'fundamental research' will have been completed and the basic technology for the product is available. Nevertheless, considerable creativity and innovation is needed to develop a marketable product. As such, these projects have a clear goal—developing a product which can be produced and sold *profitably*. Prior to setting up such a project, there will be a 'business case' setting out the product specifications, its functionalities, its expected selling price and production costs, and the budget for the product development process—in terms of both time and money. In some cases, especially in the past, such projects would have been undertaken within the OEM, although some specific development tasks or the subsequent production might have been outsourced. However, in collaborative product development, multiple parties will take part in the product development process itself.

As we will see in one of the cases in this chapter (the Phenom project), the project may be organised as a temporary organisation (see Kenis et al., 2009), in which the various collaborating parties allocate to the project individual employees from their own organisations. These individuals work full time on the project for an agreed period of time and together comprise the project team. In this way, they form a temporary organisation for a specific period of time (Lundin and Söderholm, 1995). However, in our second case (the Lunaris project), a separate organisation was set up to undertake the project, and the various parties provided individuals on a contract basis to that organisation. In collaborative product development projects, one of the collaborating parties usually provides the project leader, as we will see in our two cases. Within the project team, there is likely to be a function-based structure (i.e., based on specific knowledge or technologies), with the leaders of the operational teams drawn from the collaborating organisations. In addition, there will usually be a monitoring committee, comprising representatives from each of those organisations, which meet periodically to review the project's progress and to resolve any issues which may be causing problems for the project or to make decisions about possible developments which would go beyond the product's original specifications.

In our previous papers, we have discussed the role of minimal structures in the governance of lateral relationships (van der Meer-Kooistra and Scapens, 2008, 2015), with the latter paper focusing specifically on product development projects. We suggest that there are four types of minimal structures—institutional, economic, technical, and social—and together they provide the 'firmness and flexibility' which are needed in the governance of the relationships between the independent organisations which work together on specific projects. These structures are needed to stimulate creativity and at the same time coordinate the activities of the various organisations involved in the product development process. The economic and institutional structures provide the setting in which product development activities and processes take place, while the technical and social structures provide the boundaries for the day-to-day activities of the product development process. The combination of the four structures leaves sufficient room for innovation and creativity and thereby balances firmness and flexibility. We will refer to these minimal structures when discussing the two cases.

As we will see later, our two cases enable us to distinguish three different types of relationships and to describe the governance of each of these relationships. On a day-to-day basis, there is the governance of the operational teams and individuals working on the project. The project leader, together with the operational team leaders, has the primary responsibility for ensuring that the various specialists are able to work together effectively. Then there is the governance of the 'overall' project, which is the responsibility of the monitoring committee, mentioned earlier. Finally, there is also the governance of the employees of the collaborating organisations who are working on various projects, probably in different locations. Here, the individual organisations want to ensure that their employees keep in mind the interests of their employing organisation, as well as focusing on the goals of the product development project on which they are working.

In this chapter, in addition to discussing generic governance issues in collaborative product development projects, we will specifically focus on the three above types of governance and the relationships between individuals involved in the projects. These relationships form the social structure which is crucial for knowledge sharing and the integration of knowledge. In our two case studies, we describe the different relationships and how they were governed. The formal organisation of these two projects differs somewhat, but they share a number of common characteristics. Furthermore, there may be other ways of organising such projects, but we would expect some of the common characteristics of these two cases to apply elsewhere. The first case concerns the development of a desktop electron microscope—the Phenom project. The local development agency (BOM) was influential in bringing together the various parties which collaborated on this project, and one of the collaborating suppliers took the leadership role. In the second case, a separate company was set up by the OEM to undertake the development of a printer capable of printing the printed circuit boards used in computers and other electronic equipment—the Lunaris project. BOM was also involved in this project, but here it contributed funding and assisted in raising funds from other parties to finance this separate company. However, the company itself had relatively few employees, as the specialist knowledge came from the other collaborating parties who provided individual experts to work on the project.

The next two sections will describe the two case studies. Then, drawing on these cases, we will discuss the governance of collaborative product development projects; first, by discussing the generic governance issues in such projects in the context of the four minimal structures introduced earlier, and second, by discussing the governance of the three types of relationships mentioned earlier. Finally, we will draw out the implications and suggest possible directions for future research.

Phenom Product Development Project

As mentioned earlier, the aim of the Phenom project was to develop a desktop electron microscope. The basic technology for such a microscope had previously been developed by Philips Research (also located in the southern part of the Netherlands, in the city of Eindhoven), but it needed developing into a marketable product. FEI Electron Optics, a US-based OEM producing and selling large electron microscopes, also located in Eindhoven, had purchased the technology from Philips Research, as it was interested in extending its product range to include a desktop electron microscope. However, at that time, it did not have the necessary financial and human resources to develop a marketable product on its own. An initiative taken by the regional development agency (BOM—mentioned earlier), however, provided an opportunity for FEI to work with other companies in the region in developing the Phenom.

At the beginning of the new millennium, BOM had initiated its *Collaborative Product Innovation in Manufacturing* project, which was designed to find ways of increasing collaboration among OEMs and the small- and medium-sized companies in the region around Eindhoven. As product innovation activities of OEMs have become increasingly dependent on external specialist suppliers, the project aimed at improving the capabilities of the suppliers within the region to strengthen the product innovation supply chain. One particularly interesting aspect of this initiative was the risk-reward model proposed by BOM. It was becoming increasingly common for suppliers to bear some project risk, for instance, by agreeing a fixed fee for developing a particular part or component for a product. If the development costs are less or more than the agreed fee some or all of the profit/loss would accrue to the supplier. However, the risk-reward model proposed by BOM went further and incorporated market risk as well as project risk. This meant that key suppliers would only recover their development costs from the revenues earned when the product was eventually sold in the market.

After preliminary discussions in the autumn of 2004, the Phenom product development project began in April 2005. Much of the development work was done by the suppliers, while FEI was to be responsible for selling the new product. The development work required a range of engineering skills, principally in mechatronics, software, electronics, and electron optics, along with design skills. FEI (the OEM and owner of the technology), NTS (the mechatronics developer), and Sioux (the software developer) shared the risks of the project. NTS and Sioux were to be paid for their development work through a share of the profits from FEI's sales of the Phenom. Benchmark (the electronics developer) and Van Berlo Studios (the product designer), however, were unwilling to accept the BOM risk-reward model, although Benchmark agreed to undertake the development work for a fixed fee, thereby accepting some of the project risk.

These parties came together to collaborate on the project, in what could be termed a temporary organisation (Bakker and Janowicz-Panjaitan, 2009; Engwall, 2003; Lundin and Söderholm, 1995). Although the parties were separate, independent organisations, they are part of a regional network—most of them had worked together on other similar collaborative projects in the past (but in other settings) and/or could expect to work together again on future projects. As such, although the Phenom project had a finite life, it had a history and a future—in other words, it was temporally embedded (Bakker and Janowicz-Panjaitan, 2009; Engwall, 2003; Lundin and Söderholm, 1995; see also van der Meer-Kooistra and Scapens, 2015).

In a recent paper, we discussed the role of minimal structures in the governance of product development projects undertaken by several independent organisations,[2] and specifically pointed to the institutional, economic, technical, and social structures (see van der Meer-Kooistra and Scapens, 2015). In the case of the Phenom project, the regional network and its organisational context formed the institutional structure of the project. The main economic structure was the risk-reward model, coupled with the agreements between the parties about the development time/cost budget and the planned cost/selling price of the Phenom. The specifications for the Phenom were derived from its expected functionalities and the electron optics technology bought from Philips Research. These specifications provided the technical structure, which also included the stage-gate model[3] for the project. Together the economic and technical structures provided the boundaries within which the project activities had to take place.

However, as a desktop electron microscope was a new product, the boundaries created by the technical and economic structures left substantial room for manoeuvre in the development of the Phenom. This required the participants to share their knowledge and expertise while developing the product, to discuss actual issues and problems as they arose, and to agree solutions. Over time new functionalities were added to the product to improve its marketability, but this increased the development costs and increased the expected production costs and planned selling price for the Phenom. However, the lack of tight boundaries did not create particular tensions in the relationships between the parties as the institutional context and the temporal embeddedness of the project in the regional network created institutional trust at the organisation level. Nevertheless, there also had to be trust among the individuals working within the project on a day-to-day basis, i.e., trust in the expertise, capabilities, and commitment of the others with whom they were working. This developed through the social structure which evolved as the project got underway and progressed.

Each of the parties collaborating in the Phenom project assigned a number of individuals from their own organisations to work full time on the project. These individuals worked together in the project office, which was located at the NTS site,[4] and NTS provided the project leader. The day-to-day work of the project was overseen by the project management team, chaired by the project leader from NTS and comprising the senior persons assigned to the project by the collaborating parties; FEI, NTS, Sioux, Benchmark, and Van Berlo. Within the project, there were three operational teams: a mechanical team (leader from NTS), a software team (leader from Sioux), and an electrical team (leader from Benchmark). The individuals who were assigned to the project by Van Berlo, the product designer, participated in both the mechanical team and the software team.

As well as possessing expertise and technological knowledge, the various individuals working on the project needed to have the necessary social skills to work closely together in order to share their expertise and knowledge and to discuss technical problems, not only within their operational team but also with the other teams. Working on the project in the same location stimulated this sharing of expertise and knowledge and facilitated the search for solutions to technical problems. By so doing, the team members were able to quickly develop good personal relationships as well as trust in each other's capabilities and commitment to the project. As well as various *ad hoc* meetings within and between the operational teams, the project management team held weekly meetings to review progress, to discuss issues and problems, and to monitor the work of the operational teams.

The collaborating parties held meetings every three or four months, chaired by the CEO of NTS. These meetings discussed design and financial issues and included brainstorming sessions to find solutions to difficult problems, especially problems which spanned the activities of the different parties. In addition, they were joined by the project management team and the leaders of the operational teams to discuss issues and problems which had to be 'escalated' by the operational management, such as when decisions to deal with specific problems or to add new functionalities were likely to involve exceeding the development budget and/or the planned costs/selling price of the Phenom. In addition, management meetings of the risk-reward parties (FEI, NTS, and Sioux), also chaired by the CEO of NTS, were held two or three times a year. These brought together the senior managers of FEI, NTS, and Sioux to discuss contractual matters, review the progress of the project, and consider financial and sales related issues. The organisation of the project as a whole, together with these various types of meetings, helped maintain trust-based relationships at the individual and organisational levels.

As the individuals assigned to the project by the collaborating parties worked full time on developing the Phenom, their own organisation's management organised various informal activities during which lessons learned from the project could be passed onto their colleagues and advice could be obtained from those colleagues about particular issues and problems in developing the Phenom. As such, these informal activities provided opportunities for knowledge sharing *within* the collaborating organisations and helped to maintain social relationships *within* those organisations.

The Phenom was developed quite quickly, and technically, it was a very good product. However, the initial sales were disappointing. As a desktop electron microscope, the Phenom is much smaller and much cheaper than conventional electron microscopes (and its users can be trained within a day instead of several weeks). However, its level of magnification is correspondingly lower and, as such, it competes with optical microscopes rather than the larger electron microscope. Consequently, the market for the Phenom is rather different to the market for FEI's conventional products. Unfortunately, FEI had been unable to develop a new sales and marketing organisation for the Phenom. This was a very serious concern for the other two risk-reward parties, NTS and Sioux, as they would only recover their development costs when sufficient numbers of the Phenom had been sold. After substantial discussions and negotiation, the risk-reward parties decided to set up a new marketing company, named Phenom World, to distribute the Phenom worldwide and it is now selling successfully.

In this case, the collaborating parties came together through a contractual arrangement which did not create an independent legal entity, although it could be described as a temporary organisation which came to an end when the Phenom was developed, even though some of the parties continued to collaborate in its marketing and sales. A key feature of the business model was the way in which some of the key suppliers shared the risk and rewards of the project. In our next case, the sharing of risk and rewards is also a feature of the business model, but its organisational form was somewhat different, as we will see.

Lunaris Product Development Project

The Lunaris project began initially in 2006, when Océ, a Canon Group Company, was seeking new applications for its existing inkjet technology. Océ has considerable experience in inkjet technology for graphic arts applications, but it wanted to extend its product range. The aim of the Lunaris project was to develop inkjet technology for the production of the inner layers of the printed circuit boards (PCBs) used in computers and other electronic products. Using inkjet technology, the Lunaris would replace 11 of the 15 steps in the lithographic process currently used to produce PCBs, making the production of inner layers less complex, much faster, fully digital, more environmentally friendly, and 30% cheaper.

A project team was set up in Océ's Inkjet Application Centre in Eindhoven. The team comprised members from Océ, Sioux, NTS, and Ramaer (a PCB company in the Eindhoven region). However, this project team was set up outside Océ's normal corporate structure, as it was believed that developing such a completely new product needed people who were able 'to think outside of the box', and this would not be possible within the existing business structures with their short-term targets. At the outset, the project was concerned primarily with technology development, and there were only some very general ideas about the nature of the product and its market. However, by the beginning of 2009, the technology had been sufficiently developed, along with more concrete ideas about the product and the market. At this time, Océ decided to spin off the Lunaris project to a new company, called MuTracx, which would be dedicated to developing and then marketing the new product.

Using a convertible loan from Océ, MuTracx purchased this new inkjet technology from Océ. In addition, Océ provided a start-up loan. However, as external investors were reluctant to invest in the business, MuTracx's management team decided on a relatively modest project with limited expectations regarding sales of the Lunaris in the initial years. On this basis, the management team produced a business case for the project and were then able to obtain a bank loan and a government subsidy. In addition, they invited the key parties in the product development to become risk-reward partners – based on BOM's risk-reward model. These risk-reward parties were Sioux (software), TMC (civil engineers), 3T (electronics), and CCM (mechatronics). These parties would only receive payment for their development costs out of the sales revenues of the Lunaris. Sioux also took an equity stake in MuTracx.

In contrast to the Phenom project, in which there was a temporary organisation, in this case, MuTracx is a separate legal entity and the 'owner' of the Lunaris project. As an entity, it was responsible for both the development and the subsequent marketing of the Lunaris. However, the key suppliers assigned members of their staff to work on the project at the MuTracx site. As a result, most of the people working at the MuTracx site were employed by these key suppliers, and MuTracx only had a small number of systems architects who planned, monitored, and coordinated the project. Consequently, the governance of the relationships among the collaborating parties was very important.

Again, drawing on van der Meer-Kooistra and Scapens (2015), we can see the institutional, economic, technical, and social structures which governed the project. Although the project initially started within Océ, when it was spun off and MuTracx was formed, the various collaborating parties were drawn from the same regional network as the Phenom project. This network provided the institutional structure and the temporal embeddedness of the project. The business case prepared by the MuTracx management team and the BOM risk-reward model provided the economic structure for the project. The business case included the planned cost for the production of the Lunaris as this would be critical for its pricing and competitiveness.

Furthermore, the limited funds available to MuTracx meant that the time available for the development of the Lunaris was very constrained. As a result, cost and time budgets were very important in the economic structure.

For purposes of the development process, the Lunaris was decomposed into functional units, each with an operational team responsible for its development. In this way, the individual functional units could be developed in parallel, and this shortened the development time. However, it also had the potential to create problems as decisions taken by one team could have consequences for the work of the other teams. The technical structure of the project comprised the planned functionalities of the Lunaris and the technical specifications of each of the functional units. These were translated into budgets for the development cost and a projected bill of materials for the eventual product. Initially, the economic and technical structures provided considerable flexibility for the individual teams, but as the project developed and decisions were taken about the functional units and how they would be integrated to form the Lunaris, the boundaries within which the operational teams could work became much tighter, and the flexibility which was available in the early phases of the project declined.

Both in the early stages, when there was considerable flexibility for the individual teams, and in the later stages, when the boundaries of the project became much tighter, the social structure played an important role in the relationships between the operational teams and the collaborating parties. The collaborating parties knew each other from the regional network, and most of them had worked together on previous and/or ongoing projects. This contributed to trust-based relationships between these parties at an organisational level. In addition, the organisation of the operational teams stimulated the development of good relationships at the level of the individual participants, who brought their knowledge and expertise to the project on a day-to-day basis. All these participants, from the various collaborating parties, worked at the MuTracx site, except a small number from Océ, which had set up an operational team based in its Applications Centre, nearby in Eindhoven.

MuTracx's management team and system architects managed the activities of the operational teams, and each of the collaborating parties assigned a leader for their own teams who was also responsible for relationships with the other teams and with MuTracx. As all teams (except the Océ team) were located at the MuTracx site, there was intensive and extensive sharing of knowledge, and unforeseen problems could be easily discussed and solutions found. Furthermore, MuTracx's managers could easily see how the project was developing by walking around, observing and talking, and they encouraged the teams to be creative but within the financial and time constraints.

In addition, there were regular meetings during which the ongoing activities and problems could be discussed. Each team had a meeting every morning to discuss the day's activities, and every week or two weeks all the teams came together to discuss what had been achieved and to plan the next steps in the development process. There were also various *ad hoc* meetings between parties, which were organised to discuss and resolve specific problems. Furthermore, there were quarterly meetings of senior managers from all the collaborating parties to discuss both technical and commercial issues, and both Sioux and TCM organised meetings at which their own team members could discuss and share experiences with colleagues from their own organisation who were working on other projects.

In the Lunaris case, although the product development activities took place within a specific organisation—i.e. MuTracx—the parties taking part in the development processes were drawn from several different organisations. In this sense, it is similar to the Phenom project. In both cases, the regional network of suppliers provided an institutional structure which governed relationships between the collaborating parties, while the risk-reward model (originally proposed by BOM) provided a similar economic structure in each case. Although the form of organisation differed (the Lunaris project taking place within MuTracx, while the Phenom was developed in a temporary organisation), the governance of the collaborative product development activities and the relationships between the collaborating parties was quite similar, as we will discuss.

Generic Governance Issues in Collaborative Product Development Projects

As we saw earlier, although the business models of the Phenom and Lunaris projects had different organisational structures, they both involved the collaboration of a number of parties which were independent organisations. The relationships among these independent organisations are a particular form of lateral relationships. As we have argued in previous papers (van der Meer-Kooistra and Scapens, 2008, 2015), this form of lateral relationships can be governed by four minimal structures—institutional, economic, technical, and social—which together stimulate creativity and knowledge exchange and at the same time coordinate the activities of the collaborating organisations. As we indicate in those previous papers, we prefer to use the term *governance* rather than *control* when discussing lateral relationships between independent organisations. Control implies that there is some form of hierarchy in which a superordinate authority exercises control over subordinate parties. However, in lateral relationships between more or less equal parties, the role of a superordinate authority (if there is one), and, in particular, its ability to impose controls over the other parties, is far less clear. Consequently, the collaborating parties have to work closely together to govern their collaborative projects.

In the following subsections, we will discuss the generic governance issues in collaborative product development projects in the context of the four minimal structures. We will start by elaborating on the generic governance issues related to the institutional and economic contexts of these projects, followed by a discussion of the generic governance issues related to their technical and social contexts. In so doing, we will refer to the governance issues in the two cases. We will finalise this section by discussing the role of the four minimal structures in creating firmness and flexibility in the governance of collaborative product development projects.

Institutional and Economic Contexts

The institutional and economic contexts of the parties collaborating in product development projects determine the boundaries within which the projects are set up and executed. These contexts comprise the institutional and economic structures which not only structure the activities during the initiation and execution of the development processes but also structure the decision-making processes of the various parties in the pre-project phase when the parties are considering whether or not to participate in such a project. We agree with Engwall's (2003) claim that the 'inner life' of a project cannot be fully understood without giving proper attention to the pre-project phase and the influences of the wider institutional and organisational contexts during that phase. In collaborative product development projects, the collaborating parties are usually OEMs and small- to medium-sized specialist organisations which possess their own particular technical knowledge and expertise.

To become involved in a collaborative product development project means that OEMs and the specialist organisations must be prepared to take on quite new roles. OEMs have to change the way they have previously worked with their suppliers, moving away from the traditional hierarchical mode of working to a more lateral or horizontal mode in which the OEMs and the specialist organisations (the suppliers) are equal partners in the product development process. The specialist organisations have to be willing to bring their technical knowledge and expertise to the project. Furthermore, as they will be collaboratively developing the new product, together with the other specialist organisations, they have to be willing to share this knowledge and expertise with those other organisations. Moreover, they may have to accept more responsibility for the development activities, which could include some of the project risk (i.e. development costs and development time) and possibly also some of the market risk (arising from the sale of the new product), which they would not have done in more traditional forms of subcontracting. As they take more responsibility for the development activities, the financial situation of these specialist organisations must be sufficient to enable them to accept this additional responsibility and the risks involved. Funding from governmental research and development (R&D) programmes can sometimes be available to help these (relatively small) specialist organisations to become involved in such product development projects.

In the two cases we described earlier, the institutional and economic contexts in the pre-project phase stimulated the parties to become involved in these collaborative product development projects. BOM, the regional development agency, had taken an initiative aimed at strengthening the regional supply chain, and this had consequences, not only for the business models of the specialist suppliers but also for the OEMs themselves. In collaborative product development projects, the OEMs and their specialist suppliers become equal partners, and this means, among other things, that the specialist organisations and the OEMs have to share knowledge and technology with the other project parties and that developing the new product is the responsibility of all the collaborating parties. The BOM's report (see Loeh et al., 2007) was discussed in detail by the regional network of OEMs and their suppliers. As a result of the BOM initiative, and particularly its support for the small- and medium-sized specialist organisations in the region, the members of the regional network indicated their willingness to participate in collaborative product development projects. In some instances, this required them to improve their technical, project management, and social capabilities, and some of the specialist organisations recruited more highly qualified employees to extend their core competences.

As they were part of a regional network, the parties involved in the two projects knew each other, some very well. Most of them had worked together on previous product development projects or they were collaborating in other projects or supply chains. As the parties knew each other, it was easier for them to accept the new business model and the new types of relationships with the other parties which the BOM initiative implied. In addition, the key specialist parties accepted the risk-reward model, and as a result, they became jointly responsible for the project and market risks of the new product.

As in our two cases, the management of project and market risks is often an important governance issue in the execution phase of collaborative product development projects. Because of their joint responsibility for these risks, it is in the parties' interests to complete the product development activities within both the development cost budget and the planned development time and at the planned cost of producing the new product. Therefore, if the individual participants working on the project on a day-to-day basis want to go beyond the economic boundaries, as agreed at the outset by the collaborating parties, the approval of senior managers of these parties will be needed. As such approval is likely to be needed quickly, there have to be regular meetings of senior representatives of the collaborating parties. These meetings can also help to develop the trustworthy relationships which are needed to facilitate the collaborative process.

The Phenom project provides a particularly good illustration of the role played by the institutional and economic contexts in the initiation and execution phases of the project. As the parties were enthusiastic about the new business model proposed by BOM, they wanted to start the development activities as soon as possible. All parties, including the risk-reward parties, were willing to start the Phenom project without having formally agreed and signed a contract. These parties already knew each other very well.

They had worked together in the past and anticipated that they would work together in the future. There was institutional trust between the parties, and consequently, they did not feel they had to wait for the contract to be signed.

With collaborating parties located in the same geographical region, communication is relatively easy. There are likely to be local (informal) communication channels which can provide information about the various parties' involvement in other projects. Furthermore, this means that the parties will want to be perceived as being 'good' collaborative partners, as negative information about their involvement in a particular project could affect their involvement in future projects. Thus, the institutional context of a project can both stimulate and discipline the collaborating parties. This was very important in the Phenom project when it started to become clear to the risk-reward parties that the OEM had been unable to set up the necessary sales network for the new product, with the result that the initial sales were disappointing. This was a significant problem for the specialist parties, as it threatened their ability to recover their development costs. Therefore, they decided to jointly set up a new marketing company to market the Phenom worldwide.

Technical and Social Contexts

The technical and social contexts provide the boundaries for the day-to-day activities of the product development process. The main technical boundaries are determined by the technical competences of the members of the operational teams as well as the required functionalities of the new product. These functionalities determine the technical specifications for the new product and a stage-gate model is usually drawn up to monitor the development process (Cooper, 1990; Hertenstein and Platt, 2000).

Meeting the planned timeline (set out in the stage-gate model) is essential in collaborative product development projects as it is usually very important, for competitive reasons, to get the new product to market as quickly as possible. Furthermore, extending the timeline will increase development costs, require more human resources than originally planned, and lead to delays in parallel projects and/or the start of new projects. Consequently, meeting a strict timeline is a common feature of collaborative product development projects. This means that there is little time during a project to develop the necessary technical competences. This does not mean that the individual participants (and the collaborating organisations) cannot learn lessons and develop new knowledge in the course of a project, but it does mean that the individual participants need to have the necessary technical competences at the outset. Consequently, if it emerges that a particular participant does not have the necessary technical competences (or even social competences—see later), his/her employer (which will be one of the collaborating parties) must be prepared to quickly withdraw him/her from the project team and to appoint someone more competent.

The members of the operational teams have to be fully committed to the development process. Without being willing to openly sharing their knowledge with others, the members of these teams will not be able to integrate their respective expertise and knowledge in the development of the new product. This implies that all participating organisations, including OEMs, must be willing to allow others to use their knowledge and technology.

In addition to having the required technical competences, the individual participants need to have adequate social skills to be able to collaborate intensively with other participants who have a similar or different technical background (Kamoche and Cunha, 2001; van der Meer-Kooistra and Scapens, 2015). Each has to respect the other's expertise and to be open to the other's knowledge and ideas. There also needs to be openness about 'failure', and when things go wrong (or do not work out as expected), everyone must be prepared to discuss them. It is crucial to create an atmosphere in which all the participants are ready to meet together and discuss issues and problems as, and when, they arise. Thus, it is essential that there are good working relationships among all the participants in the project—participants from different organisations and with different technical backgrounds. These working relationships are usually developed during the execution of the project. In the next section, 'Governance of Relationships', we will elaborate on the governance of these working relationships, but first we will discuss how the minimal structures provide the firmness and flexibility which are needed in the governance of collaborative product development projects.

Firmness and Flexibility

The institutional, economic, technical, and social structures have to create structure (firmness), as well as room for manoeuvre (flexibility) for the participants involved in collaborative product development projects. In this subsection, we will discuss how these minimal structures enable the participants to be creative and to successfully develop a new product and bring it to the market. In addition, we will point out how these structures can evolve over the lifetime of a product development project.

At the start of a project, the aim is usually quite clear, i.e. to develop a marketable and profitable product, but how to achieve this aim may be far less clear. For example, in the two projects described earlier, it was very clear what had to be developed, namely, a desktop electron microscope and a printer capable of printing PCBs, respectively. Nevertheless, there were many technical problems which had to be solved and marketing issues which needed to be addressed, as the products were developed. Consequently, there needed to be sufficient space to allow the operational teams room for manoeuvre so they could be creative in finding innovative solutions to the problems they encountered (Kamoche and Cunha, 2001; van der Meer-Kooistra and Scapens, 2015). Room for manoeuvre is especially important when a project involves new technology, as in our two cases, or when the project parties have limited experience with the particular technology, such as when an existing technology is applied in a new area. The collaborating parties bring to the project diverse capabilities and knowledge, which have to be integrated in the development of the new product (Wallin and Von Krogh, 2010).

In many collaborative product development projects, the technical structure (e.g., the technical specifications and product functionalities) and the economic structure (e.g., development cost/hours budget and the planned cost/price of the new product) can only provide a broad framework (i.e., loose boundaries) at the start of the project. These structures will evolve during the product development process. However, as the project progresses, decisions will be taken which 'fix' various aspects of the product specifications and, thereby, the ultimate cost of producing the new product. Through these decisions, the technical structure, as well as the economic structure, become firmer and, as a result, limit the extent to which the members of the operational team(s) can be creative. Consequently, it may be necessary to avoid the technical structure becoming too firm too early, so as to provide the flexibility which is needed for creativity.

In the two projects described earlier, the boundaries provided by the technical and economic structures were quite loose, but they were supported by an institutional structure in the form of the regional network and the temporal embeddedness of the project. This institutional structure provided the basis for the institutional trust which allowed the parties to begin the project, even in the absence of a formal contract in the Phenom case. Although the collaborating organisations and their senior managers knew each other, as they had worked together before, many of the individual members of the operational teams had not previously collaborated with each other. However, social relationships were developed, and this built trust among the participants at the day-to-day operational level while they were working together on the project, sharing their knowledge and expertise and openly discussing issues and problems as they arose. Because of the tight timelines of such projects, social relationships have to be developed and trust built rather quickly. It is through the social structure that the members of the operational teams come to feel jointly and personally responsible for developing the new product as a whole rather than for some specific element of it (as would be the case in traditional subcontracting).

In this section, we have discussed generic governance issues which arise in collaborative product development projects. These issues stem from the lateral relationships between independent organisations which are the central feature of collaborative product development. In the next section, we will outline the governance of the relationships among participants at various levels in collaborative product development projects.

Governance of Relationships

The core of collaborative product development projects is the contribution and sharing of knowledge by the parties which have agreed to develop a new product *together* (see e.g. Garriga et al., 2013; Menon and Pfeffer, 2003;

Spaeth et al., 2010; Wallin and Von Krogh, 2010). However, such knowledge largely resides within the individuals assigned to the project by the various parties. These individuals need to collaborate as the different types of knowledge which they each bring to the project have to be integrated in the product development process. Much of this knowledge is tacit in nature, as it is gained through experience and the development and repeated application of individual skills. As such, it is stored in the individual's cognition and can only be shared through face-to-face collaboration. Furthermore, Wallin and Von Krogh (2010) argue that the knowledge required for successful collaborative product development[5] projects consists not only of the technical knowledge derived from the different domains (mechanics, electronics, software, manufacturing, sales, marketing, and so on) but also knowledge about how to organise the contribution, sharing, and integration of that technical knowledge.

Organising the contribution, sharing and integration of the knowledge of the individual participants working day to day on a collaborative product development project, requires the creation of conditions which encourage and enable those individuals to work closely together and the development of good working relationships among the individuals concerned. In the two collaborative product innovation projects described earlier, there were three levels at which these working relationships were organised: (1) between the senior managers of the collaborating parties, (2) between the individual participants working together on a day-to-day basis, and (3) between the individual participants allocated to the project and their colleagues in the same organisation working on other projects. The first two levels extend beyond the boundaries of the individual collaborating organisations, while the third level relates to relationships *within* each of those collaborating organisations. Below we will describe the relationships at these three levels and discuss how they can be governed.

Relationship Between the Senior Managers of the Collaborating Parties

The senior managers of the collaborating parties are responsible for the overall management of collaborative product development projects. To exercise this responsibility, these senior managers need to have knowledge about how to organise the contribution, sharing, and integration of the knowledge required for the project. Their responsibility begins with the decision of their organisation to participate in a collaborative product development project.

Having taken the decision to participate, other decisions have to be taken *together* with the other project parties. Examples of such decisions are the terms of the contract; the sharing of project risks; the organisation of the project; the assignment of key individuals to the project (and possible replacements over time); the development cost/time budgets; the functionalities and the planned cost/selling price for the product; the process for approving changes to the development budgets and the functionalities, cost, and price of the product;

and so on. These decisions shape the form of the product development process and the way in which the operational teams work together on the project. However, it is important that the operational teams are given sufficient room for manoeuvre to enable them be creative and to innovate in developing the product. Once this is done, the senior managers should leave the day-to-day activities to the project's operational teams but monitor the project's progress through regular senior management team meetings. However, they (the senior managers) play a key role when issues or problems faced by the operational teams need to be escalated to a higher management level, for example, when the operational teams propose adding new features to the product which will increase the development costs and/or the cost/price of the product. In such instances, the senior managers of the collaborating parties need to discuss and, if they consider it appropriate, approve (or reject) the proposal.

Because of the tight timelines of product development projects (discussed earlier), decisions about such escalated issues need to be made quickly. So, to avoid delaying the project, the senior management committee has to meet regularly and, when necessary, arrange *ad hoc* meetings. Product development projects undertaken within OEMs are usually subject to the various hierarchical levels, with their formal decision-making procedures, regulations, and responsibilities. This can complicate decision-making processes and create delays in the product development process, especially when new ideas and new technologies are involved. This was the primary reason for Océ's decision to spin off MuTracx to develop the Lunaris.

To exercise their responsibility for the overall management and monitoring of the project, the senior managers need to be kept fully informed by the project leader about the project's progress and about issues and problems encountered by the operational teams. In addition to the regular senior management meetings, the senior managers need to stay in close contact with individuals from their own organisations, who are leaders of operational teams, and have regular (and also *ad hoc*) meetings with their own employees who are working on the project. For the senior management team to be able to take decisions *together*, there must be trust-based working relationships among the senior managers involved. If they do not already exist, as a result of the institutional context, they must be built quickly. Regular and *ad hoc* meetings of the senior managers are a formal mechanism which can help in building and maintaining trust-based relationships. In addition, social activities and events for all the participants in the project can be a more informal mechanism but one which can be very important for the senior managers to get to know the others taking part in the project.

Relationship Between the Individual Participants Working on the Project

The individual participants work together on the development of the product on a day-to-day basis. Usually, they work in operational teams, each of which is responsible for specific development tasks. These teams normally consist mainly of individuals having a similar knowledge background, but individuals with different knowledge backgrounds can also be members of an operational team. Even though these teams are usually formed around similar domain knowledge, since knowledge from the different domains has to be integrated, the team members need to understand the interfaces between the domains and be open to the insights and ideas of the other teams. As already mentioned, the operational teams need room for manoeuvre if they are to be creative. The boundaries, within which they have to work, are set by the senior managers of the collaborating parties. Although these boundaries will contain a certain amount of flexibility, the operational teams will need senior managers' approval to go beyond them.

The day-to-day management of the various operational teams is the responsibility of the project leader. The project leader usually comes from one of the key collaborating parties (not necessarily the OEM), and his/her appointment is a joint decision of the senior managers of the collaborating parties. Each of the operational teams will have a team leader. In collaborative projects, each operational team is likely to comprise primarily individuals from one of the collaborating parties. This party will normally nominate the team leader, but his/her appointment will be made by the senior managers of all the collaborating parties, in consultation with the project leader. Although the project leader is responsible for the project as a whole and, as such, manages the activities of the operational teams, he/she has no 'direct' hierarchical relationship, as most of the members of these teams will be employed by other organisations. Furthermore, as the members of the operational teams bring specific technical knowledge to the project (knowledge which the project leader may not possess), the project leader cannot exercise 'tight' control over their work. Instead, he/she has to create the conditions in which there is sufficient flexibility for the operational teams to be creative while at the same time providing sufficient structure so that the work of the various operational teams can be integrated in developing the new product.

As pointed out by van der Meer-Kooistra and Scapens (2015), a project leader has to avoid 'micro-managing' the teams and the team members. Instead he/she has to allow them (as professionals) to do their own work, as well as stimulate day-to-day interactions among team members and among the various teams. This requires interpersonal trust in the relationships among the individual team members and among the various teams, including trust in their expertise and competence. The project leader has to create the conditions in which trust-based relationships among the team members can be built. This can be facilitated by all (or most of) the participants working in a single location so that they can readily meet each other to discuss issues and solve problems as they arise, and also come together regularly in both formal and informal meetings. One of the typical mechanisms a project leader will use to structure the project activities over time is the *stage-gate model*, which sets out all the necessary steps (stages) in the product development process, as well as the achievements and authorisations (gates) which are necessary to move from one stage to the next. The project leader has to ensure that all the individual participants are fully committed to the project as a whole (and not just to their specific element or elements) and to moving through the various stages of the project and passing each of the gates within the planned timeframe.

As the individual participants working on a collaborative product development project come from a number of different organisations, their relationships with other participants can be characterised as lateral relationships. Consequently, their relationships are not controlled as they would be in a hierarchy; instead, they are governed by minimal structures which include the boundaries set by the senior managers of the collaborating parties and the mechanisms used by the project leader. These structures, however, leave sufficient room for manoeuvre to allow them to be creative and to use their knowledge in developing the new product. However, trust-based relationships with the other participants are crucial for the success of the project.

Relationship Between Individual Participants and Their Colleagues From the Same Organisation

The close working relationships which develop between the individual participants who work on a collaborative product development project on a day-to-day basis create a form of *a-temporality*, as they can come to identify themselves more with the project, than with their employing organisation (Janowicz-Panjaitan et al., 2009). This a-temporality separates the project from its temporal embeddedness, as the project becomes the 'site' for the collaborative product development project, even where it is not 'a site' in the sense of a physical location. As such, it encourages the individual participants to become professionally and personally identified with the project and with the development of the new product, and this creates the project as something separate from their employing organisations. This can sometimes create problems for the individuals and their employing organisations, as potentially there can be competing interests, and balancing these interests can sometimes be problematic.

To avoid such problems, the senior managers of individual collaborating organisations can arrange regular, but quite informal, meetings for their employees who are participating in different projects (van der Meer-Kooistra and Scapens, 2015). Such meetings create a parallel social structure (i.e., parallel to the social structure within the collaborative product development projects) which can help to (re-)integrate their employees into their employing organisations. In these meetings, individuals who are working on different collaborative product development projects meet with their colleagues and discuss problems, lessons learned, and knowledge created in their specific projects. In this way, they are encouraged to continue to identify with their own (employing) organisation and to be aware of that organisation's interests. In this way, the organisation's employees learn from each other's experiences and can then use the lessons learned in their own project and/or in the organisation's future projects. As such, not only the employees but also the organisation can increase their or its capabilities in collaborative product development projects. In addition, these informal meetings help to strengthen (existing) relationships among colleagues and to make it easier for them to identify with their own organisation.

Conclusions and Research Implications

In this chapter, we have discussed the governance of collaborative product development projects in which independent companies collaborate in developing new products. This particular form of product development differs in many respects from traditional subcontracting, and it has led to the emergence of new business models. We illustrated two of these new business models with two cases in which a number of independent companies, comprising an OEM and smaller specialist organisations, developed a new marketable product. In the first case, the Phenom project, the project was organised as a temporary organisation, whereas in the second case, the Lunaris project, a separate organisation was set up to develop the new product. In each of these projects, we discussed the contributions and responsibilities of the collaborating parties, the role of minimal structures in providing flexibility as well as structure, the influence of the institutional context on the collaborating parties' willingness to participate and to accept project and market risks, and the importance of the project organisation. We also drew attention to the importance of good working relationships among the participating parties at three different levels: among the senior managers of the collaborating parties, among the individual participants working together on the project on a day-to-day basis, and among the individual participants allocated to the project and colleagues in their employing organisation who are working on other projects. By so doing, we were able to discuss the structures and practices used in the two cases and, moreover, by drawing on concepts from various literatures, we were able to understand the governance of these collaborative product development projects.

However, as both our cases were in the high-tech electronics industry and, in both, the new product was developed in a relatively short period of time (two to three years), further studies are needed to ascertain whether there are similar processes in other industries and in more complicated and time-consuming projects. However, there are likely to be collaborative product development projects in other industries, especially when specialist knowledge and expertise from different domains is needed. In such projects, the sharing and integration of knowledge and expertise will require governance mechanisms, as well as trustworthy working relationships at the level of the individual participants and at the inter-organisational level. In our cases, the regional network stimulated and supported the development of such relationships at the inter-organisational level, as the senior managers of the organisations involved knew each other and had worked together in the past and/or expected to work together in the future. However, the trustworthy relationships at the level of the individual participants working on the projects on a day-to-day basis had to develop during the execution of the projects. Further studies are needed to explore how such trustworthy relationships are sustained in other types of collaborative product development projects.

When collaborative product development projects extend beyond the regional setting, possibly internationally, or when the collaborating parties have no previous experience of working together, it is likely that the institutional structure will be weak and probably insufficient to support the type of trustworthy working relationships we observed in our two cases. In such projects, further mechanisms and processes are likely to be needed, possibly during the process of selecting collaborative partners and when drawing up the contract, to develop trustworthy working relationships at both the individual and organisational levels. For example, it has been recognised in the literature that learning about potential partners' competences, norms, and values, and their working methods and decision-making procedures, before the execution of a project, can stimulate the development of trustworthy relationships (see van der Meer-Kooistra and Vosselman, 2000; Dekker, 2008). However, developing trustworthy working relationships among the members of operational teams is more likely to be done during the execution of the project. In addition, projects in wider or international settings may face other challenges, such as cultural differences and geographical distances, which can limit the temporal embeddedness of the project. Further studies of the governance of collaborative product development projects in different industries and, more specifically, in projects in an international setting, are needed. In these studies, the following questions could be addressed: how can good working relationships be built and maintained, both at the organisational level and at the level of the operational teams, and what are the implications of the temporal embeddedness and the institutional context of such projects?

Where projects are more complex or spread over longer periods of time, the level of uncertainty will increase, which leads to higher levels of project and market risk and to less complete contracts. Small(er) specialist organisations may not be willing (or able) to accept such levels of risk and so the risk-reward model used in the two cases illustrated in this chapter may not be suitable. What does this imply for risk sharing and the position of the specialist organisations vis-à-vis OEMs in collaborative product development projects? And what does this imply for the financing of such projects? Is more public funding required for such projects? In each of our two cases, the local development agency (BOM) played an important role in stimulating or raising funding for the project. In many developed countries, governments are increasingly seeking to promote innovation, with initiatives ranging from such small-scale activities as university linked incubators, to the funding of major research and development activities. A potential area for research could be the governance of collaborative product development projects with significant public sector involvement. In such projects, it would be interesting to explore how the economic interests of private sector organisations can work alongside the social (and potentially political) interests of public sector organisations.

In this chapter, we have discussed the role of the economic and technical structures in setting boundaries for collaborative product development projects, including the role of accounting and management control. However, in our cases, the role of accounting and management control was limited to setting the boundaries for the development activities in terms of the development time/cost budgets and the cost/selling price of the new product. These budgets and costs/prices could only be exceeded with the approval of the senior managers of the risk-reward parties. The financial aspects of both projects were the responsibility of the project leader and were monitored by the senior management of the risk-reward parties. None of these managers had any management accounting background; instead they all had technical backgrounds and were responsible for both the technical and financial aspects of the projects. As our studies focussed on the broader governance arrangements for the project as a whole, we did not investigate the influence of the senior management of the collaborating parties on decisions concerning the initial development time/cost budgets and the cost/selling price targets. Neither did we study in detail their decision to accept the risk-reward model and, in the Phenom case, the decision to set up a new organisation, Phenom World, to market the new product. To gain in-depth insights into the role of accounting and management control in collaborative product development projects, further research is needed into the decision-making processes within the individual collaborating organisations. Thus, we believe there remain many interesting areas for study in relation to the governance of collaborative product development projects.

Notes

1. In English, this agency is the Brabant Development Agency and in Dutch Brabantse Ontwikkelings Maatschappij. It is usually known as BOM—the abbreviation of its Dutch name.
2. In that paper, we termed such collaboration *co-development*, but here we use the term *collaborative product development*. However, the two terms have a similar meaning.
3. A stage-gate model identifies all the steps (stages) in the product development process, as well as the achievements and authorisations (gates) which are necessary to move from one stage to the next (see e.g. Cooper, 1990 and Hertenstein and Platt, 2000).
4. These individuals from the collaborating organisations spent at least 3/4 days working in this project office, with just a small amount of time (if any) spent in their own organisations.
5. They use the term *open innovation*.

References

Bakker, R.M. and Janowicz-Panjaitan, M., 2009. Time matters: The impact of 'temporariness' on the functioning and performance of organizations. In Kenis, P., Janowicz-Panjaitan, M. and Cambré, B. (eds.), *Temporary Organizations: Prevalence, Logic and Effectiveness*. Cheltenham: Edward Elgar, 121–141.

Cooper, R.G., 1990. Stage-gate systems: A new tool for managing new products. *Business Horizons*, 33, 44–54.

Dekker, H.C., 2008. Partner selection and governance design in interfirm relationships. *Accounting, Organizations and Society*, 33, 915–941.

Engwall, M., 2003. No project is an island: Linking projects the history and context. *Research Policy*, 32, 789–808.

Garriga, H., von Krogh, G. and Spaeth, S., 2013. How constraints and knowledge impact open innovation. *Strategic Management Journal*, 34(9), 1134–1144.

Hertenstein, J.H. and Platt, M.B., 2000. Performance measures and management control in new product development. *Accounting Horizons*, 14, 303–323.

Janowicz-Panjaitan, R.M., Kenis, P. and Vermeulen, A.M., 2009. The atemporality of temporary organizations: Implications for goal attainment and legitimacy. In Kenis, P., Janowicz-Panjaitan, M. and Cambré, B. (eds) *Temporary Organizations: Prevalence, Logic and Effectiveness*. Cheltenham: Edward Elgar, 142–154.

Kamoche, K. and Cunha, M.P., 2001. Minimal structures: From jazz improvisation to product innovation. *Organization Studies*, 22, 733–764.

Kenis, P., Janowicz-Panjaitan, M. and Cambré, B., 2009. *Temporary Organizations: Prevalence, Logic and Effectiveness*. Cheltenham: Edward Elgar.

Loeh, H., Pels, H. J., Ebeling, F. and Faber, E. (2007). *Collaborative Innovation in Dommel Valley: From Subcontracting to Collaborative Innovation in High Tech Systems*. This report can be accessed at various places online, including www.scribd.com/document/159518841/Collaborative-Innovation-in-Dommel-Valley

Lundin, R.A. and Söderholm, A., 1995. The theory of the temporary organisation. *Scandinavian Journal of Management*, 11, 437–455.

Menon, T. and Pfeffer, J., 2003. Valuing internal vs. external knowledge: Explaining the preference for outsiders. *Management Science*, 49(4), 497–513.

Spaeth, S., Stuermer, M. and von Krogh, G.F., 2010. Enabling knowledge creation through outsiders: Towards a push model of open innovation. *International Journal of Technology Management*, 52(3/4), 411–431.

van der Meer-Kooistra, J. and Scapens, R.W., 2008. The governance of lateral relations between and within organisations. *Management Accounting Research*, 19, 365–384.

van der Meer-Kooistra, J. and Scapens, R.W., 2015. Governing product co-development projects: The role of minimal. *Management Accounting Research*, 28, 68–91.

van der Meer-Kooistra, J. and Vosselman, E.G.J., 2000. Management control of interfirm transactional relationships: The case of industrial renovation and maintenance. *Accounting, Organizations and Society*, 25(1), 51–77.

Wallin, M.W. and von Krogh, G.F., 2010. Organizing for open innovation: Focus on the integration of knowledge. *Organizational Dynamics*, 39(2), 145–154.

14 The Allure of Innovation

Assembling a Novel Public–Private Partnership

Paul Andon, Jane Baxter and Wai Fong Chua

Introduction

The aim of this chapter is to encourage research that helps us to understand how affect and accounting are intertwined in the functioning of inter-organisational networks concerned with innovation. This chapter explores how affect is mobilised to enrol actors into an inter-organisational network designed to address the New South Wales (NSW) State Government's social housing needs in an innovative but economically defensible way. We argue that accounting was not enough to convince and enrol actors: it was the co-mingling of accounting and affect that strengthened the associations in this innovation network. The empirical focus for our study is a novel public housing public–private partnership (PPP) in Sydney, Australia, formed in 2007. This long-term, multi-million-dollar project among the public, private, and non-governmental sectors aimed to transform an existing public housing estate, promising substantial community renewal.

But what counts as innovation? We do not use the term *innovation* to refer to the invention of a new object only. In common with others (see Abernethy and Bouwens, 2005; Rogers, 2003; Zaltman *et al.*, 1973), an innovation may involve 'repackaging' existing ideas, products, or processes to offer improved or simply different forms of service or functionality. The key to defining an innovation is that the relevant actors attribute an element of 'newness' or 'difference' to their projects. Correspondingly, using a PPP as a vehicle to deliver social housing was a hitherto unexplored option in NSW.

Further, we adopt a position that innovation is seldom comprised by the acts of single, isolated individuals. Latour (1996) states that innovation is materialised only if it "*holds humans and non-humans together, continuously*" (p. 213; emphasis in original). That is, innovation is constituted by actor-networks comprising human and non-human actors, spanning physical and virtual worlds. More recently, innovation networks have been formalised as inter-organisational alliances (see Das, 2014; Sampson, 2007; Wassmer, 2010). These alliances have grown in scale and scope, in part because the necessary financial resources can be immense, and limited funding therefore needs to be pooled. Also, innovation does not arrive fully formed. The adoption of a new idea invariably entails a series of experiments and trials as an idea is adapted. Innovation is thus networked and distributed over space and time, comprising the connected efforts of many actors. Accordingly, the innovative social housing PPP recounted in this chapter occurred in a network (of politicians, government bureaucrats, financiers, members of the media, residents, maps, risk matrices, spreadsheets with net present value calculations, and government policy manuals), which was anticipated to operate for over 30 years.

Whether situated in a single organisation or in a network of interlinked entities, innovation settings are arguably affective arenas comprised by various "passionate interests," reflecting the intensity of the attachments between actors (Latour and Lépinay, 2009, p. 433). Passionate interests sustain the hope, excitement, and belief associated with an innovation. Passionate interests help to mobilise and enrol many, inspiring them with visions of what might and could be built by the collective. But in addition to hope, passionate interests are also often synonymous with interceding anxiety and frustration. Whilst some accounting researchers argue that accounting numbers can help to produce and transport feelings of 'comfort' in complex and uncertain settings (Catasús *et al.*, 2016; Marginson and Ogden, 2005; Pentland, 1993), accounting practices may amplify anxiety and fear. Actors are confronted with the impossibility of correctly calculating the risks, costs, and financial benefits of a project that will be years in the making. Moreover, accounting numbers can be quite fragile and unstable in many situations (Andon *et al.*, 2007; Mouritsen *et al.*, 2009).

Given this, we are interested in how affect and accounting connect in innovation settings, especially those that are organised as inter-organisational networks. What do we know of these connections?

Insights From the Literature

There has long been interest in how accounting and innovation connect. Early research (Brownell, 1985; Rockness and Shields, 1984) suggested that financial measures did not play an important role in research and development (R&D) departments and their performance. However, a little over a decade later, there was some suggestion that control systems, by imposing rules and financial hurdles, inhibit the creativity necessary for innovation (Amabile, 1998). This concern was allayed to some degree by subsequent research suggesting that the relation between financial control and innovation was more complex. Indeed, in certain settings, financial controls increase performance (Bisbe and Otley, 2004; Davila, 2005; Ditillo, 2004; Muller-Stewens *et al.*, 2016). That is, a range of intermediary and contingent factors (such as product strategy and levels of uncertainty) influence the deployment and effects of controls; thus, the link between accounting and innovation is not necessarily negative.

Other research has explored the consequences of using different accounting performance measures, such as market share, internal rates of return, or a technology roadmap, during different phases in the materialisation of an innovation (Christner and Stromsten, 2015; Davila, 2000; 2005; Miller and O'Leary, 2007; Mouritsen *et al.*, 2005; Mouritsen *et al.*, 2001; Power, 1994). Christner and Stromsten (2015), in particular, recount an interesting case. They studied a technology start-up, finding that management focussed initially on estimating the market share of a new technology. However, when venture capitalists became involved, the focus shifted to using a financially based internal rate of return. Ultimately, this led to discontent among the original inventors (who were highly committed to their original product vision), with one of the inventors leaving the company. Whilst the authors did not discuss the concept of affect, there are hints that the passionate interests of inventors may have run counter to the demands for quicker financial returns from the venture capitalists.

Growing research interest has been observed also in understanding the role of accounting in managing inter-organisational relations (see Caglio and Ditillo, 2008 for a review). For example, informed by transaction cost economics, researchers have characterised: the control archetypes used to manage interorganisational relations (e.g., market-based and hierarchical or bureaucratic), the contextual elements affecting the suitability of these archetypes, and the design of accounting controls with respect to these archetypes (e.g., Håkansson and Lind, 2004; Speklé, 2001; Van der Meer-Kooistra and Vosselman, 2000). Studies have also taken a particular interest in how accounting is shaped by the nature of trust in the inter-organisational relationships (e.g., Free, 2008; Langfield-Smith and Smith, 2003; Tomkins, 2001; Vosselman and Van der Meer-Kooistra, 2009). Recent research has sought to highlight how accounting contributes to the establishment of complex interfirm relations (Mouritsen and Thrane, 2006; Thrane and Hald, 2006) and how accounting can be a conduit for both order and controversy in these relations (Chua and Mahama, 2007).

As this suggests, there is a reasonably large body of work seeking to understand the linkages between accounting and innovation, as well as accounting and the functioning of inter-organisational networks. In comparison, investigating the connection between accounting and affect is a relatively nascent project. Boedker and Chua (2013) argued that accounting is an affective technology—meaning that accounting techniques, such as budgeting and performance measurement, generate affective reactions in networks of actors. Boedker and Chua argued that affect is relational, inhering in links among people, objects, and events. In their study of the Australian subsidiary of a multinational corporation, they highlighted how a stretch revenue target seduced actors not only to comply with the target but also to actively co-produce their subjection to it. And the performance target produced diverse affects—a loss of pride (the company was no longer a global leader measured in terms of sales revenue), anxiety (that the revenue target would not be reached), excitement (what if the growth target were reached?), and hope (for improved status and promotion when, and if, they had achieved their targets). Thus, accounting performed as a mode of 'affective engineering' (Thrift, 2008), generating desired passionate interests between the goals of the US Head Office and the activities of the Australian subsidiary.

More recently, Cooper and Johnston (2012) and Carlsson-Wall *et al.* (2016) investigated the affective consequences of public performance measures. In particular, they outlined how football league table rankings generate a range of affective effects—a mixture of joy, frustration, or resignation, depending on how one's team is performing. More recently, Baxter *et al.* (2016) studied a Swedish football club. They write that accounting not only generates affect, the very deployment and significance of accounting techniques is influenced by the passionate interests connecting a network of fans, rival fans, sponsors, patrons, league officials, club managers, and players. They argue that the (at times) violent passionate interests of a certain segment of fans (such as the ultras and "the firm") make ticket sales difficult for management to budget, harming also the reputation of the club and dissuading others from providing much needed sponsorship revenue. This resulted in the club's having little financial flexibility, selling players in the transfer windows to avoid insolvency (see also Cooper and Joyce, 2013). As such, the circulation of affect within this network of actors had a major influence on the strategic and day-to day financial management of the football club.

This emerging focus on affect and accounting is encouraging. However, these studies do not address innovation settings. How are affect and innovation connected? A recent study by Vouri and Huy (2015) is instructive. They argued that shared fears were central to Nokia's exit from the smartphone market. Top managers feared external competitive threats and adverse shareholder reactions, while middle managers feared demanding senior managers and their peers. Together, these collective fears led to information blockages, resulting in top management's developing an overly optimistic view of Nokia's technological prowess. This contributed to a lack of appropriate investment in product innovation. Vouri and Huy (2015) point out that emotions can be shared—and it was this shared fear that prevented Nokia offering innovative products equal to those of rivals, Apple and Samsung.

Having said this, as far as we can ascertain, there is no research exploring how affect, accounting, and innovation interrelate. We seek to contribute by exploring these interconnections, especially in the context of an inter-organisational network.

Field Evidence From an Innovative Social Housing Project

The Field, Innovation, and Affect

The empirical analysis focuses on a PPP formed to revitalise an 81-hectare public housing estate in the western Sydney suburb of Bonnyrigg (NSW Department of Housing, 2007). The PPP was an inter-organisational venture among public, private, and non-governmental actors to deliver social housing infrastructure and services. We conducted fieldwork for two years starting in February 2007. Numerous documents were collected during this time, including media articles, parliamentary records, transcripts and reports from various housing inquiries, and budget committee transcripts from Parliament. Further, 31 semi-structured interviews, totalling 42 hours of interview time, were conducted with actors who were knowledgeable about public housing and the Bonnyrigg Estate.

Public housing has been a long-standing matter of concern in NSW because of the state's deteriorating housing stock (Hayward, 1996; Kemeny, 1983). A renewed focus on public housing emerged in 2003 with the appointment of Carl Scully as Minister for Housing. (Scully was previously the Minister for Transport.) At the time of his appointment, a highly emotional discourse of disadvantage characterised public housing. Estates were described as "troubled," "depressed," "shameful," "slum-like," "dysfunctional," and "bastions of crime and vandalism" (Anonymous, 2004; General Purpose Standing Committee No. 4, 2004; Skelsey, 2003a, 2003b, 2003c, 2004). Accordingly, Scully announced his innovative vision for public housing in NSW:

> Mr Scully wants to put the private sector deals he pioneered in building tollways, such as the Eastern Distributor and cross-city tunnel, into practice in public housing. "Ultimately, the best result is if some are bulldozed and replaced with high-quality modern housing. We could create renewed communities that for all intents and purposes look like a normal aspirational suburb. The aim of the exercise to increase public housing stock and increase the mix and have Department of Housing dispersed among the aspirational housing community. I see big problems in our housing estates—we don't get enough money to maintain them, they are rundown and there's a stigma."
>
> (Skelsey, 2003a, p. 19)

As such, Scully mobilised a set of passionate interests conveying 'betterment' through the physical and social renewal of estates. This was highly compelling to actors being enrolled in this project.

Scully was attached to PPPs because of the 'success' he had achieved with them as the Minister or Transport. Similarly, actors in NSW Treasury were comforted by the performance of PPPs delivering 'social infrastructure' in the state's educational sector. Actors in Housing were buoyed by the British experience of public housing PPPs, although much smaller in scale. These antecedent affective attachments contributed to a general understanding of the value-for-money (VFM) achievable from a public housing PPP. VFM would accrue from: economies of scale and scope (aggregating conventionally outsourced activities such as building and maintenance in one contract), the competitive pressures of the tendering process, and the leveraging of estate land values. Moreover, private partners would release Housing from delivery concerns; government attention would be focused on housing policy and administration.

However, anxieties circulated, too, within this network of actors. First, there had been high-profile PPP 'failures' in NSW, such as the Sydney Airport Rail Link. Would this PPP fail, too? Second, how would the public, particularly residents, *feel* about the private development of a housing estate and the sale of public land? Would this undermine political support for the government? Third, would the combination of construction, maintenance, and tenancy management services within one contract fail to enrol private sector interests? It was stated:

> The banks, the financiers and the lawyers that are in property development are used to thinking short term, high gain, high return, more inherent risk. [Property Developers] never think about PPPs, so they've never got their head around it. . . . And for the PPP guys, they've got to get their head around it, geez, they're now exposed to the residential housing market and all the bloody vagaries there.
>
> (Housing Interviewee 1)

Fourth, even if the private sector showed an appetite for this type of long-term risk, would the highly emotive stereotype of public housing tenants (as "crims" with "feral kids") weaken their attachment to the project? Nevertheless, these shared anxieties were not viewed as sufficiently serious to halt the materialisation of a public housing PPP. As a housing expert stated:

> What we care about is that people get affordable, secure housing, that's of reasonable quality. . . . [Housing] were up shit creek without a paddle, and we knew that they had to try and do something different.
>
> (NGO Interviewee)

It was generally recognised that innovation was required in the provision of public housing and that a PPP offered the best chance of accomplishing this. Yet a PPP must offer VFM to be (at least financially) acceptable and to justifiably sustain its allure.

Accounting, Affect, and Innovation

The determination of VFM expected from this proposed PPP was outlined in Working with Government (WWG) policy and guidelines (NSW Government, 2001a, 2001b). First, the vision for a renewed housing estate was to be inscribed in the form of a Reference Project, released as part of the tender documents. Second, the Reference Project was to be passed to Treasury to develop the Public Sector Comparator (PSC), a forecast of the PPP's likely NPV. The PSC was then used as a benchmark for evaluating the proposals received from the various competing private consortiums. Before a

PSC was constructed, however, a suitable site for the proposed PPP needed to be selected. The selection of the site was characterised by a process of 'end-gaming' (Clegg *et al.*, 2006; Pitsis *et al.*, 2003), which tested a site's feasibility in relation to the reference project's espoused benefits. It was in the process of end-gaming that various forms of accounting (listing, measuring, sorting, ranking) were inextricably inter-twined with the affective dimensions of the envisioned innovation in social housing.

An array of non-financial measures was mobilised by Housing to identify 12 priority sites to be scrutinised for their possible VFM. The measures used to screen existing social housing sites in Sydney for their potential development included: estate size; the capacity for improvement in social and physical amenity; the loss of public housing; the change in the mix of public and private housing; and the general appeal of an estate for development. But, as an interviewee from Housing stated, these measures were augmented by "a fair bit of subjective stuff" that coupled affect, and its circulation, to the evaluation process. To illustrate, in a listing of the 12 sites (see Table 14.1), the Bonnyrigg Housing Estate (the eventual choice for redevelopment) was portrayed as a "crime haven" (Skelsey, 2003a, p. 19). Part of the allure of the Bonnyrigg site resided in an imagined future that would replace this negative affective milieu with a set of passionate interests amplifying aspirational social values within the community and beyond to other potential developments.

Table 14.1 A comparison of the potential development sites

Site	*Description*
Redfern-Waterloo	It's unlikely the two 30-storey aged housing towers would be removed, but significant other State, land holdings would be attractive to a private developer.
Glebe	The southern end has a heavy concentration of public housing. Some people say crime is retarding the Glebe Point Rd strip but redevelopment could be hindered by heritage issues.
Mt Druitt	About 8000 dwellings for 32,000 people were built near the station during the 1960s. Many of the dwellings sit on large blocks ripe for redevelopment.
South-Eastern Sydney	There are several housing estates in sought-after south-eastern Sydney, including South Coogee, South Maroubra, and Chifley. Police say public housing estates do not have more crime, but some residents complain of anti-social activity.
Riverwood	An estate with more than 1300 dwellings, close to a railway station, in an area subject to strong redevelopment pressures.
Campbelltown	There are 7758 dwellings, many clustered in large estates—Claymore, Minto, or Airds.
Bonnyrigg	An estate where houses face laneways that can be crime havens. Redevelopment makes sense.

Source: Adapted from Skelsey, 2003a

The 12 potential sites were then subjected to more traditional forms of accounting measurement comparing the 'business as usual' NPV of an estate (that is, maintaining the existing buildings and facilities) to a 'development' option. These calculations permitted Housing to assess the affordability and viability of each site's redevelopment. But again, the numbers were not enough to corral and convince actors on their own: the numbers needed to be strengthened through their association with the prevailing passionate interest of community renewal. Anticipated increases in property values were valorised by actors because they enabled a more precise assessment of the amplification of this passionate interest rather than the accumulation of financial benefits alone. An interviewee from Housing stated:

> So in a sense we're also using property value as a proxy for social change. So as we manage to improve the estate area then the property values go up. So it was almost like a measure of how much we were improving the social outcomes for the tenants.
>
> (Housing Interviewee)

And Bonnyrigg was a particularly appealing site in this regard because of its large tracts of open land, uninterrupted by major roads and existing concentrations of private housing.

Despite the seeming allure of this innovation, there were risks and anxieties that co-mingled with the financialisation of the proposed PPP. In part, these were managed through the formalisation of a risk matrix, wherein many potential hazards, adverse effects, and complications were imagined and their management anticipated, for example, construction and interface risks. However, these risks were characterised as being predominantly 'boilerplate', following a "well-trodden path." More difficult to contain and manage were the affective overflows of the envisaged estate development. How would the Bonnyrigg residents react to an unsettling of their passionate interests tying them to 'family', 'home', and 'community'? How could Housing shift their attachments to align with the passionate interests embedded in an aspirational community? Correspondingly, Housing engaged in affective engineering activities, conducting an extensive program of information sessions, community BBQs, newsletter communications, workshops ("Our Bonnyrigg Dream"), and other meetings with Bonnyrigg residents. A Community Reference Group was established to monitor the 'mood' of the community, acting as a "canary in a mine." Despite these extensive efforts, it was recognised that there were still lingering anxieties about the impact of the redevelopment on residents.

After both extensive financial scrutiny and community engagement, 'Bonnyrigg Partnerships' was named as the preferred bidder in October 2006.[1] While the preferred bid's value was expressed in financial terms, promising a NPV of \$392.8M and expected savings of 6.3% when compared with the most likely PSC, this enumeration was, again, strengthened by a passionate interest in community renewal:

> This project is not just about the housing, or the parks, or the availability of services, but all those things that make for a sustainable and vibrant community. The project is also about the process of community renewal and how change is managed for the overall benefit of the community, with particular regard to the existing residents.
>
> (Contracts Summary, p. 1)

Only part of the allure of this innovative social housing project stemmed from its promised savings from private sector and non-governmental involvement in the financing, design, construction, maintenance, and servicing of a redeveloped Bonnyrigg Estate. The allure of this innovation resided also in the prospect of a shared attachment to a passionate interest that would disassociate a community from its supposedly dismal past, replacing this with an interest in a transformative future for a network of residents, politicians, government departments, private sector organisations, and non-government organisations alike.

Discussion

The adoption of a PPP to deliver social housing in NSW was characterised as an innovative project by those who championed its materialisation, such as Minister Scully. This innovation was materialised by an inter-organisational network spanning governmental, private sector, and non-governmental actors. Key actors were the Minister, Treasury officials, staff from the Department of Housing, members of community housing organisations, private financiers, building contractors, and members of the Bonnyrigg community. But, as Latour (1996) cautions us, the materialisation and functioning of this inter-organisational innovation network was also an effect of non-human actors, such as calculative artefacts (e.g., non-financial performance measures, the PSC, NPV calculations, and risk matrices), discourses (e.g., the anti-social nature of public housing estates), documents (e.g., the tender documentation released by Housing to potential and short-listed bidders), and procedures (e.g., WWG guidelines). Clearly, there was great concern about the financialisation of this innovation—that it offered a clearly justifiable NPV. However, the promise of a positive NPV was not enough. The numbers were given strength through their association with a passionate interest in social renewal, that is, the prospect of transforming Bonnyrigg into an 'aspirational community'.

As such, this study supports previous work, in part. This case gives credence to the claims of Jordan and Messner (2012, p. 545) that actors do not rely "blindly" on accounting information in capital budgeting and innovation contexts. Further, Boholm and Corvellec (2015), for example, have argued that there is widespread use of 'gut feel' and judgment in decision making within the public sector. Nonetheless, this study also challenges previous work, especially that by critical researchers who have claimed that calculative practices, collectively referred to as 'accountingisation', have colonised the materialisation of PPPs, favouring financial considerations over other qualities (Broadbent *et al.*, 2008; Cooper and Taylor, 2005; Shaoul, 2005). We did not observe this. Rather, we witnessed manifold attachments to a passionate interest in the 'social' in the formation of a PPP to redevelop the Bonnyrigg estate.

Our study adds evidence that passionate interests matter in the constitution of an innovation. Housing estates were an obligatory passage point to community renewal. They were the places where social problems connected with public housing (such as crime and vandalism) were to be found. Estates had to be fixed if public housing was to be improved and communities transformed. But why was a PPP the vehicle for this transformation? The adoption of a PPP stemmed from a shared passionate interest (between members of government departments and other organisations) in the potential of inter-organisational networks to deliver innovation. Such interests also materially influenced the type of calculative practices enacted. But the non-financial performance measures and NPV calculations were incomplete and imperfect. However, they became strong enough to convince when coupled to a passionate interest in the accomplishment of an 'aspirational community'. Moreover, the potential for influential, countervailing interests further informed the innovation process. For example, extensive workshopping and consultation processes were enacted within the Bonnyrigg community, deliberately reengineering the passionate interests (such an anxiety about the impact of change on their lives) that residents attached to the proposed development.

Clearly, the research agenda connecting affect, accounting, and inter-organisational innovation remains large. Our research is quite particular. This suggests a need to study the role of affect in other innovation settings, both inter- and intra-organisational, to better understand how different configurations of actors, passionate interests, and practices (such as accounting calculations, procedures, and narratives) become materialised in the name of 'innovation'. The question for the future will be whether functional, situated configurations of actors, devices, inscriptions, and interests (rather than universal combinations) can be identified and more clearly delineated, informing us which ecologies of human and non-human actors work in different contexts (Schatzki, 2010). For example, how do innovation, accounting, and affect become embedded in the workings of agile, global networks of contractors coordinated by virtual aggregators? How is this different from or similar to the working of such assemblages in more established, bureaucratic, multi-national corporations?

In conclusion, we hope this chapter encourages other accounting researchers to consider how shared passionate interests both shape and are shaped by accounting practices, whether it is in relation to inter-organisational, networked innovations, or other settings. As our chapter and emerging research suggest, this is an important step in understanding how accounting operates in the contemporary world.

Note

1. The Bonnyrigg Partnerships consortium included Westpac Banking Corporation (investor and lead financier), Becton Property Group (investor and lead property developer), Spotless (facilities management), and St George Community Housing Co-operative (tenancy management, community improvement, and rehousing activities) (NSW Department of Housing, 2007).

References

Abernethy, M. and Bouwens, J. (2005). Determinants of accounting innovation implementation. *Abacus*, *41*(3), pp. 217–240.

Amabile, T. (1998). How to kill creativity. *Harvard Business Review*, *76*, pp. 77–87.

Andon, P., Baxter, J. A. and Chua, W. F. (2007). Accounting change as relational drifting: A field study of experiments with performance measurement. *Management Accounting Research*, *18*(2), pp. 273–308.

Anonymous. (2004). Vision gives hope. *Fairfield Advance*, 15 December, p. 1.

Baxter, J., Carlsson-Wall, M., Chua, W. F. and Kraus, K. (2016). Accounting, financial managing and attachments in affective nets: The case of a Swedish football club. *Working Paper*.

Bisbe, J. and Otley, D. (2004). The effects of the interactive use of management control systems on product innovation. *Accounting, Organizations and Society*, *29*(8), pp. 709–737.

Boedker, C. and Chua, W. F. (2013). Accounting as an affective technology: A study of circulation, agency and entrancement. *Accounting, Organizations and Society*, *38*(4), pp. 245–267.

Boholm, A. and Corvellec, H. (2015). The role of valuation practices for risk identification. *GRI-rapport 2015:4, Managing Big Cities*. Gothenburg Research Institute.

Broadbent, J., Gill, J. and Laughlin, R. (2008). Identifying and controlling risk: The problem of uncertainty in the private finance initiative in the UK's National Health Service. *Critical Perspectives on Accounting*, *19*(1), pp. 40–78.

Brownell, P. (1985). Budgetary systems and the control of functionally differentiated organisational activities. *Journal of Accounting Research*, *23*(2), pp. 502–512.

Caglio, A. and Ditillo, A. (2008). A review and discussion of management control in inter-firm relationships: Achievements and future directions. *Accounting, Organizations and Society*, *33*(7), pp. 865–898.

Carlsson-Wall, M., Kraus, K. and Messner, M. (2016). Performance measurement systems and the enactment of different institutional logics: Insights from a football organization. *Management Accounting Research*, 32, pp. 45–61.

Catasús, B., Ferri, P. and von Laskowski, S. (2016). Accounting and the hope of action. *European Accounting Review*, *25*(2), pp. 403–419.

Christner, C. and Stromsten, T. (2015). Scientists, venture capitalists and the stock exchange: The mediating role of accounting in product innovation. *Management Accounting Research*, *28*(1), pp. 50–67.

Chua, W. F. and Mahama, H. (2007). The effect of network ties on accounting controls in a supply alliance: Field study evidence. *Contemporary Accounting Research*, *24*(1), pp. 47–86.

Clegg, S., Pitsis, T., Marosszeky, M. and Rura-Polley, T. (2006). Making the future perfect: Constructing the Olympic dream. In Hodgson, D. and Cicmil, S. (eds.), *Making Projects Critical*. New York, NY: Palgrave Macmillan.

Cooper, C. and Johnston, J. (2012). Vulgate accountability: Insights from the field of football. *Accounting, Auditing & Accountability Journal*, *25*(4), pp. 602–634.

Cooper, C. and Joyce, Y. (2013). Insolvency practice in the field of football. *Accounting, Organizations & Society*, *38*(2), pp. 108–129.

Cooper, C. and Taylor, P. (2005). Independently verified reductionism: Prison privatization in Scotland. *Human Relations*, *58*(4), pp. 497–522.

Das, T. K. (ed.) (2014). *Strategic Alliances for Innovation and R&D: Research in Strategic Alliances*. New York, NY: Information Age Publishing.

Davila, T. (2000). An empirical study on the drivers of management control systems' design in new product development. *Accounting, Organizations & Society*, *25*(4/5), pp. 383–409.

Davila, T. (2005). The promise of management control systems for innovation and strategic change. In Chapman, C. (ed.), *Controlling Strategy: Management, Accounting, and Performance Measurement*. Oxford, UK: Oxford University Press, pp. 37–61.

Ditillo, A. (2004). Dealing with uncertainty in knowledge-intensive firms: The role of management control systems as knowledge integration mechanisms. *Accounting, Organizations and Society*, *29*(3/4), pp. 401–421.

Free, C. (2008). Walking the talk? Supply chain accounting and trust among UK supermarkets and suppliers. *Accounting, Organizations and Society*, *33*(6), pp. 629–662.

General Purpose Standing Committee No. 4. (2004). Examination of proposed expenditure for the portfolio areas Roads, and Housing (transcript of committee proceedings, 15 September). *NSW Legislative Council*.

Håkansson, H. and Lind, J. (2004). Accounting and network coordination. *Accounting, Organizations and Society*, *29*(1), pp. 51–72.

Hayward, D. (1996). The reluctant landlords? A history of public housing in Australia. *Urban Policy & Research*, *14*(1), pp. 5–34.

Jordan, S. and Messner, M. (2012). Enabling control and the problem of incomplete performance indicators. *Accounting, Organizations and Society*, *37*(8), pp. 544–564.

Kemeny, J. (1983). *The Great Australian Nightmare*. Melbourne: Georgian House.

Langfield-Smith, K. and Smith, D. (2003). Management control systems and trust in outsourcing relationships. *Management Accounting Research*, *14*(3), pp. 281–307.

Latour, B. (1996). *Aramis or the Love of Technology*. Cambridge, MA: Harvard University Press.

Latour, B. and Lépinay, V. A. (2009). *The Science of Passionate Interests: An Introduction to Gabriel Tarde's Economic Anthropology*. Chicago, IL: Prickly Paradigm Press.

Marginson, D. and Ogden, S. (2005). Managers, budgets and organisational change: Unbundling some of the paradoxes. *Journal of Accounting & Organizational Change*, *1*(1), pp. 45–61.

Miller, P. and O'Leary, T. (2007). Mediating instruments and making markets: Capital budgeting, science and the economy. *Accounting, Organizations and Society*, *32*(7/8), pp. 701–734.

Mouritsen, J., Hansen, A. and Hansen, C. (2009). Short and long translations: Management accounting calculations and innovation management. *Accounting, Organizations & Society*, *34*(6/7), pp. 738–754.

Mouritsen, J., Hansen, A. and Jonsson, S. (2005). Target costing and coordination: Framing cost information sharing in new product development. *Accounting in Scandinavia*, pp. 219–241.

Mouritsen, J., Larsen, H. T. and Bukh, P. N. D. (2001). Intellectual capital and the 'capable firm': Narrating, visualising and numbering for managing knowledge. *Accounting, Organizations and Society*, *26*(7/8), pp. 735–762.

Mouritsen, J. and Thrane, S. (2006). Accounting, network complementarities and the development of inter-organisational relations. *Accounting, Organizations and Society*, *31*(3), pp. 241–275.

Muller-Stewens, B., Widener, S., Steinmann, J. and Moller, K. (2016). The role of controls in innovation: An examination of diagnostic Use, interactive use, and dynamic tension. Paper presented in the *Annual Conference for Management Accounting Research*, March 10–11, Koblenz, Germany.

NSW Department of Housing. (2007). *Bonnyrigg 'Living Communities' Public Private Partnership Project: Summary of Contracts*. Sydney: NSW Government.

NSW Government. (2001a). *Working with Government: Guidelines for Privately Financed Projects*. Sydney: NSW Government.

NSW Government. (2001b). *Working with Government: Policy for Privately Financed Projects*. Sydney: NSW Government.

Pentland, B. T. (1993). Getting comfortable with the numbers: Auditing and the micro-production of macro-order. *Accounting, Organizations and Society*, *18*(7/8), pp. 605–620.

Pitsis, T., Clegg, S., Marosszeky, M. and Rura-Polley, T. (2003). Constructing the Olympic dream: A future perfect strategy of project management. *Organization Science*, *14*(5), pp. 574–590.

Power, M. (1994). From the science of accounts to the financial accountability of science. *Science Context*, 7(3), pp. 355–387.

Rockness, H. and Shields, M. (1984). Organizational control systems in research and development. *Accounting, Organizations and Society*, *9*(2), pp. 165–177.

Rogers, E. (2003). *The Diffusion of Innovations* (5th Edition). New York, NY: The Free Press.

Sampson, R. (2007). R&D Alliances and firm performance: The impact of technological diversity and alliance organization on innovation. *The Academy of Management Journal*, *50*(2), pp. 364–386.

Schatzki, T. (2010). *Site of the Social: A Philosophical Account of the Constitution of Social Life and Change*. University Park, PA: Pennsylvania Press.

Shaoul, J. (2005). The Private Finance Initiative or the public funding of private profit? In Hodge, G. and Greve, C. (eds.), *The Challenge of Public Private Partnerships: Learning From International Experience*. Cheltenham, UK and Northampton, MA: Edward Elgar, pp. 190–206.

Skelsey, M. (2003a). Adding aspiration to public housing. *Daily Telegraph*, 15 September, p. 19.

Skelsey, M. (2003b). Bulldozing tactics for estate problem. *Daily Telegraph*, 15 September.

Skelsey, M. (2003c). Private plans for public housing. *Daily Telegraph*, 15 September, p. 7.

Skelsey, M. (2004). Dead-end estates face axe. *Daily Telegraph*, 13 December, p. 10.

Speklé, R. F. (2001). Explaining management control structure variety: A transaction cost economics perspective. *Accounting, Organizations and Society*, *26*(4), pp. 419–441.

Thrane, S. and Hald, K. S. (2006). The emergence of boundaries and accounting in supply fields: The dynamics of integration and fragmentation. *Management Accounting Research*, *17*(3), pp. 288–314.

Thrift, N. (2008). *Non-Representational Theory: Space | Politics | Affect.* Oxford, UK: Routledge.

Tomkins, C. (2001). Interdependencies, trust and information in relationships, alliances and networks. *Accounting, Organizations and Society*, *26*(2), pp. 161–191.

Van der Meer-Kooistra, J. and Vosselman, E. (2000). Management control of interfirm transactional relationships: The case of industrial renovation and maintenance. *Accounting, Organizations and Society*, *25*(1), pp. 51–77.

Vosselman, E. and Van der Meer-Kooistra, J. (2009). Accounting for control and trust building in interfirm transactional relationships. *Accounting, Organizations and Society*, *34*(2), pp. 267–283.

Vouri, T. and Huy, Q. (2015). Distributed attention and shared emotions in the innovation process: How Nokia lost the smartphone battle. *Administrative Science Quarterly*, *61*(1), pp. 1–43.

Wassmer, U. (2010). Alliance portfolios. A research review and agenda. *Journal of Management*, *36*(1), pp. 141–171.

Zaltman, G., Duncan, R. and Holbek, J. (1973). *Innovation and Organizations*. New York, NY: Wiley.

15 *Accounting, Innovation and Inter-Organisational Relationships*

Insights From the 13 Empirical Cases

Martin Carlsson-Wall, Håkan Håkansson, Kalle Kraus, Johnny Lind and Torkel Strömsten

Since few organisations control all resources needed to innovate, the concept of innovation is often characterized as an inter-organisational phenomena (c.f., Powell et al., 1996). This book explores the interconnections between accounting, innovation and inter-organisational relationships. Since this topic has been relatively neglected in prior research, this book takes its point of departure in 13 empirical cases. An overall message from all chapters is that the relationship between accounting and inter-organisational innovation is recursive, i.e., accounting shapes inter-organisational innovation processes and vice versa.

The first three empirical cases related to a start-up context (Chapters 2–5). Chapters 6–8 detailed a more traditional production context. In Chapters 9–11, a services context is examined. Finally, Chapters 12–14 include a discussion of governmental agencies when analysing accounting and inter-organisational innovation. How can accounting represent the inter-organisational innovation activities that we have observed in this book? And how do companies develop and use accounting in order to manouvre in this economic landscape of blurred organisational boundaries, resource heterogeneity and activities that are highly interdependent? From the empirical cases, two broad themes emerge: 1) the issue of incomplete performance indicators and 2) accounting as an engine for interaction, negotiation and compromise.

First, many of the chapters have described how actors struggle to find performance measures that can capture the value of the various inter-organisational innovations and new products being developed. Accounting metrics and calculations are incomplete (Dambrin and Robson, 2011; Jordan and Messner, 2012; Busco and Quattrone, 2017) as the different organisations represented in this book have difficulty capturing the value of the underlying inter-organisational innovation activities. In some chapters, this *incompleteness* creates problems during inter-organisational innovation processes; in others, it opens up new opportunities for innovations to emerge. Performance incompleteness is nothing new to accounting, management or marketing scholars, but as the empirical cases clearly show, the problems and opportunities related to such incompleteness are accentuated when inter-organisational innovation is at the core of the analysis.

Second, because of the empirical chapters' focus on how new technologies and production systems create interdependencies, a central theme has been to study the role of accounting in relation to interaction and negotiation (c.f., Burchell et al., 1980). The empirical chapters in the book show that accounting often work as the "engine" of change and innovation (borrowing the term used by Mouritsen and Hald in Chapter 8). Given the conflict in integrating different types of knowledge, one may even claim that accounting was used to provoke in some of the chapters. Relatedly, accounting often facilitated fruitful and workable compromises during inter-organisational innovation. Interaction, negotiation and compromise are nothing new to accounting, management or marketing scholars, but as the empirical chapters clearly show, the interconnections among accounting, negotiation and compromise are accentuated when inter-organisational innovation is at the core of the analysis.

The Issue of Incomplete Performance Indicators

Discussions around incomplete performance indicators have been ongoing for a long time (e.g., Ridgway, 1956). Accounting is never a perfect representation of the underlying activities of, for instance, innovation; it has never been and will never be (Dambrin and Robson, 2011). There are numerous studies that make this point and illustrate how individuals and organisations try to cope with such incompleteness (Chapman, 1997; Dambrin and Robson, 2011; Hall, 2010; Jordan and Messner, 2012; Mouritsen et al., 2009). As Jordan and Messner (2012, pp. 544–545) put it: "Accounting information—even if available in detailed form—provides only a limited understanding and handling of the complexity of organisational life." From the empirical chapters in the book, we can conclude that the issue of incomplete performance indicators becomes accentuated when inter-organisational innovation is at stake. The incompleteness will create frustration and anger but also hope for a better and more prosperous future. Inter-organisational innovation thereby seems to create intense emotion among entrepreneurs and other stakeholders, and accounting is intertwined in these emotional innovation processes (see Andon et al., Chapter 13).

All chapters detail that inter-organisational innovation involves the combination of old and new resources. Given that resources are heterogenous and that resource combination involves several actors, accounting faces a great challenge; it is difficult to measure the value of a specific resource or object. The challenges of measuring the value or the profitability of an inter-organisational innovation is shown in many of the empirical studies reported in the chapters. One obvious example is the Pyrosequencing innovation in Chapter 3 (Christner et al.). In this chapter, different calculations were used at different phases of the innovation process. During the innovation process, the content of the innovation changed, and the different calculations were intertwined with these changes. Most of the calculations showed a future that looked bright for the innovation, and they indicated a high potential for financial success. For a long period, the innovation was a success, and it ended up as a highly valued company on the stock market. However, when the next generation of the innovation should be developed, large obstacles occurred. The next generation of the innovation was much more complex compared with the previous one, and the number of physical interfaces that needed to be adopted to each other had increased dramatically. The accounting representation of the innovation emphasised growth and a need to target a customer segment that would demand high volumes of DNA sequencing. The technical requirements, in combination with a strong time pressure, became for some of the suppliers too hard a task, and they failed to deliver these functions on time. In the end, the company was merged with another organisation, owned by the same venture capital firm.

Another example of the difficulties of measuring inter-organisational innovation is presented by Mouritsen and Hald in their study of HearingCorp and some of its key suppliers in Chapter 8. HearingCorp used a supply chain scorecard to measure supplier performance and to simulate possible future actions and their financial consequences. However, the key suppliers were very dissatisfied with the supply chain scorecard and argued that it only measured cost and transactional performance. One key account manager stated that "the measures that currently define our performance are in our opinion much too superficial." It was also the purchasing unit within the HearingCorp that owned the supply chain scorecard, and it was mainly used for commercial negotiations. Measures that captured innovation was absent in the scorecard. The key suppliers argued that it was necessary to include such measures to be able to capture the supplier performance. Hence, the accounting used did not capture or represent a valid reality from the suppliers' perspective. They wanted other features of the resources that they brought to the table to become more visible and thereby valuable. The intervention from the key suppliers resulted in a new supplier performance system, a system that much more emphasised the suppliers' competencies and their ability for driving innovation. The measures in the new system focused less on transactions and more on the suppliers' capabilities. The involved organisational units within HearingCorp and its key suppliers found the new accounting system as an acceptable tool for measuring supplier performance.

In Chapter 12 by Eklinder-Frick and Waluszewski, the issue of how to measure what is successful from a governmental policy perspective is discussed. The chapter is written from a policy perspective, in which control and accounting is used very much "at a distance." For the governmental organisation, it is critical to be able to identify and see what innovations that eventually will be valuable. But this turned out very difficult. The evaluation focused on if those who have received innovation support are behaving in accordance with the supporting policy organisation's model of innovation—and not at all if they are engaged in establishing producer–user interfaces, necessary for the innovation to succeed.

An additional aspect of the incompleteness of performance indicators is related to indirect effects. Dubois and Gadde (Chapter 11) show how new calculations in support of a restructuring project resulted in dramatic changes of the company's maintenance, repair and operations. The new calculation focused on indirect costs of handling the supplier relationships such as orders, goods receiving and payment. The new calculation indicated that a dramatic reduction of the supplier base would significantly reduce the indirect supplier cost. Consequently, the company initiated single sourcing within the different purchasing categories. The single sourcing strategy also resulted in a reduction of the direct costs for the item bought when the company was prioritised by its selected suppliers. The new calculus extended the unit of analysis in the purchasing decisions. Before the changes, the attention was directed to the single transaction and its efficiency. After the changes, the unit of analysis had extended in two dimensions. First, the single transaction was considered as a part of a series of transactions within a long-term buyer–supplier relationship. This enabled the involved companies to jointly work with both companies' cost structures. Second, the items exchanged in one relationship were used in combination with items from other suppliers. The suppliers also supplied these items to other customers, and the company could reduce its costs by adopting to these customer demands. Sometimes the company could change the other customers' demand so it better fitted the company's need. Dubois and Gadde stated that "the costs in the relationship become driven not only by firm internal activities and joint undertakings of the two, but also by how the focal relationship was connected to the rest of the network." Consequently, the combination of resources, both physical and organisational, were taken into consideration in this case. The calculations were adopted to fit the network of combined resources, rather than the opposite.

Incomplete performance indicators are also an issue in the case presented by Andon, Baxter and Chua (Chapter 14). The authors provide a case that involved actors from different spheres of the society with different competencies and goals with the cooperation. In this situation, "the numbers were not enough to corral and convince actors on their own: the numbers needed to be strengthened through their association with the prevailing passionate interest of community renewal." It was not enough with the number; the actors also needed to accept the larger goal of the project. In this case, the emotions added to the resource features facilitated a successful project and made it possible for the actors to accept the way accounting represented the value of the combined resources.

Another way to approach the phenomenon of incomplete performance indicators is to identify a theoretical construct that help coping with such incompleteness. Van der Meer-Kooistra and Scapens (Chapter 13) use the concept of minimal structures to provide an analysis on how individuals use accounting as a fixed point and something to rely on, to create some order in the otherwise chaotic every day of inter-organisational innovation processes.

One of the cases is organised as a joint project, while the other is organised within a company. Interestingly, even if the organisational boundaries are set differently in the two cases, minimal structures play an important role in both cases to coordinate activities and make things more predictable and manageable for the companies.

Accounting as an 'Engine' for Interaction, Negotiation and Compromise

The role of accounting as an 'engine' for interaction, negotiations and compromise has been extensively discussed in prior work. Burchell et al. (1980), for instance, discuss this in a general sense based on the dimensions uncertainty of objectives and uncertainty of cause and effect. In the light of Burchell et al.'s (1980) classification, this makes perfect sense. The chapters detail how the uncertainty of cause and effect was high during inter-organisational innovation, but the uncertainty of objectives was low (everyone wanted a successful innovation). Given this, Burchell et al. (1980) suggest that accounting works as a 'learning machine'. The empirical chapters in the book indeed support this; accounting played a critical role in forcing and shaping interaction and thereby also dialogue and learning among the different actors involved in inter-organisational innovation.

When we think of networks, often the actor dimension and the relationships that actors create with each other come to our minds. Relationships between actors come in many different forms. Some relationships are close and have evolved over long periods of time, while others are more short term, transactional relationships. From the chapters in this book, we can see how the role of accounting as an 'engine' is complicated because innovation takes place in many different types of relationships, and the "engine" is therefore sometimes hard to locate as well as hard to turn on (or turn off when needed). Innovation is conducted within complex network structures of inter-organisational relationships that involve a number of heterogeneous actors from different spheres of society and with different competencies and technologies. The actors often interact with each other in tortuous processes over a long period of time. Such a situation is dramatically different to the classical market-hierarchy dichotomy in which accounting is supposed to co-ordinate the activities within the hierarchy and the market co-ordinate activities beyond the company boundaries.

Ditillo and Caglio state in Chapter 9 that "the most crucial aspects of the project were inter-firm interdependencies and tight time constraints." They also put forward the iterative nature of the innovation process. An example of the importance of activities that spans across several organisational units from heterogeneous actors form different spheres was detailed in Andon, Baxter and Chua's Chapter 14. They state: "This innovation was materialised by an inter-organisational network spanning governmental, private sector, and non-governmental actors."

The chapters provided by Christner, Lind and Strömsten (Chapter 3) and Olsen (Chapter 4) show how capital market actors (directly and indirectly) play an important role in inter-organisational innovation processes. The financial resources, but also the experience and contacts, that venture capitalist provide to entrepreneurs will in one way or the other become intertwined with the innovation journey. Christner, Lind and Strömsten further illustrate that Pyrosequencing was highly dependent of its suppliers for innovation success and a failure from one of the suppliers was a critical ingredient in an unsuccessful innovation. Simultaneously, accounting reinforced the hierarchy and created a situation of conflicting demands for the Pyrosequencing management. Olsen (Chapter 4), on the other hand, discusses how the venture capital firms provide an infrastructure for rapid growth and scalable innovation. Since time is critical for these type of actors, there is little time for exploration; venture capitalists supported ventures that were exploitative in nature. The evaluative infrastructure that the venture capitalists provided (certain metrics and tools) supported innovative solutions that fit into this type of framework, while other potential innovations were turned down since they did not offer high growth and value potentials. Relatedly, Wouters and Pelz in Chapter 5 provide an interesting example of a corporation providing an infrastructure for internal start-ups. Bosch provides resources, experiences and contacts (internally but also externally) to spur radical innovation. This is another type of blurred organisational reality since, even if the start-ups are created around a shared vision, explorative activities are encouraged and can take the new ventures in unforeseen directions.

In addition to this spatial blurriness, many of the chapters also point to another type of blurriness; time-related blurriness. Time is constantly present in start-up endeavors. The chapters that bring forward how venture capital firms work (Christner, Lind and Strömsten, Chapter 3; Olsen, Chapter 4), both illustrate the heaven and peril of this type of ownership. As long as things work smoothly, having a venture capitalist on your side is heaven. When things don't work as planned, the venture capitalist must go in and protect the investment. The role of accounting in interaction and negotiation in these cases is therefore interesting to analyse. Since control from the venture capitalist perspective very much is conducted "at a distance," even if board membership is very common, the performance measurements are adapted to suit at a distance control. Accounting clearly will have an impact on the operations and strategic decisions of these firms.

Time is also crucial in inter-organisational innovation more generally. Thus, companies have different spatial horizons but also different time-related horizons. Periods of relatively stable development activities are followed by very hectic and stressful development work. An inter-organisational innovation is often a long and tortuous process that moves back and forth between the involved organisations and in which it is often a necessity to extend the time horizon to many years. Since multiple actors are involved in the innovation process and all these actors have their own time horizon, the coordination problem will not only be a spatial one but also something that will involve how actors perceive and measure time. Since accounting calculations can visualise the time value of money, calculations will mediate these different views on what is valuable and not. Being active in setting the agenda and to choose what calculation to use, or to influence an existing accounting calculation, will be critical to maneuver in the inter-organisational network. This was illustrated nicely in the chapter provided by Mouritsen and Hald (Chapter 8), who showed how the new accounting system created a need for interaction between the companies about the innovation. It was a compromise, and the purchasing department and the key suppliers needed to jointly discuss more frequently with the product development function. The new accounting system "helped develop a new language concerned more with technology and innovation than with cost, commercial and transactional performance." Relatedly, van Triest and Blom (Chapter 10) illustrated how accounting was used as an 'engine' for interaction and negotiation during inter-organisational innovation. A supplier, through the introduction of an open book accounting arrangement, wanted to change the relationship with its major customer. The buyer placed separate orders that in the end were very costly for the supplier. The supplier initiated an innovation project, in which accounting played an important role. New accounting metrics were introduced to serve as a basis for dialogue and negotiation to change the inter-organisational relationship.

Ditillo and Caglio (Chapter 9) described an innovation project within the telecom industry. The formal management controls were important "tools to create a space in which to orient innovation endeavours." The involved companies used, for example a GANTT chart that specified the project activities and it was used to keep control of time. The GANTT chart showed when actors from different companies should be involved in the project and their respective contributions. Hence, the GANTT chart fostered integration between the involved companies in project from a time perspective. Another crucial ingredient in the co-ordination of the project was the regular meetings between individuals from the involved companies. It included formal meetings and ad hoc informal contacts. The acceptance test manager interacted on a daily basis with the project team. As mentioned earlier, to manage an innovation project is often a matter of coordinating time, when a certain activity must be performed. The nature of activities is therefore important to make clear. When the activities to be performed are sequential, the challenge and control mechanisms will be of one sort. If the activities are, or can be, performed in parallel, other types of mechanisms must be used, and the coordination and exchange of information become more complex and multifaceted. Where the van Triest and Blom case provides an example of sequential activities, the Ditillo and Caglio case illustrates the complexities when activities are both sequential and parallel.

Wouters and Pelz (Chapter 5), studying Bosch and its "start-up factory," found that even if Bosch encouraged entrepreneurial activity, the ideas that were seen as valuable and eventually got funding were aligned with the previous "idea structure" and history of Bosch. Hence, even if a great idea came up, the Bosch model favoured what fitted into the current vision and strategy. As such, accounting was used to negotiate compromises. The issue of compromises is also discussed in Carlsson-Wall and Kraus (Chapter 7), when they show how engineers and sales managers from ABB Robotics and engineers and purchasing managers from General Motors together used calculations as a baseline when they negotiate compromises. It was necessary to find re-designs for the industrial control system that was perceived as satisfactory solutions by both companies. The compromises needed to fit with the companies' previous decisions. Thus, compromises that in the Wouters and Pelz case were related to history and a company's vision, but the Carlsson-Wall and Kraus case related to the interdependencies and resource constellations that already existed in the companies' network. Accounting served, according to the authors, "as an anchor that framed the compromises" between the companies. The individuals within Robotics and General Motors found the calculations good enough for capturing the resource heterogeneity and the interdependencies and for guiding them in the joint innovation process.

Moll and Harrigan (Chapter 6) showed the difficulties in reaching compromises in large development project. Boeing introduced a new integrated accounting system that would make it possible to co-ordinate its global suppliers on a real-time basis. It was an information system that all the suppliers had access to and all of them were expected to report progress of their specific part in the development project. The intention of the system was to make it possible for all involved suppliers "to provide a representation of remote supplier events that other in the supply chain can act upon." The idea behind the integrated system was good, but in practice, it did not work as planned. Some suppliers did not fulfil their commitments according to plan, and others redesigned their sub-parts so they did not fit with the other parts of the airplane.

To overcome some of the difficulties in reaching compromises, many of the chapters detail the use of 'structural compromises' by clarifying and separating roles, responsibilities and accounting for inter-organisational innovation projects. Perna and Waluszwski (Chapter 2) described how the organisations first created a boundary between them and then later designed two separate accounting systems to save one of the companies from bankruptcy. The creation of the 'new unit' was thereby formed to deal with a specific part of the environment—the military sector with its special financial and legal requirements. Another example of structural differentiation was detailed by Wouters and Pelz (Chapter 5), who showed how Bosch created a separate unit that was allowed to pursue different types of innovative project than the 'rest' of the company. The existence of a very distinct company structure made it impossible to have certain type of inter-organisational innovation projects within the company. For instance, when a start-up wanted to sell its services on-line, the Bosch accounting system was not adapted for these activities and needed to be altered, since a digital service was sold and not physical products. Hence, the 'new unit' designed an accounting system that was adopted to the new way of doing business by the start-up.

Relatedly, Olsen (Chapter 4) showed structural arrangements on an industry level. The venture capital industry created an infrastructure to speed up and scale up inter-organisational innovation. The system was clearly a compromise as it 'closed the door' for some innovations that did not fit into the administrative accounting system and time requirements that the venture capital industry put on innovations. Andon, Baxter and Chua (Chapter 14) also illustrated how accounting can be used to guide structural compromises in innovative endeavors. The authors provide a case on a private–public partnership that in itself is a compromise, in which the public has to rely on the private to fulfil its contract to the citizens of a country. The whole idea of public–private partnership is to pool resources and to stretch governmental budgets. Accounting is therefore at the very core of the design and development of public private partnerships.

Summary

Increased blurriness of the spatial boundaries between the involved organisations and the extended time horizon of an inter-organisational innovation make it more difficult to identify and measure the value of the joint output from the innovation. As a consequence, it is more difficult to fairly distribute the created value. In other words, the incompleteness of performance indicators is highly evident. A dissatisfied organisation can hinder the innovation, and it is important that the involved organisations perceived the value of an innovation as clearly and fairly distributed (Tomkins, 2001). An organisation that invests more resources than the benefits it receives from the innovation and find itself unfairly treated by the other ones in the innovation process will in the long run leave the collaboration. Accounting therefore has an important role—to be a 'learning machine' and a carrier of "fairness" as the accounting information used has to be trusted and the reality it represents shared among the involved actors. It will often work as an 'engine', guiding dialogue and compromises and thereby facilitating and 'enabling' inter-organisational innovation. But too rigid accounting systems run the risk of 'hindering' such innovation. Therefore, the tension that accrual and period accounting creates for inter-organisational innovation processes that often are organised in projects must be dealt with. This will directly lead to different time horizons and different ways to evaluate different organisational units, the firm in the period reports and the project that might take several years before it is ready to launch. How this tension is managed is an important area of concern that the chapters in this book have shed light on, and it is summarised in the two themes set out in the beginning of this chapter: the issue of incomplete performance indicators and accounting as an engine for interaction, negotiation and compromise.

References

Burchell, S., Clubb, C., Hopwood, A., and Hughes, J. (1980). The roles of accounting in organizations and society. *Accounting, Organizations and Society*, 5, 5–27.

Busco, C., and Quattrone, P. (2017). In search of the perfect one: How accounting as a maieutic machine sustains inventions through generative 'in-tensions'. *Management Accounting Research*, forthcoming.

Chapman, C.S. (1997). Reflections on a contingent view of accounting. *Accounting, Organizations and Society*, 22, 189–205.

Dambrin, C., and Robson, K. (2011). Tracing performance in the pharmaceutical industry: Ambivalence, opacity and the performativity of flawed measures. *Accounting, Organizations and Society*, 36, 428–455.

Hall, M. (2010). Accounting information and managerial work. *Accounting, Organizations and Society*, 35, 301–315.

Jordan, S., and Messner, M. (2012). Enabling control and the problem of incomplete performance indicators. *Accounting, Organizations and Society*, 37, 544–564.

Mouritsen, J., Hansen, A., and Hansen, C. Ø. (2009). Short and long translations: Management accounting calculations and innovation management. *Accounting, Organization and Society*, 4(6–7), 738–754.

Powell, W.W., Koput, K.W., and Smith-Doerr, L. (1996). Interorganizational collaboration and the locus of innovation: Networks of learning in biotechnology. *Administrative Science Quarterly*, 41, 116–145.

Ridgway, V.F. (1956). Dysfunctional consequences of performance measurements. *Administrative Science Quarterly*, 1, 240–247.

Tomkins, C. (2001). Interdependencies, trust and information in relationships, alliances and networks. *Accounting, Organizations and Society*, 26(2), 161–191.

16 *Accounting, Innovation and Inter-Organisational Relationships*

Avenues for Future Research

Martin Carlsson-Wall, Håkan Håkansson, Kalle Kraus, Johnny Lind and Torkel Strömsten

It is now time to return to the figure from the introduction chapter and discuss contributions and future research opportunities for the domains of accounting and inter-organisational relationships (Caglio and Ditillo, 2008; Håkansson et al., 2010), accounting and innovation (Davila et al., 2009; Chenhall and Moers, 2015; Moll, 2015) and inter-organisational innovation (Håkansson and Waluszewski, 2002; La Rocca and Snehota, 2014; Öberg, 2013).

Contributions to the Literature on Accounting and Inter-Organisational Relationships

Extending the Spatial Dimension With a Multi-Level Perspective

The spatial dimension has always been central to the literature on accounting and inter-organisational relationships. Many studies have focused on individual dyads (Gietzmann, 1996; Dekker, 2004), while other have problematised the role of accounting in supply chains (Dekker, 2003; Cooper and Slagmulder, 2004; Seal et al., 2004; Free, 2008), networks (Tomkins, 2001; Håkansson and Lind, 2004; Mouritsen and Thrane, 2006) and wider ecosystems (Miller and O'Leary, 2007). As the chapters in this book have demonstrated, inter-organisational innovation connects individuals, teams and organisations, both within firms as well as in dyads, supply chains and networks. This is why the issue of incompleteness of performance indicators are accentuated when inter-organisational innovation is at the core of the analysis.

An explicit recognition, empirically as well as theoretically, of a multi-level perspective (see Figure 16.2) would therefore help to develop the literature on inter-organisational relationships in several ways. Even though some studies focus on the interconnection between intra- and inter-organisational accounting (i.e. Mouritsen et al., 2001; Thrane and Hald, 2006; Carlsson-Wall et al., 2011; Kraus and Strömsten 2016), they have not explicitly addressed the spatial complexity when individuals, teams and organisations are connected. Important questions that can be asked with a multi-level perspective is how accounting is related to reward systems for boundary spanning individuals

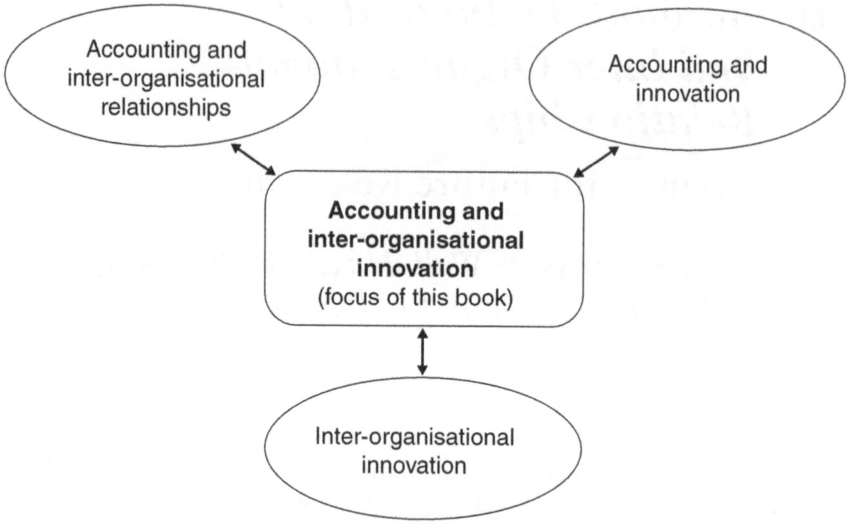

Figure 16.1 Focus of this book and related research domains.

(Dekker, 2016; Moll, 2015) or the role accounting plays in coordinating multiple development projects spanning numerous inter-organisational relationships (c.f., Moll, 2015).

Making the Temporal Dimension More Explicit

Another fruitful area for further research is to make more explicit the temporal dimension of accounting and inter-organisational relationships. Many of the chapters in this book stress the importance of "dynamics" and "non-linear developments." We know that many inter-organisational innovation projects are about re-using previous innovations in a creative way. This can be related to Miller and O'Leary (2007) and their study of Intel. Theorising accounting through the notion of 'mediating instrument', they showed how Moore's Law and technology roadmaps created shared expectations among semiconductor companies of how historic paths could be utilised in future investments. Within industrial marketing, a number of scholars have demonstrated the importance of linking different time perspectives. Håkansson and Waluszewski (2002) showed how actors on a network level re-used earlier investments to improve the business case and profitability of current investments. This re-use was an essential component in understanding how new technological paths emerged and gained momentum. Within accounting, Mouritsen and Kreiner (2016) further highlight the importance of forgetting and forgiving for making promises about the future. If we return to the Boeing Dreamliner project, we can see how individuals, teams and organisations need to integrate specialised and distributed knowledge. This is a highly

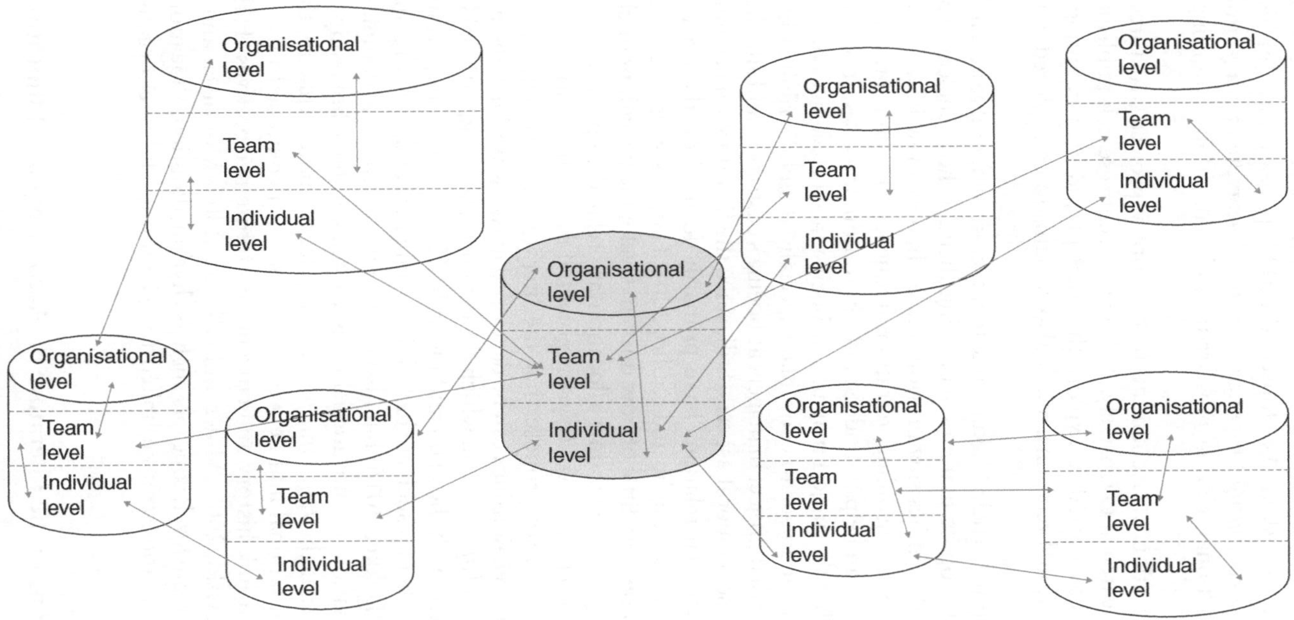

Figure 16.2 Extending the spatial scope to include individual, team and organisational levels.

uncertain project with large risks. As Moll and Harrigan describe in their chapter (Chapter 6), Boeing went too far, but they also learned from it. If we change unit of analysis and focus on the team level, another set of temporal questions can be asked. As Hopwood (2005, p. 586) noted in his 30-year editorial for *Accounting Organizations and Society*, temporary projects and inter-organisational relationships are unexplored within accounting:

> The operation of accounting in temporary project structures has not been researched extensively. Although recent research published in this journal has started to explore the roles played by accounting in inter-organizational relations, much also remains to be explored in this field.

In the conceptual article "Taking time to integrate temporal research," Ancona et al. (2001) propose that an overarching theme is how one can map activities to time. By synthesising previous research, they show how concepts such as pace, rhythm, scheduling, duration, frequency, entrainment, ordering and synchronising can help to understand innovation processes. It is not difficult to imagine that the project manager at Boeing faced challenges of scheduling, synchronising and pace to coordinate specialised and distributed knowledge or to imagine that project managers at Boeing's customers and suppliers struggled with these temporal aspects. Still, since the literature on accounting and inter-organisational relations have primarily focused on the organisational and network levels (Caglio and Ditillo, 2008; Håkansson et al., 2010; Dekker, 2016), we know very little of how uneven development rhythms or challenges with inter-organisational time allocation are related to performance metrics on the team level. Here we see great potential for further work.

To summarise, we propose that the literature on accounting and inter-organisational relationships can be developed in two ways. First, there is a need for a *multi-level approach* in which the network and organisational levels are complemented with the team and individual levels. This is important to further develop themes such as the link between inter- and intra-organisational accounting (Dekker, 2016) but also to portray the empirical complexity that inter-organisational innovation brings to accounting scholarship. Second, we propose that the *temporal perspective* can be more explicitly theorised. On an organisational and network level, one can continue to develop perspectives that link history and current and future perspectives (Håkansson and Waluszewski, 2002; Miller and O'Leary, 2007; Mouritsen and Kreiner, 2016). On a team level, concepts such as rhythm, duration, allocation of time and synchronisation can be linked to accounting and inter-organisational relationships.

Contributions to the Literature on Accounting and Innovation

The literature on accounting and innovation shares many characteristics with the literature on inter-organisational accounting in terms of growth, positioning and research design. For example, both literatures emerged in the mid-1990s and have grown steadily during the 2000s. Both literatures find inspiration in positioning themselves as opponents to the traditional, and more hierarchical, view of accounting, and both literatures have predominantly used qualitative case studies focusing on large companies with a high degree of product complexity. But the two literatures are also different. Although they both criticise hierarchical forms of accounting, they do it from different angles. While core themes within the literature on accounting and inter-organisational relationships are interaction and negotiations, the central focus within the literature on accounting and innovation is about coping with *complexity* and *uncertainty* (Davila et al., 2009; Chenhall and Moers, 2015). To put it simply, the literature on accounting and inter-organisational relationships argues that traditional accounting models are less relevant because there is a need to manage interaction and negotiation, while the literature on accounting and innovation argues that traditional accounting models are difficult to apply because innovation processes require flexibility and improvisation. However, since complex products such as a Boeing airplane or an ABB robot are developed in multi-party networks (Garud et al., 2013), these literatures have started to address more of the same control problem—interaction and negotiations in uncertain situations.

Studying How Enabling and Coercive Controls Operate in Inter-Organisational Innovation Settings Involving Multiple Suppliers

From prior research (e.g., Ahrens and Chapman, 2004; Wouters and Wilderom, 2008; Jordan and Messner, 2012; Englund and Gerdin, 2015; Jörgensen and Messner, 2009), we know that enabling and coercive control captures how project members *perceive* the control. This can be particularly useful when analyzing inter-organisational innovation activities, since, as the empirical cases in this book suggest, there is a constant need to balance efficiency and flexibility, and this balance is related to multiple levels. For example, regarding space, there is a need to balance efficiency and flexibility in each supplier relationship or to define a portfolio of suppliers and customers involved in developing the product (Tomkins, 2001; Lind and Strömsten 2006). Interestingly, there seems to be potentially complementary views of how this can occur. The chapter provided by van der Meer-Kooistra and Scapens (Chapter 13) indicates that efficiency and flexibility is primarily balanced through a relatively low degree of formalisation. In contrast, the empirical case that Jörgensen and Messner (2009) presented show that the balance between efficiency and flexibility is achieved through a high degree of formalisation, so called enabling control consisting of stage-gate models and process manuals. Since neither one of the studies focus on enabling or coercive control for a portfolio of inter-organisational relationships, this is an interesting avenue for future research.

Furthermore, one can study if, and how, the control pattern dynamically changes during an inter-organisational innovation project. In line with this, Moll and Harrigan (Chapter 6) showed that in the beginning of the Boeing Dreamliner project, many supplier relationships seemed to have been managed with a minimal structure type of approach. However, because of quality problems and time delays, it seems that Boeing changed and initiated more formal controls. What are the effects of these changes? Are they perceived as enabling or coercive by the suppliers? What negotiations occur and what compromises are reached? These questions can be linked to the discussions by Free (2007) and Neu et al. (2014). Free (2007) shows how supply chain accounting in two UK retailers combined elements of both enabling and coercive controls and how there was a considerable heterogeneity among practices. This would indicate that it can be difficult to have the same "minimal structure" or "enabling control" during inter-organisational innovation. Furthermore, studying the low-price apparels industry, Neu et al. (2014) describe how coercive controls are used on an individual level to deal with time pressure and uneven development rhythms in the sweatshops that produce the clothing. How enabling and coercive controls are combined throughout an innovation project with multiple suppliers is therefore interesting because it addresses both the spatial (multi-level) and temporal challenges of inter-organisational innovation.

More Explicit Recognition of the Individual Level

Some of our empirical chapters highlight the importance of certain individuals during inter-organisational innovation. Yet previous literature on accounting and innovation has seldom theorised the individual level. One way to address this limitation is to highlight the subjective dimension of time. Ancona et al. (2001) introduce the two concepts of *temporal perception* and *temporal personality*. Temporal perception is defined as "by perception of time, we mean the understanding and knowledge about time acquired through the senses. For individuals, vision, hearing, and touch—through their tight interconnections with the brain—all contribute to a sense of time" (Ancona et al., 2001, p. 518). If Dekker (2016) highlighted the need for more research on boundary spanners in general, temporal perception is a theoretical concept that can be of use to further build on such ideas. Temporal perception can also be complemented with temporal personality. Ancona et al. (2001, p. 519) define temporal personality as "the characteristic way in which an actor perceives, interprets, uses, allocates, or otherwise interacts with time." This means that temporal perception is about perceiving time while temporal personality is about how an individual acts based on this perception (Ancona et al., 2001). Future research could explore, for instance, how subjective temporal orientations are related to budgeting, performance measurements and other management control devices during inter-organisational innovation.

To summarise, the literature on accounting and innovation has paid great attention to complexity and uncertainty. Being inspired by management scholars such as Adler and Borys (1996), this literature has shown how accounting can play an enabling role in innovation processes. Acknowledging recent calls for more research on inter-organisational innovation (Chenhall and Moers, 2015; Moll, 2015), we suggest that new questions can be asked by studying how enabling and coercive controls operate in inter-organisational innovation settings involving multiple suppliers. Furthermore, on the individual level, temporal perception and temporal personality (Ancona et al., 2001) can help us develop our understanding of how boundary-spanning individuals relate to different types of accounting.

Contributions to the Literature on Inter-Organisational Innovation

The literature on inter-organisational innovation has a long history. Early studies of how companies interact and develop new products started to occur in the late 1960s and in 1982 the book "International Marketing and purchasing of industrial Goods: An Interaction Approach" was published as an edited volume (Håkansson, 1982). Since then, scholars have highlighted how inter-organisational innovation is an interactive process where there is a need to both plan and improvise (i.e. Håkansson and Snehota, 1995; Håkansson and Waluszewski, 2002, 2007; Dubois and Araujo, 2006). An important theoretical point of departure within this research stream is Penrose (1959) and the idea that value is created when heterogeneous resources are combined for new uses (Håkansson and Waluszewski, 2002). This means that the value of a resource (regardless if it is a physical or some other kind) is highly dependent on knowledge integration of how a resource can be used. If we take a Boeing airplane, there are thousands of individual resources that need to be combined (see Moll and Harrigan, Chapter 6). Since an individual company cannot take the financial risk of such an endeavour, there is a need for inter-organisational innovation. However, since the complexity of combining all the resources in the Boeing Dreamliner is a highly uncertain process, there is also a strong need to *re-use* previous technologies to avoid unnecessary quality problems and delays. This means that interaction processes are difficult to delimit in time. On the one hand, they are dependent on an organisational memory to ensure re-use; on the other hand, there is a need to envision a prosperous future.

Despite studying many process characteristics, the inter-organisational innovation literature has paid limited attention to accounting (Baraldi and Lind, 2017). In fact, the literature has traditionally seen accounting as hindering the innovation process (Baraldi and Strömsten 2009; Dubois 2003). In the empirical studies in this book, however, it has been demonstrated the enabling and well as constraining roles of accounting in inter-organisational innovation.

Adding More Explicit Theorising of the Enabling Role of Accounting

A first starting point is to draw on degree of formalisation and type of formalisation from the Adler and Borys (1996). If we start with degree of formalisation, there are several accounting concepts that can be used. For example, the idea of *minimal structure* (Brown and Eisenhardt, 1997; Kamoche and Cunha, 2001; van der Meer-Kooistra and Scapens, Chapter 13) can be used to describe how companies balance needs for efficiency and flexibility in inter-organisational innovation processes. As van der Meer-Kooistra and Scapens show (Chapter 13), minimal structures help to facilitate the knowledge integration process that is necessary in combining and recombining heterogenous resources. Another interesting concept is *mediating instruments* (Miller and O'Leary, 2007; Revellino and Mouritsen, 2009; Christner and Strömsten, 2015). Studying the coordinating role of Moores Law and technological roadmaps, Miller and O'Leary (2007) show how these non-financial controls mediate different interest and help actors synchronise important investment decisions. Studying biotechnology and the link to venture capital, Christner and Strömsten (2015) show how accounting calculations are part in shaping the development trajectory of the company Pyrosequencing. Other accounting concepts with a relatively low degree of formalisation are overlapping accountabilities (Håkansson and Lind, 2004), accounting as a promise (Mouritsen and Kreiner, 2016) accounting as evaluative infrastructure (Kornberger et al., 2017) and accounting as a maieutic machine (Busco and Quattrone, 2017). Given the long and rich empirical tradition of the literature on inter-organisational innovation, it seems that these new accounting concepts could provide interesting perspectives in future studies within this domain.

Another development path is to focus on type of formalisation (Adler and Borys, 1996) and more carefully study how inter-organisational accounting systems are designed and implemented. During inter-organisational innovation processes, there is a need to keep track of all the resources that are combined. When the Boeing Dreamliner is developed, it is not enough to use result controls because there are so many resources that need to be combined in an exact and timely way. This is where Adler and Borys' (1996) concept of *enabling bureaucracy* can be further developed. First, from a spatial perspective, one can study the portfolio of relationships which are part of the Boeing Dreamliner project. How does Boeing coordinate the many different suppliers, and is there an explicit intention to develop enabling forms of control? Having studied Boeing's intentions, one can collect data from the supplier perspective and see how they perceive the inter-organisational control. Do they think that that there is room for repair and flexibility and does the information exchange ensure internal and global transparency? Within the inter-organisational innovation literature, there is a long history of acknowledging the importance of seeing both sides of a relationship (Håkansson, 1982; Håkansson and Snehota, 1995; Håkansson and Waluszewski, 2002).

This means that this literature could be a suitable case for addressing the methodological critique put forward by Caglio and Ditillo (2008), that accounting studies have focused too much on one part of the relationship. Thus, given that the literature on inter-organisational innovation has primarily focused on the coercive role of accounting, we see a large potential to explore new, more enabling, type of accounting concepts such as minimal structures, mediating instruments, evaluative infrastructures and accounting as a promise.

Adding the "Constitutive" Aspect of Accounting

Another perspective is to study the aspects of accounting that shapes the processes and outcomes in inter-organisational innovation (Mouritsen et al., 2009; Dambrin and Robson, 2011; Christner and Strömsten, 2015). Rather than seeing accounting as an answering machine that portrays an objective world, the chapters in the book have demonstrated how accounting is involved in shaping development paths and trajectories. If we return to Penrose (1959) and the view that innovation is a process of combining heterogeneous resources, the constitutive perspective opens up new avenues. To start with, one can ask—what is the role of accounting for how an object becomes a resource? In the article "Creating something from nothing: resource construction through entrepreneurial bricolage," Baker and Nelson (2005) draw on Penrose (1959) and ask how entrepreneurs can develop unique services from seemingly worthless resources. The authors show that objects become valuable resources because the entrepreneurs draw on their imagination and intimate knowledge of the resource(s) to identify new and innovative uses. With a constitutive lens of accounting, Baker and Nelson's way of thinking can be extended. For example, Christner et al. (Chapter 3) detailed how accounting calculations such as internal rate of return and discounted cash flow have clear impact on *which* heterogeneous resources that are combined and *when* this occurs but also *where* (inside the organisation or as an outsourced activity). In a similar way, Mouritsen et al. (2009), through their concepts of short- and long translations, demonstrate how accounting actively shapes the resource combination process. In short translations, "innovation activities are mobilized by a single calculation and related to a variance from a standard or budget whether the deviation is positive or negative" (Mouritsen et al., 2009, p. 739). In long translations, "calculations challenge each other and develop organizational tensions and dialogues beyond innovation activities. Long translations develop new possible versions not only of preferred types of innovation activities, but also about their location in time and space" (Mouritsen et al., 2009, p. 739). In relation to resource heterogeneity, Mouritsen et al. (2009, p. 754) write:

> The problem of heterogeneity of components is not visible before it has been made a calculation. If someone would claim, say, that innovation should be 'more efficient', another voice would immediately say 'show me

> what you mean' and then the calculation has to emerge. Mere cognitive interpretations of innovation is not collectively actionable; innovation has to be inscribed and made a calculation before it can be acted on.

This view of the role of accounting in inter-organisational innovation can be connected with a sub-stream of the inter-organisational innovation literature that focuses on market practices (i.e. Kjellberg and Helgesson, 2006; Hagberg and Kjellberg, 2010; Harrison and Kjellberg, 2016; Kjellberg and Olsson, 2017). These researchers draw on Actor Network Theory and Science and Technology Studies to theorise the inter-organisational innovation process. Sharing similar theoretical interests, marketing and accounting researchers have also begun to bridge perspectives regarding valuation practices (Kjellberg et al., 2013; Mennicken and Sjögren, 2015). In the recently launched journal *Valuation Studies*, Helgesson and Muniesa (2013) describe in the first editorial how innovation and valuation(s) are closely related. They illustrate their argument with the movie *Moneyball* and how the detailed measuring of baseball performance not only created a new innovative way of managing baseball teams; it also showed how financial valuation was closely related to identity and values.

To summarise, the inter-organisational innovation literature has historically contributed with great empirical and theoretical richness when it comes to inter-organisational innovation. However, despite the practical importance of financing and coordinating the inter-organisational process, accounting has received little attention. Based on the findings from the chapters in this book, we point out two directions that could be of interest for the literature on inter-organisational innovation. First, focusing on the enabling role of accounting, there are a lot of new accounting concepts: minimal structures (van der Meer-Kooistra and Scapens, Chapter 13), mediating instruments (Miller and O'Leary, 2007), accounting as a promise (Mouritsen and Kreiner, 2016), accounting as evaluatory infrastructures (Kornberger et al., 2017) and accounting as a maieutic machine (Busco and Quattrone, 2017). These theoretical concepts do not see accounting as a tool for hierarchical control and have been applied in creative and innovative settings. Here we see potential for inter-organisational innovation researchers to incorporate an accounting perspective. Second, focusing on the constitutive aspects of accounting, we see a potential to study how resources come to existence through accounting technologies. The literature on inter-organisational innovation has theorised the innovation process as a process of combining heterogeneous resources. With a constitutive lens, this stream of research can analyse how an object becomes a resource with value and how these resources are combined.

Beyond the Three Domains: Exploring After-Market Services and Digitalisation

When studying accounting, innovation and inter-organisational relationships, we also see great possibilities for future research to explore two themes that were touched upon but not extensively dealt with in the empirical chapters: *after-market services* and *digitalisation*. Starting with after-market services, this is interesting because there is a general lack of service studies in the literature but also because there is an interesting temporal tension with the physical product. In many industries, after-market services have become the holy grail for both increased revenues and profitability (Kowalkowski et al., 2017; Luoto et al., 2017). A main reason for this is that purchasing departments have increased the use of inter-organisational cost management (Cooper and Slagmulder, 2004; Agndal and Nilsson, 2009). With reduced prices, many companies need to identify additional revenues to increase growth and profitability. This is where after-market services come in. From an innovation perspective, there is an interesting temporal dimension to this problem because at a certain point in time, a company is more dependent on after-market services compared with the physical product. This symbolic milestone can have large implications for a company, its identity and the innovation process. For example, if after-market services are prioritised, how do companies design the product so that sales of after-market services can be optimised? Which performance metrics are used in the innovation projects to ensure that this happens? Currently, there is lack of studies that explore accounting and inter-organisational innovation through the interrelationship between the physical product and the after-market service. After-market services change the interaction dynamics between companies. When a company sells a product such as an industrial robot, there is intense interaction before and directly after the sale. However, during the life-cycle, there is considerably less interaction. Sometimes, this can be an advantage because the customer might want help that is included in a guarantee and increases costs. However, other times, this lack of interaction is a clear disadvantage because it opens up for competing suppliers to form a relationship with the customer.

A second theme is digitalisation. Even though many innovations in prior literature surely have software elements in their physical products, few studies have focused on software development. This is raised by Ditillo and Caglio (Chapter 9) in their analysis of management control for knowledge integration. When digitalisation changes existing business models, this is an interesting avenue for further research. First, there is a natural connection between accounting, innovation and strategy, which Davila et al. (2009) point out in their review. How does digitalisation affect how accounting and innovation is interrelated? Do companies focus more on digital components in their business models? As an illustration, within the newspaper industry, several companies are now starting to see their online version as the key product and the paper product as a complement. With such a shift, does the innovation process within the newspaper industry change? If so, how, and what are the consequences for accounting?

Related to digitalisation, we suggest "Internet of Things" as a promising avenue for further research. If one goes to the *Oxford Dictionary* and searches for this term, it defines Internet of Things as: "The interconnection via the Internet of computing devices embedded in everyday objects, enabling them to send and receive data."

What is intriguing with "Internet of Things" is that it involves both technical and institutional disruption. When Uber and Volvo collaborated to pilot test self-driving cars in San Francisco, this was not only a technical endeavour; it was also a highly institutional endeavour because it stretched boundaries not only in the technical field but also in relation to laws, regulation and what it means to take responsibility. For example, on December 14, 2016, before Uber and Volvo did the first test drive, the California Department of Motor Vehicles issued a statement saying:

> The California DMV encourages the responsible exploration of self-driving cars. We have a permitting process in place to ensure public safety as this technology is being tested. Twenty manufacturers have already obtained permits to test hundreds of cars on California roads. Uber shall do the same.

Arguing that Uber was not testing a self-driving car, Uber's vice president of Advanced Technologies, Anthony Levandowski, said to the press:

> Nor is it clear why the DMV is requiring that we apply for a permit now, when they've known that self-driving Ubers have been on the streets of San Francisco over a month? We have been safely driving self-driving Ubers in the same manner in Pittsburgh for months, where policymakers and regulators are supportive of our efforts.

The empirical phenomena of "Internet of Things" therefore provide a great platform for further analyzing the digitalisation aspects of accounting, innovation and inter-organisational relationships. It also implies that inter-organisational innovation is highly emotional. The two lines directly below the definition of "Internet of Things" in the *Oxford Dictionary*: "if one thing can prevent the Internet of Things from transforming the way we live and work, it will be a breakdown in security."

Such technological and institutional disruption is related to strong emotions. The emotional aspect of inter-organisational innovation is stressed in Andon et al.'s chapter (Chapter 14). When Uber and Volvo conduct inter-organisational innovation, there are high hopes on organisational, team and individual levels. Surprisingly, as noted by Andon et al. (Chapter 14), research on accounting and innovation often lack an explicit focus on emotions. Within accounting more generally, however, there is an emerging literature on emotions (see Boedker and Chua, 2013; Bourmistrov and Kaarbøe, 2013; Chenhall et al., 2017; Guénin-Paracini et al., 2014; Carlsson-Wall et al., 2016; Catasús et al., 2016; Taffler et al., 2017). These studies have begun to explore the relationship between accounting and emotions. For example, Boedker and Chua (2013) describe how performance metrics affect employees' emotions in a global multinational company. A breakdown of security in "Internet of Things" can clearly result in nightmares. This actually happened on December 14, 2016, because during the first test day, it was documented how Uber's Volvo XC90 ran a red light. Who was to blame for this breakdown in security? Was it even a breakdown or "just" a personal mistake? As we noted, the Internet of Things is intriguing because it deals with both technological and institutional disruption.

Related to digitalisation, one can also follow the lead by Kornberger et al. (2017), who study the role of accounting in platform organisations such as Uber, eBay and Airbnb. These organisations are interesting because they have a very small balance sheet. Instead, they use the digital platform to create a marketplace where users and producers can meet. Drawing on the literature on accounting and inter-organisational relationships and the literature on accounting and rankings, Kornberger et al. (2017) introduce the concept of evaluative infrastructure to show how accounting operates in this setting. Highlighting how platform organisations could be the new frontier for how accounting scholars could challenge hierarchical forms of control, the authors write:

> It is this paper's contention that the focus on these evaluative infrastructures helps to equip accounting scholars with critical instruments to study a set of emerging phenomena that are related to platforms as new organizational form, including distributed innovation, crowd sourcing, big data and other burgeoning phenomena.

Platform organisations and their focus on artificial intelligence are also interesting in relation to the multi-level perspective of innovation that we have proposed. For example, what happens to innovation processes when the goal is to reduce the number of individuals and rely on artificial intelligence? How does a platform organisation use performance metrics to evaluate artificial rather than human intelligence? Is there a need for a combination of artificial and human intelligence as suggested by Quattrone (2016)? What happens in the future? Are platform organisations and artificial intelligence the new research frontier?

References

Adler, P.S., and Borys, B. (1996). Two types of bureaucracy: Enabling and coercive. *Administrative Science Quarterly*, Vol. 41, pp. 61–89.

Ahrens, T., and Chapman, C. (2004). Flexibility and efficiency in a UK restaurant chain. *Contemporary Accounting Research*, Vol. 21, Issue 2, pp. 271–301.

Agndal, H., and Nilsson, U. (2009). Interorganizational cost management in the exchange process. *Management Accounting Research*, Vol. 20, Issue 1, pp. 85–101.

Ancona, D.G., Okhuysen, G., and Perlow, L. (2001). Taking time to integrate temporal research. *Academy of Management Review*, Vol. 26, Issue 4, pp. 512–526.

Andon, Baxter and Chua. Chapter 14 in this book.

Baker, T., and Nelson, R. (2005). Creating something from nothing: Resource construction through entrepreneurial bricolage. *Administrative Science Quarterly*, Vol. 50, Issue 3, pp. 329–366.

Baraldi, E., and Lind, J. (2017). Value measuring and value appropriation in business networks. In *No business is an island: making sense of the interactive business world*. Håkan Håkansson and Ivan Snehota (eds.), Emeraldinsight.com, pp. 47–66.

Baraldi, E., and Strömsten, T. (2009). Controlling and combining resources in networks – From Uppsala to Stanford, and back again: The case of biotech innovation. *Industrial Marketing Management*, Vol. 38, pp. 541–552.

Boedker, C., and Chua, W.F. (2013). Accounting as an affective technology: A study of circulation, agency and entrancement. *Accounting, Organizations and Society*, Vol. 38, Issue 4, pp. 245–267.

Bourmistrov, A., and Kaarbøe, K. (2013). From comfort to stretch zones: A field study of two multinational companies applying "beyond budgeting" ideas. *Management Accounting Research*, Vol. 24, Issue 3, pp. 196–211.

Brown, S., and Eisenhardt, K. (1997). The art of continuous change: Linking Complexity theory and time-paced evolution in relentlessly shifting organizations. *Administrative Science Quarterly*, Vol. 42, Issue 1, pp. 1–34.

Busco, C., and Quattrone, P. (2017). In search of the perfect one: How accounting as a maieutic machine sustains inventions through generative 'in-tensions'. *Management Accounting Research*, forthcoming.

Caglio, A., and Ditillo, A. (2008). A review and discussion of management control in inter-firm relationships: Achievements and future directions. *Accounting, Organization and Society*, Vol. 33, Issue 7–8, pp. 868–898.

Carlsson-Wall, M., Kraus, K., and Lind, J. (2011). The interdependencies of intra- and inter-organisational controls and work practices: The case of domestic care of the elderly. *Management Accounting Research*, Vol. 22, pp. 313–329.

Carlsson-Wall, M., Kraus, K., and Messner, M. (2016). Performance measurement systems and the enactment of different institutional logics: Insights from a football organization. *Management Accounting Research*, Vol. 32, pp. 45–61.

Catasús, B., Ferri, P., and von Laskowski, S. (2016). Accounting and the hope of action. *European Accounting Review*, Vol. 25, Issue 2, pp. 403–419.

Chenhall, R.H., Hall, M., and Smith, D. (2017). The expressive role of performance measurement systems: A field study of a mental health development project. *Accounting, Organizations and Society*, Vol. 63, pp. 60–75.

Chenhall, R., and Moers, F. (2015). The role of innovation in the evolution of management accounting and its integration into management control. *Accounting, Organizations and Society*, Vol. 47, pp. 1–15.

Christner, H., and Strömsten, T. (2015). Scientists, venture capitalists and the stock exchange: The mediating role of accounting in product development. *Management Accounting Research*, Vol. 28, pp. 50–67.

Christner, Lind and Strömsten. Chapter 3 in this book.

Cooper, R., and Slagmulder, R. (2004). Interorganizational cost management and relational context. *Accounting, Organization and Society*, Vol. 29, Issue 1, pp. 1–26.

Dambrin, C., and Robson, K. (2011). Tracing performance in the pharmaceutical industry: Ambivalence, opacity and the performativity of flawed measures. *Accounting, Organizations and Society*, Vol. 36, pp. 428–455.

Davila, A., Foster, G., and Oyon, D. (2009). Accounting and control, entrepreneurship and innovation: Venturing into new research opportunities. *European Accounting Review*, Vol. 18, Issue 2, pp. 281–311.

Dekker, H. (2003). Value chain analysis in interfirm relationships: A field study, *Management Accounting Research*, Vol. 14, Issue 1, pp. 1–23.

Dekker, H. (2004). Control of inter-organizational relationships: Evidence of appropriation concerns and coordination requirements. *Accounting, Organizations and Society*, Vol. 29, Issue 1, pp. 27–50.

Dekker, H. (2016). On the boundaries between intrafirm and interfirm management accounting research. *Management Accounting Research*, Vol. 31, pp. 86–99.

Ditillo, and Caglio. Chapter 9 in this book.

Dubois, A. (2003). Strategic cost management across boundaries of firms. *Industrial Marketing Management*, Vol. 32, pp. 365–374.

Dubois, A., and Araujo, L. (2006). The relationship between technical and organisational interfaces in product development. *The IMP Journal*, Vol. 1, Issue 1, pp. 28–51.

Dubois and Gadde. Chapter 11 in this book.

Eklinder-Frick and Waluszewski. Chapter 12 in this book.

Englund, H., and Gerdin, J. (2015). Developing enabling performance measurement systems: On the interplay between numbers and operational knowledge. *European Accounting Review*, Vol. 24, Issue 2, pp. 277–303.

Free, C. (2007). Supply-chain accounting practices in the UK retail sector: Enabling or coercive collaboration? *Contemporary Accounting Research*, Vol. 24, pp. 897–933.

Free, C. (2008). Walking the talk? Supply chain accounting and trust among UK supermarkets and suppliers. *Accounting, Organizations and Society*, Vol. 33, pp. 629–662.

Garud, R., Tuertscher, P., and Van de Ven, A. (2013). Perspectives on innovation processes. *Academy of Management Annals*, Vol. 7, Issue 1, pp. 775–819.

Guénin-Paracini, H., Malsch, B., and Paillé, A.M. (2014). Fear and risk in the audit process. *Accounting, Organizations and Society*, Vol. 39, Issue 4, pp. 264–288.

Hagberg, J., and Kjellberg, H. (2010). Who performs marketing? Dimensions of agential variation in market practice. *Industrial Marketing Management*, Vol. 39, pp. 1028–1037.

Håkansson, H. (Ed.), (1982). *International Marketing and Purchasing of Industrial Goods: An Interaction Approach*. New York: Wiley.

Håkansson, H., and Lind, J. (2004). Accounting and network coordination. *Accounting, Organizations and Society*, Vol. 29, Issue 1, pp. 51–72.

Håkansson, H., Kraus, K., and Lind, J. (2010). *Accounting in Networks*. New York: Routledge.

Håkansson, H., and Snehota, I. (1995). *Developing Relationships in Business Networks*. London: Routledge.

Håkansson, H., and Waluszewski, A. (2002). *Managing Technological Development: IKEA, the Environment and Technology*. London: Routledge.

Håkansson, H., and Waluszewski, A. (2007). *Knowledge and Innovation in Business and Industry: The Importance of Using Others*. London and New York: Routledge.

Harrison, D., and Kjellberg, H. (2016). How users shape markets. *Marketing Theory*, Vol. 16, pp. 445–468.

Helgesson, C.-F., and Muniesa, F. (2013). For what it's worth: An Introduction to valuation studies. *Valuation Studies*, Vol. 1, pp. 1–10.

Hopwood, A. (2005). After 30 years. *Accounting, Organizations and Society*, Vol. 30, Issue 7–8, pp. 585–586.

Gietzmann, M.B. (1996). Incomplete contracts and the make or buy decision: Governance design and attainable flexibility. *Accounting, Organizations and Society*, Vol. 21, No. 6, pp. 611–626.

Jörgensen, B., and Messner, M. (2009). Management control in new product development: The dynamics of managing flexibility and efficiency. *Journal of Management Accounting Research*, Vol. 22, Issue 1, pp. 99–124.

Jordan, S., and Messner, M. (2012). Enabling control and the problem of incomplete performance indicators. *Accounting, Organizations and Society*, Vol. 37, pp. 544–564.

Kamoche, K., and Cunha, M. (2001). Minimal structures: From jazz improvisation to product innovation. *Organization Studies*, Vol. 22, Issue 5, pp. 733–765.

Kjellberg, H., and Helgesson, C.-F. (2006). Multiple versions of markets: Multiplicity and performativity in market practice. *Industrial Marketing Management*, Vol. 35, pp. 839–855.

Kjellberg, H., Mallard, A., Arjaliès, D.-L., Aspers, P., Beljean, S., Bidet, A., Corsín, A., Didier, E., Fourcade, M., Geiger, S., Hoeyer, K., Lamont, M., MacKenzie, D., Maurer, B., Mouritsen, J., Sjögren, E., Tryggestad, K., Vatin, F., and Woolgar, S. (2013). Valuation studies? Our collective two cents. *Valuation Studies*, Vol. 1, pp. 11–30.

Kjellberg, H., and Olsson, D. (2017). Joint markets: How adjacent markets influence the formation of regulated markets. *Marketing Theory*, Vol. 17, pp. 95–123.

Kornberger, M., Pfluger, D., and Mouritsen, J. (2017). Evaluative infrastructures: Accounting for platform organization. *Accounting, Organizations and Society*, Vol. 42, pp. 79–95.

Kowalkowski, C., Gebauer, H., and Olivia, R. (2017). Service growth in product firms: Past, present and future. *Industrial Marketing Management*, Vol. 60, pp. 82–88.

Kraus, K., and Strömsten, T. (2016). Internal/inter-firm control dynamics and power – A case study of the Ericsson-Vodafone relationship. *Management Accounting Research*, Vol. 33, pp. 61–72.

La Rocca, A., and Snehota, I. (2014). Relating in business networks: Innovation in practice. *Industrial Marketing Management*, Vol. 43, pp. 441–447.

Lind, J., and Strömsten, T. (2006). When do firms use different customer accounting? *Journal of Business Research*, Vol. 59, pp. 1257–1266.

Luoto, S., Brax, S.A., and Kohtamäki, M. (2017). Critical meta-analysis of servitization research: Constructing a model-narrative to reveal paradigmatic assumptions. *Industrial Marketing Management*, Vol. 60, pp. 89–100.

Mennicken, A., and Sjögren, E. (2015). Valuation and calculation at the margins. *Valuation Studies*, Vol. 3, pp. 1–7.

Miller, P., and O'Leary, T. (2007). Mediating instruments and making markets: Capital budgeting, science and the economy, *Accounting, Organizations and Society*, Vol. 32, Issues 7–8, pp. 701–734.

Moll, J. (2015). Editorial: Special issue on innovation and product development. *Management Accounting Research*, Vol. 28, pp. 2–11.

Moll and Harrigan. Chapter 6 in this book.

Mouritsen, J., Hansen, A., and Hansen, C.Ø. (2001). Interorganizational controls and organizational competencies: episodes around target cost management/functional analysis and open book accounting. *Management Accounting Research*, Vol. 12, Issue 2, pp. 221–244.

Mouritsen, J., Hansen, A., and Hansen, C.Ø. (2009). Short and long translations: Management accounting calculations and innovation management. *Accounting, Organization and Society*, Vol. 34, Issues 6–7, pp. 738–754.

Mouritsen, J., and Kreiner, K. (2016). Accounting, decisions and promises. *Accounting, Organizations and Society*, Vol. 49, pp. 21–31.

Mouritsen, J., and Thrane, S. (2006). Accounting, network complementarities and the development of inter-organisational relations. *Accounting, Organizations and Society*, Vol. 31, Issue 3, pp. 241–275.

Neu, D., Rahaman, A.S., and Everett, J. (2014). Accounting and sweatshops: Enabling coordination and control in low-price apparel production chains. *Contemporary Accounting Research*, Vol. 31, pp. 323–346.

Öberg, C. (2013). Competence integration in creative processes. *Industrial Marketing Management*, Vol. 42, pp. 113–124.

Olsen. Chapter 4 in this book.

Penrose, E. (1959). *The Theory of the Growth of the Firm*. Oxford: Oxford University Press.

Perna and Waluszewski. Chapter 2 in this book.

Quattrone, P. (2016). Management accounting goes digital: Will the move make it wiser? *Management Accounting Research*, Vol. 31, pp. 118–122.

Revellino, S., and Mouritsen, J. (2009). The multiplicity of controls and the making of innovation. *European Accounting Review*, Vol. 18, Issue 2, pp. 341–369.

Seal, W., Berry, A., and Cullen, J. (2004). Disembedding the supply chain: Institutionalized reflexivity and inter-firm accounting, *Accounting, Organizations and Society*, Vol. 29, Issue 1, pp. 73–92.

Taffler, R.J., Spence, C., and Eshraghi, A. (2017). Emotional economic man: Calculation and anxiety in fund management. *Accounting, Organizations and Society*, Vol. 61, pp. 53–67.

Thrane, S., and Hald, K. (2006). The emergence of boundaries and accounting in supply fields: The dynamics of integration and fragmentation. *Management Accounting Research*, Vol. 17, Issue 3, pp. 288–314.

Tomkins, C. (2001). Interdependencies, trust and information in relationships, alliances and networks. *Accounting, Organizations and Society*, Vol. 26, Issue 2, pp. 161–191.

Van der Meer-Kooistra and Scapens. Chapter 13 in this book.

Wouters, M., and Wilderom, C. (2008). Developing performance-measurement systems as enabling formalization: A longitudinal field study of a logistics department. *Accounting: Organizations and Society*, Vol. 33, pp. 488–516.

Contributors

Paul Andon is an Associate Professor in Accounting at the UNSW Business School, Sydney, Australia.

Jane Baxter is an Associate Professor in Accounting at the UNSW Business School, Sydney, Australia.

Jacco Blom graduated from the Accountancy & Control programme at the University of Amsterdam, the Netherlands.

Ariela Caglio is an Associate Professor in the Department of Accounting, Bocconi University, Italy.

Martin Carlsson-Wall is an Associate Professor in the Department of Accounting at the Stockholm School of Economics, Sweden.

Carl Henning Christner is a post-doctoral researcher at the Stockholm School of Economics Institute for Research, Sweden.

Wai Fong Chua is a Professor in the Department of Accounting at the University of Sydney, Australia.

Angelo Ditillo is an Associate Professor in the Department of Accounting, Bocconi University, Italy.

Anna Dubois is a Professor of Industrial Marketing and Purchasing at the Department of Technology Management and Economics, Chalmers University of Technology, Gothenburg, Sweden.

Jens Eklinder-Frick is an Assistant Professor of Business Studies at the Business Administration Faculty, University of Gävle, Sweden, and a post-doctoral researcher at the Science & Technology Studies Center, Uppsala University, Sweden.

Lars-Erik Gadde is an Emeritus Professor at Chalmers University of Technology, Gothenburg, Sweden.

Håkan Håkansson is a Professor of International Management at the BI Norwegian Business School, Norway.

Kim S. Hald is a Professor with special responsibilities in Performance Management in Organisation, Business Relationships and Supply Chains in the Department of Operations Management at Copenhagen Business School, Denmark.

Fiona Harrigan is a College Lecturer in Accountancy at University College Dublin, Ireland, and holds a PhD from the University of Manchester, UK.

Kalle Kraus is a Professor in the Department of Accounting at the Stockholm School of Economics, Sweden, and in the Department of Accounting at Monash University, Monash Business School, Australia.

Johnny Lind is a Professor in the Department of Accounting at the Stockholm School of Economics, Sweden.

Jeltje van der Meer-Kooistra is an Emeritus Professor of Financial Management at the University of Groningen, the Netherlands.

Jodie Moll is a Senior Lecturer of Accounting at Alliance Manchester Business School, University of Manchester, UK.

Jan Mouritsen is a Professor of Management Control in the Department of Operations Management at Copenhagen Business School, Denmark.

Per Ingvar Olsen is a Professor in the Department of Strategy and Entrepreneurship, BI Norwegian Business School, Norway.

Michael Pelz is a PhD student and research assistant at the Karlsruhe Institute of Technology, Germany.

Andrea Perna is an Associate Professor at Polytechnic University of Marche, Italy, and a visiting researcher at Uppsala University, Sweden.

Robert W. Scapens is an Emeritus Professor at the Alliance Manchester Business School, UK, and a Visiting Professor of Management Accounting at the University of Birmingham, UK.

Torkel Strömsten is an Associate Professor in the Department of Accounting at the Stockholm School of Economics, Sweden.

Sander van Triest is an Associate Professor at the Amsterdam Business School, University of Amsterdam, the Netherlands.

Alexandra Waluszewski is a Professor in the Science & Technology Studies Center, Uppsala University, Sweden.

Marc Wouters is a Professor of Management Accounting at the Karlsruhe Institute of Technology, Germany, and Visiting Professor at the University of Amsterdam, the Netherlands.

Index

Note: Page numbers in *italic* indicate a figure and page numbers in **bold** indicate a table on the corresponding page.